*Fateful Beauty*

From Robert Edis's *Decoration and Furniture of Town Houses*, 1881.
Courtesy of the Division of Rare and Manuscript Collections, Cornell
University Library.

# Fateful Beauty

AESTHETIC ENVIRONMENTS, JUVENILE DEVELOPMENT,
AND LITERATURE 1860–1960

Douglas Mao

PRINCETON UNIVERSITY PRESS

PRINCETON AND OXFORD

Copyright © 2008 by Princeton University Press
Published by Princeton University Press, 41 William Street, Princeton, New Jersey 08540
In the United Kingdom: Princeton University Press, 6 Oxford Street, Woodstock,
Oxfordshire OX20 1TW

Library of Congress Cataloging-in-Publication Data

Mao, Douglas, 1966–
Fateful Beauty : aesthetic environments, juvenile development, and literature, 1860–1960 /
Douglas Mao.
   p.  cm.
Includes bibliographical references and index.
ISBN 978-0-691-13348-5 (hardcover : alk. paper)
1. Literature, Modern—19th century—History and criticism. 2. Literature, Modern—20th
century—History and criticism. 3. Literature and society. 4. Literature—Aesthetics. I. Title.
PN761.M26 2008
801′.93—dc22     2007034637

British Library Cataloging-in-Publication Data is available

This book has been composed in Galliard

Printed on acid-free paper.

press.princeton.edu

Printed in the United States of America

10 9 8 7 6 5 4 3 2 1

For Chip

# Contents

## Preface

This book could not have come into being without the help of several generous institutions and many generous souls. My institutional debts begin with three universities, and three English departments within them: Princeton, Harvard, and Cornell supported this project with leave time, funding, and facilities the mere thought of which makes me count myself fortunate in the extreme. I am also grateful beyond measure to the John Simon Guggenheim Foundation for the fellowship year during which the most crucial work on this project was completed. On the side of souls, I would like to thank first my colleagues and students at Princeton, Harvard, and Cornell for teaching me so much that has made its way, directly or indirectly, into these pages; next, the interlocutors who have listened to parts of this book's story—at Dartmouth, Emory, Yale, Connecticut College, Johns Hopkins, Penn State, Rutgers, the Society for the Study of Narrative Literature, the James Joyce Symposium, the Modern Language Association, and the Modernist Studies Association—and responded with incalculably valuable suggestions. More particular appreciation for references, queries, reflections, and assistance needs to go to Edward Adams, Katherine Biers, Laura Brown, Jonathan Culler, Kevin Dettmar, Jay Dickson, Mary Esteve, Jed Esty, Philip Fisher, Deborah Garfield, Matthew Gold, Ellis Hanson, Molly Hite, Oren Izenberg, Scott Klein, Jim Longenbach, Jesse Matz, Sean McCann, Natalie Melas, James Najarian, Doug Payne, Todd Porterfield, Shirley Samuels, Daniel Schwarz, Harry Shaw, Rebecca Walkowitz, Mark Wollaeger, and Louise Yelin. For the superlative research around which many parts of this book are built, my admiration and sempiternal gratitude to Runal Mehta, Katy Croghan Alarçon, and Kathleen Hames; for their eloquent, thoughtful, and magnanimous assessments, my very warmest thanks to the readers of this study's manuscript.

Much of the final chapter of *Fateful Beauty* is drawn from an essay that appeared in *Paideuma*; I am grateful to the editors for publishing that piece. For permission to print the illustration in chapter 6, my thanks to Harcourt Education, and for permission to reproduce the Ingres painting in chapter 6, to the Réunion des Musées Nationaux and Art Resource, New York (and Tricia Smith and Robin Stolfi at Art Resource more particularly). I am indebted to the Cornell Library Rare and Manuscript Collections for permission to print the illustrations in chapter 1 and for the production of those images, and to Rhea Garen, Eileen Heeran, and Fiona Patrick for their kindness during my Rare Books adventures. For assistance with the illustration in the introduction, my sincerest thanks to Scott

Stowell and Open Studios. For their extraordinary care in bringing this book into the world, I am obliged to Natalie Baan, Bob Bettendorf, Lorraine Doneker, Alison Eitel, Adithi Kasturirangan, and Heath Renfroe at Princeton University Press—and thankful beyond words for the patience and immense copy-editorial insight of Marsha Kunin. This book about lovely things most owes its materialization, of course, to the faith and care of Hanne Winarsky, who has been the best of editors from the moment of our first exchange. And it owes its own loveliness to the production team at Princeton and to its brilliant jacket designer, Susan Barber.

Let me thank, finally, all the friends and relatives who have dispensed so much forbearance and encouragement through this project's long gestation. A few require special mention. Matt Bremer, there when thoughts of this study first glimmered, was a fount of solace through many of its writing's most difficult passages. My mother, Evelyn Schwarz, has offered love and understanding whose unboundedness continues to stagger me. My enthusiastic siblings, Debra Mao and Edmund Mao, were always, I think, somewhere in my mind as I wrote. And then there is Chip Wass, who never failed to make me feel that hours devoted to *Fateful Beauty* were hours well spent; who makes life incandescent; whose own beauty has been, just miraculously, my fate.

*Fateful Beauty*

# Talking about Beauty

Why, I have seen wallpaper which must lead a boy
brought up under its influence to a career of crime; you
should not have such incentives to sin lying about your
drawing-rooms.

A baby's a baby! It's the environimonament
that molds 'em.

The first of these epigraphs comes from "The Decorative Arts," a lecture
Oscar Wilde gave on his North American tour of 1882. In a sense, the
book before you does no more than elaborate some broader contexts for
this witticism, asking what meanings it may have had for its utterer, what
made it intelligible to its first hearers, and why it might still say something
to us today. Answering these questions in depth, however, means tracking
a set of ideas about environment's work on the young through a range of
appearances, on terrains as diverse as interior-decoration guides, popular
child-rearing advice, juvenile-delinquency codes, innovations in public
and domestic education, debates about determinism, the emergence of
neurophysiology and psychology, the discourse of the unconscious, the
history of aesthetics, and—centrally, in this case—some of the forms of
writing we call literature. One could also say, then, that this book describes
how a vast array of arguments, speculations, and practices converged, in
the last part of the nineteenth century and the first part of the twentieth,
around the matter of the growing human organism's molding by surroundings and circumstances.

Wilde's bon mot about wallpaper was probably not, it must be said up
front, the fruit of extended deliberation. Nor does it seem to have been
intended as much more than a throwaway. As Wilde enthusiasts know,
the lecture tour originated with Richard D'Oyly Carte, who was both a
manager of lecture-circuit talent and a producer of *Patience*, the W. S.
Gilbert–Arthur Sullivan operetta that debuted in London in April 1881,
with a parody of Wilde named Bunthorne at its comic heart. Seizing an
opportunity to combine business with business, D'Oyly Carte engaged
Wilde by way of introducing Bunthorne's original to North Americans—
who could see *Patience* in New York by late 1881 and soon after at many

venues across the country. For the first weeks of his tour, in January and early February 1882, Wilde emitted epigrams, dined with luminaries, set tongues wagging with his flamboyant costume, and enjoyed massive newspaper coverage; he also gave a relatively learned lecture entitled "The English Renaissance of Art," in which he spoke at length about the theoretical foundations of the "Aesthetic Movement" and the critics and artists who had helped, intentionally or not, to bring it to birth (John Ruskin, William Morris, Algernon Charles Swinburne, Walter Pater, James McNeill Whistler). But the response to his performances on and off stage was not altogether encouraging: attacks in print and at his lectures edged from hostile to cruel and—what was much worse—audiences sometimes seemed bored. Wilde therefore set out to tone down his outrageousness and to devise a more accessible introduction to art and beauty. The major product of the latter effort was "The Decorative Arts," which he wrote in Chicago, drawing heavily on late additions he had made to "The English Renaissance," and which he first gave in that city on 13 February. This offering, which dwelt less on high cultural names and more on the need to bring beauty, taste, and good design into the home, became Wilde's most popular lecture, the one he would give when making only a single appearance in a given locale.[1]

The wallpaper remark did not appear even in early versions of "The Decorative Arts"; it seems to have emerged as Wilde, making his way west, continued to revise. Nonetheless, it fits perfectly with the proselytizing mission of the tour and indeed with Wilde's long campaign, inaugurated well before his trip to America, to shift the ground of virtue from a narrowly conceived morality to a lush aesthetics. Hearing the phrase "incentives to sin lying about your drawing-rooms," a late Victorian would have thought first of indecent literature along the lines of the "wicked French novel" invoked by Mr. Dumby in Wilde's 1892 play, *Lady Windermere's Fan* (402);[2] that Wilde meant to exploit this commonplace is confirmed by his choice of "lying about," which obviously suits books much better than wallpaper. By so clearly redirecting concern from immoral volumes to ugly decoration, Wilde was memorably encapsulating his claim that among distinctions between good and bad, the one that really matters is the one between things that succeed as art and things that aesthetically fail.

Yet this is not quite the whole story of the witticism. For with it, Wilde was also indicating that art has a potent effect on conduct—and lending this point a certain topical character by tapping into widespread concern about the origins of criminality and the lawlessness of youth. As social historians have shown, the early years of the nineteenth century witnessed the birth of the juvenile delinquent as a social problem, while the later saw a further proliferation of efforts to address fears both of young people and on behalf of young people. In other words, Wilde's comment falls squarely within a period when solicitude about dangerous children and children in danger, to use the apt phrasing of Jacques Donzelot (96), was leading to unprecedented philanthropic and state-sponsored intervention in the lives of minors. Axiomatic for proponents of such action was that it must be possible to make better citizens by changing the environments in which young people mature—especially young people of the lower classes, whose ways of living appalled middle-class observers and from whose ranks the delinquent population was mainly drawn. Wilde's joke depends partly, then, upon an incongruous pairing of working-class destiny with middle-class milieu, of criminal career with drawing-room furniture.

Yet the main source of humor in the wallpaper remark is neither an inversion of values nor a collision of classes. It is, rather, a disproportion between large result and trivial cause. The motor of the epigram (which places it within a tradition, still very much alive, of jokes turning on the outsize portentousness of decoration, clothing, and other ephemera) is the suggestion that something as trivial as wallpaper could exert the kind of influence more usually attributed to drunken parents, thieving peers, or the deprivations of slum life. A mere domestic covering, an affair of surface by definition, wallpaper seems the very antithesis of profundity, as Wilde would recall again in his last great line, "My wallpaper and I are fighting a duel to the death. One or the other of us has to go" (Ellmann, *Oscar Wilde* 581). In the lecture auditorium as at the edge of the grave, however, the joke is much more than a joke, for Wilde's 1882 audience would have seen how it condensed the thesis of "The Decorative Arts" as a whole: that aesthetic environments (represented especially neatly by wallpaper, a furnishing that literally surrounds) have enormous power to shape the character and intellect of the young. Indeed many of Wilde's hearers would have been prepared to admit a truthfulness to the bon mot even without help from the rest of the lecture, since the thesis Wilde was staging in comic terms had been central to a discourse of moralized decoration already several decades old, quite respectable, and foundational to movements for artistic education and the beautification of schools.

Some of the specifics of that discourse will claim our attention further on, but for now we will do best to linger with this matter of small causes and large consequences. A little earlier in the text of "The Decorative Arts," Wilde observes that "the good we get from art is not what we derive directly, but what improvement is made in us by being accustomed to the sight of all comely and gracious things" ("Decorative" 161–62). What is important about art, in other words, is not the moral lesson we might draw from the narratives it represents (per a dominant nineteenth-century view), nor is it intense experience in the presence of the thing (as many theorists of the aesthetic, not excluding Wilde at other moments, would argue). What counts is something more nearly like a developed *inattention* to beauty—a taking of graciousness for granted, a becoming "accustomed" to the comely—that somehow improves our very selves. From this suggestion, Wilde moves to some thoughts on art in education, and it is here that our epigraph resides:

> Consider how susceptible children are to the influence of beauty, for they are easily impressed and are pretty much what their surroundings make them. How can you expect them, then, to tell the truth if everything about them is telling lies, like the paper in the hall declaring itself marble? Why, I have seen wallpaper which must lead a boy brought up under its influence to a career of crime; you should not have such incentives to sin lying about your drawing-rooms. ("Decorative" 162)

"How can you expect them, then, to tell the truth if everything about them is telling lies . . . ?" The ideal of truthfulness in materials did not begin or end with Wilde, certainly. Ruskin, to whom we will return in chapter 1, decried architectural elements that misrepresent structural needs and, drawing upon the ideas of the Cambridge professor Robert Willis, made "The Lamp of Truth" one of his *Seven Lamps of Architecture* (Hill 223–24). The American architect Andrew Jackson Downing, to whom we will also return, took as his great principle "the simple and obvious one that the material should *appear* to be what it is" (35). Charles Eastlake, author of the best-selling *Hints on Household Taste* (1872), stressed honesty in materials generally and specifically warned against covering "the walls with a paper stained and varnished in imitation of marble" (52). And the theorists and practitioners of architectural modernism would make correspondence of form to function one of the least contestable premises of building in the age of concrete and steel. Read in this tradition, Wilde's allusion to truthfulness can seem to explain the influence of domestic furnishings by way of a kind of moral allegory after all: false wallpaper might encourage lying by suggesting that untruths go unpunished even when in plain sight.

Yet it is not clear that the young person meeting such wallpaper would draw this kind of lesson consciously. In his previous sentence, we might notice, Wilde intimates that the sensuous environment works not by the pointing of a moral explicit to thought but in a gentler, quieter, more continuous fashion. Children are generally "susceptible . . . to the influence of beauty" and become "what their surroundings make them"; like the rest of us, only perhaps more so, they are improved not by specific lessons depicted in specific objects but by a kind of contagious loveliness in the ambience of lovely things. As he nears the end of the lecture, Wilde makes this point yet more sharply. If "all the decorative arts" are given "enormous importance" in the current "English renaissance" of art, this is so because

> we want children to grow up in England in the simple atmosphere of all fair things so that they will love what is beautiful and good, and hate what is evil and ugly, *long before they know the reason why.* If you go into a house where everything is coarse and you find the common cups chipped and saucers cracked, it will often be because the children have an utter contempt for them, but if everything is dainty and delicate, you teach them practically what beauty is, and gentleness and refinement of manner *are unconsciously acquired.* ("Decorative" 163, emphasis added)

Beautiful things work on the young, then, in a manner prior to precept and beneath the level of consciousness. The tedious and readily resisted inculcation of morals can be replaced, as a parent might be pleased to learn, by the more pleasant, efficacious, and sly technique of providing tasteful china. What lends beauty its special influence over the soul is precisely its capacity to slip in and improve the child without the child's being aware of it at all.

One main argument of this book is that from the late nineteenth century through the early twentieth, the scarcely registered workings of environment on the developing human being were a preoccupation of many kinds of people, from artists to scientists, from writers of fiction to crafters of policy, from experts pondering national problems raised by juveniles to parents gnashing their teeth over domestic ones. The book's other main argument, more specific than the first and dependent upon it, is that this preoccupation lent a special character to period speculations on the possible role of art and beauty in human life. The idea that aesthetic experience could shape the soul was not new in the years indicated by the subtitle of this book, nor was the understanding that people can be influenced (especially in their tender years) by events and forces of which they or their guardians are unaware. What *was* new was the extraordinary depth of this period's interest in the operations of unregistered experience, along with its tendency to conceive of human development as a series of transactions between an organism and its environment. The pages that follow will consider in detail the synergy between the concept of environment and the belief that any experience, no matter how fleeting or innocent, might exert incalculable influence over a person's development. They will also note how the ascent of both offered an especially promising basis for claims that the path to a better world lay in provision of beauty for the young. And they will show how this cluster of ideas bridged the diverse forms of thinking, telling, and doing mentioned in the opening paragraph of this introduction—how it linked (switching now to a more standard vocabulary of disciplines and practices) literature, art, architecture, psychology, philosophy, education, social reform, and popular advice.

Among these fields, the one privileged in *Fateful Beauty* is the kind of imaginative writing that goes by the name of literature. The topic of stealthy environmental influences can certainly be approached in ways that make other territories of human endeavor or natural process central, but a premise of this study is that literature plays an especially important part in this story, and for several reasons. One has to do with the representation of intimate experience, or rather with the intimate representation of experience. As the writings of Walter Pater (to be visited in chapter 2) irresistibly suggest, no form of talk about development may be better at capturing small transactions of life than the narration of the concrete experiences of an individual person. And because subtlety in delineation seems to suit subtlety in things delineated, literary narratives may be especially powerful in this regard, if by "literary" we mean to gesture at an unusual richness of meaning in the minutest details of language. Another way of putting this would be to say that under prevailing taxonomic habits, the detailed narrating of a life's unfolding can scarcely *escape* being marked as literary; for better or for worse, the literary is commonly understood to bear a tight affiliation to the experientially intimate.

Highly germane to this point is the historical importance of the bildungsroman, which we might succinctly define as the genre of the long narrative concerned with a fictional individual's maturation. Certainly, one aim of *Fateful Beauty* is to show that problems of development are important in imaginative writing well outside this genre as such (as in Auden's poetry and criticism), and yet the bildungsroman's eminence stands behind even this undertaking. If literature has existed since antiquity, "literature" as a category may be an invention of the last two hundred years or so, which means that its emergence roughly coincides with that of the bildungsroman—a genre most often, though ever problematically, said to find its prototype in Johann Wolfgang von Goethe's *Wilhelm Meisters Lehrjahre* (*Wilhelm Meister's Apprenticeship*) of 1795–96. Whatever the particulars of interdependence here, it is certainly difficult to imagine how anything like the regnant understanding of "literature" could have come into being apart from a sense that one of the main things literature does is to tell of the growth of an individual human being in a social context. That literature *ought* to be understood this way has, certainly, been contested by many modernist innovators and their heirs; for them, such an identification precisely misses the point that the truly literary dimension of a text must lie in its rejection of mimetic representation (including, it may be, the representation of subjectivity) in favor of the play of language. But if views on the proper hallmark of the literary differ, few would dispute that "literature" has been associated in popular opinion— and in the disciplinary partitioning of intellectual life performed by the academy since the nineteenth century—with stories about how particular people mature.

Further, literature and the bildungsroman have had a close if not always transparent relationship to faith in the benevolent power of the aesthetic, as the critic Marc Redfield has argued. Several recent readers have shown how the social hope of eighteenth- and nineteenth-century aesthetics lay in the idea that beauty—often in the company of its grander companion, sublimity—would bring human beings to some kind of reconciliation with a world that otherwise seems alien, indifferent, fragmented, or oppressive. (Terry Eagleton, to whom we will return in chapter 2, offers the most salient and extensive treatment of this aspiration.) Other readers have pointed out that the bildungsroman attempts something similar, its nominally ideal ending being one in which the protagonist comes to accommodation with a society that has thrown up obstacles to the desires and impulses of youth. (Franco Moretti, to whom we will return in a few paragraphs, presents the fullest elaboration of this argument.) Redfield, for his part, considers a number of collaborations and conflicts between these two programs for harmony, showing how the bildungsroman, as itself an aesthetic enterprise, is meant to abet the reconciliation between soul and world—even if no instance of the genre quite manages this feat, even if it can be doubted whether a true bildungsroman has ever existed. Bildungsromane are, in idea at least, "the most pedagogically efficient of novels, since they thematize and enact the very motion of aesthetic education"; because reading is "a process of *Bildung* inscribed in the text itself as the text's reflection on its own human essence," the bildungsroman becomes "a trope for the aspirations of aesthetic humanism," its concept finally having "no existence apart from . . . the post-Romantic history of aesthetics" (55, 39, 65). The texts considered in *Fateful Beauty* all negotiate in some fashion the dream of tuning subjects to their worlds. And they all draw on an understanding (so widely held in the nineteenth century as to merit the name "popular") that in any such tuning literature will assume a leading role.

All this said, it would be a mistake to subordinate the project of the present study to the question "Why literature?" Equally relevant, one might say, is the question "Why *not* literature?" For a governing assumption here is that the study of literature, as of any art, carries intrinsic interest, that it makes a contribution to knowledge requiring no apology in other terms, even if (as has been suggested in this case) other terms are eminently available. *Fateful Beauty* is not intended to constitute cultural history as opposed to literary criticism, then, nor does it aim to use literary texts merely to illustrate historical phenomena more interesting than the texts themselves. It aspires, rather, to a kind of stereoscopic effect in which one frame, wherein the object of study is a series of literary works, merges with another, wherein the object of study is a preoccupation ramifying widely through culture and society. The hope is that readers principally interested in literature will see how its readings are not just enhanced by, but inextricable from, its reconstruction of more broadly permeating convictions and trends, even as those with a primary interest in psychology, education, or social reform will see why procedures associated with literary criticism are necessary to the historiographical work it undertakes.

The first chapter of *Fateful Beauty* examines several aspects of late nineteenth- and early twentieth-century thinking about developmental environments. It begins by considering how the image of the vulnerable child figured in a variety of efforts to manage the experience of young people within and without the family, then turns to the growth of interest in the human organism's stealthy shaping by environment so named. This question of stealth requiring further elaboration, it next discusses how discoveries in physiology and early psychology enhanced interest in the mysterious, quasi-chemical processes by which character is formed—that is, in what we might call a developmental unconscious—before concluding with a look at how such preoccupations governed period hypotheses anent the nature of the aesthetic. Some elements in this wide-ranging chapter bear quite obviously on everything that follows; some resonate more strongly with some sections of the book than with others; some do not have acute application to any succeeding chapter. But the aim here is not to pave the way for later demonstrations that these phenomena were all directly registered in literary texts; it is rather to show that for the later nineteenth and early twentieth centuries, increasing anxiety about the susceptibility of the young, the rise of environment as a major term of thought, growing attention to the significance of the unconscious, and new understandings of art and beauty profoundly affected each other—that they made, even, a certain practical and theoretical constellation centered on the insight that people become who they are through experiences of which they may hardly be aware.

In its second chapter, the book turns to the developmental program of British aestheticism, as it was anticipated by figures like William Wordsworth and Ruskin, solidified by Pater, and disseminated by Wilde and his contemporaries. Here, the argument is that Pater and Wilde find in the aesthetic a double benefit, the stealthy action of the beautiful environment rendering the soul more beautiful even as highly conscious aesthetic experience provides an opening for a sense of freedom from determination by external forces. The chapter goes on to ask why aestheticism seemed driven to undercut its own best hopes for beauty, and how its recipes for gentle shaping may be understood in relation to both the ascent of discipline described by Michel Foucault and the ideology of the aesthetic explored by Eagleton.

Chapters 3 and 4 focus on James Joyce and Theodore Dreiser, both of whom grew up in the shadow of an apparently conclusive demonstration, by modern science, that an individual's acts and qualities are determined by environmental forces working upon hereditary constitution. Pater and Wilde were also immersed in this understanding, but where it led them to a certain positive excitement about the possibility of young people maturing amid beauty, it led Joyce and Dreiser to forms of rebellion against aestheticism's ideals. In Joyce's framing, the virtue of the aesthetic lies not in the habituating to fair things described in "The Decorative Arts" but in its tendering of an order of experience that—more in line with the second of the two benefits recognized by Pater and Wilde—offers a liberation from circumstances through a suspension of appetitive desire. For Dreiser, meanwhile, Joycean as well as Wildean forms of aesthetic optimism are undone by the recognition that the yearning for beauty is itself a desire of the organism and thus a means by which environmental forces extend or confirm their control of the soul. In exploring Joyce's and Dreiser's responses, the chapter considers afresh the relationship between aestheticism and literary naturalism, which has been discussed periodically over the years but little examined lately and never substantially treated in terms of beauty's stealthy shaping.

The final two chapters turn to what we might regard as a last phase of the critique of aesthetic optimism, as unfolded by two gifted makers of literary art who were also high-profile public intellectuals in the middle years of the twentieth century—figures, that is, whose work furnishes a singular record of what issues were being pondered by the kind of people whose main business was to ponder issues. Chapter 5 argues that much in the extraordinary oeuvre of the novelist and journalist Rebecca West turns upon a sharp dismissal of the belief that any milieu can remain secure against external forces of rupture. Although sensitivity to beauty is for her the quality that divides worthwhile people from disagreeable ones, West stresses—in her most famous novel, in her best-known work of nonfiction, in her Left-baiting defenses of patriotism, and in her essayistic engagement with the experiments of Ivan Petrovich Pavlov—how dangerous it is to assume that surroundings can be managed, how important to recognize that the terrain of a human organism's struggle is never reliably circumscribed. Chapter 6 turns to yet another encounter between a writer and a scientist to examine how, in the twentieth century, views of environment's power could shape a politics. Beginning by asking what W. H. Auden learned from the life and publications of his physician father, George, it shows that the poet initially addressed the question of environmental influences less by working through the mysteries of agency than by flatly declaring transcendence of one's milieu to be an imperative. The chapter goes on to survey Auden's concerns about the possible conflict between the manipulation of juvenile conditions and the nurturing of free will, and to show how his vision of the making of the artistic soul relies on dissonance rather than concord between the environment and the growing organism. A brief epilogue to the book visits some scenes from the careers of beauty and environment after the middle of the twentieth century.[3]

Given the close connection between "literature" and stories about people growing, the claim that many writers of this time were profoundly concerned with human development might not in itself seem cause for comment. Yet this assertion does, in its way, run against a common understanding of what happened to literature in this period, and particularly to the novel after about 1900. Several influential critics have argued that European and North American writers in the twentieth century turned away from the nineteenth century's delight in narrating how young people mature and devoted themselves instead to stories about how young people do *not* mature, about how life in the modern world is an affair of stagnation or regress. Patricia Meyer Spacks, for example, has written eloquently about early twentieth-century novelists' privileging of an empowering arrest affiliated with "genius" (236), while Franco Moretti has argued that even by the time of George Eliot and Gustave Flaubert, "the historical and cultural configuration which had made the *Bildungsroman* possible and necessary had come to an end" (226). Not only had it become difficult to believe that "the biography of a young individual" could be "the most meaningful viewpoint for the understanding and the evaluation of history" (227); by the turn of the century, according to Moretti, youth had begun "to despise maturity," to "define itself in revulsion from" age, to look "for its meaning within itself" because adult niches had ceased to seem remotely hospitable (231).

   That there is a great deal of truth in these assessments will be obvious to anyone familiar with the troubled young heroes of late nineteenth- and early twentieth-century novels, or with the cultural shifts that occurred between, say, 1870 and 1920. When José Ortega y Gasset, born in 1883, recalled, "In my generation, the manners of old age still enjoyed great prestige. So anxious were boys to cease being boys that they imitated the stoop of their elders" (51), he was also acknowledging how rapidly things had changed thereafter. Still, the assertion that the significant literature of the era largely replaced exuberant growth with desperate stasis has to be qualified. As we will see, the dream of the individual's flowering into harmony with society may have been subjected to new kinds of skepticism, but *interest* in how young people become the adults they become remained high. If this continuity is hard to see, one reason may be that the interest itself came to be directed at hard-to-see factors—to be governed, once again, by a feeling that the really crucial transactions occur on so molecular a scale that they resist elevation to anything recognizable as plot. Although Pater, Wilde, Joyce, Dreiser, West, and Auden all have something important to say about the shaping power of juvenile environments, they do not always say it in texts in which stories of young people take center stage.

This and preceding references to the writing of the period clearly invite another question about this book, however: Why has the term "modernism" been omitted from its title and skirted, at least so far, in this introduction? For answer, we might begin with the point that "modernism" was not a word much on the lips of the authors with whom *Fateful Beauty* is occupied. It only came into its current use around the middle of the twentieth century, referring at first to a movement, trend, or group of formal features (radical experimentation, difficulty, fragmentation, refractoriness, and malaise, among others) associated with certain innovative artists and writers. Only a little later did it come also to name a span of years. With this turn, of course, those cultural producers and works that looked more modernist in the qualitative sense came to be seen as epitomizing the age's meaningful progress, while others tended to recede from view; to have been nonmodernist in the age of modernism was, so it now seemed, to have been out of sync with the times, retrograde or irrelevant. It can also be argued that when "modernism" became the dominant temporal marker in the story of the arts, the qualitatively modernist features *within* particular works and oeuvres became the ones easiest to discern and most necessary to discuss.

Because concern with developmental environments has not heretofore been regarded as a leading characteristic of modernism in its qualitative acceptation, however, centering this study on modernism would mean either (1) deploying the term as a purely temporal designation or (2) arguing at length that this concern was a distinctive dimension, though so far little noticed, of the web of texts and writers that have been marked modernist in the qualitative sense. Both options prove problematic. Certainly, the most generous demarcations of modernism in the Anglo-American world might adopt something like 1860 (or at least Pater) as a start, 1960 (or very late West and Auden) as an end. But precisely because so large a span hovers just within the limits of the plausible, and because rival accounts might put the beginning as late as 1910 and the close as early as 1930 or even 1925, the invocation of modernism would seem to demand fuller defense here than it would in a book zeroing in on, say, the second and third decades of the twentieth century. It would appear to require some buttressing by demonstrated relevance to modernism in the less contested sense, the one that refers to groups or qualities—which is to say that option one passes directly into option two.

But option two, again, has problems of its own. To make a strong case that one is revealing a hitherto unnoticed feature of modernism (as school, style, or corpus), one would have to devote substantial attention to artists recognized as modernist—to demonstrate that the newly disclosed traits or interests accompany ones that have already put those artists securely in the modernist category. Among the writers substantially visited here, however, only Joyce has impeccable modernist credentials. In crucial respects, Dreiser, Wilde, the later Auden, and West can be understood as antimodernist, while Pater's work seems to many less an instance of modernist practice than a stimulus to modernist innovation. Nor will this book's personnel fully cooperate with an attempt to forge an intriguing trajectory, say from incipient modernism to intense modernism to attenuated modernism. Were we to rank our principal authors from most to least evidently modernist, we might come up with something like: Joyce, early Auden, Pater, West, later Auden, Wilde, Dreiser—or the fourth, sixth, first, fifth, seventh, second, and third of our writers chronologically speaking. Preferable to either of these two options, then, would seem to be a relatively sparing use of "modernism" in this study. This tack has the collateral virtue of affirming something important to those who like a certain thickness or range in readings of the culture of a given period: that the intellectual and artistic life of this era does not necessarily look less bristling or vibrant if we expand our scope beyond the figures generally regarded as most central to high modernism.

Still, it would be wrong to imply that this book has little to contribute to the ongoing critical conversation about modernism's meanings. As one of the readers of its manuscript pointed out, one way of understanding modernism is to see it as driven by a sense of a contest over who was best equipped to describe and amend human relations, a contest in which artists (still drawing inspiration, at some level, from earlier ideals of the poet-sage) saw their opponents as social scientists, natural scientists, and other professional analysts of the modern world. In such a frame, the six writers principally discussed here would be inescapably or even essentially modernist, though their ways of joining the contest in question clearly vary. West and Auden enter the fray most directly, perhaps, inasmuch as they most visibly arrogate to themselves the right to critique and adapt extraliterary theories about human behavior for their own projects. But Pater ingeniously suggests that the modern worldview is at once a product of science and that which confirms the necessity of art, while Wilde, Joyce, and Dreiser offer prescriptions for (or diagnoses of) living whose claims to expertise cannot quite be subsumed under poetic inspiration or empirical investigation alone.

Even at its most narrowly delimited, moreover, modernism was entangled in crucial ways with questions of beauty and receptivity to environmental stimuli. Three of these bear particular mention here. First: it will soon become clear that many of the ideas about human development examined in *Fateful Beauty* depend upon an engagement with the concept of the moment. This tiniest of temporal abstractions has always loomed large in modernist writing and writing about modernist writing, from the "awful daring of a moment's surrender" in *The Waste Land* to Virginia Woolf's "moments of being," from Ezra Pound's definition of the Image as "that which presents an intellectual and emotional complex in an instant of time" to the sweeping surveys of modernism offered by later critics like Moretti and Ronald Schleifer. Parts of this book, especially in chapters 2 and 3, nod to connections between the moment in developmental thinking and the moment as it figures in modernist art, but there is clearly more to be said on this point, and it will surely be to the good if future readers in future books say it.

A second, and closely related, impulse in modernism lies in its conviction that a single rich perception can alter a life. In chapter 3, we will situate Joyce and his elevation of quotidian experience amid the discourses of environment and development, but something similar might be done with a number of other modernist or protomodernist writers. Henry James and Virginia Woolf could each have been given a chapter here, as much for their concern with the power of the impression as for their sensitivity to the ways surroundings resonate through souls; so perhaps could William Carlos Williams, ever anxious for a fresh seeing that would renew the world. And so, for that matter, could Pound, whose absorption of Pater and Wilde in this area is betrayed by numerous passages in his work. In one, from 1916's *Gaudier-Brzeska*, Pound declares that James McNeill Whistler and the Impressionists have made him "more conscious of the appearance of the sky where it juts down between houses, of the bright pattern of sunlight which the bath water throws upon the ceiling," and that "[a]ll this is new life, it gives a new aroma, a new keenness for keeping awake" (126).

This testimony to aesthetic resurrection leads to a third and rather different point of entanglement: the importance of the not traditionally beautiful and the ugly in modernist aesthetics. On the first page of her study of the modernist cult of ugliness, Lesley Higgins quotes the following epistolary comment, March 1918, from John B. Yeats to his son William: "The poets loved of Ezra Pound are tired of Beauty, since they have met it so often in plays and poems and novels and in ordinary life. . . . It has ceased to be unintelligible, so very naturally and inevitably they turn to the ugly, celebrating it in every form of imitation" (quoted in Higgins 1). Pound might have taken exception to the elder Yeats's terms—as Higgins notes, he and many other modernists were often ready enough to promote beauty as such (145)—but it is clear, all the same, that in the early part of the century beauty suffered from its very positivity, which allied it with qualities disdained by moderns and allegedly beloved by philistines (spiritual elevation, sexual decorum, piety, cheerfulness). As the century wore on, interestingness displaced beauty as the essential quality of valid art; praise of beauty in art came to seem ever more anachronistic and recherché; and—in a development astutely noted by Denis Donoghue—casual allusions to beauty receded ever farther from the legitimate conversational terrain of heterosexual men (29). As if this were not enough, the last decades of the century saw trenchant critiques of the ideological work of the aesthetic and of sensuous pleasure (Pierre Bourdieu, Laura Mulvey, Paul de Man, Eagleton) that made it difficult to offer a judgment of beauty without recalling the exclusions, injustice, and violence perpetrated in its name.

Recently, however—and perhaps partly because these critiques made the aesthetic look more blooded and forceful than it had for some time—beauty has enjoyed a certain return to favor. Against the charge that aesthetic judgment has always been an implement in the class warfare practiced by the high upon the low (adaptations of Bourdieu) and that the sensuous pleasure taken in an object amounts to a violation of it (extensions of Mulvey), well-known critics such as Wendy Steiner, Elaine Scarry, and Donoghue have mounted eloquent defenses. They have pleaded that attacks on pleasure perform their own suspect kinds of ideological work; that the feeling for beauty and the feeling for justice augment each other; that we have much to gain not only from the unsettling experience of beautiful things but also from irresolvable debates about the value of beauty.[4] This impetus toward a theoretical reevaluation seems, further, to have encouraged or dovetailed with an efflorescence of interest among novelists and poets. Zadie Smith's novel *On Beauty* (2005), for example, plays off Scarry's *On Beauty and Being Just*, while Alan Hollinghurst's Booker-prize-winning *Line of Beauty* (2004) draws its titular conceit from an ingredient of aesthetic success apprehended by William Hogarth in the eighteenth century.

Yet the claims for beauty whose devising is described in the earlier chapters of this book, and whose calling into question is described in the later ones, have not so far figured prominently in the twenty-first-century turn. As should be clear by now, these claims were informed by a social optimism according to which conscious aesthetic experience on the part of adults might be no more crucial than scarcely registered aesthetic experience on the part of the young. Though these claims accorded beauty an important role in the fashioning of a better world, they did not rely solely on encounters between informed audiences and works of art as such, nor did they accord the highest importance to the cultivation of taste or to some mimetic (or antithetical) relation between art and society. And though they often touched on a certain dream of resuturing life to art (dreamt by figures as diverse as the anthropologist Jane Harrison and the art critic Clement Greenberg), these claims did not exactly repose on that dream, either.[5] To the way of thinking that they expressed, what art could make people know or feel was not necessarily more important than what aesthetic environments could make people insensibly become.

In this strand of a program, in this strain of a social vision, beauty and environment clearly worked together. As the notion of environment became more and more central to thinking about juvenile development and the destiny of humanity, it enhanced the aesthetic's bid to nurture future possibility; promoters of the beautiful may be said to have returned the favor. But the fortunes of the two soon diverged. If beauty's hold declined in the early years of the twentieth century, the same cannot be said of environment's. In the 1920s a radical yet appealing behaviorism briefly made environmental conditions the concern of every parent up on the latest in child rearing; in the 1930s widespread social misery lent prestige to the view that nothing was as important as socioeconomic circumstances in determining the life courses of individuals. But it was the decades after World War II that arguably witnessed the height of environment's triumph. Revulsion at Nazi eugenic policies helped make inquiry into hereditary and even physiological influences on human development broadly unpalatable, which meant that in serious research (and in popular understandings growing out of new science) environment had the field largely to itself. Not until the end of the century—with the arrival of newly sophisticated genetic analysis, explosive innovation in psychopharmacology, and a certain sense of generational distance from the era of the Third Reich—would the dominance of environment begin to recede.

The reach of environment in the popular imagination of the postwar era is nicely illustrated by the second of this introduction's two epigraphs, drawn from a text appearing around the end of the period treated in *Fateful Beauty*. That text is the 1953 Warner Brothers cartoon "A Mouse Divided," directed by Isadore "Friz" Freleng with story by Warren Foster, and the line is spoken by a drunken, baby-delivering stork. Having overindulged at a "Stork Club" in the sky, and believing himself therefore incapable of carrying an infant mouse all the way to its proper parents, the inebriated avian leaves the winsome rodent on the nearer doorstep of Sylvester the Cat and his bride. Sylvester is at first tempted to devour the new

Figure 0.1. The drunken stork.

arrival ("I've given birth to a breakfatht!"), but ends up defending his so unusually acquired bundle of joy from other hungry felines. The last scene finds Sylvester himself being pushed in a stroller far too small for him by the rodential parents, to whom *he* instead of the infant mouse has now been delivered in the stork's no less bungled attempt to correct his earlier mistake.

As uttered by the stork, "A baby's a baby! It's the environimonament that molds 'em" rationalizes a dereliction of duty. Under its intoxicated and intoxicating logic, no hereditary differences among offspring can really matter because environment determines everything in the fate of the young; kitten or baby mouse, the scion of the Sylvesters will be the scion their parenting produces. But the affective consequences here are just the opposite of those usually engendered by a conviction of environment's great power: among parents, as not among besotted messenger storks, such a belief tends to heighten anxiety about the conditions under which precious offspring will mature, since it is precisely those conditions that fall to parents' charge.

The cartoon does not endorse the stork's pronouncement, of course: all manner of calamity follows the Sylvesters' adoption of the baby mouse. What is instructive for our purposes is that the stork makes the remark at all. Incorporating the line about environment into an absolutely mass-cultural form, its author or authors had to assume that it would be comprehensible to most Americans, just as Wilde had to assume that his audience would make sense of his wallpaper quip.[6] To pass from the earnest aesthete on wallpaper in 1882 to the cartoon stork on the fungibility of parents in 1953, therefore, is not only to pass from the absurdly sublime to the sublimely absurd, or from a tendentially middle-class spectacle to a thoroughly cross-class entertainment. It is also to move from an indication that certain ideas about environment were widely diffused near the end of the nineteenth century to a confirmation that environment's power had achieved something like universal recognition, if not universal assent, in the postwar United States. By the middle of the twentieth century, it was clear that beauty's own fate had not been to dominate thinking about the raising of children in the new age. But environment had fared extraordinarily well.

## CHAPTER ONE

# Stealthy Environments

## GUARDED MOMENTS

On the threshold of the twentieth century, the Swedish reformer Ellen Key gave the title *Barnets århundrade*, or *The Century of the Child*, to a book that would become a runaway international bestseller. In so naming it, Key meant to forecast, or to prescribe, what the new century might be: the age when humanity would recognize how completely a society's character is determined by the way its children are raised and, by devoting its best resources to the perfecting of juvenile conditions, at last transcend the violence and misery that had constituted its sorry history thus far. Yet the title of Key's book—which was published in Swedish in 1900, enjoyed a hugely successful release in English in 1909, and had been translated into nine European languages by the end of the decade— seems no less appropriate to the century just ending when she wrote. For it was in the nineteenth century that children and childhood obtained a certain radical importance.

To be sure, the difference between historically earlier and historically later understandings of the first years of human life can be overstated. Philippe Ariès's provocative 1960 proclamation that "the idea of childhood did not exist" in the European Middle Ages has not withstood scrutiny, at least not in its most literal form, and it seems clear that all human cultures have taken note of sharp differences between mature people and those not fully grown. But it was only in the nineteenth century, arguably, that children (and adolescents as such) became the objects of sentimental, theoretical, and practical attention that they remain today.

The reasons why this happened are multiple; they are also contested, as in the question, not definitively settled, of whether intense parental devotion to the individual child led to or followed from a decline in infant mortality rates in Europe. One thing that does seem clear is that the chief philosophical inspiration for the new valuing of the child came from Romanticism, especially the writings wherein Jean-Jacques Rousseau and William Wordsworth countered a long-standing Christian emphasis on original sin with a compelling elaboration of original innocence. Especially influential in nineteenth-century Britain and English-speaking North America was Wordsworth's "Ode: Intimations of Immortality," which accrued a cultural potency matched by few other poems after antiquity. Its resounding lines, "But trailing clouds of glory do we come / From God, who is our home: / Heaven lies about us in our infancy!" were widely quoted and ubiquitously contemplated (Heywood 27), and the poem as a whole helped to make children both the bearers and the symbols of innocence in a morally doubtful world. The historian John Gillis has even argued that in the nineteenth century, for the first time, it was not those about to die who furnished the principal "window on eternity," but rather those just born ("Birth" 90).

As Judith Plotz has observed, the Victorians themselves credited Wordsworth and other Romantics with discovering (in the words of Horace Elisha Scudder, 1885) "childhood as a distinct individual element of life" (quoted in Plotz 1). And this verdict referred to prescription and practice as well as description and poetizing. "Love childhood; promote its games, its pleasures, its amiable instincts," Rousseau had directed in 1762's *Émile*, adding in rhetorical flourish, "Why do you want to deprive these little innocents of the enjoyment of a time so short which escapes them and of a good so precious which they do not know how to abuse?" (79). Rousseau's doctrine that the young ought not to be pushed to mature too soon was variously adapted by later educators on the Continent and then in Britain and America; it also accompanied the wide diffusion of Wordsworthian sentiments through the English-speaking world. With the help of Rousseau, Wordsworth, and other key witnesses, childhood became a phase of life ideally free from grown-up cares and duties, indeed a possession to which every person could seem eminently entitled.

In the nineteenth century, this understanding helped underwrite a breathtakingly complex array of efforts to protect the moral and physical well being of young people. Educators, reformers, journalists, clergy, scientists, physicians, government officials, and parents sponsored this work, and though their objects and long-range goals were diverse, these parties were united by a feeling that all was not right in juvenile environments as they stood. In *Émile*, Rousseau had envisioned a manipulation of circumstances so artful that almost nothing in the early years would be left to chance; the succeeding century witnessed something like an attempt to translate this plan into terms suitable to whole societies. Propelled by a concern that any moment in the young life might have lasting developmental consequences, and that damage to the juvenile might go unrecognized until all hope of correction was gone, solicitous adults took on the task of safeguarding the young from every kind of experience likely to nourish depravity, vice, shiftlessness, or failure.

Solicitude about the susceptibility of young persons was not in itself a nineteenth-century invention, or even a Romantic one. In *A Mother's Blessing or the Godly Counsaile of a gentlewoman, Not Long since Deceased, Left behind for her Children*, which went into a dozen editions before 1640 (Staub x), Dorothy Leigh aspires to show her sons the "right way" she has gleaned from scripture, "lest for want of warning they might fall where I stumbled, and then I should think my self in the fault, who knew there were such downfalls in the world, that they could hardly climb the hill to Heaven without help, and yet had not told them thereof" (quoted in Pollock 174). In a document of 1745, Eliza Pinckney of South Carolina resolves to "be careful" of her children's bodies and souls, "to watch over their tender minds, to carefully root out the first appearing and buddings of vice . . . ; to spare no pains or trouble to do them good, to correct their errors what ever uneasiness it may give [her] and never omit to encourage every virtue [she] may see dawning in them" (quoted in Pollock 175). And in a passage typical of the correspondence that would be published shortly thereafter as a model of paternal counsel, Lord Chesterfield tells his son in 1748, "your welfare, your character, your knowledge, and your morals, employ my thoughts more than anything that can happen to me, or that I can fear or hope for myself" (67).

Nor did it take until the later eighteenth century for commentators to register the developmental significance of experiences little remarked at their occurrence: in his 1693 *Thoughts concerning Education*, John Locke avers that "little, and almost insensible Impressions on our tender Infancies, have very important and lasting Consequences" (83). But it was in the age of Romanticism, with its heightened care for the moments of juvenile life, that this empiricist observation can be said to have come into its own. In *Émile*, Rousseau insists that "[f]rom the moment the child begins to distinguish objects, it is important that there be selectivity in those one shows him," since "the very choice of objects presented to him is fit to make him timid or courageous" (63). In his *Plan for the Conduct of Female Education in Boarding Schools*, 1797, Erasmus Darwin reports that a difference in learning among equally industrious children might "arise from some trivial circumstance, which determined the inclination of the fortunate student; and that it is possible, that the means may sometimes be discover'd of governing these incidents, and thus producing a new era in the art of education!" (93). The following year, Maria and Richard Lovell Edgeworth cautioned in *Practical Education* that "the first impressions which infants receive, and the first habits which they learn from their nurses, influence the temper and disposition long after the slight causes which produced them are forgotten" (8–9).

Also published in 1798 was *Lyrical Ballads*, the collection by Wordsworth and Samuel Taylor Coleridge in which the poem known to posterity as "Tintern Abbey" first appeared. Many writers before Wordsworth had written about the response of the soul to landscape, but none, arguably, had turned so keen an eye on the intimate and indeed invisible shaping performed by the experience of the natural world. In "Tintern Abbey," Wordsworth writes famously of owing to the "beauteous forms" of nature relief in times of distress, and of finding in

> hours of weariness, sensations sweet,
> Felt in the blood, and felt along the heart;
> And passing even into my purer mind,
> With tranquil restoration:—feelings too
> Of unremembered pleasure: such, perhaps,
> As have no slight or trivial influence
> On that best portion of a good man's life,
> His little, nameless, unremembered, acts
> Of kindness and of love. (*Poetical* 260)

It is not only that beauteous forms bring about tranquil restoration quietly; it is also that the very deeds nurtured by pleasurable feelings, though constituting the best portion of a life, go unremembered. As any scholar of the period will affirm, the famous Romantic obsession with consciousness decidedly encompassed a fascination with what consciousness as such does not quite hold. A poem like "Tintern Abbey" could be treasured for what it discloses about the inner life, but this disclosure includes a gesture to what has been lost to vision or never beheld at all.

In *The Prelude*, first drafted in two books in 1799 but expanded into fourteen before its posthumous publication in 1850, Wordsworth would write yet more expansively of childhood experiences whose consequence may be registered only long after, if at all. Describing youthful encounters with mountains, trees, birds, live people, and dead bodies, he stakes their claim to general interest on a revelation of how they have shaped that most interesting thing, the adult (poet's) mind. But he also stresses that we can never know exactly which childhood moments exercised what kinds of powers: "Who knows the individual hour in which / His habits were first sown, even as a seed? / Who that shall point as with a wand and say / 'This portion of the river of my mind / Came from yon fountain?'" (77). When in the famous "spots of time" passage from book twelve he declares that "[t]here are in our existence spots of time, / That with distinct pre-eminence retain / A renovating virtue," his reference is to times of depression when "our minds / Are nourished and *invisibly* repaired" (emphasis added). And this "efficacious spirit chiefly lurks / Among those passages of life that give / Profoundest knowledge to what point, and how, / The mind is lord and master—outward sense / The obedient servant of her will. Such moments / Are scattered everywhere, taking their date / From our first childhood" (429, 431). The healthy mind knows its strength and the limits of its strength, but this bright certainty depends on a shadowy process, an invisibly working renovation whose virtue or spirit does not stand forth from the backdrop of earlier passages of life but "lurks" within them.

The connection between childhood experience and what lurks is brought out yet more unsettlingly by Wordsworth's contemporary and friend Thomas De Quincey. In his 1821 *Confessions of an English Opium-Eater*, De Quincey notes that in the dreaming accompanying his opium addiction, the "minutest incidents of childhood . . . were often revived": if he "had been told of them waking, [he] should not have been able to acknowledge them as parts of [his] past experience," but appearing as they did in dreams, he "*recognised* them instantaneously." He is thus led to conclude that "there is no such thing as *forgetting* possible to the mind; a thousand accidents may, and will interpose a veil between our present consciousness and the secret inscriptions on the mind; accidents of the same sort will also rend away this veil; but alike, whether veiled or unveiled, the inscription remains for ever" (68–69). In his 1845 *Suspiria de Profundis*, De Quincey describes the brain as a "natural and mighty palimpsest" on which "[e]verlasting layers of ideas, images, feelings, have fallen . . . softly as light," and where, though "[e]ach succession has seemed to bury all that went before," yet "in reality not one has been extinguished." The whole array of moments of life, though "covered up . . . in forgetfulness," can "revive in strength" at the "hour of death," or "by fever," or "by the searchings of opium." And this means that we are never free of any of the passages of childhood, least of all the most shattering ones: "the deep, deep tragedies of infancy, as when the child's hands were unlinked for ever from his mother's neck, or his lips for ever from his sister's kisses, these remain lurking below all, and these lurk to the last" (144–46).

In so attending to the shaping powers of early experience, Wordsworth and De Quincey were responding to, if not also helping to augment, a certain shift in understandings about what young children needed in and around the home. In the early modern European household, the work of forming the child had devolved principally on the father, and it was still the father whom Locke addressed in his late seventeenth-century treatise. As primary responsibility shifted to the mother over the course of the eighteenth century, however, recommended techniques of cultivation shifted as well: forbidding lost ground to cozening; subtle and stealthy methods supplanted direct and forceful ones.[1] The Edgeworths were vigorous on the superiority of the gentle way, though this did not exclude firmness at times: promoting an associationist conditioning in which the very young would be led to link pleasure with good actions and pain with bad, they assured the young mother that the "first steps require rather caution and gentle kindness, than any difficult or laborious exertions" and that "the female sex are from their situation, their manners, and talents, peculiarly suited to the superintendence of the early years of childhood" (713). In her *Letters on the Elementary Principles of Education*, Elizabeth Hamilton too recommends the method of association: having quoted another writer on the need to watch over "the impressions and associations which the mind receives in early life, to secure it against the influence of prevailing errors" (18), she affirms that consistent preparedness for their duties on the part of mothers "would do more towards the progressive improvement of the human race, than all the discoveries of science, and researches of philosophy!" (21).

Similar counsel, sometimes explicitly beholden to the Edgeworths, was offered on the other side of the Atlantic,[2] and by the 1820s, the time of the first flood of domestic advice manuals from American publishers, maternal and quotidian "influence" had become a central concern. As Lori Merish recounts, the antebellum United States saw influence as

> a form of authority, exercised on the passions rather than reason, which oper-
> ated through persuasion instead of force. . . . Influence was seen to be both
> so subtly and habitually exercised as to be imperceptible and irresistible: in
> the words of the conduct book author Rufus Bailey [1837], influence "per-
> suade[s], and compel[s] . . . so gently that there . . . seem[s] to be the absence
> of all authority or irksome constraint." Influence, numerous antebellum au-
> thors claimed, was exercised by pleasing and refined material forms—such as
> gracious, cultivated women and elegant artifacts. (103)

Lydia Maria Child (better known today as a novelist and abolitionist and the original editor of Harriet Jacobs's *Incidents in the Life of a Slave Girl*) declares in *The Mother's Book*, her widely circulating guide of 1831, that a "silent influence, which they do not perceive, is better for young children than direct rules and prohibitions" (24) and that it "is impossible to exaggerate the importance of the spiritual atmosphere of home; of the thousand little things done and said without calculation of results; of the daily and hourly emanations from our own characters" (174–75). Indeed she borrows, for an opening hortatory flourish, the words of her brother Convers Francis, Jr., who asks in his "Discourse on Errors in Education,"

> Who can tell what may be the effects of a single good principle deeply fixed,
> a single pure and virtuous association strongly riveted, a single happy turn
> effectually given to the thoughts and affections? It may spread a salutary and
> sacred influence over the whole life and through the whole mass of the charac-
> ter of the child. Nay, more, as the characters of others, who are to come after
> him, may, and probably will, depend much on his, the impulse we give may
> not cease in him who first received it: it may go down from one generation
> to another, widening and deepening its influence as it goes, reaching forth
> with various modifications, more or less direct, till the track of its agency
> shall be completely beyond human calculation. (quoted in Child vii–viii)

The price of such a capacity for influence, however, is an extraordinary responsibility. Child also warns that mothers must spare the young every scene of anger and passion—for "who can tell how much of *moral* evil may be traced to the states of mind indulged by a mother, while tending the precious little being, who receives everything from her?" (4).[3]

Further, if even the most ordinary event in the life of the young person could be extraordinary in its consequences, the solicitous parent might have to do more than exercise an improving influence in her own person and manners. She might also have to arrange the moments of the child's day with some care. Evangelical Puritan educators had recommended disciplining children to strict regimens since the seventeenth century (Cleverley 28–29), but it was over the course of the nineteenth that good management of the home took on the character of a professional enterprise. As Ann Hulbert points out in *Raising America: Experts, Parents, and a Century of Advice about Children*, by the end of the century, children were being prepared for a future in a world "set up increasingly along managerial and professional lines," so that it "stood to reason . . . that middle-class motherhood should become a vocation more akin to professional management, and in an era awed by Frederick Winslow Taylor's efficiency studies, that meant 'scientific'" (36). Hulbert quotes, among other sources, a speaker at the first National Congress of Mothers, held in Washington in 1897, who urged her hearers to "become students of childhood and students of every system, scheme, plan, and practice of the development of the body, mind, and character of the child" (32, quoting Dickinson 18).

We might supplement Hulbert's point by noting the lack of irony with which other participants at the Congress proclaimed the mother's first duty to be "the duty of the organizer," called "the need of an organized home life" the "one great need of many women," and emphasized the unparalleled importance of learning "how to organize our children morally" and "how to organize their bodies" (Miller 118; Newton 149; Miller 118; Miller 118). Nor was it only at the very end of the century or in the American context that authorities employed such a vocabulary. A contributor to the *American Journal of Insanity* in 1850–51 praises the mother who has "faith in useful knowledge"—as of how "right growth of the brain" is promoted by habits "formed in the nursery"—and who applies such knowledge "diligently to the gentle training of the bodily functions" (John Fonerden, quoted in Caplan 15); James Kincaid notes that "management" was often used to cover "the whole range of what one did with children" in British guides from the middle of the century forward (87–88).

It is by no means clear that many mothers (or fathers) were able to impose on their offspring's days the dramatic organization recommended by experts; indeed Hulbert cites much anecdotal evidence to the contrary. But it does seem that as the century went on, the days of young people became more systematic on another front: that of school. In England, the elite "public" schools underwent a transformation between 1840 and 1880, as reformers following the famous Thomas Arnold of Rugby moved to diminish chaos, raise the moral tone, and further organize the pedagogical day. By the 1880s, according to Edward Mack, the public school boy "was supervised so continuously from morning to night that he found very little leisure for the independent action which he had indulged in previously" (124).

Even for less affluent children, the philosophy of schooling changed in ways that paralleled developments on the domestic side. Innovations such as the "Madras" system of Andrew Bell stressed, in Alan Richardson's words, "clockwork regularity and . . . constant surveillance" (93), and as Joseph Kett observes of the American case, "concepts of moral education and practices in Sunday schools, private schools, and public schools were" modified under the view that "internalization of moral restraints and the formation of character were more likely to succeed in planned, engineered environments than in casual ones" (112). Engineering in this sense did not always mean overt regimentation: given the wide dissemination of ideas from progressive educators such as Johann Heinrich Pestalozzi and Friedrich Froebel, play and mobility could certainly be incorporated. It was not that all educators were bent on making the daily schedule of pedagogy more rigid; it was that, like parents, they were becoming more deliberate in arranging juvenile environments so as to produce desirable developmental outcomes.

No less significant than reorganization was the spread of compulsory education for the masses. Several Western European countries had tried to require schooling for children in the eighteenth and early nineteenth centuries,[4] but it was only in the later nineteenth that the movement strongly took hold (Cunningham, *Children and Childhood* 123). In the 1880s the French government passed a series of *lois scholaires* mandating free schooling for children six through thirteen (Colón, 399); in the United States, twenty-eight states enjoined compulsory education in the years following the Civil War, though enforcement lagged into the twentieth century (Cunningham, *Children and Childhood* 158); in 1880, the school-leaving age for English children was set at ten, and in the following decade there were nearly a hundred thousand truancy prosecutions each year in England and Wales (Cunningham, *Children and Childhood* 158). These statutes do not signify that prior to their enactment education was only for the privileged, of course; in England, the Education Act of 1870 had laid the foundations for a national school system, and schools run by and for members of the working class had been providing literacy training for decades.[5] What the laws do mean is that by century's end, young people across classes in Britain and the United States had, at least in theory, become beings whose major occupation was supposed to be learning in a structured institutional setting.

This is to say, of course, that they had become beings whose major occupation was not supposed to be factory work, domestic servitude, or vagabondage—a principal motive for compulsory education having been the protection of children from dangerous labor (and no less dangerous idleness). Other legal and institutional augmentations of control over young people's lives, meanwhile, were designed to protect them not from exploitative employers but from careless or abusive parents. In *The Policing of Families*, Jacques Donzelot shows how this intervention burgeoned in France after the middle of the nineteenth century, from societies for child protection, which began to enter working-class households in the 1860s, to a series of acts passed between 1889 and 1912 that effected "a gradual transfer of sovereignty from the 'morally deficient' family to the body of philanthropic notables, magistrates, and children's doctors" (83). Similar developments occurred elsewhere. A Society for the Prevention of Cruelty to Children was founded in New York in 1874, while in Britain, reformers' targeting of parental neglect waxed especially intense in the ambitious 1880s, which decade culminated in the founding of the National SPCC in Britain and the enactment of laws against cruelty to children (Heywood 107–08). By the end of the century, opinion was gravitating toward the view that although the best place for children in danger was often with their own or foster families, the state should still have the power to remove them if conditions warranted (Illick 89). As Rachel Fuchs has summarized matters, late nineteenth-century politicians in a number of Western countries "became increasingly willing to position the state between the family and the child to protect children" even as "they glorified and sought to protect motherhood" (180).

The most insistent provocation to larger-scale management of the young came not from home, work, or school, however, but from the streets themselves. For in urban areas, where population growth was outpacing planning, and where crime and criminality were staple topics of an increasingly powerful popular press, what seemed most to clamor for remedy was the specter of masses of unsupervised lower-class juveniles. In a speech to Parliament in 1848, Lord Ashley, who had campaigned against the exploitation of poor children since the mid-1830s, captured the state of alarm when he estimated that London was home to thirty thousand "naked, filthy, roaming, lawless, and deserted children" (Cunningham, *Children of the Poor* 106). In New York the following year, the chief of police warned that the number of "vagrant, idle and vicious children," already "almost incredible," was "constantly increasing" (Cunningham, *Children and Childhood* 145). And from roughly the second decade of the nineteenth century on, the problem of youthful disorder enjoyed medicolegal embodiment in a new a kind of person, or rather a new juridical construction: the juvenile delinquent.[6]

As social historians have noted, the category of the delinquent comprehended not only the young person who had committed a criminal offense but also the one who might be headed in that direction. "Statutory definitions of 'delinquency,'" writes Anthony Platt, "included (1) acts that would be criminal if committed by adults, (2) acts that violated county, town or municipal ordinances, and (3) violations of vaguely defined catchalls—such as 'vicious or immoral behavior,' 'incorrigibility,' 'truancy,' 'profane or indecent language,' 'growing up in idleness,' 'living with any vicious or disreputable person,' etc.—which indicated, if unchecked, the possibility of more serious misconduct in the future" (138). Measures designed to combat delinquency tended, that is, to conflate the young person who had committed a crime with the young person who might become a criminal through deprivation, abuse, endangerment, or mere refractoriness. Thus an 1866 act in England permitted authorities to place in Industrial Schools orphans, children with parents in prison, and juveniles who were just generally troublesome (Steedman 116), while a New York City statute of 1886 recommended assignment to a reform home not only for any girl above twelve "found in a reputed house of prostitution or assignation" but also for any deemed "willfully disobedient to parent or guardian and . . . in danger of becoming morally depraved" (Colón, 464). When independent systems of juvenile courts were at last established (the first in the United States in Illinois in 1899, the first in Britain in 1908), they were explicitly authorized to deal with children who had not yet committed statutory crimes and to impose reformatory terms of indefinite length.[7]

One key reason why juvenile delinquents seemed to merit treatment different from that dispensed to adult offenders lay in their evidently greater susceptibility to environmental influences. The 1819 report of the Society for the Prevention of Pauperism in New York, an early document in the literature of juvenile delinquency, asked rhetorically, "Shall we send convicts in the morning of life, while the youthful mind is ardent and open to vivid and durable impressions," to the same penitentiaries housing adults, there "to be taught in all the requisites that will enable them to come forth when their terms of imprisonment expire, more prepared to invade the peace of cities and communities?" (Hawes 33). In succeeding years, it was this sense that young people could be especially dangerous *because* endangered that made it seem reasonable to accord governmental and philanthropic institutions a power to dispose of them far more extensive than any system's power over adults. By the later nineteenth century, errant children were coming to be seen as patients more than offenders, juvenile court judges were increasingly expected to take on attributes of the doctor-counselor or scientific researcher, and (as Robert Nye points out with respect to France but in terms that would apply to the United States and Britain as well) "the medicalization of crime" was making "the doctor an indispensable figure in the treatment of juveniles, displacing both 'paternal correction' and traditional legal processes in the 'punishment' of young delinquents" (130). In *The Young Delinquent* of 1925, Cyril Burt observes that the "outworn maxim of traditional justice that the punishment should fit the crime" is "now giving place to the sounder principle that the treatment must fit the delinquent" (586), but a version of this wisdom had been active for many years.

The clinical cast of juvenile jurisprudence was further heightened by the introduction of an array of other specialists tasked with bringing to light the factors influencing the individual child, and by the installation of the case study at the new justice's procedural heart. Indeed in *The Individual Delinquent* of 1915, William Healy, the first psychiatrist to serve an American juvenile court (Burt 592), pressed the point that "[d]ata about family traits, early characteristics, and environment may be worth much for explanation of the offender's tendencies" and insisted that "understandings of beginnings and foundations of misconduct in general, and knowledge of them as existing in the individual career" should be "a required qualification of anyone who sits in legal judgment" (Healy 12, 8). In his book of ten years later, Burt agreed that "the special method which the scientific investigator adopts in search for the causes of any particular misdeed" should be "nothing less than the taking of a complete case history," an "intensive inquiry into the whole psychological situation with a survey, as detailed and as comprehensive as he can make it, of the past, the present, and the future" (5). Offering extensive guidance on information-gathering in light of current knowledge about delinquency's causes, Burt, like Healy, contributed to a line of theory and practice elegantly summarized by Michel Foucault in *Discipline and Punish*: "The delinquent is to be distinguished from the offender by the fact that it is not so much his act as his life that is relevant in characterizing him" (252). Or as Burt himself puts it, "With the misdeeds of immature boys and girls, the main issue to be answered is not—by whom was this crime committed? but, why did this particular child commit any crime at all?" (5).

For some, the answer to this question was most often to be found in the urban milieu, where even children who attended school might spend part of each day exposed to the lure of new, inexpensive, and vicious entertainments. The 1830s saw the rise of the "penny theater" in Britain, the 1860s that of the "penny dreadful" in Britain and the "dime novel" in the United States; later on came motion pictures, which disseminated lurid images and narratives in poorly lit places of public assembly.[8] Solicitous custodians tried to counter with alternative recreations: the settlement houses, led by Toynbee Hall in London's East End (established 1884) and Chicago's Hull House (established 1888), offered counseling, gymnasiums, art galleries, kindergartens, and club meetings, while "play organizers," as Dominick Cavallo has named them, began in the American 1880s to gather funding for urban playgrounds, where the natural inclination of the young (especially boys) toward physical contest might be directed into team sports supervised by adults. Arms of the social purity movement published juvenile literature designed to compete with the more scurrilous penny dreadfuls and dimes; other reformers, including Hull House founder Jane Addams, tried theaters showing elevating rather than sensational pictures (Nasaw 15). Meanwhile, organizations like the Boy Scouts, founded in 1908, strove to channel adventurous instincts into self-discipline and patriotism. (The model figure for the Scouts was the helpful native colonial, whose skills at tracking and pathfinding served the noble cause of empire.)

But it was not only the idle hour that seemed to threaten the health and morals of the young; at least as worrisome was the fraught moment, in which an impression or experience—reading, or even briefer encounters with stimulating images—could wreak decisive harm. "No doubt the destiny of individuals has often been decided by volumes accidentally picked up and eagerly devoured at a period of life when every new impression is powerful and abiding" (144), wrote Child, recommending domestic oversight in *The Mother's Book*, and the dangers of impressionability soon became a basis for restrictions outside the household. In 1857 the influential Cockburn ruling in Britain named as the criterion of obscenity in literature "[w]hether the tendency of the matter is to deprave and corrupt those whose minds are open to such immoral influence and into whose hands a publication of this sort may fall" (quoted in Geller 22). In 1897 Anthony Comstock of New York's Society for the Suppression of Vice warned the National Congress of Mothers,

> However well we may guard our children, there are dangers of a fearful character surrounding them. Evil exists everywhere; it meets children on the public street . . . ; and every news stand furnishes material that is photographed upon the eye of the child, the negatives being carried to the chamber of imagery, where the spirit of evil may either hold them in abeyance or constantly reproduce from them pictures for the injurious entertainment of the child's mind. (179)

Healy's 1915 volume on delinquency similarly stresses the power of the visual and the special danger of sexually arousing images, whose effect may be felt not only "at the moment" but also in "the establishment of memory pictures which come up at other quiet times, such as when the individual is in bed" (307–309).

Censorship and other forms of governmental restriction could be marshaled against such threats, of course. The Cockburn ruling provided a
template for the 1873 Comstock Act in the United States, which prohib-
ited "every obscene, lewd, lascivious, or filthy book" from passing through
the mails (Geller 22). Meanwhile American libraries, beginning with the
Indianapolis Public in 1881, developed separate catalogs of books suitable
for issue to children (Geller 35), and in Britain, intensified enforcement
of laws against selling indecent pictures commenced in the mid-1880s
(Bristow 202). In addition to institutional restrictions, however, came all
manner of exhortations to vigilance on the part of individual adults and
young people. Since the days of Thomas Arnold, at least, masters and boys
at elite schools had been encouraged to maintain close watch over student
morals; in the 1880s, social-purity campaigns suggested that right-spirited
ladies might "keep a watchful eye on the hayfields at meal-times" and
investigate sleeping arrangements in their parishes (Bristow 130–31); the
purity movement also sponsored the dissemination of books and pam-
phlets assisting the young in maintaining guard over their own bodies.
As the title *Scouting for Boys* suggests, further, the skill that took pride of
place in the original manual of the Boy Scouts was keen watching—not
merely for outbreaks of vice, but for every kind of threat and sign of trouble: "Remember that it is a disgrace to a scout if, when he is with other
people, they see anything big or little, near or far, high or low, that he has
not already seen for himself" (21; see also Boehmer at xx). Part of the
genius of scouting, one might say, was that it proposed vigilance itself as
the recreation of choice.

There was another way of observing children that took flight in the later
nineteenth century, one involving not the solicitous oversight of their behavior but the scientific description of their growth and development. Indeed if the period of the late nineteenth through the early twentieth century could be called the Age of the Child Managed, it could with equal
justice be named the Age (or the dawn of the Age) of the Child Studied.
Prior to the late 1870s, there was, certainly, a literature of childhood recol-
lected in more or less fictive terms (including Saint Augustine, Goethe,
Wordsworth, and the Brontës); there was also an ample body of conduct
books and other prescriptive matter, and an array of treatises on education.
But apart from a few anticipatory documents, careful recording of the development of actual children became a print phenomenon only in the last
quarter of the nineteenth century. Seminal here were Hippolyte Taine's
1876 study of language acquisition by his daughter and, in the following
year, the appearance in the journal *Mind* of an English translation of Taine
and of Charles Darwin's "Biographical Sketch of an Infant." In the wake

of the "Sketch" (a digest of notes on his son's first months of life that Darwin had made thirty-seven years earlier), fathers in numbers began to apply their scientific curiosity to their offspring; by 1881 James Sully could observe wryly in the *Cornhill* magazine, "Men who previously never thought of meddling with the affairs of the nursery have been impelled to make periodic visits thither in the hope of eliciting important psychological facts. The tiny occupant of the cradle has had to bear the piercing glance of the scientific eye" (343). The next year saw the publication of a book marking both a culmination of the "baby biography" form and a powerful impetus to the scientific study of child development: in *Die Seele des Kindes* (*The Mind of the Child*), the German physiologist William T. Preyer gave a detailed account of his son's first three years and promoted systematic methods for the observation of children. In the 1890s, figures such as Wilhelm August Lay helped foster the experimental study of pedagogy, and within a couple of decades this too was a consuming enterprise, producing volumes of research every year (Bringmann 158).

If Darwin was a spur for fathers and Preyer for nonparental scientists, the figure who did most to inspire *mothers* to detailed observation was the American G. Stanley Hall. In 1883 Hall—who also introduced Preyer's work to the United States—published *The Contents of Children's Minds*, which synthesized information from oral questionnaires administered to six-year-olds entering the Boston school system. Adapting the method of a survey conducted in 1869 by the Pedagogical Society of Berlin, Hall tested children's recognition of a variety of objects and concepts (beehives, the growing of apples, the location of the lungs) to argue that learning is shaped to a high degree by social environment, and that pedagogy should turn on skillful direction of children's attention rather than demands for the recital of facts (Bronfenbrenner 151; Hall, "Contents" 136–37). More important than Hall's particular conclusions on this occasion, however, was that his questionnaire studies—of which he supervised more than a hundred (White 56)—supplied a focus of practice for the child-study movement. Led by the Child Study Association (founded, as The Society for the Study of Child Nature, by a group of upper-middle-class mothers in New York City in 1888), this unusual collaboration between professional and amateur researchers invited parents and teachers to submit data on many features of children's life and behavior, compilations of which were published in venues like the journal *Pedagogical Seminary*, founded by Hall in 1891.[9]

Although friction between parents and professional researchers was not long in developing, the CSA remained vital for many participants well into the twentieth century (Breeuwsma 186–89; Hulbert 29, 58–60, 98–102), and numerous publications with "child study" in the title combined sum-

maries of scientific data with advice for the individual mother. A typical
volume, William A. McKeever's *Outlines of Child Study: A Text Book for
Parent-Teacher Associations, Mothers' Clubs, and All Kindred Organizations* (1915), notes in its chapter on "the laboratory idea in child study"
how "[c]hance incident, good fortune or bad fortune in our childhood
environments, teachers who were wise or otherwise, parental thought and
carefulness or lack of it, and countless other matters, all impressed themselves upon our nerves in peculiar ways during the period of our growth
and tended to shape our personalities as we possess them to-day" (34).
Once again, the capacity of any event to shape the soul is crucially assumed,
and once again what follows from this assumption is an exhortation to
careful watching: there follow sections headed by imperatives such as
"LEARN TO OBSERVE THE CHILDREN," "STUDY THE NEIGHBORHOOD
CHILDREN," and "VISIT THE PLAYGROUND" (34–37). Another typical
manual, Ruth Strang's behaviorist-inflected *Introduction to Child Study*
(1930), offers "to show parents and teachers how to study children more
scientifically—how to make accurate, impersonal, systematic observations
over a period of time, and to record them promptly; and how to use various physical and mental tests in studying the normal development or the
special problems of a given child" (2).

In the decades around the turn of the century, developmental psychologists helped immeasurably to reinforce the belief that there are always
powerful causal links between the deep past of childhood and the present
of mature personality. According to Jerome Kagan (critiquing this view
in 1983), all theorists "assumed a structural link between the phases of
development," and many "implied that no part of the child's past could
ever be lost; every psychological property in the adult could, in theory,
be traced to a distant origin" (40). The famous psychologist Edward L.
Thorndike, for example, asserted in *The Elements of Psychology* (1905) that
"nothing of good or evil is ever lost; we may forget and forgive, but the
neurones never forget or forgive. . . . [E]very worthy deed represents a
modification of the neurones of which nothing can ever rob us" (quoted
in Kagan 41). E.E.R. Mumford, in *The Dawn of Character in the Mind of
the Child* (1925), argued that since "by the time we are grown up, 99
hundredths of our actions" are determined by habit, "we cannot exaggerate the importance of the formation of right habits in childhood, neither
can [we] exaggerate our own responsibility, as parents, in their formation"
(quoted in Kagan 40). And in *Parenthood and the Newer Psychology* (1926),
F. H. Richardson observed that "the mind of any person, child or adult,
is made up of the sum total of all of the experiences through which he has
passed since birth, plus every impression that has ever touched him in

passing, no matter how fleeting and transitory some of these may have seemed" (quoted in Kagan 40).

All of these explanations, Kagan notes, build on a premise already available in Locke's *Thoughts concerning Education*: that even insensible impressions can have important consequences (Kagan 42). As we have seen, many authorities between the time of Locke and the great age of child study (Rousseau, Erasmus Darwin, the Edgeworths, Wordsworth, De Quincey, Hamilton, Child) had stressed the power of fleeting experiences; writers after Child but before Thorndike did likewise. In *The Century of the Child*, for example, Key warned against excessive meddling in children's activities yet also recommended "devoting one's whole vigilance to the control of the environment in which the child is growing up, to watching the education which is allowed to go on by itself" (113). For, she cautions, "the ways of injuring the child are infinite, while the ways of being useful to him are few. . . . The slightest mistrust, the smallest unkindness, the least act of injustice or contemptuous ridicule, leave wounds that last for life in the finely strung soul of the child" (114).

In her prescription of vigilance, her anxiety about the power of small emotional interchanges, and her maintenance of a Rousseauistic tension between the desiderata of free, natural development and minute governance, Key distills splendidly the wisdom of the preceding decades. In her emphasis on control over environment as such, however, she seems especially attuned to turn-of-the-century priorities, her rhetoric on this point chiming neatly with speeches from the first National Congress of Mothers and with another best seller on juvenile concerns published shortly after: G. Stanley Hall's *Adolescence* of 1904. For while helping to energize the child-study movement, Hall was also engaged in other projects centered on psychology and children, among them the collating of virtually every obtainable report—scientific and unscientific, ancient and modern—on the years between childhood and full maturity. Publishing this compendium in the massive two-volume *Adolescence*, he made the case that this phase of life is biologically and psychologically distinct from childhood, and therefore requires its own special handling by physicians, parents, educators, and makers of policy. Not only was the book a phenomenal marketing success; it also established "adolescence" so firmly as a term of common use that few today would question the category's naturalness. In the words of Patricia Meyer Spacks, *Adolescence* "quickly acquired an international audience and inaugurated a period, still continuing, in which the adolescent assumed a place of pivotal importance in sociological, psychological, and literary thought and in the popular imagination" (228).

Part of the volume's appeal lay in its depiction of adolescence as a time of enormous possibility—when, for example, religious and altruistic feelings substantially emerge. Yet the adolescent that Hall brought before the public was a fragile creature too, vulnerable to the corporeal and mental ill health associated with a changing body, tinglingly receptive to vice as well as virtue. Winding up the first chapter of his book, Hall defends the importance of its project in the following terms:

> Dominant in all these aspects of adolescence is the note of an equilibrium relatively less secure than what has preceded, of an old anchorage broken, of elements less harmonized, of coordinations yet incomplete, of adjustment to the environment less fine and less settled, of insecurity and ever-impending danger of mental or physical relapse, and at the same time, of the promises and potencies of a slow but ever higher development. Hence there is need of the most careful study of consummate practical wisdom, in providing the most favorable environment and eliminating every possible cause of arrest or reversion. This is indeed the practical problem of this book.
>
> Could we solve the problems of adolescence, which these aspects of growth alone propound . . . we should thus best be able to settle the deeper problems of education in the large sense that considers it as coextensive with all the environment. (1: 49)

In spite of Hall's frequent admonition that adolescents need room to flex their dawning powers, the overall tenor of *Adolescence* can fairly be described as protective: the book not only extends the period of intense vulnerability (and thus adult solicitude) well past childhood as such but arguably makes vulnerability the leading property of the new, postchildhood phase in question. Danger is ever impending; every obstacle to development's proper trajectory must be eliminated; and it would seem desirable, were it possible, to control "all the environment" of maturation. This last conviction bespeaks Hall's debt to Rousseau, who had argued that damagingly artificial civilization is best combated by yet more ingenious artifice, that the only way to educate a child as nature dictates is to contrive surpassingly intricate approximations of once natural processes. And indeed in the preface to *Adolescence* Hall nods approvingly to Rousseau's belief that children should be raised in accordance with "primal hereditary impulses" (1: x)—which desideratum, according to Hall, is even more difficult to achieve in the urbanized contemporary world than it was in the eighteenth century.

But what was at stake, we might ask, in conceiving of the task of educators and parents as a controlling of environment? Why did it seem to Hall right to say that "education in the large sense" might be "coextensive with all the environment," and why would such a statement have made sense to Key and many others? Whence the authority and reach of this concept?

## Significant Surroundings

The major reason environment became so critical in thinking about the young over the course of the nineteenth century was that it was becoming critical in thinking about everything. To be sure, ideas about milieu can be said to figure in any empirically grounded approach to the world, in any theory or practice that attributes causal significance to circumambient conditions. But during the period on which this book focuses, environment as such became a cornerstone of Western approaches to social problems and indeed of inquiry into the nature of the universe, as important in its way as more famously nineteenth-century obsessions such as history and evolution (and childhood). When and where environment's ascent meaningfully began might be debated, but a good case can be made for the French Idéologues' pursuit of a general science of ideas at the end of the eighteenth century, which was grounded in the belief that all thoughts have their sources in the material surroundings and conditions of those who think them. For the next century at least, intense awareness of the power of milieu would set the contours of French intellectual life, from the groundbreaking evolutionary theory of Jean Baptiste Lamarck (*Philosophie Zoologique*, 1809) to the destiny-configuring settings in fictions by Hugo, Balzac, Baudelaire, and Zola; from the antihereditarian stand taken by French criminologists to French jurisprudence's keen interest in the conditions conducing to form each particular delinquent.

The concept of environment quickly became central to British and American thinking as well. The first English deployment of the term to mean "the conditions under which any person or thing lives or is developed; the sum-total of influences which modify and determine the development of life or character" recorded in the Oxford English Dictionary comes from Thomas Carlyle in 1827—three years prior, as it happens, to the first OED citation in which the term means simply "that which environs; the objects or the region surrounding anything" (also Carlyle). From the beginning, in other words, "environment" was bound up with development, redolent not only of physical location but also of the formative power exerted by a totality of influences. Nor was it merely that environment impinged on life's courses; in the view of many important scientists and literati, life was to be *defined as* the series of interactions between an organism and its environment or medium.[10] This, at any rate, was the view advanced by Auguste Comte and heavily disseminated by British and American popularizers of science such as George Henry Lewes. Particularly emphatic about the need to consider social influences on the human organism, Lewes characteristically opens the final part of his *Problems of Life and Mind* (published posthumously, in the late 1870s, under the editorship of his companion George Eliot) by marking as "the first common fact and the most fundamental" of human experience that "our psychical activity is the expression, 1°, of the action of the external medium on the organism, and, 2°, of the reaction of the organism" (3).

Yet more decisive in the rise of environment was Herbert Spencer, in some respects the most influential English intellectual of the later nineteenth century. Testimony to his role can be found in the 1901 *Dictionary of Philosophy and Psychology,* where the entry for "environment" records that it was "[r]endered current as a technical term in biology by Herbert Spencer, who conceived the organism and its environment as constantly acting and reacting upon each other" (Morgan 328). Yet this attention to unceasing interaction—nicely encoded in Spencer's 1855 definition of life as "the continuous adjustment of internal relations to external relations" (*Principles of Psychology* 374)—was not, as such, Spencer's major contribution. In itself, the formulation closely echoed Comte; it owed much also to Lamarck's belief (later confuted by Darwin, though Spencer and many others did not fully appreciate the reversal) that adaptations to environment made during an organism's lifetime could result in traits heritable by that organism's offspring. Spencer's great innovation lay rather in his use of the environment-organism interchange to ground a cosmology, at once dazzlingly ambitious and magnificently reductive, according to which all processes in the universe conform to the rule that systems proceed from unorganized homogeneity to organized diversity. Spencer developed a psychology, a biology, an ethics, and a sociology on this basis, and argued (in his massive *Principles of Sociology* and elsewhere) that society is itself an organism that will continue to improve until individuals' capacities for harmonious interaction obviate all need for coercive interference (and hence government becomes unnecessary).

Part of the appeal of any Lamarckian approach to social problems lay in a sort of optimism that transcended anxieties about demonstrated failures of human effort or competence: though there might be much suffering along the historical way, such approaches implied, the trajectory of things was inevitably toward higher, more perfectly functioning forms. Indeed what has come to be called Social Darwinism was grounded less in Darwinian natural selection than in Spencer's vision of a beneficent progress that might in small ways be assisted by human effort but could never be beholden to it. At the same time, however, there is a sense in which recognition of environment's power permits a more active and generous grappling with social ills. Where it is imagined that environment can have little effect on an organism's destiny, as in the hereditarian assumptions of eugenics, the amelioration of society has to be conceived principally in terms of discouragement to breeding by inferior human stock; there is little to look forward to for the less congenitally gifted apart from the hope that their descendants will eventually vanish. Where environment is taken to have a substantial power over human destinies, however, there remains at least some promise for any individual, especially the young and unformed. Environmental conditions may, after all, be changed.

The mention of eugenics reminds us, of course, that environment did not simply rule the day, unchallenged, in nineteenth-century thinking about the maturation of the human individual and the destiny of "the race" (where this last could signify either the totality of humanity or one particular group). "Nature" was at least as imaginatively potent in this field as was "nurture," and many of the tensest debates about social engineering, especially in the later decades, turned on an opposition between the view that heredity is the principal or even sole determinant of the course of a life and the assumption that environment is. Fin-de-siècle criminology, to which we will return shortly, staged this debate especially starkly, pitting the sometimes rigidly hereditarian views associated with Italian experts against the environmentalist inclinations of the French.

When it came to actual young people on the verge of falling into crime, however, it was difficult—no matter what one's theoretical commitments—to do anything but retain some hope that positive change might come with altered conditions. Certainly, this was the wager of delinquency law, with its emphasis on the removal of juveniles from unpromising surroundings; and it was a venture embodied above all in the case history, which tried to ascertain as thoroughly as possible the environmental factors conspiring to produce each young offender. In *The Individual Delinquent*, Healy not only makes the standard suggestion that "all adolescents showing criminalistic tendencies" be placed "in some environment that creates healthy interests and is free of stimulation towards misconduct"; he also reminds the reader that "the adolescent is in a peculiar situation in regard to control of his own environment" because unlike the theoretically mobile adult he must "be satisfied with the environmental circumstances given him" (728, 726). In *The Young Delinquent*, Burt takes pains to dismiss the view that delinquency is purely hereditary; rather, he reiterates, each case will reveal a different proportion of hereditary and environmental factors (56, 581–82).

Interest in bad environments' capacity to produce social evils was not, of course, confined to those focused narrowly on the problem of delinquency. The influential critic John Ruskin worried amply about the miserable housing conditions of the urban poor; like Octavia Hill—who, with his financial assistance, began a project of London tenement renovation in the 1860s—he believed that the love of beauty had to be cultivated among the less fortunate, and that recreation rooms, playgrounds, and gardens must therefore be provided in the East End and other zones of want (Nord 120). Other figures such as George Godwin, editor of the journal the *Builder*, felt the same: stressing that "the health and morals of the people are regulated by their dwellings" and that overcrowding was the leading cause of crime, shortened life expectancy, and drunkenness among the lower classes, Godwin too advocated the bringing of greenery to urban spaces (quoted in Winter 196). After about 1870, vice and pauperism were less and less frequently attributed to innate qualities of the impoverished, more and more to, in Nye's apt phrasing, "the pathological ecology of the urban slum" (332). And this trend was soon abetted by exposés of life among the London poor from investigators such as Charles Booth and Andrew Mearns. Urban conditions became the stuff of scandal not least by virtue of their capacity to deform the vulnerable young.[11]

By the last years of the nineteenth century, therefore, one could scarcely talk about the raising of children of any social class without referring to environment. The proceedings of the first and second National Congresses of Mothers, 1897 and 1898, furnish fine testimony on this score, revealing a broad consensus that though heredity sets limits on possibility, "environment does and must act as the one tremendous and vital power to develop unduly or to control happily the inheritance which parents stamp upon their children" (2.64). In her presidential welcome to the First Congress, Mrs. Theodore W. Birney declared that "[c]hildren of so-called depraved or vicious parents born into surroundings which develop the inherited tendency to crime should be given a better environment to secure improved results" (1.9), while in his speech on the dreadful dangers facing the young, Comstock described his topic as nothing other than "the environment of the children in our nation" (1.178). In the opening address of the Second Congress, Helen R. Wells told the assembled that children "have rights of birth, of environment, and of education" and that the "crowning right of childhood's environment is love" (2.13–14). Later in that meeting, Horace Fletcher charged that "[u]ntil the new era of good environment is established this is not a Christian, nor even a civilized country" (2.203).

As these comments suggest, a key advantage of the term "environment" was that it migrated freely between the largest set of factors affecting youth and the conditions of the individual household. This duality of meaning made it especially handy for the National Congress, whose twin aspirations were to disseminate the latest research on parental practice and to articulate a sweeping vision for children across the country. But the scope of the term also made "environment" serviceable to many others interested in juvenile issues around the turn of the century, when there was immense currency to the notion that the future depended on right nurture cooperating with healthy nature in the lives of those who would literally constitute society in years to come.

Two factors helping to increase the prominence of environment in thinking about the young, then, were a widespread tendency to associate life itself with the organism-environment interaction and the concept's ready applicability to both home and street. But environment seems to have had another, subtler allure for those worried about malleable persons. To get a handle on this additional source of its appeal, we might begin with a contemporaneous opinion from a different but related discourse. In the famous criminological debates that raged in the last three decades of the nineteenth century, French researchers, led by the anthropologist Léonce Manouvrier, famously insisted on the importance of milieu as a source of crime—this in contradistinction to the view, promoted by the Italian school associated with Cesare Lombroso, that criminal propensities are innate and can be recognized by certain bodily markers.[12] At the Second International Congress of Criminal Anthropology, held in Paris in 1889, Manouvrier admitted that criminals were slightly less anatomically perfect than noncriminals, but held insistently (and in the view of many, heroically) to the line that environment was the major factor leading to criminality. As Marie-Christine Leps reports, Manouvrier at one point in the debates "actually narrowed the definition of social milieu by claiming that no two individuals could be said to belong to the same one; he insisted that a single word, gesture, or look could significantly alter anyone's environment" (37).[13]

Part of what makes this assertion so striking is that it simply dissolves the distinction between developmental environment and unfolding experience. Events in time here become features of a kind of causal space encompassing the subject, as also happens (more prosaically and less noticeably) when we deploy the spatiotemporal noun "circumstances." But what follows from such a framing of experience? Narrowly, a position like Manouvrier's could be taken to discourage efforts to control the conditions of development: after all, if one look can alter a milieu, what chance is there of arranging things so as to keep a person from fatal courses? Yet the fact that it is possible to think of everything that impinges upon an individual as an environment seems historically to have had something like the opposite effect—to have sponsored a kind of working optimism much more in line with Manouvrier's hopes for social progress. For when a vocabulary of unpredictable occurrences in time is replaced by a language of surrounding space, the project of experiential management suddenly seems more plausible. It is manifestly the case that a person in the "environment" of a school, home, or prison is removed from the complete unpredictability of encounters in a wider world, and from this recognition it is but a short analogical step to the dream of controlling environment or milieu in a more abstract and encompassing sense. Where a sort of mad hubris might attach to the belief that one could protect a growing soul from every damaging event, thinking in the spatial terms of environment makes the exclusion of everything that would wound or deprave seem, if not easy, still an aspiration of which one need not quite despair. To speak of environment is to evoke wise arrangement rather than unrelenting watchfulness and luck.

And there is yet an additional advantage to the language of environment (or milieu), emanating from yet another duality in the term's meaning. As some of the previously quoted admonitions against uncontrolled parental emotion attest, human beings' very changefulness could seem to make them a danger to the delicate young, as in Child, where there is no telling what moral evil may be traced to the moods of an emotionally labile mother, or in Key, where the smallest unkindness can leave lifelong wounds in the juvenile soul. Given that constantly admirable behavior is hardly to be expected from most human beings, it would seem that few young people have a chance of escaping such injury. Yet here again, environment comes to the rescue. For that term can designate not only the sea of social relations in which the child matures but also, or alternatively, the complex of inanimate physical entities that surround it. And where the kind of goodness emanating from human beings is subject to interruption, there seems a reliable continuousness in the goodness belonging to objects and locations—a leading name for which, of course, is "beauty." Certainly, beauty is far from invulnerable; things can be lost, destroyed, or worn down. But the aesthetic quality of an object or a place does not fluctuate in the way a parent's fairness or a teacher's tolerance can. It would seem that if a beautiful environment can improve a child at all, it can improve that child unremittingly.

In the United States, interest in the moral effects of young people's aesthetic environments reached back at least to the eighteenth century. Then, as Merish points out, key American theologians "stressed the importance of beauty in the emotional experience of piety and endeavored to assimilate neoclassical aesthetic categories into the matrix of Protestant theology, thus tempering traditional Calvinist sanctions against luxury and art." By the 1830s, an array of Protestant authors could be found proclaiming the "'civilizing' influence of luxury and tasteful surroundings, especially domestic surroundings" (91); it was not only "cultivated women" but also "elegant artifacts," again, that were credited with improving effects.

Among architects, the most celebrated spokesman in this line was Andrew Jackson Downing, who in volumes such as *Victorian Cottage Residences* (1842) and *The Architecture of Country Houses* (1850) provided plans for buildable dwellings and moral rationales to go with them. "What an unfailing barrier against vice, immorality, and bad habits, are those tastes which lead us to embellish a home," he exclaims in a typical passage, adding that the words of God "in all his material universe, are written in lines of Beauty" (*Victorian* ix). In the same period, William Ranlett, an-

other author of plan books, wrote of the "intimate . . . connection between taste and morals, aesthetics and Christianity" (quoted in Clark 25),
while the influential minister Horace Bushnell spoke of how the child
"breathes the atmosphere of the house," and of how his parents' objects
become his own, their "life and spirit mold[ing] him" (quoted in Clark
25). According to Clifford Edward Clark, Jr., "the domestic housing cru-
sade had reached its full power" by the 1850s (28), and indeed the wed-
ding of spiritual well-being to practical domestic health can be found in
many American writers of the middle of the century, including Gervase
Wheeler (*Rural Homes*, 1851) and the collaborators Catherine Beecher
and Harriet Beecher Stowe (*The American Woman's Home*, 1869).

The moral force of domestic furnishings seems to have entered British
public discourse just a little later, on the whole, than it did American.
According to Deborah Cohen in *Household Gods*, her marvelously illuminating study of the meanings of decoration in the Victorian age, it was just
after the middle of the century that design reformers began to articulate
vigorously the position that "instruction in taste was a moral necessity . . .
because things had the power to influence people for good or ill" (19).
By the 1860s or 1870s, Cohen notes, the idea "that domestic goods helped
to shape character" had been "well established" (24), partly with the aid
of clergymen such as the Reverend W. J. Loftie, who in his 1876 *Plea for
Art in the House* sought "to provide a religious basis for home decoration"
(27). Cohen persuasively traces much of the power of this idea to a change
in prevailing modes of Christian thinking, from a worldly goods-rejecting
theology of atonement to an incarnationalist view according to which
human beings—and by extension their possessions—bear the divine
within them.

Other elements of British tradition also abetted the moralizing of domestic beauty in Victorian Britain. There was, first, the history of inquiry
into the relations between morality and taste, which had assumed immense
importance for philosophers of the English and Scottish eighteenth century such as Burke, Kames, Shaftesbury, and Hume, and which descended
to nineteenth-century British intellectuals who were absorbing, in addition, the ideas of continental aestheticians such as Kant, Schiller, and (later
on) Hegel. The hugely popular Wordsworth early helped to make the influence of the "beauteous forms" of nature familiar to audiences of many
kinds, as we have seen, and then there was the linkage between architecture and morality elaborated by commentators such as A.W.N. Pugin (a
Catholic convert who hoped that a Gothic architectural revival would support a reanimation of the Christian spirit of the Middle Ages). Above all,
there was the towering and complicated figure of Ruskin.

In his hugely influential *Seven Lamps of Architecture* (1849), the man
who would later become the first Slade Professor of Fine Art at Oxford

insisted that good architecture must be the "beginning of arts"; that it is the "embodiment of the Polity, Life, History, and Religious Faith of nations"; that with poetry it is "one of the two strong conquerors of the forgetfulness of men" (170, 165, 148); and that it is all these things insofar as it attests to a feeling of meaning and purpose in their labor on the part of those who actually build it. In his famous statement on Gothic architecture from *The Stones of Venice* (1851–53), Ruskin contrasted the deadening instrumentalization of workers under nineteenth-century mass production with the construction of the medieval cathedral, the very imperfections of which bespeak both its makers' humanity and the ordained imperfection of the human soul. But beauty's moral power was not only for artists and artisans; it was there for anyone primed to receive it, and it might minister in stealthy ways as well as more overt ones. In *Stones*, Ruskin observed that "the eye is continually influenced by what it cannot detect; nay, it is not going too far to say, that it is most influenced by what it detects least" (*Works* 10. 154). And of the *Iliad* he wrote in 1869, "all pieces of such art are didactic in the purest way, indirectly and occultly," so that when you are bettered by them "it shall be partly with a general acceptance of their influence, so constant and subtle that you shall be no more conscious of it than of the healthy digestion of food; and partly by a gift of unexpected truth, which you shall only find by slow mining for it" (quoted in Landow 67).

Ruskin's ideas were soon as influential in North America as they were in Britain. Roger B. Stein has argued, for example, that a reading of the first volumes of his *Modern Painters*, published in the 1840s, nudged Downing from a neoclassical emphasis on rules toward an appreciation of proportion as a matter of feeling (50–56); clearly Downing's comment about God's words being written in lines of Beauty echoes Ruskin's sense of beauty as theophany. Ruskin was also embraced by religious leaders who saw him as, in Stein's words, an "ally in teaching men the morality of art" (230), and best-selling books such as Charles Eastlake's *Hints on Household Taste* disseminated his ideals of sincerity in craft. Thus although Ruskin's influence over practicing architects waned in the latter decades of the century, he was widely known to the public at large, possibly as famous in the United States as he was in Britain. Indeed an American critic of 1898 named him "one of the four most famous living authors" (Stein ix).

Nor was Ruskin the only spokesman for the virtues of art and design to have American adherents. The pre-Raphaelite Brotherhood and William Morris were well known by the time of Wilde's lecture tour, and several North Americans were quick to note that Bunthorne's original appropriated phrases from Pugin, Ruskin, Eastlake, and Pater (O'Brien 68). Meanwhile, the elevating effects of art and beauty were being promoted across the continent by art schools from Philadelphia to Toronto and from Saint John to San Francisco; by little magazines produced in places like Omaha and Fort Worth; and by organizations that included decorative-arts associations in New York and Montreal as well as the "Aesthetic Society" of Jersey City and similar groups across the country (Blanchard xii; O'Brien 31; Freedman 113). It was even the case that Wilde had been preceded in Canada by another apostle of beauty. As Kevin O'Brien points out, Professor Walter Smith, principal of the Normal Arts School of Boston and state director of arts education in Massachusetts, had lectured (to much smaller audiences) on "Household Taste" in various Canadian locales the previous year. A renowned educator, the author of several books on art teaching, and a devotee of Ruskin ("the greatest art master this century has produced" [318]), Smith brought along actual household articles to illustrate his points, as Wilde did not, and stressed, as Wilde did, "the importance of beautiful homes in moulding the minds of children and making them love the good and the beautiful" (O'Brien 40, 119).[14]

Although Wilde claimed to be bringing the gospel of aestheticism to North America, then, many of those attending or reading about his lectures would already have heard that gospel in some other version. And these auditors would have been primed to take seriously not only the premise that domestic furnishings shape character but also the idea that beauty's influence will not be fully apparent to the child it is so decisively affecting (Wilde's "love what is beautiful and good, and hate what is evil and ugly, long before they know the reason why"). In *The Architecture of Country Houses*, Downing had alluded to "the partially concealed sources of that power" that architecture "exerts over our hearts and understandings" and ruminated that "[i]t would be a boon to the age, if some gifted artist would show the world the secret sources of the influence which Architecture wields in all civilized nations" (3, 2). Readers who had picked up the American printing of Loftie's *Plea for Art in the House*—a copy of which Wilde sought, incidentally, when working up his new lecture (Gere 92)—would have learned not only that the cultivation of taste "may be a moral [and] . . . even a religious duty" (89) but also that children's "taste may be warped unconsciously by some piece of poor design or some gaudy inharmonious coloring," leading them "in after life to complain of an inability to judge of colour, or a deficient eye for form owing to our neglect" (69). And those who had encountered Clarence Cook's 1878 *House Beautiful* would have heard that "the children's eye is forever being educated," so that "what they do see ought to be of a character to refine the taste, accustom the eye to harmonies of color and form, and insensibly help it to form standards of judgment" (279).

When Wilde arrived, in fact, the religious and moral motives of good furnishing were already yielding ground to the idea that the artisticness

Figure 1.1. From Clarence Cook's *House Beautiful*, 1878. Courtesy of the Division of Rare and Manuscript Collections, Cornell University Library.

of the home and its inhabitants might be an end in its own right; as Clark points out, the new emphasis of the 1870s and 1880s lay upon domestic creativity, family members' self-expression, and an ideal of the house as work of art (108, 125, 127). Still, there was no sharp break between the earlier rationale for care in home decoration and the later, nor did there seem an appreciable diminishing of the importance attached to beauty's quiet ministry. The governing principle of 1897's *Decoration of Houses*, by Edith Wharton and Ogden Codman, Jr., is not that God's words are written in beauty or that the cultivation of taste might be a religious imperative, only that architecture and decoration should work together. Yet at the end of their chapter on the schoolroom and nursery, the authors declare that "the child's visible surroundings form the basis of the best, because of the most unconscious cultivation: and not of aesthetic cultivation only, since, as has been pointed out, the development of any artistic taste, if the child's general training is of the right sort, indirectly broadens the whole view of life" (183).

Children should be helped to love what is beautiful and good, and hate what is evil and ugly, long before they know the reason why. In all civilized nations, architecture wields secret sources of influence. Children's taste may be warped unconsciously by bad design. What children do see ought to help insensibly to form their standards of judgment. The best cultivation is the most unconscious. Clearly, those affirming the formative power of beautiful environments tended to see that power as stealthy in its operation—a curious view, at first blush, because it depends on a scenario in which vivid perceptions do their meaningful work in ways unperceived. Why should the aesthetic be associated with this style of action, with sly insinuation into the soul instead of transformations taking place in the light of full awareness? To answer this question, we will need first to examine in a little more depth the later nineteenth century's interest in silently formative transactions between subject and world—in what we might call the developmental unconscious. Only then will we turn to some period hypotheses about the subtle potency of the aesthetic.

## THE UNCONSCIOUS BEFORE FREUD

At one point in his massive *On Intelligence* of 1870, Hippolyte Taine (the prolific French intellectual who, as we saw, helped to initiate the vogue for infant observation) writes as follows of the movement of molecules in the brain:

> [B]esides the mental events perceptible to consciousness, the molecular movements of the nervous centres also arouse mental events imperceptible to consciousness. These are far more numerous than the others, and of the world which makes up our being, we only perceive the highest points, the lighted-up peaks of a continent whose lower levels remain in the shade. . . .
>
> Having settled this, we see the moral world extending far beyond the limits assigned to it. We are accustomed to limit it to events of which we have consciousness; but it is now plain that the capacity of appearing to consciousness belongs only to certain of these events; the majority of them do not possess it. Outside a little luminous circle, lies a large ring of twilight, and beyond this an indefinite night; but the events of this twilight and this night are as real as those within the luminous circle. (1: 180–81)

Others had used similar language in treating of the unconscious. Lectures by the Scottish philosopher William Hamilton, published posthumously a decade before, had included a vision of "the sphere of our conscious modifications" as "only a small circle in the centre of a far wider sphere of action and passion, of which we are only conscious through its effects" (83). Gustav Fechner, one of the founders of psychophysics, was fond of comparing the mind to an iceberg whose tip is played upon by the winds of awareness but whose greater mass lies beneath the surface (Whyte 160). Lewes had affirmed that "unconscious processes in the region of thought or of action" form "by far the larger part of our psychical activity" (139). And many other authorities agreed.[15]

Yet what the unconscious meant for these writers was not quite what it connotes for most people today. A twenty-first-century nonspecialist might—in the wake of a hundred years of dissemination and reinterpretation of the work of Sigmund Freud—think of the unconscious as a dark place in the mind where desires and drives inadmissible to consciousness carry on a largely unseen activity that occasionally erupts into symptoms or analytic revelations. From the middle of the nineteenth century up to the Great War (after which Freud's formulations began to assume their preeminence), however, the unconscious covered a much wider range of elusive phenomena, including the unwilled operations by which we synthesize sense data into meaningful forms, the knowledge that we seem to store even while sleeping or thinking of other things, the cognitive operations that transpire away from the light of consciousness, the capacities that our bodies develop without explicit direction, and the neurophysiological changes that subtend experience and the evolution of personality. At once exemplary of the meanings held by the unconscious in the second half of the nineteenth century and critical in shaping those meanings was William Carpenter's 1855 proposal of "unconscious cerebration," a kind of thinking that occurs outside of awareness but whose existence is attested by (for example) the fact that we may be unable to recall some name or phrase when we try hard, only to have it flash unbidden into recollection later on ("Power" 99–100). A similarly significant proposal was that of "unconscious inference," by which process—according to Hermann von Helmholtz, possibly drawing on earlier speculation by John Stuart Mill—the atomistic stimuli falling on neural receptors are integrated into perceptions without our deliberately assembling them (Reed 117–18, 131–32).

There were even, arguably, ideas of the unconscious well before the nineteenth century. In his 1960 classic *The Unconscious before Freud*, L. L. Whyte assembled hundreds of snippets from writers as early as Galen to demonstrate the antiquity of the recognition that many operations of thought occur outside the purview of full attention. Whyte suggests that the need to posit an unconscious became acute after Cartesianism made awareness central to consciousness; that the adjective "unconscious" first received something like its contemporary psychological acceptation in the late eighteenth century; and that both noun and adjectival forms came into more frequent use during the first part of the nineteenth, especially in writing associated with Romanticism. (The same holds for *Unbewusst-sein* and *bewusstlos* in German.) In the later middle of the nineteenth century, propelled by theories like those of Carpenter and Helmholtz, the unconscious became a topic of general fascination: by the 1860s, it was the subject of numerous articles in periodicals, not to mention books such as Eduard von Hartmann's *Philosophy of the Unconscious*, which after its publication in 1869 sold fifty thousand copies in Europe, making it the best-selling late-century book of German philosophy (Whyte 170, Shuttleworth 20, Reed 141). According to Jenny Bourne Taylor and Sally Shuttleworth, the "notion of latent thought" became "absolutely central to mid-Victorian notions of the self" (xvi); according to Whyte, talk about the unconscious as such had by 1870 become common among Europeans eager to exhibit their cultural literacy—which is to say that "the general conception of unconscious mental processes was *conceivable* (in post-Cartesian Europe) around 1700, *topical* around 1800, and *fashionable* around 1870–1880" (163, 169, 63).

One important piece of nineteenth-century inquiry into the unconscious concerned conspicuous physical interactions between individual and environment that seemed to occur in the absence of conscious decision. In reflexes, instincts, and habits, the external world impinges on the person and the person responds, but in a manner that circumvents deliberation, bypasses the will, and sometimes amazes the response's executor. Consider, first, the reflex. In 1786 Luigi Galvani had demonstrated that frogs' muscles could be induced to contract by the application of electricity; in the 1820s Pierre Flourens showed that a bird with its entire cerebrum removed would lose perception, instinct, and volition, but could still draw away if touched and indeed fly if thrown into the air (Harrington 9). In the 1830s Marshall Hall reported the yet more dramatic finding that the human spinal cord governs a series of partly independent reflex arcs integrating the sensory and motor nerves—in other words, that in human beings stimuli applied to the extremities can lead to responses without any participation by the brain. Given that the brain had by this time been confirmed as the seat of mind, Hall was providing physiological confirmation that the body has a quasi-mental life of its own, that it can answer the world around it without always waiting for the imprimatur of consciousness. As J. D. Morrel wrote in a review of several books of psychology in 1856, the reflex mechanism "has begun to claim for itself the origination of many phenomena which were before attributed to the direct effort of the mind, or the will," so that "many actions are performed by us, and performed *consciously*, which are not in any way the result of purpose, forethought, desire, or adaptation" (quoted in Rylance 196). Or as Alexander Bain had put it the previous year in *The Senses and the Intellect* (one of the books reviewed by Morrel and still considered in some quarters the departure point of modern psychology), reflex movements furnish an important example of how "certain arrangements not included in the sphere of consciousness, or mind proper . . . yet form links in our mental actions" (256).

Bain's work, in *Senses* and elsewhere, has often been described as an attempt to harmonize new discoveries in physiology with the associationist psychology developed by David Hartley and others beginning in the middle of the eighteenth century. (Following on ideas from Locke, Hartley had proposed that early experience builds up the mind's basic structures, which subsequently sort incoming stimuli by linking "ideas" on the basis of innate resemblance or contiguity [Rylance 57–58].)[16] The remark just quoted, with its treatment of reflex in terms of "links in our mental actions," neatly instantiates Bain's project at the micro-level; another illustration, on a larger scale, lies in his treatment of instinct—"the *untaught* ability to perform actions of all kinds, and more especially such as are necessary or useful to the animal" (256)—which forms the major subject of the same chapter of *Senses*. Bain's hypothesis in this area (several pieces of which were developed decades earlier by Thomas Brown of the University of Edinburgh, as Edward Reed has shown [64–79]) is that the human behaviors labeled "instinctive" in fact develop through a process akin to what later researchers would call conditioning. Under this view, the young organism produces motor acts that are at first simply random but quickly come to be associated with pleasures or pains that result from them, as when an infant feeling cold happens to touch the nurse lying next to it and feels the alleviation provided by the nurse's warmth. Once such associations are forged, movements targeted to the avoidance of pain and the inducement of pleasure can be initiated without the participation of higher consciousness (296).

Like the phenomena of reflex and instinct, habit (described by one of Spencer's American disseminators, E. L. Youmans, as a process in which "voluntary actions are constantly becoming reflex" [381]) seemed to show how a person could respond correctly to environmental stimuli without willing the response or even being aware of its occurrence. The history of engrossment with habit is a long one: in his *Thoughts concerning Education*, Locke had observed that habits work "more constantly and with greater facility, than reason" (171); in his *Analogy of Religion* (1736), one of the most widely read texts in the English-speaking world through the nineteenth century, Joseph Butler noted that "[w]hatever we do on the call of duty we do easier next time; whatever we fail to do we find more difficult, that is we are still less disposed to do it. We fall back on the sure law of habit" (quoted in Newsome 13). Habit was discussed by Erasmus Darwin, Carpenter, Spencer, and Lewes; and in his famous "Belfast Address" of 1874, the apostle of science John Tyndall named as "a fact of

supreme importance" that "actions, the performance of which at first requires even painful effort and deliberation, may, by habit be rendered automatic" (185). Henri Bergson associated habit with a deadening dimin-
ishment of perception that could be combated by a certain conscious
activity, while in later years delinquency theorists such as Burt, and educators such as John Dewey, stressed as Locke and Butler had how in proper
deployment of habit's automatism lay an essential tool for living.[17]

No treatment of habit, however, was as spirited as that of William James,
who in the first volume of *Principles of Psychology* (1890) not only named
the capacity to acquire habits the "most important feature" of brain physiology (from the point of view of psychological inquiry) but also described
the "laws of Nature" themselves as "nothing but the immutable habits
which the different elementary sorts of matter follow in their actions and
reactions upon each other" (103–104). For James, the brain is "an organ
in which currents pouring in from the sense-organs make with extreme
facility paths which do not easily disappear" (107), which is to say that
each experience cuts channels through the mind's expanse of possibility
that deepen further when the experiences recur. (This image of grooves
made through the mind was not James's invention; it can be found in
Spencer, Lewes, and Carpenter as well [Taylor 69; Youmans 391–92;
Lewes 17, 58].) As the means by which environment and our early choices
narrow the possibilities for the future of the self, then, habit veritably *is*
psychological development in James's scheme. And appropriately, no other
passage in *Principles* equals for rhetorical pyrotechnics the famous one in
which James describes habit as "the enormous fly-wheel of society," that
alone which "keeps us all within the bounds of ordinance, . . . saves the
children of fortune from the envious uprisings of the poor," and "dooms
us all to fight out the battle of life upon the lines of our nurture or our
early choice" (121).

Of course, this understanding has tremendous prescriptive consequences. "Could the young but realize how soon they will become mere
walking bundles of habits," James declares,

> they would give more heed to their conduct while in the plastic state. We are
> spinning our own fates, good or evil, never to be undone. Every smallest
> stroke of virtue or of vice leaves its never so little scar. The drunken Rip
> Van Winkle, in Jefferson's play, excuses himself for every fresh dereliction by
> saying, "I won't count this time!" Well! he may not count it, and a kind
> Heaven may not count it; but it is being counted none the less. Down among
> his nerve-cells and fibres the molecules are counting it, registering and stor-
> ing it up to be used against him when the next temptation comes. Nothing
> we ever do is, in strict scientific literalness, wiped out. . . . If he [any youth]
> keep faithfully busy each hour of the working-day, he may safely leave the
> final result to itself. (127)

The smallest stroke of virtue or vice leaves a scar; acts that consciousness might wish to banish still find a corporeal location among the nerve cells and fibers; nothing we ever do is wiped out. Here, in other words, Child's and Key's visions of wounding by the thoughtless parental act find a complement in the damage we do to ourselves in adopting bad habits, while the theory advanced by De Quincey and others—that no experience fails of permanent registration—is echoed in the warning that not one of our actions is, strictly speaking, erasable.

Theorists of education and juvenile improvement in succeeding decades would extend this line of thinking in various ways, whether building on James or drawing from other sources. We have already noted the formulations of the twentieth-century developmentalists cited by Kagan, and Dewey would rest his plea for an education attentive to each experience's power to shape subsequent experience on "the fact of habit, when *habit* is interpreted biologically" (*Experience* 35). In the third chapter of *Adolescence*, meanwhile, Hall supports his case for "the importance of muscular development and regimen" with a claim by the British alienist (and ardent proponent of physiological materialism) Henry Maudsley that "character is simply muscle habits." Hall also invokes modern psychology's discovery that "every change of attention and of psychic states generally plays upon them [the muscles] unconsciously, modifying their tension in subtle ways," so that they become "the vehicles of habituation, imitation, obedience, character, and even of manners and customs" (1.131–32). As Cavallo has shown at length, ideas like Hall's were vital to the push for playgrounds, where (it was theorized) character would be built up through proper exercise. Such convictions were important too for the physical culture movement—which did not, by the way, fail to receive its nod at the First National Congress of Mothers: "The idea that the body is to be educated," Julia King told that gathering, "is sweeping over the country like a tidal wave. . . . [A] true system of physical culture properly taught aids in building up ideal character" (1.193–94).

Some might object to systems like James's hortatory ethics, of course, on the ground that they simply cede too much control to lower faculties or powers. James believed that his scheme was rendered proof against such a charge, however, by the very breadth of his definition of consciousness: having stated in unmissable italics that "*habit diminishes the conscious attention with which our acts are performed,*" he also stresses that attention never diminishes quite to zero, since habitual actions are always accompanied by muscular sensations "to which we are *usually inattentive*, but which immediately call our attention if they go *wrong*" (114, 118). This distinction is highly significant to *Principles* as a whole, because one of James's major efforts there is to refute the very idea that there *is* an unconscious. In addition to scattering dismissals of the concept throughout the book, he devotes a whole chapter to rebutting arguments that phenomena such as somnambulism and hysteria prove the unconscious to exist.

It is clear, nonetheless, that much in James's psychology could be described in terms of the unconscious, since that term had often been extended to processes such as bodily learning and the absorption of stimuli at the periphery of attention. One writer who parsed the meanings of consciousness differently from James was Morton Prince, the founder of the *Journal of Abnormal Psychology* and a physician considered by some to be the leading American experimental psychiatrist of his day (Howells 451). In 1914 Prince, who had previously published a book on the dissociation of personality, brought out *The Unconscious*, which provides a matchless synthesis of thinking on the topic as it stood in the years just before Freudian psychoanalysis achieved its dominance in the United States and Britain. Prince there defines habit as the repetition of dispositions acquired not through "conscious memory" but through "unconscious memory, i.e. a physiological memory" (136) and places what we would call conditioning—as in the "reflex stimulation of saliva in dogs" being studied by Ivan Petrovich Pavlov and his team—under a category he calls "psycho-physiological" memory (139).

According to Prince, in fact, "*dormant ideas are . . . equivalent to conserved physiological complexes*" because it is only as "physiological complexes that ideas that have become dormant can be regarded as existing" (133). Bodily memory and what we think of as memory in the mind are of a piece, in other words, inasmuch as both are predicated on the neural modification that occurs in experience. And this leads Prince to his central concept of the "neurogram," which, on the analogy of the "telegram, Marconigram, and phonogram," names the "alteration left in the brain by life's experiences" (131). For Prince, the unconscious is nothing other than "the great storehouse of neurograms" (149), the region where "may be conserved a vast number of life's experiences ranging in time almost from the cradle to the grave. The hopes, the wishes, the anxieties of childhood may still be there, lying fallow, but capable of injecting themselves under favoring conditions into our personalities" (256). The unconscious is moreover so capacious and thorough, in Prince's view, that even "perceptions of the environment which *never . . . entered the fringe of the personal consciousness, i.e., of which the individual was never even dimly aware*, may be conserved" (52).

In according so large a role to retention in his characterization of the unconscious, Prince not only glances backward to De Quincey's palimpsest and the grooves and channels of Carpenter, Spencer, Lewes, and James but also looks forward (or rather sideways, given his acquaintance with Freud's work) to the formulations of psychoanalysis. For Freud, one might say, the most interesting moments in psychic life are precisely those at which the fallow hopes, wishes, and anxieties of childhood "inject themselves under favoring conditions into our personalities." In the exemplary "Wolf Man" case study, which was written in the year *The Unconscious* was published but not itself published until 1918, Freud describes the effect of the "primal scene" witnessed (or imagined) by his patient in terms of "*deferred action*. At the age of one and a half the child receives an impression to which he is unable to react adequately; he is only able to understand it and to be moved by it when the impression is revived in him at the age of four; and only twenty years later, during the analysis, is he able to grasp with his conscious mental processes what was then going on in him" (17.45). In this scenario, the mystery confronting psychology—that of how and why certain experiences are stored—finds a counterpart in the mystery confronting the child, the incomprehensibility of the scene of sex. And the experience comes into its meaning, as it were, not at the instant of its occurrence but on the occasion of its recovery.

The patient in this study presented many puzzles soliciting explanation, but the one that gave "From the History of an Infantile Neurosis" its informal title was the terror he had experienced in dreaming of white wolves. As it happens, the exemplary history Prince presents in *The Unconscious* is also one in which white animals provoke alarm. It is the case of a woman, identified as B. C. A., "who suffers from an intense fear or phobia of cats" but

> can recall no experience in her life which could have given rise to it. Yet when automatic writing is resorted to the hand writes a detailed account of a fright into which she was thrown, when she was only five or six years of age, by a white kitten which had a fit while she was playing with it. The writing also describes in minute detail the furnishings of the room where the episode occurred, the pattern of the carpet, the decorative designs of the window shades, the furniture, etc. . . . [T]his observation is typical of many others. . . . (16)

B. C. A. could not consciously remember the room at all, since her family had moved shortly after the incident in question, but her depiction was, Prince notes, corroborated by an older family member. This "minute description, by a special technic, of the furnishings of a room which had not been seen since childhood . . . and which were totally forgotten" must count, then, as "a sufficient demonstration of the principle of conservation of conscious experiences that cannot be voluntarily recalled" (19).

One intriguing feature of B. C. A.'s recollection is its rendering of the scene of her fright, which reads like a baroque confirmation, or gothic revision, of Wilde's and others' claims for the influence of decoration on the maturing soul. Prince does not describe B. C. A. (or any patient recovering a memory) as being dramatically affected by domestic accoutrements themselves, but it does seem that solicitude about such furnishings' effects on the young intensified in the wake of Freud's and other experts' emphasis on the power of early experience: according to Clifford Clark, "interest in the traditional notion of the shaping power of the home environment was reinforced by psychological theories that stressed the importance of childhood and the subconscious" (153). More significant for our overview of the unconscious, however, is that B. C. A.'s childhood incident surfaced through automatic writing—a practice wherein the subject does not consciously direct the writing hand, either because exposed to some distraction or because in some other unusual state such as hypnosis (B. C. A.'s situation, in fact, at the time she drew forth the incident of the kitten) (15). Analysis, hypnosis, and automatic writing were indeed three of the "favoring conditions" that had for some time been recognized as conducive to recovery of otherwise inaccessible memories or abilities.

Other such conditions included a variety of abnormalities and disorders. Discussing mental latency in 1859, for example, William Hamilton had observed that the mind may contain knowledge or habits "which are revealed to consciousness in certain extraordinary exaltations of its powers" such as "madness, febrile delirium, somnambulism, catalepsy, &c." (81). In his *Principles of Mental Physiology* of 1874, Carpenter had remarked that any "trace" left by ideational states as a physical change in the cerebrum, "although remaining so long outside the 'sphere of consciousness' as to have *seemed* non-existent, may be revived again in full vividness under certain special conditions,—just as the invisible impression left upon the sensitive paper of the Photographer, is developed into a picture by the application of particular chemical re-agents. . . . Thus, the revival, in the delirium of fever, of the remembrance of a Language once familiarly known, but long forgotten, has been often noticed" ("Memory" 155). Many observers had described unusual situations in which lost memories returned, and indeed it is hard to imagine how the conception of the unconscious as a repository could have gained the hold it did apart from such exhibitions. As the British psychologist Frederic Myers summed matters up in his posthumously published *Human Personality and Its Survival of Bodily Death* (1903), "[I]nfancy, idiocy, sleep, insanity, decay;—these breaks and stagnancies in the conscious stream were always present to show us . . . that the first obvious conception of man's continuous and unitary personality was wholly insecure" (16–17).

There is not space here to rehearse the countless ways in which the young field of psychology was affected by experiments on distraction and attention; by the documentation of cases of multiple personality; by public demonstrations and private performances of hypnosis, spiritism, and automatic writing; by innumerable confrontations with hysteria, somnambulism, *idées fixes, automatisme ambulatoire*; and by other pathologies that seemed to offer tantalizing attestation to the dividedness of even the non-pathological subject. But our focus on how environments shape the self in ways unnoticed does require us to glance at one key region of this fascinating terrain, that of suggestion. The suggestibility of hypnotized persons had been recognized from the first demonstrations of hypnosis, or mesmerism, in the eighteenth century: in the trance, subjects could be made to act in accordance with suggestions put by the hypnotizer, even in ways that would be grossly out of character, and subjects could remain suggestible even after the session had ended. In the late nineteenth century, Jean-Martin Charcot in Paris, and his rival Hippolyte Bernheim of Nancy, helped to make hypnosis a central topic of psychological investigation, Charcot first limiting its importance to patients suffering from hysteria, Bernheim later countering that all human beings are suggestible in varying degrees.[18] In his preface to his 1888 German translation of Bernheim's *De la suggestion et de ses applications à la thérapeutique*, a young Freud credited the Nancy school with establishing suggestion as "the nucleus of hypnotism and the key to its understanding" and "stripping the manifestations of hypnotism of their strangeness by linking them up with familiar phenomena of normal psychological life and of sleep" (1.75). By 1890, it seems, the idea that all people are subject to suggestion had become a commonplace (R. Gordon 118).

In his 1899 volume, *The Psychology of Suggestion*, which carries an introduction by William James, the Russian-born American psychologist Boris Sidis describes the "suggested idea" as "*forced* on the stream of consciousness . . . a strange, an unwelcome guest, a parasite, which the subject's consciousness seeks to get rid of" (11). But Sidis also stresses that these unwelcome guests fill our days: suggestibility is a "a constituent of our nature" that "never leaves us" (16), the essence of a "subwaking, reflex consciousness" (89) always coexisting with the waking mind. Indeed Sidis begins his book by noting how suggestibility manifests itself in ordinary life: "I hold a newspaper in my hands and begin to roll it up; soon I find that my friend sitting opposite me rolled up his in a similar way"; or one can induce someone abstracted in a problem to drink from a glass he hardly perceives by drinking from a nearby glass oneself (6). Turning to the phenomenon of crowd behavior (which Gustave Le Bon, in *The Crowd* of 1895, had associated with the dominance of the spinal cord over the brain), Sidis even goes so far as to declare, "Not sociality, not rationality, but suggestibility is what characterizes the average specimen of humanity, for *man is a suggestible animal*" (16, 17).

Not surprisingly, research into suggestibility led to concerns about its misuse as well as hopes for its beneficial application. Many worried that hypnotized subjects could be induced via suggestion to break the law, though other experts deemed such an abuse impossible; reviewing the debate in a book of 1891, Bernheim declared it likely though not certain that suggestion could "directly induce the accomplishment of a criminal act" and went on to note that it "plays a role in many crimes," even "in every action, good or bad" (107, 108, 119). It was widely known by 1890, meanwhile, that neuralgias, rheumatism, gout, dysmenorrhea and other medical conditions could be relieved through hypnotic therapy (Ellenberger 115; see also Elliotson 396–401 and Martineau 406–10), and some imagined using suggestion to enhance pedagogy. "Intellectual education," wrote Myers, "includes the training of perception, memory, and imagination; and all these faculties will be found to have been sometimes much heightened by hypnotic suggestion." Bernheim argued that if education in general would take its cues from "the doctrine of suggestion," it would cease trying to force the same uniform program upon all pupils: "to adapt each one's education to its special suggestibility . . . is the role of pedagogy as clarified by the light of psychology" (23).

Others believed that suggestion could be used to reform criminals and delinquents. According to Myers, hypnosis had already demonstrated "triumphs" in "[m]oral education"; indeed if the subject can be properly hypnotized, "no depth of previous baseness and foulness need prevent the man or woman whom we charge with 'moral insanity' or stamp as a 'criminal-born,' from rising into a state where he or she can work steadily, and render services useful to the community" (174, 199). Sidis claims no less confidently, "A knowledge of the laws of the subconscious is of momentous import in education, in the reformation of juvenile criminals and offenders, and one can hardly realize the great benefit that suffering humanity will derive from a proper methodical use of the subconscious within the province of therapeutics" (3). Among the publications advertised on the back leaves of Sidis's book, notably, are William Douglas Morrison's *Juvenile Offenders*, Enrico Ferri's *Criminal Sociology*, Cesare Lombroso's *The Female Offender*, and several volumes on pedagogy.[19]

Yet there were also objections to educational deployments of suggestibility, among them that the subject so trained by the well-intentioned would be unable to resist suggestions from less benevolent quarters. In his 1907 *L'Art et l'Hypnose*, for example, Émile Magnin (who insisted that magnetism and magnetic therapy, often associated with mesmerism, were utterly different from hypnosis) objected to the use of hypnosis in moral education in the following terms: "I do not see what one would gain in availing oneself of the hypnotic method, which, on the one hand, would cure a child of vicious tendencies while, on the other, it would have made him an impulsive being, absolutely unable to resist the injunctions and influences of the environment" (57).[20] To use hypnosis to cure vicious tendencies would only be to render the child more dangerously susceptible to environmental forces—clearly an inadequate solution if a bad environment had led to the problem in the first place. But if there were serious objections to deploying so highly invasive a form of suggestion, could a gentler version be used with success?

### SECRETS OF THE AESTHETIC

Some possibilities in this direction are suggested by Magnin himself, whose topic is not the use of suggestion in education (the previous quotation in fact figuring only as a passing remark in his book) but the link between suggestion and art. *L'Art et l'Hypnose* reports the case of Magdeleine G., a woman allegedly without training in dance who, when hypnotized, responded bodily to music in a way that many observers found at once uncanny and riveting. Magnin, who staged a series of public performances featuring Magdeleine G. at the turn of the century, hypothesizes in *L'Art* that she brought to her gestures elements of music, the plastic arts, photography, and literature that she had heard or seen at earlier points in her life but did not recall. Partly on the basis of spectators' readiness to compare the often toga-clad Magdeleine to figures from Greek statuary, further, Magnin ventures that ancient Greek prophetesses and sculptors achieved their effects through a like attunement to suggestion—a resource from which, he avers, modern artists might profitably draw (284–85).

More richly theoretical treatments of the connection between suggestion and art had already appeared by the time of Magnin's book. In 1893's *La Suggestion dans l'art*, Paul Souriau had proposed to systematize a set of ideas, which he described as already in wide circulation, concerning "the suggestive value of certain works, . . . the fascination exercised upon us by certain spectacles, . . . musical hypnosis," and so on (3). Souriau devotes much attention to the likenesses between intense contemplation of art and the hypnotic state: "all activity ceases; we do nothing except look. . . . We keep the same vague smile on the lips, the same joyous emotion in the heart, the same image suspended in the spirit. It is pure contemplation. Is it not also hypnosis?" (6). Yet he also stresses that the power of suggestion is not limited to hypnotized subjects—that it operates in everyday life (as when, walking along the street, one takes to humming a tune someone else has been whistling without being aware that one has heard it) and that, like animals adopting the colors of their surroundings, "[w]e take on, little by little, the air, the appearance, the ways of speaking and of feeling of the people who surround us" (72, 242). The process by which we adopt qualities of our moral environment, which he names "*le mimétisme moral*," is clearly of a piece with the effect of art: "we therefore have a natural tendency to make ourselves like the objects of our contemplation" (243).

Figure 1.2. Madeleine Guipet, Magnin's "Magdeleine." Sequence originally captioned "Marche Funèbre de Chopin." Photographs by Frédéric Boissonnas. From Magnin, *"Magdeleine": Étude sur le geste au moyen de l'hypnose*. Courtesy of the Division of Rare and Manuscript Collections, Cornell University Library.

In 1889's *Essai sur les données immédiates de la conscience* (translated into English as *Time and Free Will*), Henri Bergson had already argued, in a passage quoted with approval by Souriau, that "the object of art is to put to sleep the active or rather resistant powers of our personality, and thus to bring us into a state of perfect responsiveness, in which we realize the idea that is suggested to us and sympathize with the feeling that is expressed. In the processes of art we shall find . . . a refined and in some measure spiritualized version of the processes commonly used to induce the state of hypnosis" (14; quoted in Souriau 72). As part of his argument against the tendency to express as quantitative or categorical distinctions what are in truth subtle qualitative differences in emotional life, Bergson goes on to insist that "the feeling of the beautiful is no specific feeling, but . . . every feeling experienced by us will assume an aesthetic character, provided that it has been *suggested*, and not *caused*" (16–17). Suggestion is the very essence of the aesthetic, then, and the aim of the artist is to share complex emotion, to enable "us to experience what he cannot make us understand . . . by choosing, among the outward signs of his emotions, those which our body is likely to imitate mechanically, though slightly, as soon as it perceives them, so as to transport us all at once into the indefinable psychological state which called them forth" (18).

If aesthetic feeling involves a certain weakening of barriers against external psychic forces, as Bergson and Souriau claim, then it would certainly be closely allied to hypnotic suggestion. But in such a case the general operation of art and beauty would also resemble the maternal influence touted by advice-givers like the Edgeworths and Lydia Child; it would encompass the wholesome effects of furnishings described by proponents of moralized decoration; and it would be of a piece with the mysterious powers of architecture mentioned by Andrew Jackson Downing. Indeed one might say that the theorists of suggestion offered a precise late answer to Downing's midcentury question about the "secret sources of the influence which Architecture wields in all civilized nations." A drawing out of sympathetic responsiveness, "*le mimétisme moral*": art as suggestion seems once again to open the way to a moral pedagogy divested of pedagogy's usual association with tedious constraint and incitements to rebel.

In this sense, formulations such as Bergson's and Souriau's speak to a line of thinking that reaches back to antiquity, according to which one of art's powers is to smuggle instruction into the soul under the cover of pleasure. From Plato to Horace to Philip Sidney, it had been argued that while many may turn to art for delight rather than instruction, the latter will be imbibed along with the former provided the work enjoyed be of an elevating kind. But *La Suggestion dans l'art* and the *Essai sur les données immédiates de la conscience* speak yet more nearly, in some respects, to philosophical aesthetics in the tradition of Immanuel Kant and Friedrich Schiller, wherein judgments of taste serve to mediate between the pleasures of sensation and the claims of reason or morality. For like Bergson's and Souriau's reflections on the element of suggestion in art, such theories of mediation finally depend upon a certain mystery, a certain eluding of the grasp of consciousness, that obtains in aesthetic experience. In Kant's *Critique of Judgment* (1790), for instance, the aesthetic seems affiliated with elusiveness on at least three fronts: in the making of aesthetic judgments, which exceed explanation in terms of concepts; in the experience of sublimity, where the mind is momentarily overwhelmed by confrontation with something so immense that it exceeds comprehension; and in the work of art imbued with genius, which seems to carry off its success without reference to recoverable rules or guidelines of taste.

The elusiveness of the aesthetic is even more important in the work of Schiller, who transformed Kant's relatively static vision of the faculties into a sort of narrative of passage from the coarsely sensuous to the truly moral. In his 1795 *Letters on the Aesthetic Education of Man*, Schiller argued that it is only by means of the aesthetic that an individual or a whole society can rise from a condition in which mere response to sensation governs all to one characterized by autonomous thought. Humankind must, according to Schiller, "be momentarily free from all determination and pass through a condition of mere determinability"— must pass, that is, through the aesthetic condition—if "under the influence of a barbarous constitution" the character is ever to "become enno-bled" (98, 50). Significantly, Schiller allows that this civilizing effect of beauty can emerge not only from the grave contemplation of great art but also from a more general immersion in the tasteful: though speaking of "the race" as a whole, he seems to be referring to the individual as well when he declares that "just as form gradually approaches him from without, in his dwelling, his furniture, his clothing, it begins finally to take possession of Man himself, to transform at first only the outward but ultimately the inward man" (136).

Elsewhere Schiller remarks that "[p]oetry sets out from the uncon-scious" (quoted in Whyte 129); and in a lecture from 1784 (or seven years before he began reading Kant), he can be found arguing, in reference to the moral power of dramatic art, that images "transmitted by the [theatri-cal] stage eventually become one with the morality of the common man and in certain cases determine his sensations. . . . These impressions are indelible and the slightest stimulus can recall the whole cautionary aes-thetic image to the hearts of men as if it had returned from the grave" (quoted in Hart 28). Once again, we find the soul laid open to improve-ment by art; once again, the activity of the aesthetic involves a stealthy penetration and a permanent change in the subject, a working via what we may think of as a developmental unconscious.

Nineteenth-century British critics seldom declared themselves be-holden to Schiller, in part because Thomas Carlyle, who did most to intro-duce that writer's work to Britain, also warned that Schiller's aesthetic theory was (like much in German Romanticism) too idealist and abstract to be embraced wholeheartedly (Sharpe 36).[21] Yet as we have seen, many Anglo-American writers echoed in one way or another Schiller's claims anent the formative virtues of the aesthetic. Insisting on the importance of built environments to societies as well as persons, Ruskin supplemented Wordsworth's rendering of individual development with a Schillerian at-tention to the civic importance of beauty's shaping of souls. Builders, dec-orators, and aesthetes, including Oscar Wilde, echoed Schiller's remark on the morally transformative powers of dwellings and furnishings. And, as we will see in chapter 2, Walter Pater evoked Schiller in a different way, connecting beauty with both a quiet refining of the soul and a hope for freedom from determination by the forces that impinge upon us.

The wealth of these adaptations should not lead us to conclude, how-ever, that all critics who linked art with the unconscious emphasized the moral gains that could accompany pleasure. It was also possible to focus on pleasure alone. In his 1866 treatise, *The Gay Science*, Pater's contemporary Eneas Sweetland Dallas charges that German critics, Schiller paramount among them, go wrong in assuming all art to take "the idea of the beau-tiful" for its theme (85). For what in fact unites the arts, according to

Dallas, is that they have pleasure for their object, as we can discern if we probe science's discovery that the sphere of the unconscious is far larger than that of consciousness. "We live," he writes (with William Hamilton's observations especially in mind),

> in two concentric worlds of thought,—an inner ring, of which we are conscious, and which may be described as illuminated; an outer one, of which we are unconscious, and which may be described as in the dark. Between the outer and the inner ring . . . there is a free and a constant but unobserved traffic for ever carried on. . . . What passes in the outside world of thought, without will and for the most part beyond ken, is just that which we commonly understand as the inscrutable work of imagination; is just that which we should understand as the action of the hidden soul. (1.207–1.208)

Imagination, it turns out, is simply what transpires mentally but away from the light of consciousness; it is a name for the operation of the "Hidden Soul," for "the automatic action of the mind or any of its faculties" (1.194).

This insight then permits Dallas to explain the effects of works of art. For while "the object of science is to know and to make known, the object of art is to appropriate and to communicate the nameless grace, the ineffable secret of the know-not-what" (1.314). The "true artist," according to Dallas, recognizes "however dimly, the existence within us of a double world of thought," and attempts "by subtle forms, tones, words, allusions, associations, to establish a connection with the unconscious hemisphere of the mind, and to make us feel a mysterious energy there in the hidden soul" (1.316). Such action one can see demonstrated wonderfully in Wordsworth, whose writing "abounds with passages that vividly refer to the concealed life of the mind and the secret of poetry" (1.321–22). And it is this commerce with the unknowable that produces pleasure, "a sensible possession or enjoyment of the world beyond consciousness. We do not know that world, yet we feel it—feel it chiefly in pleasure, but sometimes in pain, which is the shadow of pleasure. . . . It is in the hidden sphere of thought, even more than in the open one, that we live, and move, and have our being; and it is in this sense that the idea of art is always a secret" (1.313).

Yet the aesthetic is linked to the secret by more than the general opacity of the unconscious; reinforcing the connection is the obscurity of the processes by which environing stimuli alter us. Like other writers we have encountered, Dallas insists that no experience fails to leave its traces, that "whether we know it or not, the senses register with a photographic accuracy whatever passes before them, and . . . the register, though it may be lost, is always imperishable" (1.215). For De Quincey, this meant that the unconscious could be a storehouse of pain, but for Dallas it becomes a hoard of strange treasures, no less valuable for the fact that it has been assembled without will or selection: "the memory grips and appropriates what it does not understand—appropriates it mechanically, like a magpie stealing a silver spoon, without knowing what it is, or what to do with it. The memory cannot help itself. It is a kleptomaniac and lets nothing go by" (1.216). For examples in support of this point, Dallas turns to somnambulism, to De Quincey on his dreams, to reports of persons on the edge of death seeing their whole lives in an instant, and to the case of the Countess of Laval, who could speak Breton (to which she had been exposed in childhood) while sleeping but not while awake. "So," Dallas concludes, "in the days of our feebleness we have witnessed scenes and events for which we have seemed to have no eyes and no ears, and a long time thereafter we describe as from imagination what is really a surrender of memory. Looks and tones come back upon us with strange vividness from the far past; and we can picture to the life transactions of which it is supposed that we have never had any experience" (1.218). For Dallas, the hidden world unclosed by art takes form through stealthy processes and stores up experiences, especially of our early years, that we may not recall and may scarcely have noted when they occurred.

Although Dallas is not overtly concerned with children or their development, then, his book illustrates neatly how, in the later nineteenth century, insights into the formative consequence of juvenile experience could help frame thinking about the significance of beauty and art. And in this it gestures to a larger point: that ideas about children's malleability, the power of environments, the mysteries of the unconscious, and the office of art all hung together in this period. Treatments of any of these matters (which correspond, of course, to the four sections of this chapter) implicitly drew upon assumptions about the others; none could have been understood precisely in the way it was had the others not commanded substantial attention and provoked extensive commentary and debate.

At this juncture, it may be worth stressing that few if any late nineteenth-century observers would have regarded beautiful environments' formative power as the guiding premise of a specific institution, a distinct social movement, or a cleanly delimited trend. Belief in the positive influence of aesthetically estimable surroundings was always tied to a broader interest in the effects—moral, psychological, social, expressive, theatrical—of domestic space, and it would have been inconceivable apart from a cultural valuation of the arts and the artistic generally whose amplitude inhabitants of later eras may not easily comprehend. Certainly, claims for the necessity of art to life continue to be broadcast today, and we can be fairly sure that the number of people in late nineteenth- and early twentieth-century Britain and the United States who thought art essential to humanity's redemption was, as a proportion of the total population, less than immense. Nonetheless, it is clear that faith in the power of the aesthetic was unusually widely diffused during this period, something between an essential component of the spirit of the age and an exceptionally long-lasting vogue. We have seen that Ruskin was for a time one of the best-known authors in the Anglo-American world and that Wilde was in the fullest sense a celebrity; less remembered is that Walter Pater, popularly associated with the idea that one ought to live life for its beautiful moments, also enjoyed wide recognition on both sides of the Atlantic around 1900.[22] It is hard to imagine someone in the twenty-first century obtaining such radical prominence by disseminating a gospel of beauty, just as it is difficult to envision masses of parents today worrying about the moral influence of home decoration, aesthetic societies attracting devotees in small towns as well as large cities, or undergraduates finding a conventional way to be unconventional in the pose of the aesthete, languidly maundering on the superiority of art to life.

If claims for the power of beauty in human development depended on a wider cultural privileging of the aesthetic, however, it was also true that this wider privileging gained much from its capacity to respond to developmental concerns. Art and beauty could not have become the repositories of so much hope had they not seemed naturally in tune with the project of improving the course of maturation—especially not in an age when progress and evolution so saturated thinking about major practical and metaphysical questions. Clearly, the aesthetic drew some of its power to captivate from its association with possibility itself, its intimations of a social fertility whose limits could not be charted because beauty's mysteries could never be fully plumbed.

With this summary point on the table, it would seem time for this section, and this long chapter as a whole, to close. Before we quite leave the secrets of the aesthetic, however, we need to draw one more element into the picture. We have seen how in Dallas's *Gay Science*, the unconscious with which art connects us is essentially a mental phenomenon; but we have also seen that some theorists regarded the unconscious as including the sphere of corporeal activity carried on without conscious direction. As it turns out, this idea of a bodily unconscious also had its effect on conceptions of the aesthetic. It is clearly at work in Bergson's remark about the artist's choosing emotions "which our body is likely to imitate mechanically, though slightly, as soon as it perceives them," and other writers too considered such effects. In "Beauty and Ugliness," published in the *Contemporary Review* in 1897, for instance, the aesthetes Vernon Lee and Kit Anstruther-Thomson argued that a subject contemplating a beautiful object replicates, in subtle muscular and respiratory movements, stresses or rhythms dimly or unconsciously perceived to be at play in the object. When one beholds the agreeable form of a beautiful jar, for example, one's sense of its wholeness leads to "bodily sensations . . . extraordinarily composed, balanced, co-related in their diversity": "one accompanies the *lift up*, so to speak, of the body of the jar by a *lift up* of one's own body; and one accompanies by a slight sense of downward pressure of the head the downward pressure of the widened rim on the jar's top. Meanwhile the jar's equal sides bring both lungs into equal play," and so on (175).

In his *Physiological Aesthetics* of 1877, the novelist and journalist Grant Allen had advanced another kind of theory about bodily response in the person absorbed by beauty. When a stimulated organ cannot discharge its function on an appropriate object, according to Allen, purposeless activity of either an active-motor or a passive-sensory kind results; we call the active-motor kind play, but we call the passive-sensory kind aesthetic experience. "Aesthetic Pleasure," therefore, may be "defined as the subjective concomitant of the normal amount of activity, not directly connected with life-serving functions, in the peripheral end-organs of the cerebro-spinal nervous system" (34). Like Lee, Allen considered sensitivity to the beautiful an evolutionary adaptation,[23] but in his formulation aesthetic experience's usefulness to the organism is associated with activity that lacks an immediate aim: for Allen, something like the purposiveness without purpose that the Kantian observer senses in the beautiful object transpires at the level of the organs themselves. What this suggests is that even conceptions of the aesthetic that insisted on its corporeal grounding could align it with a form of *resistance* to the continuous, unseen transactions between organism and environment—with a certain movement of consciousness *against* a body willing to satisfy itself without the mind's lucid assent.

Something like this possibility had already been articulated in the philosophy of Arthur Schopenhauer—which, though never vigorously embraced by British or American intellectuals, seems to have become a popular topic of discussion after receiving extended consideration in an 1853 number of *The Westminster Review* (Reed 88). In *The World as Will and Representation* (1819, revised 1844), Schopenhauer had offered a striking picture of existence in which human beings are driven to ever new cravings by manifestations within themselves of an eternally restless universal will, and in which art proffers one of the few forms of temporary release from this endless urging. Drawing on Kant's attribution of disinterestedness to aesthetic judgments, Schopenhauer stressed that in true aesthetic experience, appetitive desire gives way to a pure contemplation in which the urge to devour, to possess, to make over what is before one dissolves. In such intervals, the self is transcended, the restive will calmed, the yearnings of the animal body stilled.

Yet Schopenhauer did not conceive of this transcendence as a sheer triumph on the part of spirit over the bonds of physiology; rather, he saw it as part of the functioning of a mind embedded in the corporeal. In his telling, the "sight of beautiful objects" is certainly "a *phenomenon of the brain*" that will vary with the brain's "form and size, the fineness of its texture, and the stimulation of its activity through the energy of the pulse of its brain-arteries" (24), and aesthetic experience is made possible by the physical evolution of the human organism. Indeed for Jonathan Crary, Schopenhauer's understanding of the aesthetic indexes how pervasively important to the nineteenth century was the view that knowledge is "conditioned by the physical and anatomic functioning of the body" (79). But how, more specifically, does this philosopher explicate the relation between aesthetic feeling and corporeal substrate?

In the second volume of *The World as Will and Representation*, published in 1844, Schopenhauer explains that if we reflect on the increasing diversification of the elements of the nervous system in higher animals, we will observe "the *motive separated* . . . more and more distinctly *in consciousness* from the *act of will* it calls forth, as is the *representation* from the *will*." And on

> the degree of this separation ultimately depends the difference and gradation of the intellectual abilities between the various species of animals, as well as between individual human beings. . . . [T]he animal perceives things only in so far as they are *motives* for its will. . . . On the other hand, even the stupidest person comprehends things to some extent *objectively*, since he recognizes in them not merely what they are with reference to him, but also something of what they are with reference to themselves and other things. . . . The objectivity of knowledge, and above all of knowledge of perception, has innumerable degrees, depending on the energy of the intellect and its separation from the will. The highest degree is *genius*. (290–91)

This genius is, for Schopenhauer, that from which spring "all genuine works of the arts, of poetry, and even of philosophy" (392). Indeed within his own philosophy, he says, it is at the question of genius that "physiological considerations" meet up with "the metaphysics of the beautiful. Really aesthetic comprehension, in the higher degree peculiar only to genius, is . . . the state or condition of pure, that is to say wholly will-less, knowledge. . . . [T]he enhancement of intelligence from the dullest animal consciousness to that of man is a progressive *loosening of the intellect from the will*, which appears complete . . . in *genius*" (290–92). And this complete loosening is not without its particular physiological requirement: if a person is to possess genius, "the cerebral system must be clearly separated from the ganglionic" (376), the higher circuits strongly distinct from the lower—as might be expected given Schopenhauer's emphasis on the differentiation of the nervous system. Adapting these formulations a little freely, we might say that aesthetic experience in Schopenhauer is affiliated with something like a temporary abrogation of the course of the reflex, a pause in the relay between stimulus and response in which the intellect both differentiates itself from and recalls its continuity with the will.

The corporeal had never been wholly exiled from aesthetic theories, of course. As Denise Gigante recalls in *Taste: A Literary History*, a number of eighteenth-century commentators grounded judgment in the body: Alexander Gerard and David Hume, for instance, identified failures of the palate with corruption of the organs and laid so much stress on the likeness between "bodily" and "mental" taste that the analogy seemed to modulate into an identity (54–60). Still, it would be fair to say that in the early years of the discipline of aesthetics, the most important link between mystery and the aesthetic lay not in the latter's association with the nondiscursive body but rather in its flexibility—in a resistance to schematization by rules that made it a plausible intermediary between the teeming sensuous world and the realm of reason, morality, and law. By the middle of the nineteenth century, however, science was pressing very hard the point that daily life itself is permeated by mystery in the form of the countless physiochemical transactions shaping each one of us, only a fraction of which can be analyzed or known. Under this dispensation, aesthetic transactions between subject and world could come to seem paradigmatic of the subtle, secret processes that change the character of every person from minute to minute—or, as in Schopenhauer, of experience whose *distinctness* from mere animal existence aligns it not with the unknown but with a special kind of knowing.

All of this implies that there was more than one way of adapting Schillerian ideals to the revelation that human beings are organisms molded unceasingly by their environments. It was possible, on the one hand, to extol art and beauty for their capacity to improve the developing being, to focus on how innumerable unregistered interactions between organism and milieu might affect the growing personality in favorable ways. On the other hand, it was possible to identify the aesthetic with resistance to the demands of the appetitive body, to link it to some form of delay between stimulus and response and to embrace something along the lines of Schopenhauer's (physiologically grounded) subversion of physiology. In other words, one could imagine benefits accruing to the soul from the material determination that happens in aesthetic experience, or one could turn to the aesthetic because it permits some sort of escape from material determination. Or one could, like the subjects of our next chapter, do both.

## CHAPTER TWO

# Aestheticism's Environments

## WALTER PATER AND THE CHILD IN THE HOUSE

> Every moment some form grows perfect in hand or face;
> some tone on the hills or the sea is choicer than the rest;
> some mood of passion or insight or intellectual excite-
> ment is irresistibly real and attractive to us,—for that mo-
> ment only. Not the fruit of experience, but experience
> itself, is the end. A counted number of pulses only is given
> to us of a variegated, dramatic life. How may we see in
> them all that is to be seen in them by the finest senses?
> How shall we pass most swiftly from point to point, and
> be present always at the focus where the greatest number
> of vital forces unite in their purest energy?
>
> To burn always with this hard, gem-like flame, to
> maintain this ecstasy, is success in life. . . . Not to dis-
> criminate every moment some passionate attitude in
> those about us, and in the very brilliancy of their gifts
> some tragic dividing of forces on their ways, is, on this
> short day of frost and sun, to sleep before evening.

These lines, along with a few others also from the conclusion to *Studies in the History of the Renaissance* (1873), were the ones for which the critic and fiction writer Walter Pater was most notorious in his lifetime, and are surely the ones for which he is best known today. The powers at Oxford, where Pater was a fellow of Brasenose College beginning in 1864, were famously disturbed by their intimation that the legitimate aim of life might be sensuous pleasure; students of aestheticism have been endlessly interested in their excision from the book's second edition and the foot-note accompanying their restoration in the third: "This brief 'Conclusion' was omitted in the second edition . . . , as I conceived it might possibly mislead some of those young men into whose hands it might fall. On the whole I have thought it best to reprint it here, with some slight changes which bring it closer to my original meaning. I have dealt more fully in *Marius the Epicurean* with the thoughts suggested by it" (*Three* 217). Another enduring piece of Pateriana is that this matter of misled young men involved more than an abstract defense of hedonism: containing a number of evocations of youthful male beauty, *The Renaissance*, together with *Marius* (1885), "played in Pater's Oxford the part played more widely a few years later by Whitman's *Calamus* poems," according to Denis Donoghue. Copies of both "were given as presents from one Uranian to another and became passwords, tokens, signs of recognition between men who came together on the authority of their difference" ("Oxford" 114). Wilde, for his part, called *The Renaissance* "the golden book of spirit and sense, the holy writ of beauty," recommended it widely, and plagiarized from it at need (quoted in Donoghue, "Oxford" 103).

As several of its many explicators have observed, the conclusion radiates a remarkable combination of exuberance and *tristesse*, its powerful evocation of the richness of experience balanced by a plangent sense of loss. Every moment some form grows perfect, but the moment goes; a limited number of pulses only is given us to enjoy. What is perhaps most curious about Pater's unfolding of this vision, however, is that it relies so heavily on a vocabulary of superlatives and maxima. Given his promotion of aesthetic pleasure in *The Renaissance* and elsewhere, one might expect the accent in such a sketch to fall on quality and arrangement, on how the moments of one's life may be composed into something that would itself constitute a valid aesthetic whole. In fact, however, the rhetoric is more quantitative than qualitative, more accumulative than compositional. Pater sets the mood by referring to a *counted* number of pulses of life, then suggests that we do best by seeing in them *all* that can be seen by the *finest* senses; there follow recommendations to be present *always* at the focus where the *greatest* number of vital forces unite in their *purest* energy, to burn *always* with this hard, gemlike flame, and to discriminate *every* moment some passionate attitude in those about us. Pater wields the phrase "success in life" against the view that life's value can be assessed according to measures other than the subjective experience of moments' richness, yet because he avails himself of the language of mosts, his "success" seems not quite immune to external standards, comparative or even competitive.

Nor is this point merely rhetorical. For what could we say of someone inspired by these words to change direction in life—to give up a lucrative business career in favor of unremunerative contemplation, for instance? We could not say that such a person had decided not to worry about success, only that she had exchanged one view of what constitutes success for another. And we would have to add that Pater sets the bar for success in life exceedingly high, demanding an almost unthinkably continuous maintenance of ecstasy, a life that never fails of exquisiteness from beginning to end. Indeed more than one reader has noticed that this charge to live fully can look like a prescription as exacting, in its way, as anything the sternest Victorian moralist could devise. As James Eli Adams observes in discussing the only apparently unlikely convergences between Pater's aestheticism and muscular Christianity, "Paterean observation is indeed a labor: 'To burn always with a hard gem-like flame,' which is how Pater defines 'success in life,' is the goal of a remarkably strenuous hedonism" dependent upon a strikingly unrelenting "disciplinary impulse" (221, 229). If Pater abjured a high Victorian stress on how moral failure might occur at many junctures in a life, he did so only, we might say, to replace it with the prospect of an infinite number of failures in the form of an infinite number of moments less than intensely lived.

Pater's design for living thus presents an interesting counterpart, at the very least, to the expressions of anxiety we have seen coming from parents, educators, and reformers concerned with keeping the young on proper course: in both cases, the sense that any moment can be developmentally crucial seems to lead to a fantasy of protecting *every* moment of experience. Of course, Pater does not treat experience in precisely the same way as those pondering the management of juveniles' formative milieux: where he looks toward an ideal life in which every moment would go right, they would ensure that no moment in the temporality of youth goes wrong. Where for him the responsibility for shaping a life lies with the individual doing the experiencing, for them it is the province of adults entrusted with the care of the maturing soul. And where his ambition is a life legible as an accumulation of superb moments (an abstract diachronicity), they take as their goal the creation of a healthy adult (a vividly concrete outcome). Pater seems concerned not with relations of cause and effect in development, in other words, but with a relation of part to whole in which each moment contributes to the sum of moments that make up a fine existence.

Or at least so the conclusion to *The Renaissance*, taken on its own, might suggest. A review of Pater's larger body of work reveals a more complicated story, however; for although he does not take up the question of how modern adults should organize the lives of modern juveniles, much of his writing on behalf of the vocation of the senses does fall within fictional or quasi-fictional narratives tracing the growth of a young person, the development of a sensitive individual. And these narratives reveal an intense interest in the soul's continuous shaping by the stimuli it meets.

Among these narratives, the longest, and the one most closely resembling the traditional bildungsroman, is *Marius*. Following its eponymous hero from boyhood on a farm in the Roman countryside to young adulthood in the orbit of Marcus Aurelius (and thence to an untimely but noble death), this historical fiction turns on the evolution of its hero's philosophy of life, which acquires new refinements and emphases as he reflects on experiences, acquaintances, and teachings encountered on his journey. Yet though it continues to evolve, Marius's thinking seems to acquire its core principles in the third chapter, when at the temple of Aesculapius he imbibes the precept "of a diligent promotion of the capacity of the eye" mandating a self-discipline in which one aspires to "keep the eye clear by a sort of exquisite personal alacrity and cleanliness . . . ; to discriminate, ever more and more fastidiously, select form and colour in things from what was less select; to meditate much on beautiful visible objects, on objects, more especially, connected with the period of youth" (53–54). Reflecting on this "'aesthetic' education, as it might now be termed" (117), some chapters later, Marius does indeed seem to carry out Pater's intention, expressed in the footnote to the third edition of *The Renaissance*, to explain more fully what had been condensed in that volume's conclusion: "Such a manner of life," he thinks, "might come even to seem a kind of religion—an inward, visionary, mystic piety, or religion, by virtue of its effort to live days 'lovely and pleasant' in themselves, here and now, and with an all-sufficiency of well-being in the immediate sense of the object contemplated." Such a life might be one in which "one's existence, from day to day, came to be like a well-executed piece of music" (118).

A piety of living days lovely and pleasant in themselves, an existence that comes to resemble fine music: as in the conclusion to *The Renaissance*, the faint paradox attending this program is that it seems to mandate living wholly within each moment of life for the sake of the whole life, a fidelity to the future and the past that works by preventing them from bearing too heavily on the present. For Marius, ultimately, this will mean holding as an ideal not consummate maturity but unceasing growth. Having been exposed late in the narrative to a Christianity carrying enormous aesthetic and moral appeal, he comes to find inadequate his old fashion of attending to the visible of this world to the exclusion of worlds beyond, and it seems as though he may be about to renounce the cultivation of the eye. Yet when in his final moments he offers a verdict on his life of seeing, the verdict is favorable—and not because it has led him to some kind of perfection. The virtue of his cultivation is rather that it has inspired "a kind of candid discontent," a gentle unease that must be the "aim of a true philosophy" because it helps the soul to leave the world "with the same fresh wonder with which it had entered" and to look expectantly toward the next (294).

Something similar seems to transpire at the climax of the "Lacedaemon" chapter of *Plato and Platonism* (1893). In this idiosyncratic, historically tenuous, and oddly entrancing vision of ancient Sparta, Pater imagines an Athenian inquiring about the devotion to rigorous bodily and mental discipline for which Sparta was famous. Why expend so much effort; why show such loyalty to a system whose rewards are less than immediately evident? Why "this laborious, endless, [*sic*] education, which does not propose to give you anything very useful or enjoyable in itself?" Pater offers as the likely reply of an "intelligent young Spartan": "To the end that I myself may be a perfect work of art, issuing thus into the eyes of all Greece" (209). It does seem that what counts in Lacedaemon is the making of a model person, the end product rather than the process of ascetic discipline. And yet even here the education of the paragon is "endless," as though what would be really impossible to perfection is a sense of having been perfected, of having nowhere else to go.

From all of this, we might gather that for Pater there is no stark or implacable opposition between valuing the moments of a life for themselves and valuing them for the quality of the person they fashion. Indeed separating the good of experience as such from the good of its formative work could be a philosophically dubious enterprise inasmuch as the very fabric of identity or subjectivity might require to be understood as experiential. This last possibility—that the self might best be conceived as a texture of experience—appears to receive especially intricate airing in "The Child in the House," a short prose piece that Pater first published in 1878 (a year after Darwin's "Biographical Sketch of an Infant") and that continues to be anthologized both for the luminousness of its prose and for its astonishing evocation of childhood's passages. Here, Pater's autobiographically inflected protagonist, Florian Deleal, sets out to note "some things in the story of his spirit—in that process of brain-building by which we are, each one of us, what we are." And thinking back upon the house of his childhood, he observes in his mind's eye

> the gradual expansion of the soul which had come to be, there—of which indeed, through the law which makes the material objects about them so large an element in children's lives, it had actually become a part; inward and outward being woven through and through each other into one inextricable texture—half, tint and trace and accident of homely colour and form, from the wood and the bricks; half, mere soul-stuff, floated thither from who knows how far. (*Imaginary* 4)

Not the least remarkable feature of this quotation is the way it engages nineteenth-century science's revelations about the physiology of mind. That Pater, like many Victorian intellectuals, was preoccupied by the implications of these discoveries cannot be doubted; as we will see shortly, his first published essay treats them as the central fact of modern thought, and he makes clear in other writings that he understands human existence to be, in the most basic sense, a matter of molecular interactions governed by natural laws. In an 1868 essay on William Morris, for which he may have drawn on Spencer's *Principles of Biology* (1864–67), Pater describes our physical life as "but a perpetual motion" of "natural elements," of "phosphorous and lime and delicate fibres . . . present not in the human body alone" but also "in places most remote from it." The "passage of the blood, the wasting and repairing of the lenses of the eye, the modification of the tissues of the brain by every ray of light and sound" are but "processes which science reduces to simpler and more elementary forces," and "[l]ike the elements of which we are composed, the action of those forces extends beyond us; it rusts iron and ripens corn." Indeed our life is "but the concurrence renewed from moment to moment of forces parting sooner or later on their ways" (quoted in Donoghue, *Walter Pater* 48–49). Pater would later use this same passage, with minor modifications, for the beginning of his conclusion to *The Renaissance*—thus impelling readers to associate him, as Donoghue puts it, "with high-toned corruption" (48).[1]

In the passage from "The Child in the House," Pater presents something between an allegory and an example of this continuity of the mind with the rest of the universe's matter. Here, the soul is not a unitary and ethereal spirit contained in the child's body, but a texture woven of phenomena of the habitation (elements of "colour and form" from the wood and the bricks) and quasi-physical substances coming from unknown distances ("mere soul-stuff, floated thither from who knows how far"). Moreover, the house itself—which is the likely, though not the certain, referent of the pronoun "it"—seems "actually" to have "become a part" of Florian's soul. We speak routinely of places becoming part of people in a figurative sense, but how to understand this "actually," which suggests a more literal integration?

The modifier could be taken to indicate that particles of the house have been incorporated into the soul by being incorporated directly into the body; this would align with the view that our whole physical life is but a combination of elements such as phosphorous and lime. Or it could mean that the house has become part of the soul in the sense that perceptions of it, as of anything, occur as changes in the chemistry of the nervous apparatus. This would align with the point that the brain's tissues are modified by every ray of light and sound, and moreover would stand as the modern equivalent of the Platonic doctrine subtending Marius's "diligent promotion of the capacity of the eye," which holds that "fair things or persons visibly present—green fields, for instance, or children's faces" diffuse influences into the air that act "in the case of some peculiar natures, like potent material essences" and conform "the seer to themselves as with some cunning physical necessity" (53–54). Either way, the effect of the "actually" is to reinforce the entanglement of the soul with the material world, so that the "one inextricable texture" seems a kind of Paterian alternative to the image of mental groove cutting favored by theorists like Carpenter and James and to the neurogram envisioned decades later by Prince.

That Pater treats the child's incorporation of the house as an instance of a law—the law that "makes the material objects about them so large an element in children's lives"—implies that the process he is describing is subject to scientific necessities beyond our power to evade. And yet though this law must be unalterable in an absolute sense, Pater also suffuses the passage with a feeling of casualness and contingency. The soul stuff comes from uncertain distances and is subject to the haphazard currents of the air, while color and form appear in the delicate manifestations not only of "tint" and "trace" but also of "accident"—with which word Pater deftly links aesthetic appearance to chance, since "accident" means both a contingent event and, in philosophical discourse, a feature of an object not integral to its essence (exemplified for many epistemologists by color or "tint"). Is the "brain-building by which we are, each one of us, what we are" to be understood, then, as lawful and determined or as lawless and unfixed?

The answer, of course, is that which it seems to be will depend on one's frame of reference. Lawful in the strictest ontological sense, development can look lawless to us because we can never know all the forces and events that have conspired to build a certain brain in a certain way. This view runs in structural parallel, as it happens, to a definition of determinism that Pater might have encountered as an Oxonian and which is still cited in the Oxford English Dictionary: in the words of a contributor to the *Oxford Essays* of 1855, "determinism" is the theory that "the will is . . . determined . . . to a particular course by external inducements and formed habits, so that the consciousness of freedom rests chiefly upon an oblivion of the antecedents to our choice." Determinism holds, in other words, that we do not really possess free will but ordinarily feel as though we do because we remain unaware of most of the countless causes that have led us to each action.[2] But Pater's physiologism does not link him only to philosophical determinists. It also links him to chapter 1's worriers over childhood, with whom he shares the conviction that an individual's maturation will be affected by factors far too numerous to be known completely, that anything in the environment of childhood may have immense consequences for the growing soul.

A few paragraphs later, Pater reiterates this point in another remarkable characterization of the building of the brain. "How insignificant, at the moment," he writes,

> seem the influences of the sensible things which are tossed and fall and lie about us, so or so, in the environment of early childhood. How indelibly, as we afterward discover, they affect us; with what capricious attractions and associations they figure themselves on the white paper, the smooth wax of our ingenuous souls. . . . Our susceptibilities, the discovery of our powers,

manifold experiences . . . belong to this or the other well-remembered place in the material habitation—that little white room with the window across which the heavy blossoms could beat so peevishly in the wind, with just that particular catch or throb, such a sense of teasing in it, on gusty mornings: and the early habitation thus gradually becomes a sort of material shrine or sanctuary of sentiment; a system of visible symbolism interweaves itself through all our thoughts and passions; and, irresistibly, little shapes, voices, accidents—the angle at which the sun in the morning fell on the pillow—become parts of the great chain wherewith we are bound. (*Imaginary* 6)

Perhaps no passage in nineteenth-century writing captures more compellingly the conviction that in the formative experience of childhood every moment counts. Nothing is too insignificant to impress itself on the soul, nothing too "little" to become part of the chain that binds us.

This point about the possible consequence of every smallest stimulus could be framed much less calmly than Pater frames it, of course: as we have seen, many of those concerned with what we have been calling the developmental unconscious stressed danger instead of possibility. If Pater's rendering permits admiration to predominate over alarm, if what radiates most is the wonder rather than the peril of it all, one reason is surely that the ensemble of environmental factors he presents is dominated by nonhuman things. When people enter the picture—at least, people in the condition of unpredictable moral beings rather than mere bundles of phenomena—questions about negative influence seem to arise at once. We have seen Lydia Maria Child and Ellen Key worrying that adults can at any time injure a child via poor example or failures of emotional control, and Maria and Richard Edgeworth even devote an early chapter of *Practical Education* to the destructive effects of family acquaintances. ("It will be found impossible to educate a child at home unless all interference from visitors and acquaintance is precluded" [149].) In "The Child in the House," however, human beings do not play the strong leading roles they do in most dramas of maturation, and when external entities shape the soul of Florian Deleal they do so largely through their aesthetic qualities.

Pater's brief quasi-memoir thus rehearses a lesson also dispensed by Wilde's "Decorative Arts" lecture and other treatises on the morality of decoration: that aestheticism's brief for the special power of beauty draws some of its persuasive force from the incorruptibility of the nonhuman, the inanimate world's heartening freedom from moral inconsistency. While there can be ugly things and ugly environments, it is still easier to imagine keeping children away from uncomely objects and places than to imagine protecting them from all outbreaks of temper, injustice, or gracelessness in persons. And for Pater in particular, almost any perceived object—even one that would commonly be dismissed as lacking in beauty—can offer something to the young. As he writes elsewhere in "The Child in the House,"

> it is false to suppose that a child's sense of beauty is dependent on any choiceness, or special fineness, in the objects which present themselves to it . . . ;
> . . . the child finds for itself, and with unstinted delight, a difference for the sense, in those whites and reds through the smoke on very homely buildings, and in the gold of the dandelions at the road-side, just beyond the houses, where not a handful of earth is virgin and untouched, in the lack of better ministries to its desire of beauty. ( *Imaginary* 5)

Not only this statement but the whole unfolding of Florian's development (in which things like hawthorn trees explode in vividness while adults are relegated to the shadows) attests to a conviction that children can find their way to beauty without adult assistance, and that indeed such unmanaged exploration may be especially healthy.

In so indicating Pater picks up closely on Wordsworth, whose narratives of his own younger self have him learning chiefly from country rambles that many parents today would deem appallingly, even criminally, unsupervised. There can be no question that period readers would have recognized strong echoes of *The Prelude* and other Wordsworth poems in "The Child in the House": steeped as they were in Wordsworth's rendition of childhood, they would have found in the little story of brain-building an apt counterpart to the vast Wordsworthian treatment of the growth of a poet's mind. Yet it is not clear that Pater was wholly at one with his age on the question of what in Wordsworth mattered most. As Kenneth Daley and other critics have pointed out, the apparent self-centeredness of Wordsworth's ruminations, what Keats called the "egotistical sublime," sorted ill with the middle nineteenth century's emphasis on humility and the care of others. And if early and mid-Victorians had problems with a certain largeness in Wordsworth, they seem to have been no less ambivalent about his attention to the small. Though Victorian esteem for what ennobles fit well with the poet's feeling for natural beauty and for the proximity of children to the divine, it did not always admit easily his claims for the significance of things routinely passed over.

Thomas Arnold (the famous reforming headmaster of Rugby), for example, was deeply attracted to his friend Wordsworth's sense of relation between nature and the soul, and loved flowers in particular. But of the last lines of the "Intimations" ode—"To me the meanest flower that blows can give / Thoughts that do often lie too deep for tears"—he declared, "There is to me something in them of a morbid feeling—life is not long enough to take such intense interest in objects in themselves so little" (Stanley 168).[3] Ruskin exhibits a similar division. Often at odds with prevailing complacencies himself, he had been an enthusiast of Wordsworth from early on, venturing in a letter of 1843 that the latter "may be trusted as a guide in everything, he feels nothing but what we ought all to feel" (*Works* 4.392). Yet his eventual verdict on Wordsworth's excesses echoes Arnold's. In 1880 he faulted the poet for evading the true somberness and terror of religion, describing him as "incurious to see in the hands the print of the Nails," instead "content with intimations of immortality such as may be in skipping of lambs and laughter of children" and inclined to pass "a good deal of time in wishing that daisies could see the beauty of their own shadows, and other such profitable mental exercises" (*Works* 34.320, quoted in Daley 29–30).

Ruskin's younger (and rivalrous) Oxford colleague saw things differently. In an 1874 essay on Wordsworth (which in its revised form would be named by Wilde the best thing in the collection *Appreciations* [Donoghue 105]), Pater insists that the "peculiar function of Wordsworth's genius" is "to open out the soul of apparently little or familiar things" and thus to prove that "the end of life is not action but contemplation—*being* as distinct from *doing*" (*Three* 420, 428). In Pater's view, Wordsworth is to be admired for providing "the central and elementary expression" of a "new sense" pervading and distinguishing modern poetry, "[a]n intimate consciousness of the expression of natural things, which weighs, listens, penetrates, where the earlier mind passed roughly by" (*Three* 416–17). Indeed, Pater avers, one sifts through all the tedium of Wordsworth's less inspired passages just to get at this essential virtue, this "quiet, habitual observation of inanimate, or imperfectly animate, existence" (*Three* 417).

Not surprisingly, Pater held Wordsworth's feeling for the small seen thing to be inseparable from a feeling for the power of the moment. "In the airy building of the brain," he writes in "Wordsworth," "a special day or hour even, comes to have for him a sort of personal identity, a spirit or angel given to it, by which, for its exceptional insight, or the happy light upon it, it has a presence in one's history, and acts there, as a separate power or accomplishment; and he has celebrated in many of his poems the 'efficacious spirit,' which, as he says, resides in these 'particular spots' of time" *Three* (418). With his usual craftiness, Pater exploits the spatial sense of "spots" in Wordsworth's "spots of time" to suggest how the poet not only revitalized the spirit of place or genius loci but also gave poetry a spirit of the moment—what we might call a *genius occasionis*—that in effect underwrites Pater's own attention to the moment's power. Indeed encountering Pater on the child in the house is like encountering an intensified version of Wordsworth on the high consequence of childhood experience. The incidents Pater records seem even less striking, by adult standards, than those in *The Prelude*; the paths of influence seem stealthier; the scrutiny performed by recollection seems probing of yet smaller crannies of the self. Florian Deleal's story seems,

we might even say, the story of the young Wordsworth retuned for a time
when science has brought the molecular processes of life to center stage,
and for a sensibility impelled by beauty to attend to the sensuous world's
most intimate effects on the soul.

Yet neither Pater nor Wordsworth, it bears reiterating, was much interested in the idea of engineering the environments in which the young
mature. Their sense of the power of small events might certainly seem to
invite Rousseauistic attempts at management, but both declined to pursue
this tack for reasons that become clear upon a moment's reflection. For
Wordsworth, such maneuvers would be unnecessary because Nature has
its own plan of instruction; indeed as Judith Plotz and Alan Richardson
both note, he and his sister Dorothy deplored the surveillance recommended by authorities such as Locke, Rousseau, and the Edgeworths.[4]
For Pater, accident assumes so large a role in growth that it is hard to
imagine it overcome by studious arrangement; and in any case he no more
than Wordsworth would admit to such arrangement's necessity. Children
draw so very much, after all, from unpromising sources like the gold of
dandelions by the road.

Moreover, Pater ends the longer passage from "Child" quoted here by
stressing how childhood's transactions, just as they happen, end up becoming their own kind of law—how even an uncontrolled environment
emerges, retrospectively, as a kind of complete fact or donnée: "irresistibly,
little shapes, voices, accidents . . . become parts of the great chain wherewith we are bound." Earlier in the passage, he had emphasized contingency and spontaneity—there are powers discovered, manifold experiences, "capricious" attractions and associations—but with this surprising
final phrase he reveals how what may seem so delightfully unconstrained
amounts to an immitigable constraining. Everything that so gorgeously
fashions us also binds us; we cannot decide what our "environment of
early childhood" will be, let alone which sights or sounds will affect us
most, yet our future will be determined by the impressions such things
make on the wax of our souls. We become the creatures of our conditions
as ineluctably in this rendering as we do in the vision of Émile Zola (whose
relation to Pater will be considered further in chapter 3).

If Pater thus sets out to dignify the evanescent by stressing its formative
power over human beings, however, he seems in so doing to risk an inverse effect in which human beings lose their eminence precisely in being
enslaved to the evanescent. If from one point of view recognition of the
soul's crafting by tiny accidents elevates those accidents, from another,
such a recognition might seem to diminish the soul. And this problem
might be especially acute on the front of the aesthetic. Affiliated as it was
with obscurity, with suggestion, with unregistered physiological processes (as we saw it to be in chapter 1), the operation of aesthetic experi-

ence could seem to highlight especially unsettlingly how our characteristics and actions depend on impingements we can neither control nor discern. To reflect on beauty's stealthy power might be to recall with particular anxiety how rarely we register the forging of the links in the chain that binds us; aesthetic formation might stand as the very archetype of the processes by which environment determines destiny.

Yet it is just here that Pater will, against all odds, find a counter to this sense of our determination—a way in which the most mechanistic vision of life may become the most liberating. To see how he manages this feat, which will prove very important to the story told in the next chapters of this book, we will do best to go back a bit, to his first published essay.

In "Coleridge's Writings," which appeared in the January 1866 number of *The Westminster Review* (and was later revised into "Coleridge" for inclusion in *Appreciations*), Pater argues that since modern science has revealed human beings to be creatures of matter, what remains to us modern people is not to disavow our condition but to draw fascinated pleasure from watching our material destinies transpire. In a crucial passage near the start of the essay, he writes:

> Modern thought is distinguished from ancient by its cultivation of the "relative" spirit in place of the absolute. . . . The moral world is ever in contact with the physical; the relative spirit has invaded moral philosophy from the ground of the inductive sciences. There it has started a new analysis of the relations of body and mind, good and evil, freedom and necessity. Hard and abstract moralities are yielding to a more exact estimate of the subtlety and complexity of our life. Always as an organism increases in perfection the conditions of its life become more complex. Man is the most complex of the products of nature. Character merges into temperament; the nervous system refines itself into intellect. His physical organism is played upon not only by the physical conditions about it, but by remote laws of inheritance, the vibration of long past acts reaching him in the midst of the new order of things in which he lives. (107)

In so writing, Pater certainly indicates his familiarity with contemporary intellectual trends; the passage evokes, for example, a comment published not long after in the first issue of *Nature*, wherein George Henry Lewes refers to the "daily increasing recognition of the importance of Physiology as an element of liberal culture" and declares that the "old conception of Life as something essentially mysterious and removed from . . . the circle of natural causes, has been set aside in favour of the conception of Life as something more complex, indeed, but not otherwise more mysterious than other natural phenomena, and dependent upon the physical and chemical agencies recognized in operation in other provinces of research" (quoted in Rylance 204). Like Lewes, Pater finds no sharp division be-

tween character and the disposition of the body, between intellect and
nerves, between something radically or distinctively ours and the vibrations of heredity. All that we associate with mind, including free will and
moral responsibility, he suggests, must be reconsidered in light of the fact
that we are governed by our material substrate.

So thinking, of course, we might try to evade the problem of human
determination by shifting the frame of reference; we might speak in sociological, philological, or ideological terms instead of biological ones. But
Pater insists in his next words that if we shift the frame in any of these ways,
we still come up against the fact that we are products of our circumstances:

> When we have estimated these conditions he [man] is not yet simple and
> isolated; for the mind of the race, the character of the age, sway him this way
> or that through the medium of language and current ideas. It seems as if the
> most opposite statements about him were alike true; he is so receptive, all
> the influences of nature and of society ceaselessly playing upon him, so that
> every hour in his life is unique, changed altogether by a stray word, or glance,
> or touch. (107–08)

This passage reinforces the point that appreciation of the material basis of
mind runs together with recognition of the formative power of fleeting
experiences: the conviction that each person is every hour "changed altogether by a stray word, or glance, or touch" (with its anticipation of the
statement of Léonce Manouvrier cited in chapter 1) follows hard upon
the note that the "moral world is ever in contact with the physical." Believing the soul to be shaped constantly by material processes not only
untethers life from ethical absolutes ("[h]ard and abstract moralities") but
also makes it impossible to know which moments will be most consequential for the developing organism.

At this point in "Coleridge's Writings," recognition of our susceptibility to every stray stimulus leads Pater explicitly to the problem of free will
and necessity. If we are merely the results of interactions among material
and social forces, and if so much of our forming is not only beyond the
reach of volition but also outside the purview of consciousness, is there
any sense in which we can understand ourselves as free? What openings
for autonomy of will can remain in such a universe? Pater offers some help
in the succeeding lines, which effectively round out his striking credo:

> The truth of these relations experience gives us; not the truth of eternal out-
> lines effected once for all, but a world of fine gradations and subtly linked
> conditions, shifting intricately as we ourselves change; and bids us by a con-
> stant clearing of the organs of observation and perfecting of analysis to make
> what we can of these. To the intellect, the critical spirit, these subtleties of
> effect are more precious than anything else. (108)

An enduring objection to deterministic visions of human life has been that to see people as mere effects of the causes that converge in them must evacuate life of interest, even of substantial value: if we are only bundles of molecules performing chemical reactions according to set laws of nature, how can we believe there to be meaning in life or even anything worth contemplating? Pater answers by asserting that if recognition of the power of the forces operating on us takes something away, it also gives something back in that it puts before us unprecedentedly rich matter for contemplation—a new ampleness, intricacy, and subtlety of things to observe. If there is an opening for freedom in this world of necessity, it comes precisely with our ability to "make what we can" of the gradations and linked conditions that never cease to play upon and through us. And it is here that the modern vocation lies: in the examination of the "truth of these relations" between ourselves and our situations, in a perfecting of analysis such as occurs when we discriminate, as the conclusion to *The Renaissance* has it, "some passionate attitude in those about us, and in the very brilliancy of their gifts some tragic dividing of forces on their ways."

Pater would make these points yet more explicit, while at the same time tying them to the question of art's role in the modern world, in the chapter of *The Renaissance* devoted to Johann Winckelmann. Concluding with a gesture toward the romances of Goethe and Victor Hugo, he writes,

> What modern art has to do in the service of culture is so to rearrange the details of modern life, so to reflect it, that it may satisfy the spirit. And what does the spirit need in the face of modern life? The sense of freedom. . . . The chief factor in the thoughts of the modern mind concerning itself is the intricacy, the universality of natural law, even in the moral order. For us, necessity is not, as of old, a sort of mythological personage without us, with whom we can do warfare. It is rather a magic web woven through and through us, like that magnetic system of which modern science speaks, penetrating us with a network, subtler than our subtlest nerves, yet bearing in it the central forces of the world. Can art represent men and women in these bewildering toils so as to give the spirit at least an equivalent for the sense of freedom? . . . Natural laws we shall never modify, embarrass us as they may; but there is still something in the nobler or less noble attitude with which we watch their fatal combinations. . . . Who, if he saw through all, would fret against the chain of circumstance which endows one at the end with those great experiences? (*Three* 215–16)

Pater does not definitively say whether modern art is a wedge by which some real freedom enters the world or only a compensation for our bondage, but it is clear that in his view art can transform the otherwise stultifying knowledge of our material and social determination precisely by activating reflection on those bewildering toils. Valid modern art is just the art that enables us to "make what we can" of gradations and linked conditions, just the art that allows us to observe with fascination the shimmering of the web woven through us.

To be sure, Pater's last sentence suggests that such observing may need no validation apart from the enjoyment it gives. But the passage as a whole implies that in addition to enjoyment, this attention will provide a certain sense of freedom from the forces that shape us—that precisely insofar as we can observe the bewildering toils at work, we might gain, as Jonathan Freedman puts it in his reading of this moment, "a kind of aesthetic mastery over Necessity" (66). Whether such observation is truly free in the sense that it eludes full governance by the material processes of the nervous system (and thus by the physical laws of the universe) does not seem to matter so very much; what matters, rather, is that we feel a certain transcendence of our determinations when we contemplate them, just as we feel that we exist when we pronounce the Cartesian cogito. "There is still something in the nobler or less noble attitude with which we watch" the "fatal combinations" of "natural laws."

Pater thus locates two very different benefits in the aesthetic, one having to do with unconsciousness and stealthy processes, the other having to do with high consciousness and processes disclosed. The first benefit lies in the making of our selves by our environments described in "The Child in the House"—in that work of brain building, especially in childhood, "by which we are, each one of us, what we are." The young person may, certainly, be aware of having what we would call aesthetic experiences (Florian Deleal has many moments of intense consciousness of beauty), but this brain building will go on whether the child is aware of it or not, often beneath or out of range of consciousness. And this is perfectly fine, because such aesthetic formation is good in itself, quite apart from any observation of it. The second benefit of the aesthetic is quite different, inhering not in the making of our souls but in our capacity to observe the making of our souls. It resides in the opening of an aperture for felt freedom (amid a world of necessity) by experiences that permit a high consciousness of the forces that shape us.

In other words, Pater finds in the aesthetic an arena where the stealthy determination of our souls by outside forces might all be for the best, even did it stay stealthy, but also—in a magnificent retrieval of freedom just where one might least have thought to find it—locates in the same field of the aesthetic a way of getting some purchase on, perhaps even faintly evading, determination in general. One reason this point may be of interest is that it suggests a connection between Pater and Schopenhauer, who also wrested from the physiology of mental life a certain aesthetic path to transcendence. A second reason it may compel attention, however, is that it modifies an assumption we made earlier, when we wondered whether it is possible to distinguish between Pater's valuing of moments of heightened experience for themselves and his valuing of those moments for the subject they help to create. It turns out that the two are indeed separable, but in the sense that Pater finds distinct virtues in the stealthy fashioning of the soul by beauty, on the one hand, and the awareness of that fashioning associated with intense aesthetic experience, on the other. And there is yet a third reason why this vision of two benefits in the aesthetic—one associated with the unconscious, the other with high consciousness—may be of interest: it would prove an important legacy of Pater to some later writers, among them Oscar Wilde.

### OSCAR WILDE AND THE MAKING OF THE SOUL

In the introduction to their edition of two notebooks kept by Wilde in the mid-to-late 1870s, Philip E. Smith II and Michael S. Helfand argue that the young writer was confronted by a choice between, on the one hand, a Ruskinian stance in which philosophical idealism weds an esteem for contemplation to a sense of social mission and, on the other, a Paterian one in which philosophical materialism subtends an antitheoretical fixation on "the impressions of isolated facts or sensible things" ("Context," 16). According to Smith and Helfand, Wilde unambiguously chose the former: "Wilde's interpretation of Aristotle's *Ethics* and the importance he, like Ruskin, gave to contemplation (*theoria*) rather than Pater's *energeia* [heightened consciousness] place him firmly in the camp of the Oxford Hegelians, who used the *Ethics* to counter utilitarianism and materialism" ("Context," 17).[5]

There can be no doubt that Wilde was much more interested in the broad social consequences of art and thought than Pater, or that he pulled away from what could seem an atomizing tendency in Pater's impressionism. The claim that Wilde diverged sharply from Pater on the matter of materialism is much harder to sustain, however, in part because it depends on a representation of the older writer that seems more caricature than characterization. Smith and Helfand suggest that Pater builds a case for pure aesthetic hedonism upon premises so doggedly materialist that they virtually rule out any interest in spirit, but this is simply not so; as we have just seen, Pater is interested even in his earliest writing in what materialism does not fully compass, and particularly in the way intense contemplation can produce a feeling of liberation from material determinations. Meanwhile, the Wilde of these notebooks shows himself fascinated by nothing so much as the material basis of mind, even as he reflects in Paterian fashion on the limitations of materialism when it comes to questions of spirit and feeling.

In one entry, from a notebook clearly started during his student days at Oxford, Wilde writes, "Comparative anatomy shows us that, physically, man is but the last term of a long series which leads from the highest mammal to the almost formless speck of living protoplasm which lies on the shallow boundary between animal and vegetable life" (*Oxford Notebooks* 163–64). In an entry in the other volume reprinted by Smith and Helfand, a Commonplace Book whose period of composition at least partly overlaps that of the Oxford Notebook, protoplasm comes up again, Wilde noting science's discovery that the vehicle of life is a protoplasmic fluid whose signal attribute is "irritability." He then continues, "The problem of science is 'consciousness[.]' Is thought a property of the cerebral protoplasm in the same sense as irritability is?" (*Oxford Notebooks* 111). Elsewhere in the Commonplace Book, Wilde descends from the protoplasmic to the atomic, asking how "to a mass of nitrogen, oxygen, carbon, phosphorous and so on it can be otherwise than indifferent how they lie and move"—asking, that is, how consciousness could have arisen from matter and come to reflect upon its own condition. Some pages later he does hazard, in the idealist vein foregrounded by Smith and Helfand, that mind and matter, "Ego and . . . Non-Ego are really one . . . harmonised in the 'Original synthetic Unity' which is God . . . the Absolute Idea" (*Oxford Notebooks* 127). But he observes still a few pages further on that "modern science has shown us that both ethics and motion are results of molecular action: motion in one direction may be an ellipse, in the other a moral sentiment" (*Oxford Notebooks* 131). And in the Oxford notebook he wonders, "What is morality but the perfect adjustment of the human organism to the actual conditions of Life, and to the observance of those inexorable Laws to break which is death[?]" (*Oxford Notebooks* 156).

Most revealing anent his relation to Paterian hypotheses, however, is a note in the Commonplace Book pertaining to the passage from *The Renaissance* that we have just examined. Having transcribed Pater's lines on necessity as a web woven through us, Wilde then adds his own thought that when we combat necessity, we do so with "the weapons of its own forging, and the assertion of liberty is only the claim that from certain forms of conscious volition certain results will inevitably follow• We are indeed compassed by the high . . . [never?] leaped mountains of necessity, but for him who knows his limitations this dark horizon becomes the sunlit circle of duty" (*Oxford Notebooks* 141).[6]

To combat necessity is to do so with weapons of its own forging, and liberty means only that certain results follow from certain forms of volition: elaborating intriguingly on Pater's understanding of freedom, Wilde suggests not that consciousness and will stand in some basic ontological opposition to the world of matter and its laws, but rather that they arise from that world and work within it. We are, for Wilde as for Pater, material creatures who seem something more than material by grace of the mysterious chemical events that allowed protoplasm to begin to think about itself, the transformations that led a structure of nitrogen, oxygen, carbon, and phosphorous to be otherwise than indifferent about how its components lie and move. Wilde's closing figure is then beautifully ambiguous: it can suggest that for the person aware of the limitations imposed by necessity, duty and necessity are one (this reading hewing to the basic sense of "becomes" as "turns into"), but it can also suggest that such a person will see duty beginning precisely where necessity appears to end (this reading being more natural to the figuration Wilde uses, since it does not suggest that darkness suddenly turns into light but instead plays on the image of dark mountains meeting bright sky). Either way, however, Wilde captures the Paterian position that recognition of our determination by external forces means not the eradication of our sense of freedom but a kind of new beginning.

To be sure, Wilde takes this point in a direction Pater (at least the early Pater) would not, when he gestures to the paradox that even if we know ourselves subject to necessity we must behave as if the will were truly free. In other words, Wilde swerves from a Paterian emphasis on observation to a more familiarly Victorian (and Ruskinian) concern with action—a move consistent with his later writing, which recurs far more directly and frequently than Pater's to social effects. Yet this does not quite mean, as Smith and Helfand believe, that Wilde saw "theoretical limitations" to materialism that Pater ignored, or that his emphasis on "social responsibility" involves a superseding of the "materialist malaise" ("Context," 52). In the passage quoted, Wilde not only grounds his ethics in materialist premises but also implies that the imperative of duty is confirmed by a certain likeness between material necessity and moral necessity. In a sense, he even outdoes Pater in materialism by suggesting (in Smith and Helfand's own phrasing) that "[l]iberty exists as a conscious volition which materialists cannot exclude from the chain of necessity" and that "social responsibility (duty) can . . . not be denied as soon as liberty is acknowledged" ("Context," 52).

Clarity on Wilde's early thinking about the material basis of mind is important because it helps us to understand better his subsequent treatments of beauty's influence upon the soul. Several readers, including Smith and Helfand, have discerned a critique of materialism in Wilde's best-known nondramatic work, 1890's *Picture of Dorian Gray*, arguing either that the silver-tongued Lord Henry Wotton demonstrates the perils of a scientific vision that represses spirit or that, following the surrender of his soul to the portrait painted by Basil Hallward, Dorian becomes a

paradigm of the automaton that determinism imagines us all to be any-
way.[7] Certainly, there can be no doubt that Wotton draws his rhetoric from
Pater: "I believe," he declares in his first great set piece, "that if one man
were to live out his life fully and completely, were to give form to every
feeling, expression to every thought, reality to every dream . . . the world
would gain such a fresh impulse of joy that we would forget all the maladies of medievalism, and return to the Hellenic ideal—to something finer,
richer, than the Hellenic ideal, it may be" (29). Many pages later, Dorian
reflects on Henry's "new Hedonism" in terms borrowed still more baldly
from the conclusion to *The Renaissance*: this philosophy was "to recreate
life, and to save it from that harsh, uncomely puritanism that is having, in
our own day, its curious revival"; it was "never to accept any theory or
system that would involve the sacrifice of any mode of passionate experience"; its aim being "experience itself, and not the fruits of experience,"
it was "to teach man to concentrate himself upon the moments of a life
that is itself but a moment" (104).

Henry's words do seem to prove a disastrous influence: taken by Dorian
(not unreasonably) to denigrate the moral, the social, and the altruistic in
favor of a life given over to the pleasures of the senses and intellect, they
lead him to a denouement that calls into question both the ethical plausi-
bility and the practical wisdom of imagining the world primarily in the
new Hedonism's terms. Yet it is not clear that Wilde's placement of such
sentiments with Lord Henry constitutes a critique either of Pater's values
or of materialism's description of the nature of the universe. Pater himself
joined the ranks of those troubled by the cynical edge of Henry's philosophy in his cool review of the novel, remarking that both Henry and Dorian
are inadequate Epicureans because they neglect the pleasures of virtue.
And it bears recalling as well that "The Child in the House," though a
drama of formation mostly by experiences of inanimate things, repeatedly
stresses how those experiences lead to qualities of sympathy, to certain
kinds of piety, and to delicacy of feeling, not merely to the selfish passions
upon which Henry seems to dwell.

What we lose if we assume that Wilde is simply condemning a materialist
understanding of life is revealed most sharply, however, by another moment in *Dorian Gray* itself. When, very late in the narrative, Dorian seems
to be straying from the path of enjoyment into renunciation and regret,
Lord Henry delivers yet another Paterian peroration in order to bring him
back to the fold. "Life," he declares,

> is not governed by will or intention. Life is a question of nerves, and fibres,
> and slowly built-up cells in which thought hides itself and passion has its
> dreams. You may fancy yourself safe, and think yourself strong. But a chance
> tone of colour in a room or a morning sky, a particular perfume that you had

once loved and that brings subtle memories with it, a line from a forgotten poem that you had come across again, a cadence from a piece of music that you had ceased to play—I tell you, Dorian, that it is on things like these that our lives depend. (162)

Whatever the narrative consequences of Henry's sermonizing, the novel does not seem notably to challenge materialism's take on the nature of existence. The materialist vision may not be sufficient prescriptively (as a guide in moral matters, in other words), but there is every reason to believe that Wilde thought it descriptively on the mark. We might recall, in this regard, that a strong version of the claim that much in our lives depends on chance tones, perfumes, lines, and cadences would have come to him from Wordsworth, Ruskin, and Paterian texts like "Child"; it would also have come to him, mutatis mutandis, from the whole discourse of what we have been calling the developmental unconscious, with its stress on the potentially immense repercussions of any careless word, any trivial event, any small decorative element in the lives of the young.

Further, the idea that life is a question of nerves and fibers and slowly built-up cells was one that, on the evidence of the notebooks, Wilde took to be the central disclosure of modern science. It may therefore be the less surprising to discover how closely Henry's language evokes a statement we encountered in chapter 1, a statement that bids both to summarize the state of knowledge about the mind and to put that knowledge in the service of a particular argument: "Down among his nerve-cells and fibres the molecules are counting it, registering and storing it up to be used against him when the next temptation comes. Nothing we ever do is, in strict scientific literalness, wiped out." The source, as we saw, is William James; the topic is habit; and the text is *Principles of Psychology*—published the same year that saw the first version of *Dorian Gray* printed in the Philadelphia-based *Lippincott's Monthly Magazine*.[8]

In both the Wilde quotation and the James, what matters is a physiological process occurring at so molecular a level that it cannot be observed; and in both, the invisibility of this working invites reflection on the limits of our control over what we are and what we do. Henry declares, on this basis, that we are wrong to believe ourselves proof against the power of sensations, while James writes a few lines before, as if in anticipation of the dreadful case of Dorian's portrait, "We are spinning our own fates, good or evil, never to be undone. Every smallest stroke of virtue or of vice leaves its never so little scar." For both writers, as for many other nineteenth-century theorists, experience works unrelentingly: Wilde makes this point in his American lectures as well as in *Dorian Gray*, while James adds further on in *Principles* that "[e]xperience is remoulding us every moment," that "our mental reaction on every given thing is really a resultant of our experience of the whole world up to that date," that "*no changes in the brain are physiologically ineffective, and . . . presumably none . . . bare of psychological result*" (234). Further, both writers indicate how this sense of the continuous power of experience brings in its wake attention to the inexhaustible subtlety of experience's textures. Following Pater, Wilde commends fineness of discrimination throughout his criticism, while James posits on the next page of *Principles* that the brain's "inward iridescences must be infinite, for the brain-redistributions are in infinite variety. If so coarse a thing as a telephone-plate can be made to thrill for years and never reduplicate its inward condition, how much more must this be the case with the infinitely delicate brain?" (235).

Yet though Wilde, Pater, and James seem well agreed on the stealthiness of experience's influence, they come to somewhat different conclusions about what kind of design for living it implies. Pater, as we have seen, advocates a disciplined receptivity—an intense, self-conscious, and cultivated contemplation—in addition to an appreciation of what beauty's quieter methods do for us. James goes on to recommend making "*our nervous system our ally instead of our enemy*," rendering "*automatic and habitual, as early as possible, as many useful actions as we can*," on the ground that the "more of the details of our daily life we can hand over to the effortless custody of automatism, the more our higher powers of mind will be set free for their own proper work" (*Principles* 122). In venues such as his American lectures, Wilde takes yet a different course, outlining an arrangement of environment that would abjure overt constraint yet conscientiously exclude whatever would conduce to malformation or injury. He would, in other words, recommend complete provision of beauty for the young.

In his lecture on "The Decorative Arts," as we saw, Wilde asked his audiences to consider "how susceptible children are to the influence of beauty," how "they are easily impressed and are pretty much what their surroundings make them," and expressed the hope of those promoting an "English renaissance" that children might grow up "in the simple atmosphere of all fair things so that they will love what is beautiful and good, and hate what is evil and ugly, long before they know the reason why." The way to make children good, in other words, is to change their environments, from ones in which not all things are fair to ones in which beauty is uninterrupted. Wilde made the case for such atmospheres yet more elaborately in the lecture that the "The Decorative Arts" substantially replaced, which was in fact called "The English Renaissance of Art":

> So, in years to come there will be nothing in any man's house which has not given delight to its maker and does not give delight to its user. The children, like the children of Plato's perfect city will grow up "in a simple atmosphere

of all fair things"—I quote from the passage in the *Republic*—"a simple atmosphere of all fair things, where beauty, which is the spirit of art, will come on eye and ear like a fresh breath of wind that brings health from a clear upland, and insensibly and gradually draw the child's soul into harmony with all knowledge and all wisdom, so that he will love what is beautiful and good, and hate what is evil and ugly (for they always go together) long before he knows the reason why; and then when reason comes will kiss her on the cheek as a friend."

That is what Plato thought decorative art could do for a nation, feeling that the secret not of philosophy merely but of all gracious existence might be externally hidden from any one whose youth had been passed in uncomely and vulgar surroundings, and that the beauty of form and colour even, as he says, in the meanest vessels of the house, will find its way into the inmost places of the soul and lead the boy naturally to look for that divine harmony of spiritual life of which art was to him the material symbol and warrant. (*Aristotle* 23)

The beautiful and the good "always go together," as do the evil and the ugly: Wilde does indeed draw upon Plato here (presenting a fair translation of a passage from book three of *The Republic*) while also picking up on hopes for beauty's stealthy effects enunciated by Schiller, Ruskin, and the many enthusiasts of aesthetically improving environments described in chapter 1. He also supports this claim for beauty with a rendering of experience, evocative of Pater and James, in which the sensuous milieu more or less literally works into the crannies of the self. It is precisely because there are inmost places of the soul for material influences to penetrate that uncomely and vulgar surroundings should be avoided.[9]

Indeed the most striking feature of this passage may be Wilde's insistence, in the first sentence, on the *exclusion* of everything not delightful, a stipulation not to be found in Pater. Pater does sometimes locate moral effects, or something like them, in domestic interiors: we have seen some of this in "Child" and *Marius*, and scattered through his writings are comments like the following, from his 1885 "imaginary portrait" of Jean-Antoine Watteau, rendered through the imaginary letters of a female friend of the painter from the provinces: "I am struck by the purity of the room he has refashioned for us—a sort of *moral* purity; yet in the *forms* and *colours* of things" (*Imaginary* 31).[10] Because he stops short of advocating a thorough manipulation of surroundings, however, Pater cannot be the main source for the Wildean claim that only lovely things around the home will satisfy a child's aesthetic hunger. On the contrary: Pater insists, as we have seen, that "a child's sense of beauty" does not depend "on any choiceness, or special fineness, in the objects which present themselves to it" and even intimates that the drive toward perfecting a life or environment would be suspect in a world that rather requires gentle discontent and an openness to change.

For reasons we will consider further on, Wilde too resisted a language of completion in thinking about human development. But he was much readier than Pater to make the perfecting of environment a social imperative. In his 1890 dialogue, "The Critic as Artist," his mouthpiece Gilbert observes that the feeling for beauty "requires some form of exquisite environment" if it is "to be purified and made perfect" (1049), then delivers yet another version of the claim that fair surroundings will inspire love of the good. Notably, all three enunciations of this sentiment—the one by Gilbert in "Critic" and the two we have seen in the American lectures—are followed by calls for educational reform that make a high priority of aesthetic engagement for the young. Gilbert imagines how the Philistine would smile "if one ventured to suggest to him that the true aim of education was the love of beauty" and decries the present "education system" for "burden[ing] the memory with a load of unconnected facts" instead of "develop[ing] in the mind a more subtle quality of apprehension and discernment," as ancient Greek education did (1050, 1055). In the American lectures, where Wilde's remarks seem directed at listeners from a wider range of class positions, the emphasis is on employment of the hands rather than honing of the critical faculties, but the moral consequence remains: "The best people of all classes should be given to the pursuits of artistic industry, and everyone should be taught to use his hands. . . . And art culture will do more to train children to be kind to animals and all living things than all our harrowing moral tales, for when he sees how lovely the little leaping squirrel is on the beaten brass or the bird arrested in flight on carven marble, he will not throw the customary stone" ("Decorative" 164).

A wide effort to cultivate the sense of beauty is thus the remedy not only for a social problem Wilde wishes to bring before his audience (the impoverishing of existence where the feeling for beauty is absent) but also for a social problem already widely recognized: juvenile delinquency. Making the younger person more sensitive to beauty might make him (or her, though in the writings of the male aesthetes the archetypal youth is male) less violent, more considerate and kind.[11] And the artisanal project would also have the advantage of keeping the hands busy—always a desideratum of antidelinquency programs. Of course, Wilde was far from the first to venture that art training might occupy as well as elevate potentially lawless elements: the same claim had been disseminated for some time by other notable proponents of art education. The American Ruskinian James Jackson Jarves, for example, wrote in 1864 of how art culture might help prevent crime, improve appearance, exercise the religious faculty, expand the intellect, and refine morals (Stankiewicz 56), while in *A Handbook of*

*Pictorial Art*, 1868, Ruskin's associate Richard St. John Tyrwhitt explained that while "[n]obody expects that the whole of the working-classes will at once take to drawing and entirely renounce strong liquor," it is hoped "that a fair per-centage of them may be partly secured from temptation to excess by having a finer mental stimulus put in their reach, instead of the coarser physical one" (18).[12]

Wilde's lectures also show him rehearsing Ruskin's argument that a change in the products of labor can only come about with a transformation of labor's scene. In *The Stones of Venice*, as we saw, Ruskin presents the medieval cathedral as at once the valid achievement and the formative environment of the workman; Wilde duly stresses that good things can only be made where the makers have lived amid beauty: "And so you must seek out your workman and give him, as far as possible, the right surroundings. . . . All the teaching in the world is of no avail if you do not surround your workman with happy influences and with beautiful things" (*Aristotle* 26–27). Here, in other words, Wilde recommends for laborers the same provision he recommends elsewhere for children: immersion in beauty. But the point is not to infantilize the working classes; it is rather to give them what, presumably, those fortunate enough to possess both wealth and taste already have, at least at home.[13]

As Wilde well knew, this kind of scheme could be expounded as easily in provocation as in placation. In an 1878 pamphlet also called "The Decorative Arts," William Morris, having invoked "On the Nature of Gothic," acknowledges that it may seem perverse to bid workingmen inhabiting "hideous streets" to "study nature and the history of art" and to "care about beauty." But it is precisely such care that will drive a will to change: "If you can really fill your minds with memories of great works of art, . . . you will . . . be able to a certain extent to look through the aforesaid ugly surroundings, and will . . . be so much discontented with what is bad, that you will determine to bear no longer that shortsighted, reckless brutality of squalor that so disgraces our intricate civilization" (95).[14] Nor was Morris alone in finding the physical hideousness of modern cities a rebuke to the idea that the provision of beauty in some domains, such as upper-class interiors, could be the end point of aesthetic reform. Particularly intrepid on this score was Wilde's friend Ouida, the best-selling novelist and critic. In an 1888 article for the Wilde-edited *Woman's World*, she wrote, characteristically:

> The streets are the only education for the eyes of the populace which it is possible to give; where they are beautiful they are the best education after that of the open country itself. But what can the streets of London say to any poor lad whose instincts of genius are struggling towards light through the darkness of his ignorance? He can find no grain of thought, no ray of beauty,

anywhere in all their dreary discords. . . . London in its possessions, whether
of art or treasure or commerce, in museum, warehouse, or gallery, is incomparably rich, but its riches are invisible to those who walk the streets. . . . I am
inclined to believe that the monotony of ugliness in the London streets—
buildings constructed without an idea, without a meaning, without a single
grace, without any charm of light and shade, of proportion or of form— . . .
affects the minds of those who live amongst it, and the sickly anemia of the
factory or the serving-girl becomes the dyspepsia and the boredom of the
woman of fashion; and I believe that the hypochondria of English men and
women is due much less to climate than it is to the absence of beauty about
them in their daily lives, and to the unenjoying haste at which they live. The
influences of beauty on the mind are never sufficiently remembered or esteemed. (483–84)

At first, Ouida seems to associate aesthetic privation with the lower classes
only, not with those more welcome in museums, galleries, and nicer
streets. As the passage goes on, however, mere aesthetic poverty modulates
into aesthetic injury affecting the woman of fashion as well as the factory
girl. And by the end, distinctions between classes have been leveled by an
ugliness so extensive that it can only be escaped (and this partially) by the
lucky few who are able to remember beauty's influence.[15]

Ouida's reproof discloses neatly another reason why the dream of managing environments had so close an affinity with aesthetic theories of development. In her depiction, one can no more exist apart from aesthetic
influences than one can inhabit a nonphysical world, which is to say that
the aesthetic environment is indistinguishable from the physical environment as a whole. Because beauty and ugliness are everywhere, enclosing
every person from the first moments of life to the last, there is simply no
developing apart from the aesthetic quality of one's surroundings. From
this perspective, Wilde's prescription of a dwelling in which not the meanest vessel fails to give delight comes to look like the logical end point of a
social thinking that begins with the envisioning of life as a continuous
series of transactions between environment and organism. And it becomes
easier to see why aestheticism in its interventionist mode tended to take
as the paradigmatic aesthetic object not the discrete work of visual art
favored by eighteenth-century aesthetics or even (the Paterian piety that
all arts aspire to the condition of music notwithstanding) the composition
in sound, but rather the built and decorated environment. In chapter 1,
we remarked the appeal, for those concerned with youth's susceptibility,
of mapping the moment-by-moment continuity of temporal experience
onto the point-by-point continuity of spatial environment. But if this re-
placement of continuously perilous time with bounded space makes the

provision of a beautiful milieu an attractive option, a sense of the inescapability of the aesthetic makes such provision seem a perfect necessity.[16]

Wilde's more totalizing rhetoric did not lead only to shades of theoretical divergence from Ruskin and Pater, however; it also undergirded, at times, a different stance on what was required for social renovation. Pater largely avoided discussion of broad programs, as we have seen, while Ruskin insisted that real concern for the less privileged meant active attempts to improve the conditions under which their lives unfolded. At some points, Wilde seems to out-Pater Pater in focusing on the fine experience of the privileged individual; at others, he approaches Ruskin in recommending relatively specific changes in education and environment, especially for the working classes. At still other junctures, however, Wilde suggests that only a total revolution will do, as though the immitigable alternatives are a world tainted by compromise with ugliness and one in which only beauty remains.

Such a view may be implicit in the American lectures, but it emerges pyrotechnically in 1891's "Soul of Man under Socialism," wherein a promotion of a future of beauty for all is bound up with denunciation of more immediate and transient forms of charity. According to that essay, the privileged must aspire not to "go down to a depressing East End and distribute bad cocoa and worse blankets to starving people," but rather to "reconstruct society on such a basis that poverty will be impossible." For just "as the worst slave-owners were those who were kind to their slaves, and so prevented the horror of the system being realised by those who suffered from it, . . . so, in the present state of things in England, the people who do most harm are the people who try to do most good" (1089, 1079). In contrast to this present state, a socialist society will nourish precious Individualism. Ending the reign of private property, which had led people to think that "the important thing was to have," when in fact "the important thing is to be," socialism will release humanity from the "sordid necessity of living for others" that, going by the names of altruism and charity, does not merely cover but indeed "creates a multitude of sins" (1083, 1079).

Wilde's impatience with spot remedies for the body, as opposed to life-long remedies for the soul, is notable not least for its implication that the future lies with the young or even the unborn—that is, with those whose souls have not been damaged beyond repair. His avowedly utopian interest is in the creation of the "perfect man," by which he means "one who develops under perfect conditions; one who is not wounded, or worried, or maimed, or in danger." The note of this "perfect personality," he stresses, "is not rebellion, but peace. It will be a marvellous thing—the true personality of man—when we see it. It will grow naturally and simply, flowerlike, or as a tree grows." So far in history, however, there has not been peace; so far, "[m]ost personalities have been obliged to be rebels" and have thus wasted half their strength "in friction" (1084). What humans can be will be known only when conditions conducing to perfection have been achieved.

This line of thinking was no more unique to Wilde than was the idea that children should be raised among beautiful and tasteful furnishings; again, a staple of late nineteenth- and early twentieth-century social commentary was that the only path to a better world might be through the fashioning—or breeding—of better human beings to populate it. Eugenics, which cast its shadow over virtually all debates on social improvement from the mid-nineteenth century to its final discrediting in the wake of Nazi policies, was the most dramatic example of this reposing of hopes for the future on the quality of future people. But the sentiment was expressed everywhere, including in *The Woman's World*. In "The Children of a Great City," which appeared in an 1888 number, Mary Jeune writes that the condition of "needy men and women" forces

> the conviction, melancholy though it be, that nothing can be done, in any real degree, to repair the mischief which their own follies and weaknesses have brought on them. Their lives are made and partly over; they have settled into grooves and ways of thought and life from which no efforts can raise them to any appreciable extent. . . . [I]f we are to achieve any real and permanent good we must seek to do it among those whose lives are still before them, and who with the vigour and elasticity of youth may, if properly helped, grow up into good and healthy men and women. (27)

For Jeune as for so many others, it is not simply that the unsupervised maturation of a generation of juvenile delinquents promises trouble. It is that the carefully tended growth of the not-yet-formed represents the only conceivable route from present haplessness to a world in which vice and degradation would be no more.

Suspicion of short-term philanthropy and enthusiasm for the long-range possibilities of youth meet strikingly in *The Picture of Dorian Gray*, whose magazine printing (June 1890) and book printing (April 1891) bracketed the publication of "The Soul of Man" (February 1891). There, Lord Henry presents Dorian's stark alternatives as, on the one hand, assisting a few people through charity work and, on the other, elevating all of humankind through an exemplary practice of the new Hedonism:

> [R]ealise your youth while you have it. Don't squander the gold of your days, listening to the tedious, trying to improve the hopeless failure, or giving away your life to the ignorant, the common, and the vulgar. These are the sickly aims, the false ideals, of our age. Live! Live the wonderful life that is in you! Let nothing be lost upon you. Be always searching for new sensations. Be

afraid of nothing. . . . A new Hedonism—that is what our century wants. You might be its visible symbol. (32)

In later chapters, Henry will credit himself with rescuing his young friend from the altruistic clutches of Lady Agatha, representative of those many women of means who found purpose in "East Ending" and other efforts to improve the lives and morals of London's poor. And in his last attempt to divert Dorian from renunciation, he will gush, "You are the type of what the age is searching for, and what it is afraid it has found. I am so glad that you have never done anything, never carved a statue, or painted a picture, or produced anything outside of yourself! Life has been your art" (163).

What makes the later Dorian so appealing to Henry, then, is that he seems to have evaded the peril of becoming anything specific, to have shown how the potential might free itself from ignoble realization in the actual. In this, Dorian's endless youth speaks to a problem attending dreams of aesthetic education at least since Schiller: that the flexibility associated with aesthetic feeling can come to seem so precious as to make the materializing of any particular possibility look like a defeat instead of a victory. Something of this difficulty certainly emerges in Wilde's comment, from "The Soul of Man," that "the recognition of private property has really harmed Individualism" by making "gain, not growth, its aim," since the inevitable implication is that any terminus to growth will be undesirable (1083). In *Dorian Gray*, however, the joke is on Henry, inasmuch as his idol's air of unruffled being is not, in truth, a triumph of poise elegantly concealing maturation's costs, but rather the product of an *actual* halt to development, supernaturally induced. One of the lessons of the novel thus seems to be that it is easy to mistake an impoverishing *failure* of becoming (a lack of growth) for a fruitful *resistance to* becoming (an evasion of narrowing and ossification).

It seems hard to argue, therefore, that *Dorian Gray* endorses Henry's attraction to Dorian's endless youth in any straightforward sense. But we may still want to ask if there is some aspect of this attraction, or of this youth, that it redeems. As it turns out, another way of posing this question is to ask how *Dorian Gray* fits into the history of the European bildungsroman.

By rough and ready definition, as we have noted, the bildungsroman is the story of a young person achieving, for better or for worse, some rapprochement with a social reality that had at first seemed hostile to youth's purposes; fictions in a line that includes *Wilhelm Meister's Apprenticeship*, *Jane Eyre*, *David Copperfield*, *The Red and the Black*, and *Sentimental Education* adhere to this narrative arc with varying degrees of fidelity. As we saw in the introduction, Franco Moretti sites the beginning of the form's decline in the late middle of the nineteenth century (when "the historical and cultural configuration" that had made the *Bildungsro-man* such an important form collapsed) and observes that in fictions of succeeding decades youth repudiates maturity, striving to vest meaning in itself alone. Patricia Meyer Spacks, again, offers a similar appraisal: though a nineteenth-century narrator "might convey the melancholy of conformity," no one in that period "imagined the possibility of preserving adolescent values unchanged into adulthood." At the dawn of the twenti-eth century, in the age of G. Stanley Hall, however, it became possible to "assume that to preserve the feelings of adolescence implies genius," so that novelists "began to celebrate characters who refused to conform, and novels explored the psychology of such refusals" (236).

Neither Moretti nor Spacks mentions *Dorian Gray* specifically in this context, but Wilde's novel unquestionably fits their chronology by virtue of its fin-de-siècle fascination with developmental arrest. Indeed because its hero both ceases to age and devotes himself to the pursuit of exquisite experience, the book's very theme may seem to be the failure of experience to teach lessons meaningfully or reliably. Though Dorian has plenty of chances to learn—he discovers strange facets of desire, reacts with horror at his and others' crimes, makes numerous resolutions to be better, and allows himself to be lectured at until all hours by Basil and Henry—the tale's last movement suggests the uselessness of all these occasions for con-scious moral advance. Having nobly refrained from ruining Hetty Mer-ton, "simply a girl in a village" and "not one of our own class" (249), Dorian wonders whether his years of living have wrought some positive change in his conscience, then answers in the negative. His gesture of restraint represents no fruit of experience, he concludes, but only another grasping at sensations: "Vanity? Curiosity? Hypocrisy? Had there been nothing more in his renunciation than that? . . . No. There had been noth-ing more" (166).

Wilde leaves open the possibility that Dorian's real tragedy inheres in a failure to see that he *has* learned something or at least retains some capacity to improve; it could be that the chance for growth has not irrecoverably shifted from the once changeful world of social life to the surface of the portrait. And yet the very donnée of the magic canvas arguably makes for the most forceful of all assaults on the assumption that experience is a teacher. If the Dorian in the picture has neither consciousness nor agency, it (or he) is capable only of registering the marks of the other Dorian's sins, not of learning from them—which is to say that in this case experi-ence manages to be formative *without* being instructive. *Dorian Gray* may thus stand not only as a repudiation of the idea of moral growth on which the bildungsroman depends but also as a cunning allegory of the form's late nineteenth-century transformation (or, as Moretti would have it, dis-solution). And we can therefore say, in partial answer to our question about Henry's attraction to endless youth, that if Dorian's destiny is hardly a desirable one, it is in its way a representative one, distilling as it does a new mistrust of previously dominant views of the value of worldly experience.[17]

But something else is worth remarking here. For it is with just this matter of a formation that is not an instruction, a registering of experience that is not a conscious learning but a physical alteration, that we return to the vision of development we have been considering all through this study. Dorian may conclude that the kind of experience dear to the classical bildungsroman has done nothing for him, but as we have seen, Henry alludes to another level of experience, in which the soul is made by the stealthy engendering of passions in slowly built-up cells. In place of a direct schooling in the push and pull of human relationships—in the interpersonal consequences of one's actions, the responsibilities of citizens, and so on— Dorian's dangerous mentor has emphasized the scarcely registered workings of beauty and ugliness on the fibers and nerves. And it is worth remarking that the novel supports Henry's emphasis by means of *both* the figures of Dorian it puts before us: first, the peripatetic aesthete, a sensualist who can detect no effects of experience in himself; second, the portrait, a stand-in for the soul that is also a rigorously physical object accruing physical alterations with every sin. We might therefore consider *Dorian Gray*—which its creator later described as "an essay on decorative art" (*Artist as Critic* 247)—both a product and an allegory of the nineteenth century's engagement with the developmental unconscious, its fixing of attention on chemical or quasi-chemical transactions by which experience subtly configures the self.

Wilde's is not the only novel in which the crisis of the bildungsoman is entangled with new revelations about the physiology of experience, of course. In Pater's *Marius*, these revelations inform the construction of a hero who learns in something like standard bildungsroman fashion but seems too good to linger long in this world; in Joyce's *Portrait of the Artist as a Young Man*, they help detonate many of the bildungsroman's conventions while sustaining the protagonist's fierce resistance to reconciliation with the social world. We will return to Paterian premature death further on in this section and to Joycean bridling in chapter 3, but first we need to visit briefly one other writer whose attention to physiology raised difficulties for the form. Karen Chase has noted that in the fiction of George Eliot, "[a]ll the emphasis falls upon the trivial character of . . . corrosive influences. . . . The small, the subtle, the gradual—these are the causes of moral change" (159). And as aspects of mind and character decompose into smaller and smaller details of physiology, the human itself seems in danger of vanishing; finding that "our most fateful acts are the least perceptible," Eliot attempts to trace behavior to . . . intentions so rudimentary that they are "hardly ever told even in . . . consciousness." And the further motives are analyzed, broken into finer constituents, the closer the life of the mind approaches the life of the body. . . . What makes [Eliot's physiological metaphors for mental life] so forceful is the suggestion that they may not be metaphors at all. The workings of motive may not simply *resemble* the workings of the body: motive may *derive* from the body. (159–60)

Other critics also have noted how in Eliot "actions and details lost to consciousness are grounded and stored in the body, or in the trope of the body" (Marc Redfield, 140), how "even the most minor gestures of . . . various characters" may be described with the "vocabulary of forces, pathways, and channels . . . employed by [Eliot's companion] Lewes and his fellow physiological psychologists" (Sally Shuttleworth, 72).

Significantly, Eliot is also the writer whom Moretti credits with both the culmination of the bildungsroman in English (*Middlemarch*, 1871–72) and two spectacular demonstrations of that form's imminent impossibility (*Felix Holt*, 1866, and *Daniel Deronda*, 1876). For Moretti, again, the bildungsroman could be the central "symbolic form" only for a world that believed that "the biography of a young individual was the most meaningful viewpoint for the understanding and the evaluation of history." But this was no longer the world of the late nineteenth and early twentieth centuries, "when psychology started to dismantle the unified image of the individual; when the social sciences turned to 'synchrony' and 'classification,' thereby shattering the synthetic perception of history; when youth betrayed itself in its narcissistic desire to last forever; when in ideology after ideology the individual figured simply as a part of the whole" (227–28).

Moretti suggests that *Holt* and *Deronda* strongly record the last three of these four changes, but we might add that the first item on his list, psychology's dismantling of the unitary individual, was premised in part on the physiological discoveries that Chase, Redfield, Shuttleworth, and others find reverberating through Eliot's work. It was not only that the biologizing of mind unsettled the continuity of personhood in a general way; perhaps more important for the bildungsroman was that formative experience had come to contain so much more than passed before the eye of the mind—a point Moretti takes up in a different manner when he writes of later fictions' confrontation with the unconscious in a more specifically Freudian sense (234–39). We might say that the novel of formation had to reach a watershed when development became a matter of continuous shaping by the totality of one's surroundings, of often silent and invisible molding by factors human, inhuman, and quasi-human. The traditional bildungsroman, with its dependence on crisis, example, reflection, and socialization, could hardly have seemed adequate to this understanding of growth.

In between telling Dorian that life is a question of nerves and fibers in which thought hides itself and telling him that our lives depend on chance tones of color and cadences from music we no longer play, Henry interjects a warning: "You may fancy yourself safe, and think yourself strong." His implication, of course, is that what we are unsafe from and weak before are contingencies of experience that affect us without our observing them, factors we cannot minutely orchestrate even when we have attended carefully to (say) our aesthetic education. Henry does not, however, voice the further implication of this implication, though Pater named it exactly when he wrote of "little shapes, voices, accidents" becoming "parts of the great chain wherewith we are bound": that pondering our forming by countless unregistered phenomena can lead to a confrontation with the specter of determinism, the dissipation of our sense of free will in the face of the innumerable causes and forces that make us. In stopping short of pursuing this discomfiting line of thinking, Henry might be said to hang on after all to the remnants of the traditional bildungsroman, where the dream of autonomy gives way to compromise but where volition rarely seems in danger of evaporating completely. Similarly, *Dorian Gray* as a whole can be said to gesture toward, yet not fully take up, the question of how fictions of individual formation should adapt to the world of modern thought Pater described in "Coleridge's Writings."

With "You may fancy yourself safe, and think yourself strong," Henry also notably echoes some lines from his first sermon to Dorian, in which he insists that the latter will come to understand the value of youth when it has left him: "When your youth goes, your beauty will go with it, and then you will suddenly discover that that there are no triumphs left for you. Every month as it wanes brings you nearer to something dreadful. Time is jealous of you, and wars against your lilies and your roses. You will become sallow, and hollow-cheeked, and dull-eyed. You will suffer horribly" (32). Dorian does not suffer these particular indignities (at least not while still alive), of course. But he comes to a disastrous end all the same, and his story raises prominently the question of why Wilde subjects this aesthetically invested hero to so grim a fate when in so many other writings he recommends education by immersion in beauty.

Framed so generally, the question is surely unanswerable. Yet we may learn something useful if we think about it in somewhat more restricted terms—specifically, in relation to Henry's admonitions about vulnerability to aging and vulnerability to experiences registered and unregistered. As a preliminary to this exploration, we might notice that Dorian is not the only Wildean figure whose artistic education fails to eventuate in moral excellence. In "Pen, Pencil, and Poison," an 1889 piece on the real-life

Thomas Griffiths Wainewright, Wilde presents a person touched power-fully by Art, "peculiarly susceptible to the spiritual influences of Words-worth's poetry," "of a delicately strung organisation," "keenly sensitive to the value of beautiful surroundings" (994, 996)—and also a forger and murderer, indeed "one of the most subtle and secret poisoners of this or any age" (1003). The neatly decadent moral Wilde draws from Waine-wright's story is that there "is no essential incongruity between crime and culture" (1008), but this verdict of mere compatibility scarcely captures this criminal's capacity to undermine aestheticism's program. Waine-wright's case, even more fiercely than Dorian's, seems to mock the preten-sion that loving what is beautiful means loving what is good.[18]

Pater, we might notice, had even more trouble than Wilde in sustaining a narrative where the attempt to live for beauty leads to long years of contentment and virtue. The biographical Wainewright lived to be nearly sixty, but fictional exponents of aestheticism in the Paterian line tend to have much shorter life spans: not only Dorian but also Marius and virtually all of Pater's other aesthetically responsive protagonists die before their time. Emerald Uthwart, the eponymous hero of an 1892 tale, is especially remarked for his molding by the physical environment of his school: "The very place one is in, its stonework, its empty spaces, invade you; . . . chal-lenge you . . . to make moral philosophy one of your acquirements, if you can, and to systematise your vagrant self; which however will in any case be here systematised for you" (207). But he withers away, still young, after being dismissed from military service for an act at once heroic and disobedient. The beauty-loving heroes of Pater's four *Imaginary Por-traits*—Watteau, Denys L'Auxerrois, Sebastian van Storck, Duke Carl of Rosenmold—all die early too, again as if too fine for this life. And other aesthetic-decadent heroes from further afield, such as Villiers de l'Isle-Adam's Axel (from the prose poem of that name), appear to find in death the only route to transcendence of life's essential vulgarity.

What accounts for this high mortality rate? One form of answer, clearly, lies in the sheer challenge of representing that perfection to which a suc-cessful aesthetic discipline would theoretically lead. In "The Soul of Man under Socialism," Wilde insists that no one can yet know what the society of Individualism will look like; no more, we might say, will it be easy to describe in detail a world, or a person, sustained by an impulse of joy fresh enough to banish all the maladies of medievalism and bring on a return of the Hellenic ideal. The problem of the fall into the actual from the potential thus again arises in the vicinity of the aesthetic, and in a moment we will return to it yet once more. For now, however, we need to notice that in spite of this dilemma of flexibility, there seems no overpowering reason why a fiction of aesthetic education should not conclude with the simple note that its protagonist went on to live a long and happy life.

What does seem a little difficult to imagine is a Pater or a Wilde penning such a finale. And this is so in large part, surely, because both stake so much on the physical comeliness that youth alone seems to possess. The sensitive heroes of these writers are not only subjects formed by beauty but also beautiful objects who must—explicitly in the doctrine of Lord Henry, implicitly elsewhere—exhibit the validity of aesthetic attunement in their appealing persons. This does not mean that Pater and Wilde really held, as if resurrecting the old discourse of physiognomy, that outward appearance and inner soul would always correlate, or that those not possessed of personal beauty are denied perfect rapport with the beautiful. It does affirm, however, that the dream of aesthetic formation in the Paterian line was always haunted by the sad chiasmus according to which the same passing of time that permits expansion of the soul enjoins also a diminution of the body. Corresponding to the recognition of our chemical determination by chance tones and unnoticed experiences, in other words, is a recognition of our subordination to the corporeal limits imposed by age. It is as though the material grounding of aesthetic formation, acknowledgment of which helped make aestheticism so compellingly modern, here exacts its price, in an unbearable disjunction between the beauty-nourished goodness of maturity and the bodily beauty of youth.

In the case of Pater and Wilde, of course, captivation by youth was grounded in a desire for young men vividly enhanced by the single-sex romance of Oxbridge and the cult of Hellenic art—neither of which could be said to dominate the whole culture of the time. This did not mean, however, that the untimely deaths of Dorian, Marius, Emerald and company were utterly disconnected from more widely prevalent feelings about the young. Over the course of the nineteenth century, as we have seen, children came to be credited with a singular proximity to the divine, and the belief that childhood should be granted special opportunities for happiness became the rule. But it was not only that children had come to be regarded as having a singular claim on enjoyment; it was also that adult life for many people—indeed for parents even more strikingly than for confirmed bachelors like Pater—was coming to be organized around an association between immaturity and legitimate pleasure. As John Gillis notes, the child became the focus "of a whole host of newly invented middle-class rituals that came to constitute and maintain the meaning and sense of family from the mid-nineteenth century onward. The child's meal times, bed times, birthdays, and graduations marked the passage of what came to be called 'family time,' not only defining the increasingly tightly calibrated stages of childhood development but also determining the parents' sense of their own journey of life" ("Birth" 91).

By the turn of the century, disapprobation of a too-swift passage from youth into adulthood had also become standard. As Joseph Kett points out, American counselors' warnings about the dangers of "precocity" in children, which emerged substantively in the 1830s, had by century's end expanded to "embrace the syndrome of over-rapid development in adolescence" (135) as well as any apparent haste in taking on grown-up professional challenges; where in the 1820s and 1830s "a willingness to strike out on one's own . . . had been a precondition for success for young men," by 1900 "such desires for independence and autonomy were viewed as prescriptions for failure" (172). With respect to British education in the last third of the nineteenth century, Gillis observes that "[n]either parents nor schoolmasters were interested any longer in pushing boys in the manner common earlier. Precocity itself was in disrepute, associated with street urchins rather than respectable schoolboys" (*Youth* 103). And Viviana Zelizer has made the case (in her widely influential "precious child" thesis) that the years between 1870 and 1930 saw an extension to all classes of the conviction that the child should be seen not as a contributor to the family's economic prosperity but as an "exclusively emotional and affective asset preclud[ing] instrumental or fiscal considerations" (11)—a being adored for being a child.[19] An earnest Victorian might find something distasteful in Pater's or Wilde's particular idylls of youth, then, but to be captivated in a general way by immaturity was to run with, not against, the tendency of the age.

It is not hard to see how this allure of immaturity connects to the impulse to provide the young with protective environments, of course. Not only does the preciousness of the precious child suggest the need for yet heavier shielding from threats to proper development; for fond parents or guardians, maturation itself could come to seem a kind of disaster that one might try to forestall by insulating the child yet more thoroughly from external impingements. And there is something more. We have seen how the hope of safeguarding juveniles could draw on a reframing of unpredictable experience in the apparently less unruly terms of environment; we have seen how environment's way of modulating from the social to the inanimate could seem to mitigate the developmental peril of changeful human moods; and we have seen how the idea of surrounding the growing organism with beauty seems to take this spatial reasoning to a kind of logical end point. What we might add here is that there is not only a metonymic relationship between carefully tended surroundings and the young human being but also, crucially, a metaphorical one. For the properly arranged physical environment (say, the aesthetic home) and the juvenile within it appear to share two qualities setting them on the other side of a divide from adulthood: a certain innocence, and a certain remove from temporality. If the reposeful material milieu is free of human failings, it is also much less likely to change from benign to injurious in a flash. And if the child is free of grown-up vices, this is so because she or he has not yet accumulated the experience that, at least in the messy world we have, seems always to give rise to imperfect people.

In this kind of frame, the utopia of utopias must surely be one in which development would stand purged of temporality's unwelcome aspects, in which the adult as well as the juvenile would reflect back the beauty of continuously beautiful conditions. What would people be like if the world—the whole world—could be arranged aright? How would humanity appear should the hour of the perfect environment come round at last? Wilde suggests an answer. When the "true personality of man" finally emerges, he tells us in "The Soul of Man under Socialism," "[i]t will be as wonderful as the personality of a child" (1084).

## BEAUTY AND FREEDOM

Reading the great eighteenth- and nineteenth-century philosophers of aesthetics, Terry Eagleton has noted how the operation of the aesthetic, as they describe it, resembles the operation of ideology as defined by Louis Althusser. If one of the historical difficulties of the bourgeoisie has been that in "rendering the Law perceptible as a discourse" it allows that Law to become a site of destabilizing contestation, Eagleton writes, then it was one of the vital innovations of figures such as Schiller to imagine an aesthetic subject who "introjects the Law which governs it as the very principle of its free identity, and so, in Althusserian phrase, comes to work 'all by itself,' without need of political constraint. . . . What matters in aesthetics is not art but this whole project of reconstructing the human subject from the inside, informing its subtlest affections and bodily responses with this law which is not a law" ("Ideology" 21; see also *Ideology* 42–43).[20]

Or, to recast matters slightly, this time in relation to Kant:

> The problem with the bourgeoisie, as Charles Taylor has well argued, is that their obsession with freedom is incompatible with feeling at home in the world. Bourgeois ideology thus continually violates one of the central functions of ideology in general, which is to make the subject feel that the world is not an altogether inhospitable place. . . . But [for Kant] the fact that we can know the world at all, however grim the news which this cognition has to deliver, must surely entail some primordial harmony between ourselves and it. . . . ("Ideology" 23; see also *Ideology* 65, 85–86, 123)

What links the aesthetic and the ideological so firmly, for Eagleton, is that both make it possible for the viewpoint of the particular subject to be understood as universal in a way that dissipates friction between subject and milieu. And this is how the "ethico-aesthetic subject—the subject of bourgeois hegemony" becomes the "one who, in Kant's phrase, gives the law to itself and who thus lives its necessity as freedom" ("Ideology" 25).[21]

What our own explorations suggest is that Pater's and Wilde's treatments of the aesthetic fit Eagleton's schema in a way, or to a degree, that even Schiller's and Kant's formulations do not approach. For with aestheticism at the close of the nineteenth century, the prescriptive aesthetic education Schiller advocates effectively expands to include a descriptive vision under which formation by beauty (or ugliness) is an inescapable fact of human development grounded in physiology—indeed perhaps *the* fact of development, if it be true that the great chain wherewith we are bound is forged out of transient shapes, voices, and accidents. If for Kant and Schiller the aesthetic draws much of its power from its ability to appear less radically other to the subject than unmediated ethical or juridical law, it does so still more dramatically in Pater and Wilde, for whom the aesthetic has always been there, weaving the very fabric of every person's identity. In other words, aestheticism makes a particularly striking bid to resolve the problem of the (age of the) bourgeoisie, the feeling of not being at home in the world, by asserting that the aesthetic *is* home in the largest sense, the totality of those surroundings that have made our internal lives beautiful with their beauty or ugly with their ugliness.

Closely related to—if not warmly embraced in—Eagleton's treatment of aesthetic ideology is Michel Foucault's discussion of the regime of discipline in *Discipline and Punish*. According to Foucault, the ascent of this social apparatus (which consolidated its hold in the eighteenth century and had by the early twentieth achieved the functional completeness it still maintains) is marked by the displacement of "the juridical subject, who is caught up in the fundamental interest of the social pact" by "the obedient subject, the individual subjected to habits, rules, order, an authority that is exercised continually around and upon him, and which he must allow to function automatically in him" (128–29). For Foucault, modern education is always, among other things, disciplinary education, which is to say that it aligns functionally and structurally with that introjection of Law that Eagleton describes.

It is therefore no accident that the disciplinary regime has given birth to a figure who links, in the tightest imaginable bond, the malefactor subject to judicial process and the educable young person in general. That figure is the juvenile delinquent. In a passage already partly quoted in chapter 1, Foucault writes:

> The delinquent is to be distinguished from the offender by the fact that it is not so much his act as his life that is relevant in characterizing him. The penitentiary operation, if it is to be a genuine re-education, must become the sum total existence of the delinquent. . . . [A]ny determining cause, because

> it reduces responsibility, marks the author of the offence with a criminality all the more formidable and demands penitentiary measures that are all the more strict. (252)

Responsibility dissolves into influences even as mind dissolves into matter, then, but the price of exoneration from the burden of solitary guilt is an intensified control of environment henceforth to be exercised by educators, social workers, psychologists, physicians, judges, and other professionals. Indeed under this regime any young person vividly becomes a potential delinquent, in a transformation whose story is one of both theoretical discourse and practical implementation, told not only in the writings of those calling for more intensive monitoring of juvenile conditions but also in the historiography of the institutions and techniques that made such monitoring possible. It is also a story that may appear, especially in light of Eagleton's arguments, to encompass aestheticism in its socially interventionist mode, with its brief for the formative powers of beauty and its suggestion that delinquency might be one of the fruits of ugliness.

Is the promotion of beautiful environments for the young therefore best understood as an effort to induce good behavior—in a broadly political as well as a domestically immediate sense—by agreeable means? Do such aesthetic programs ultimately serve as another illustration of the point, made so frequently since the early days of New Historicism, that the liberation promised by works of art will often prove to shore up rather than subvert prevailing relations of power? As usual, the answer is a complex compound of yes and no. The element of yes comes partly from the fact that the very idea of an emancipatory dimension in art—an idea lately identified with a variously described liberal humanism and subjected to a panoply of demystifications—owes much to writers such as Schiller, Ruskin, and Wilde, who conceived of beauty's gentle infiltrations as promoting a gentleness of temperament that hardly seems conducive to revolution. As we have seen, Wilde says in "The Soul of Man under Socialism" that "most personalities have been obliged to be rebels" and have thus wasted half their strength "in friction" (1084), but he also makes clear that friction is not the essence of his prized Individualism at all. The note of the "perfect personality," when perfect conditions allow it to appear, will be "not rebellion, but peace."

Given Wilde's flair for baiting his society and his sometimes extraordinary claims for art and criticism as against mere life, it can seem that being antithetical to one's milieu was what Wildean aestheticism was all about. But this was not the case, or at least not consistently. For if in some moods Wilde privileged the splendid individual at odds with society, he dreamt in others of a society that would give rise to splendid individuals. In "Soul," as we have noted, this dream transpires at the level of society and history writ large, in the arrival of a utopian environment permitting the emergence of an Individualism never yet truly seen. In "The Critic as Artist," Wilde also imagines an arranging of conditions whose result would be emancipatory, but he does so at the level of individual education, and in the setting of (more or less) the world we actually have. Declaring that there is a distinctive and valuable "beauty-sense" in human beings, Gilbert adds that "to be purified and made perfect, this sense requires some form of exquisite environment" and then comes to his own translation of the program of *The Republic*, book three: "By slow degrees there is to be engendered in him [the child] such a temperament as will lead him naturally and simply to choose the good in preference to the bad, and, rejecting what is vulgar and discordant, to follow by fine instinctive taste all that possesses grace and charm and loveliness. Ultimately, in its due course, this taste is to become critical and self-conscious, but at first it is to exist purely as a cultivated instinct" (1049). From here, Gilbert proceeds to the philistine's smile at the thought of aesthetic education, and then to a claim that "for the cultivation of temperament, we must turn to the decorative arts: to the arts that touch us, not to the arts that teach us" (1050).

Two features of this sermon are especially noteworthy. The first lies in Gilbert's admiration for a soul shaping that occurs by intimate infiltration rather than direct instruction, his privileging of the arts that touch over those that teach. Here again, decorative art's virtue is that it works nondiscursively and nondidactically, quietly nurturing the sensibilities in a fashion that not only prepares "the soul for the reception of true imaginative work, but develops in it that sense of form which is the basis of creative no less than of critical achievement" (1052). Here again too, Wilde offers eloquent testimony to the interconnectedness of three beliefs: that scarcely registered experiential transactions can have immense developmental consequences; that juvenile environments stand in need of careful arranging; and that aesthetic quality affects the soul of the organism in ways that go beyond the strengthening of capacities for art appreciation per se. Gilbert's preference for touching over teaching reminds us once more that when Wilde recommends immersing children in beauty, he does so out of an understanding of milieu that encompasses not only the social but also the physical, that partly inanimate realm whose continuous provision of stimuli inevitably shapes the growing organism.

The other noteworthy feature of Gilbert's sermon is that it does not align art with either manipulation and constraint or autonomy and liberty solely. Rather, it insists on the necessity of a passage *from* constraint *to* liberty, advising that true freedom of thought in adulthood is to be promoted by wise ordering of early conditions. Rehearsing Plato's recommendation in terms evocative of the introjection that Eagleton and Foucault discuss in their different ways, Gilbert makes something like introjection the very foundation of future empowerment: "in its due course, this taste is to become critical and self-conscious." If Plato and Schiller are on Gilbert's mind here, so, surely, is the Rousseau of *Émile*—for whom, as we have seen, the way to a wise and clear-sighted grown-up lies through magnificently cunning management of the juvenile.

Of course, present-day readers may regard the schemes suggested in *Émile* as the very archetype of everything to be decried in the paternalistic state, in the covert penetrations of ideology, in the invasive micromeddling of disciplinary techniques and regimes. Yet Rousseau's volume and "The Critic as Artist" pose a question to both past and present critiques of efforts to arrange the conditions of maturation: if adults refrain from attempting such cunning nurture, have they truly liberated the growing person or merely allowed other forces (perhaps less conducive to the evolution of a critical and self-conscious judgment) to determine what kind of adult the child becomes? If one believes—as all but the most fiercely libertarian intellectuals since the nineteenth century have believed—that development will always be governed by environment, how can one imagine that refraining from trying to arrange circumstances will result in some absolute emancipation? Rightly or wrongly, Rousseau and Wilde conclude that the way to address environmental determination is to manage conditions for the best, not to flee the taint of having had a hand in determination at all.

It is this sense of urgency about conditions favorable to perfect development that takes us, strangely enough, to the element of no in the answer to our question about whether education by beauty is best understood as a way of reinforcing extant social relations and hierarchies. For it seems clear that if one aspires to a perfected environment yielding people "not wounded, or worried, or maimed, or in danger," one may feel all the more appalled at present conditions and all the more compelled to set about changing them, just as (Morris imagined) workers might be galvanized on seeing how they had been deprived of beauty. On this front, it bears recalling that when Wilde was not promoting the immediate public benefits of education by the beautiful, he was often busy enunciating a doctrine, for which "aestheticism" still remains a synonym, whose claims on behalf of art often led to important questions about prevailing customs and values—questions of the sort that had made Pater's *Renaissance* a minor scandal and that, even before the famous trials, had provoked in some quarters a detestation of Wilde going well beyond professions of shock at his paradoxes.[22]

The author elsewhere of an affectionate play called *Saint Oscar*, Eagleton himself dwells feelingly on an antithetical element in the ideology of the aesthetic, writing that "[a]esthetics are not only incipiently materialist" but "also provide, at the very heart of the Enlightenment, the most

powerful available critique of bourgeois possessive individualism and appetitive egoism. . . . For what the aesthetic imitates in its very glorious
futility, in its pointless self-referentiality, in all its full-blooded formalism,
is nothing less than human existence itself, which needs no rationale beyond its own self-delight" ("Ideology" 30; see also *Ideology* 65). Or, in
Wilde's terms: beauty helps persuade us that what matters is not having
but being.[23] In exuding the pointless self-referentiality and self-delight
that Eagleton names, works of art and other incarnations of the aesthetic
present themselves—and this even in the teeth of their vulnerability to
commodification—as things that matter for themselves, just as persons
should matter for themselves and not otherwise.

Nor is this the only sense in which art's "pointless self-referentiality"
might serve as the foundation of a certain social promise. According to
a tradition going back to the dawn of aesthetics, an object of aesthetic
appreciation is essentially noninstrumental, a thing that unlike food, shel-
ter, tools, money, and statal institutions does not support bare existence
or basic political freedom. Yet such an object may engender serious evaluation and discussion among those who contemplate it, just as if a great
deal depended on assessing it properly. As eighteenth-century philosophy
quickly discerned, this implies that there may be inherent in aesthetic experience a sense of evaluation as a kind of social practice. When we make
judgments of taste, according to Kant, we feel that they should have a
general applicability; such judgments "must have a subjective principle
which determines what pleases or displeases only by feeling and not by
concepts, but yet with universal validity. But such a principle could only
be regarded as a *common sense*," by which we mean not a common understanding judging from concepts but "the effect resulting from the free
play of our cognitive powers" (75; §21). Our feeling that others ought
to agree with our aesthetic judgments, in other words, is a feeling that
individuals can arrive at concord in a way that would be unconstrained
yet carry the essential validity of conformity to a right principle—another
kind of reconciliation between self and world and between freedom and
law. From such a recognition, it is but a short step for a writer like Schiller
(if not for Kant himself) to the claim that while "[a]ll other forms of
communication divide society, . . . the communication of the Beautiful
unites society, because it relates to what is common to" all its members.
"Beauty alone," as Schiller puts it, "makes all the world happy" (138–39).

There are several moments at which Pater and Wilde depict a general
aesthetic cultivation reconciling individual and collective—indeed reconciling them as thoroughly as Herbert Spencer claimed evolution would
when he wrote, in 1851's *Social Statics*, of "the ultimate man . . . whose
private requirements coincide with public ones. He will be that manner
of man, who in *spontaneously* fulfilling his own nature, *incidentally* per-

forms the function of a social unit; and yet is only enabled to fulfill his own nature, by all others doing the like" (quoted in Armstrong 31). In "Lacedaemon," Pater imagines in his utopian Sparta a public "ballet-dance" having "the character both of a liturgical service and of a military inspection," a collective performance that "in spite of its severity of rule, was a natural expression of the delight of all who took part in it" (*Plato* 203). In his American lectures, meanwhile, Wilde presents art as an alternative to large-scale violence, claiming not only that the boy who has come to love marble birds will not throw stones at real ones but also that "art, by creating a common intellectual atmosphere between all countries, might—if it could not overshadow the world with the silver wings of peace—at least make men such brothers that they would not go out to slay one another for the whim or folly of some king or minister" (*Aristotle* 21–22). Perhaps Wilde's most voluble attestation to art's affiliation with a dream of social concord, however, lies in a notable omission from "The Soul of Man under Socialism": the possibility that the Individualists of his future society—who, he says, are anticipated most nearly by our own artists—might have goals or beliefs that would bring their supreme individualities into conflict.

These passages, along with the others from Pater, Wilde, Kant, Schiller, and Eagleton that we have been examining, suggest that anxiety about freedom in various senses almost inevitably attends serious reflection on aesthetic experience's power to shape the soul. We have just seen how this anxiety could be addressed by the hope that consciousness of aesthetic deprivation would provoke social action, by belief in the fertility of an analogy between the noninstrumentality of the beautiful object and the self-delight of life, and by faith in art's capacity to generate social concord in ways not overtly coercive. But we have also seen that Pater ventures a rather different response to the problem of freedom, when he links the aesthetic to a liberatory intensification of awareness itself. While in texts like "The Child in the House" he dwells on the virtues of formation by scarcely noticed transactions, in texts like "Coleridge's Writings" and the Winckelmann chapter of *The Renaissance* he makes aesthetic experience paradigmatic of a heightened observation permitting a feeling of transcendence of the forces that shape us.

We might note here that although Wilde treats much more extensively the first of the aesthetic benefits Pater discerns, he picks up on the second at certain crucial junctures. In "The Critic as Artist," for example, he closely reworks the key passage from "Coleridge's Writings" (which text he saw in revised form in *Appreciations*) wherein Pater argues that contemplation of the factors that determine us provides an intimation of escape from determination: "[b]y revealing to us the absolute mechanism of all action, and so freeing us from the self-imposed and trammeling burden of moral responsibility," Gilbert observes, "the scientific principle of Heredity has become, as it were, the warrant for the contemplative life" (1040). This statement is then closely followed by Gilbert's promise that the taste of the child raised in beauty will eventually "become critical and self-conscious," though "at first it is to exist purely as a cultivated instinct." In other words, one of Wilde's moves in "Critic" is to project Pater's two benefits onto sequential phases of maturation, affiliating unconscious shaping by beauty with early life, intense conscious reflection (and hence freedom) with adulthood.

In a moment, we will consider how James Joyce took up and transformed such speculations on the liberatory possibilities of aesthetic experience. By way of closing out the present chapter, however, we might notice that the vision of aesthetic shaping Pater bequeathed Wilde implies at least one more sense in which aesthetic influence might be allied with freedom—a sense that falls on the side not of heightened consciousness but of unconscious transactions after all.

If in the Winckelmann chapter Pater recommends art that helps us watch necessity unfold, he also evokes a certain boundary to our observational capacities when he refers to a network of forces "subtler than our subtlest nerves" running through us. Similarly, in "The Child in the House," he augments rather than diminishes the mystery of brain building by representing the soul's texture as half "accident of homely colour and form . . . half, mere soul-stuff, floated thither from who knows how far." What moments like these highlight is that the infinite stealth of aesthetic influence limits not only the absolute freedom of the maturing organism but also the control that can be exercised over that organism by others. Even the shrewdest guardians of the young cannot know precisely what will result from the atmospheres they contrive, because the workings of the myriad stimuli falling on the sensorium of any individual can never be fully cataloged. The young person immersed in beauty may still turn out in any of countless ways. Yet that there can be no certainty about what will result from a particular exposure to the aesthetic (witness the case of Thomas Griffiths Wainewright, the murderer) seems only on occasion to have dampened aestheticism's enthusiasm for the power of lovely environments. For the most part, its adherents retained a faith that things could not go far wrong where surroundings were really of the right kind. Surely, beauty would see to that.

## CHAPTER THREE

# *Aesthetics of Acuteness*

AESTHETICISM, NATURALISM, PATER, ZOLA, JOYCE, DREISER

At this juncture, we need to acknowledge that aestheticism may seem a peculiar point of focus for an exploration of late nineteenth-century views of environment's power. For the literary movement or mode most often associated with environmental determinations of development has been not aestheticism, but something that from many angles looks like its antithesis: literary naturalism. The present chapter and the next will try to redress omissions in just this quarter by considering the force of beauty as registered by two English-language writers closely associated with naturalist theory and practice. But this will not mean backtracking from the claim that aestheticism is important to the story of environmental obsessions, nor will it mean undercutting the received wisdom that naturalists were preoccupied with developmental milieux. Rather, it will mean examining more closely the connections between the two modes, recognizing how they partook of a common genealogy and shared key ideas about art, society, and their interrelation.

Most definitions of literary naturalism would allow that it coalesces around statements by the brothers Goncourt and, still more crucially, Émile Zola, whose 1879 brief for the "Experimental Novel" is usually regarded as the founding manifesto of the genre. There, Zola explains that the new kind of novel he advocates will be in the nature of a scientific experiment, the writer placing characters with certain hereditary traits in certain environments and then observing the inevitable results of their interaction. The activity of the experimental novel will be "to possess a knowledge of the mechanism of the phenomena [of emotional life] inherent in man, to show the machinery of his intellectual and sensory manifestations, under the influences of heredity and environment, such as physiology shall give them to us, and then finally to exhibit man living in social conditions produced by himself, which he modifies daily, and in the heart of which he himself experiences a continual transformation" (20–21). To advance his case for the scientific approach, Zola draws upon the physiologist Claude Bernard's 1865 *Introduction à l'étude de la médecine expérimentale*, remarking that although in the eyes of many people, "[m]edicine . . . is still an art, as is the novel," Bernard has demonstrated that the experimental method, "followed in the study of inanimate bodies in chemistry and physics, should be also used in the study of living bodies,

in physiology and medicine." Zola will prove in turn that if such a method
"leads to the knowledge of physical life, it should also lead to the knowledge of the passionate and intellectual life" (2).

For the antivitalist Bernard, Zola observes further, experiment (which
"is but provoked observation") can lead to accurate knowledge of animate
bodies as of inanimate ones because the two are equally governed by material processes. The

> essence of the higher organism is set in an internal and perfected environment
> endowed with constant physico-chemical properties exactly like the external
> environment; hence there is an absolute determinism in the existing condi-
> tions of natural phenomena . . . for the living as for the inanimate bodies. . . .
> The end of all experimental method . . . consists in finding the relations
> which unite a phenomenon of any kind to its nearest cause, or, in other
> words, in determining the conditions necessary for the manifestation of this
> phenomenon. (3)

Extending the ideas of Auguste Comte, Bernard had defined life as a mu-
tually regulating interaction between internal and external milieux (Shuttleworth 18), a formulation that comes very close to Herbert Spencer's
"continuous adjustment of internal relations to external relations." Like
Comte's, Bernard's ideas were also important to George Henry Lewes,
who posited that the human organism must be understood as existing
within both a "Bioplasm" and a "Psychoplasm," the first being the totality
of conditions affecting the organism's biological state, the second the totality of influences on its psychological state (Rylance 275). And indeed
Lewes and Zola can be said to have worked in parallel inasmuch as both
adapted Bernard to a sociological and psychological terrain.

Not surprisingly, many readers of Zola's manifesto have complained
that experiments "conducted" in a novel must in fact occur in the autho-
rial imagination, and so cannot be treated as scientific. A novelist may
discern certain laws at work among people and bring these to bear in the
text, but the actual writing cannot involve testing laws of determination,
only illustrating them. And indeed there is some slippage on this point in
"The Experimental Novel" itself: in a telling moment, Zola writes of Balzac's placing a character "amid certain surroundings in order *to exhibit*
[*pour montrer*] how the complicated machinery of his passions works" (9).
Ignoring this kind of objection, however, Zola claims that the experimental novel constitutes nothing other than the next step—beyond physiology—in the march of sciences of the human: "We have an experimental
chemistry and medicine," and so "we shall have an experimental physiology, and later on an experimental novel" (16). Indeed so "inevitable" is
this "evolution" that "we can easily proclaim, without fear of being mistaken, the hour in which the laws of thought and passion will be formu-

lated in their turn. A like determinism will govern the stones of the road-way and the brain of man" (17).

Yet the elucidation of laws of thought and passion will not, as some critics charge, lead to fatalism or quietism. On the contrary: if the "experimental moralists" (among whom Zola numbers himself) can indeed show "by experiment in what way a passion acts in a certain social condition," then it is possible to "work upon . . . individuals and . . . surroundings" so as to arrive at "the best social condition." It is possible to "regulate life, to regulate society, . . . to give justice a solid foundation." And for this reason, Zola can think of no "more noble work" or "grander application" than that which he proposes for the naturalist novelist (26).

The environments actually depicted in naturalist novels tended not to illustrate the ideal condition, of course, but rather to show how far social improvement had left to go. Although Zola's program theoretically admitted virtues blossoming out of comfort as readily as vices erupting from squalor, the form gravitated overwhelmingly to the poor and dangerous quarters of the metropole, which seemed to breed misery, degradation, and crime as relentlessly as well-kept country places ministered to health. In other words, naturalism's affinity was for just those situations that would seem most destitute of the formative beauty aestheticism prescribed. And where aestheticism promoted the cultivation of an infinitely sensitive tissue of personality, naturalism dwelt on the hardening effects of bitter circumstances. Where aestheticism treasured an ideal of high self-consciousness, naturalism depicted characters driven to their doom by forces beyond their comprehension.

Moreover, aestheticism's passion for beauty, mystery, and the delicate registering of subjective experience seems to have emerged partly in opposition to naturalism's fixation on sociological precision and developmental constraints. As Peter Bürger and others have shown, the last years of the nineteenth century witnessed a reaction, on the part of many younger French writers, against naturalism's focus on the externals of social behavior. In 1889's *La Littérature de tout à l'heure*, for example, Charles Morice complained that "the romantics and naturalists of recent times do not even seem to have noticed that the real task is to draw forth from within oneself that innermost utterly particular reality which is unknown to others and to ourselves" (quoted in Bürger 95). In an 1891 essay called "The Crisis of Naturalism," Hermann Bahr reported how, on the French scene, the "curiosity of the reader and the inclination of the writer turns [*sic*] inwards once again . . . away from the 'rendu de choses visibles' to the 'intérieurs d'âmes' " (quoted in Bürger 95).

With his 1899 *Symbolist Movement in Literature*, Arthur Symons accelerated the migration of Continental trends to England, explicitly opposing Symbolism (very closely related to aestheticism by virtue of both its

personnel and its characteristic moods and devices) to the naturalism of
Zola and company. In Symons's telling, Zola is "quite sure that the soul
is a nervous fluid, which he is quite sure some man of science is about to
catch for us, as a man of science has bottled the air, a pretty, blue liquid"
(7); the epoch of Zola has been an age "of Science, . . . of material things"
in which language "did miracles in the exact representation of everything
that visibly existed, exactly as it existed" and in which "form aimed above
all things at being precise, at saying rather than suggesting" (6–7). But
that era, according to Symons, is now passing, for the newer wave called
Symbolism inverts the earlier priorities, choosing to suggest rather than to
say, treating the soul as something elusive, shimmering, beyond chemical
distillation. Three decades later, in *Axel's Castle* (1931), Edmund Wilson
would avail himself of similar terms in arguing that the literary production
of the preceding sixty years had been dynamized by an opposition between
Symbolism and naturalism. For Wilson, the rise of Symbolism showed
literature "rebounding again from the scientific-classical pole" of naturalism to a "poetic-romantic" pole suspicious of science's certainties, just as
it had rebounded a century before from Enlightenment rationalism to
Romantic turmoil (10).

And yet, Wilson stressed, the two methods could often be found at
play in a single oeuvre or even a single work. The literary history of 1870
to 1930 was "to a great extent that of the development of Symbolism
and of its *fusion or* conflict with Naturalism" (25, emphasis added), as
one can see for example in *Ulysses*, where "a master of Naturalism as great
as Flaubert" uses Symbolist methods to differentiate among "various
characters and their varying states of mind" (24–25). Nor was Wilson
the only critic to take note of convergences between aesthetes and naturalists.[1] In *The Symbolist Movement* itself, Symons placed within the epoch
of Zola not only Flaubert, the Goncourts, and Taine but also Baudelaire
(possessed of "a certain theory of Realism which tortures many of his
poems into strange, metallic shapes"), while declaring the Symbolist
spirit to be deep in Ibsen, whom many today might class with the naturalists (6). Period celebrations of "the decadence" and critiques of degeneration also attested how frequently enthrallment by the beautiful was accompanied by pursuit of the louche. And a few decades later (or shortly
after Wilson), the Marxist critic György Lukács would commence arguing that a "principle of naturalistic arbitrariness," in which psychopa-
thology is identified with *la condition humaine* instead of particular social formations, could be found not only "in the all-determining 'social
conditions' of Naturalism" but also in "Symbolism's impressionist methods and its cultivation of the exotic"—not to mention Futurism, Con-
structivism, Surrealism, and the *Neue Sachlichkeit* (34).

Lukács does not delve deeply into the sources of naturalism's continuity with this other set of modes, but his tethering of both to determinism points to a crucial commonality in intellectual origin that has otherwise nearly been lost to criticism. For as chapter 2 should have made clear, aestheticism was grounded in the same jarring scientific revelations that grounded naturalism, and was similarly led by these revelations to key questions about freedom, necessity, and environment's effects on the growing human organism. This point emerges most clearly, perhaps, in the case of Pater, who conceded early on that life may be a series of material transactions determined by natural laws, but who also stressed, as Zola did, how much space for significance is cleared by our observation of those laws at work. "Natural laws we shall never modify . . . but there is still something in the nobler or less noble attitude with which we watch their fatal combinations": if Zola's naturalism bids us look at *fatal* combinations of forces, one might say, Paterian aestheticism bids us *look* at fatal combinations of forces.

This continuity between aestheticism and naturalism can also be discerned in Ruskin and Morris, whose belief in the shaping power of the built environment underlay their efforts to transform British architecture and design and to improve the conditions of the working classes and the urban poor. And it certainly embraces Oscar Wilde, who as a young man included in his Commonplace Book a note on the possibility of elucidating "the laws which govern the phenomena of human action, the complex manifestations of that redistribution of matter and force which we call Society" (*Oxford Notebooks* 109).[2] In later years, as we have seen, Wilde would advance an ideal that reads as the inverse of the sordid actual exposed by naturalist fiction, a world in which beauty rather than ugliness would be the rule and in which Individualism would flower precisely because conditions favorable to it had been secured.

In the present chapter, we will consider how the common grounding of naturalism and aestheticism informs some of the writing of James Joyce, a writer essential to our story in part because widely credited with building something more compellingly strange on naturalism's documentary foundations. As just noted, Wilson thought this achievement central to Joyce's literary-historical significance, and in working up his critique of modernism Lukács similarly, if less approvingly, placed Joyce at a junction between naturalism's putatively austere observation and a more luxuriant representational mode. Where Thomas Mann had produced a socially useful realism, Lukács argues, Joyce presents "perpetually oscillating patterns of sense- and memory-data" and "powerfully charged—but aimless and directionless—fields of force" that fall in line with the "all-determining 'social conditions' of Naturalism" inasmuch as they reflect "a belief in the basically static character of events" (18,

34). (To complete our triad of critics, we might speculate that Symons would have discussed Joyce in these terms had his *Symbolist Movement* postdated Joyce's works. Scholarship suggests that Symons's book had a significant impact on the young Joyce, and it is a matter of record that Symons became one of Joyce's early supporters.)

Why Joyce should be regarded as a nodal point between naturalism and other, quite different, modes is evident even from the broad outlines of his oeuvre. His first volume of fiction, *Dubliners*, presents constrained lives in a bleak urban milieu, yet it also scatters items replete with symbolic meaning through the bare existences it sparely renders. In *Ulysses*, Joyce weaves the story of a single day in Dublin together with dozens of parallels to the *Odyssey* and a network of objects, phrases, and memories that resonate with each other in countless ways, thus presenting at once a triumph of naturalist precision and a touchstone of modernist allusiveness. Yet while it might be said that *Dubliners* forecasts the Joycean transformation of naturalism that *Ulysses* completes, it can also be argued that the intervening prose fiction, *A Portrait of the Artist as a Young Man*, illustrates the transformation most decisively. As Mark Wollaeger writes, "In many ways *Portrait* epitomizes modernism understood as the confluence of the symbolist and naturalist movements of the late nineteenth century: Joyce opens his fiction to the everyday effluvia of lower-middle-class Dublin while also investing naturalistic details with polyvalent symbolic significance" (12). And, it might be added, opens his fiction to aestheticism's impassioned plea for art and beauty, choosing an aesthete for his protagonist and dramatizing the conflict between Zolaesque reality and Wildean aspirations with a resoluteness unrivaled by any other writer of the period.

Or, at least, any writer aside from Theodore Dreiser. For as we will see in chapter 4, that American novelist and journalist also pitted the possibilities of beauty against the limitations of environment, and did so out of a vision of the world even more impressively mechanistic than Pater's or Joyce's. Traditionally counted among the American naturalists, Dreiser tirelessly recurred to the question of how life could retain its meaning after science had demonstrated human fates' determination by natural law, and his readers have explored this interest extensively. What has not often been remarked, however, is that Dreiser frequently turned to the aesthetic in his quest for answers to the problem of meaning, wondering whether the inclination to beauty partly redeems our animal nature, whether there might glimmer through art some faint freedom from the conditions by which we are evidently bound.

That Dreiser has almost never been read together with his contemporary Joyce comes to seem a little surprising as soon as one notes how much the two had in common. Though the latter grew up in Ireland and the former in the American Midwest, both came of age in families driven by declining economic fortunes to less and less desirable quarters, and both would write about the longings engendered by straitened circumstances in a way that made the naturalist project more intimate and autobiographical—as if the subject of Zola's experimental novel were now telling the tale from the inside. No less significantly, the imaginations of both were shaped by rebellion against Roman Catholic schooling. To be sure, Joyce retained an affection for some aspects of his Jesuit training, whereas Dreiser never ceased to excoriate the narrowness of heartland Catholic education at the end of the nineteenth century, but both came to see Catholicism as an intellectually and spiritually limiting system that had to be overcome by the soul seeking meaningful expansion. And both seem to have been driven to this position, at least initially, by Catholicism's insistence on sexual purity, with its apparent contempt for the persistent and daily experience of desire, the manifest evidence of bodily nature.

For both, moreover, what replaced Catholic doctrine as a way of comprehending the world was the picture of the universe developed by modern science, according to which the human being was not only a soul but also an organism constantly responding to stimuli and continuously adapting to environmental conditions. We will take up this point in more detail in the following pages, but up front we might notice that neither Joyce nor Dreiser came to naturalism out of a conscious urge to join a literary school. Both got there, rather, by way of a deeply felt internalization of the clash between science and religion that was setting the contours of intellectual debate in their time. Both wrote from a broadly mechanistic standpoint wherein the attempt to find human meaning had to proceed without the security provided by a received faith. And both were moved, for reasons we will explore, to put beauty at this attempt's sacrally unsacred heart.

## CHEMICAL ACTION SET UP IN THE SOUL

The preceding chapters have been much concerned with the life of a certain idea, namely, that the small transactions of ordinary experience shape the self in potent and unpredictable ways. Beyond any doubt, Joyce's writings mark a breakthrough in the literary elaboration of this belief. Joyce's best-known biographer might have pointed to any of a dozen seminal innovations as the key to his subject's achievement, but at the beginning of his monumental *James Joyce*, Richard Ellmann spotlights Joyce's attention to little things, declaring that the "initial and determining act of judgment" in his work "is the justification of the commonplace. Other writers had labored tediously to portray it, but none knew what the commonplace really was until Joyce had written. . . . Joyce's discovery . . . was that the ordinary is the extraordinary" (5). Or as Joyce himself once described his project to his brother Stanislaus, "It is my idea of the significance of trivial things that I want to give the two or three unfortunate wretches who may eventually read me" (quoted in Ellmann, *James Joyce* 163).

*Dubliners, Ulysses,* or *Finnegans Wake* might certainly have been uppermost in Ellmann's mind when he elected to commence with the commonplace, and Joyce's comment to Stanislaus singles out no one of Joyce's early endeavors. But the point about "the significance of trivial things" has a particular application to *A Portrait of the Artist as a Young Man,* which is the only major work by Joyce to approximate the form of the traditional bildungsroman or even to follow a single character's history over a long period of time. In other Joycean texts, the affirmation of the trivial may ring primarily axiomatic or metaphysical, little things being important just because they are or because they figure into some larger symbolic pattern. *Portrait,* however, encourages its reader to attend to another possibility: that apparently minor events in early life decisively mold the children or adolescents who experience them.

This possibility emerges right away, in the groundbreaking opening where Joyce seems to mime the consciousness of the very young Stephen Dedalus:

> Once upon a time and a very good time it was there was a moocow coming down along the road and this moocow that was coming down along the road met a nicens little boy named baby tuckoo. . . .
>
> His father told him that story: his father looked at him through a glass: he had a hairy face.
>
> He was baby tuckoo. The moocow came down the road where Betty Byrne lived: she sold lemon platt. (5)

Working under the assumption that what opens a narrative has special importance to the story it tells, of course, Joyce's reader will inevitably wonder why these impressions are so favored. It could be because they represent Stephen's earliest memories or ones he especially values; it could be because they figure into thematic or figural networks unavailable to Stephen but essential to the novel as a coherent work of art. (The moocow, for example, might stand in for the maternal principle; the father's hairy face and glass might allude to Caliban and the mirror in Wilde's preface to *Dorian Gray,* also remembered in the opening pages of *Ulysses.*) But it could also be that these impressions receive the distinction of the incipit because they shape Stephen's subjectivity, personality, or destiny in some causally powerful manner. In the story of a nicens little boy who proves to be Stephen, Joyce certainly reproduces on a micro scale the narrative of *Portrait* itself, but he also suggests that this early exposure to storytelling may have helped to make Stephen into a storyteller. Similar genetic possibilities then arise with every incident related in the first chapters of the novel. The reader is invited to infer, for example, that Stephen's early experiences of wetting his bed and being pushed into a ditch contribute to his later aversion to water.

The pre-Joycean bildungsroman certainly did not neglect the point that children can be keenly affected by occurrences scarcely noticed by adults: Jane Eyre in the red room, Maggie Tulliver and her abused doll, Pip at Christmas dinner, and other instances supply ample confirmation just for the British nineteenth century. Yet Stephen's experiences at the beginning of *Portrait* come still earlier in life and seem on the face of things still more trivial than those represented by Brontë, Eliot, and Dickens. Further, their power seems to have as much to do with basic stimulation of the sensorium as with interpellation in familial or other social arrangements. In this respect, Joyce seems the heir not only of Brontë, Eliot, and Dickens but also of Locke, the Edgeworths, Wordsworth, Lydia Child, and Ellen Key, as well as other theorists of education who had attributed enormous importance to the sensory stimulation of the young: Pestalozzi, Froebel, the Mayos, Spencer.

This attention to the senses also marks Joyce an heir of aestheticism, of course. Almost from the beginning of his publishing career, readers noted his variously fascinating debts to Pater and Wilde, as when in 1922 T. S. Eliot told Virginia Woolf that Joyce was "a purely literary writer . . . founded upon Walter Pater with a dash of Newman" (quoted in Moliterno 1). In the 1930s, Stuart Gilbert remarked close parallels between Stephen Dedalus and Pater's Marius (Perlis 274), while in 1941, Harry Levin heard Paterian notes in Joyce's early criticism and some purple sections of *Portrait* (24–25, 56). In more recent years, scholars have elaborated tremendously on the relations between Joyce and Pater and between Joyce and Wilde. They have not only reinforced Levin's point that some of Joyce's earliest essays exhibit a familiarity with Pater's work and attempts at Paterian style (Moliterno 2–3; Ellmann, *James Joyce* 95; Scotto 45) but also pointed out that Joyce copied long passages from *Marius the Epicurean* and *Imaginary Portraits* into his notes (Buckley 228, McGrath 231); that he could have drawn inspiration for his theory of the epiphany from Pater's "School of Giorgione" (Scholes and Kain 94); that *Portrait* contains a wealth of acutely Paterian sentences (Buckley 229, Moliterno 76); that in both *Portrait* and Pater's "Child in the House" an "older artist desires . . . to cleanse and recompose himself as a young man" (Poirier 173); that *Portrait* is "a virtual dictionary of the tropology of Pater at large," picking up figures not only from "Child" but also from "Emerald Uthwart" and "A Prince of Court Painters" (Meisel 129); that Joyce had read *Dorian Gray* by the time he was revising *Portrait* and may have registered parallels between the "exile" of the Irish artist Wilde and himself

(Manganiello 89); that at least twenty references to Wilde appear in *Ulysses* and countless more in *Finnegans Wake* (Bowen 105).[3]

Among the numerous areas of overlap between earlier aesthetes and Joyce, however, none may be more significant than the conviction that sensuous experience should be accorded high dignity and attention in art and in life. In *The Sensible Spirit*, his aptly titled reading of Pater's philosophical importance to modernism, F. C. McGrath observes that the key Paterian elements exhibited by *Portrait* include "a dialectic of sense and spirit in the pursuit of a unified sensibility, the privileging of aesthetic experience in that pursuit, an expressive orientation toward the creative process, and an awareness of the ascetic devotion necessary to forge new techniques appropriate to a new vision of experience" (236). In *The Dialectics of Sense and Spirit in Pater and Joyce*, meanwhile, Frank Moliterno points out that both writers were "pious adolescents" who "eventually escaped from sensual repression and replaced asceticism with a love of sensual beauty and a frank acceptance of everyday life" (7). Indeed Stephen's trajectory can be said to replicate that of Florian Deleal, who also develops (in Pater's words) "a certain capacity of fascination by bright colours and choice form," a "passionateness in . . . relation to fair outward objects" (*Imaginary* 8, 11), and eventually (Moliterno's phrasing) "comes to love the immaterial through the material" (31).

Stephen does seem to be an aesthete from an early age. When, a few pages into *Portrait*, he appears in a school math competition where one team's badge is the red rose of Lancaster and the other's the white rose of York, his main interest does not lie in the sums, the competition, the historical English royal houses, or the imperial relationship betokened by those houses' adaptation to an Irish schoolroom. What captures his attention are the qualities of the rose insignia themselves:

> Jack Lawton looked over from his side. The little silk badge with the red rose on it looked very rich because he had a blue sailor top on. . . . White roses and red roses: those were beautiful colours to think of. And the cards for first place and second place and third place were beautiful colours too: pink and cream and lavender. Lavender and cream and pink roses were beautiful to think of. . . . But you could not have a green rose. But perhaps somewhere in the world you could. (9)

In case the point about Stephen's precocious aestheticism is not marked clearly enough, the last sentences connect him directly to one of high aestheticism's emblems. On the first page of the novel, he had already fashioned his own song about a green flower out of lines from the nineteenth-century parlor favorite "Lily Dale": in his revision, "O, the wild rose blossoms / On the little green place" becomes "O, the green wothe botheth" (5). But the green rose is mentioned in passing (as the desire of the eponymous heroine) in Ouida's aesthetic novel *Wanda*, as Talia Shaffer has pointed out (*Forgotten* 137), and it gestures unmissably as well to the green carnation, famously associated with Wilde after he and his associates wore corsages of this flower, with conspicuously mysterious air, to the opening of *Lady Windermere's Fan* in 1892 (Ellmann, *Oscar Wilde* 365). This minor promotional gesture played, for those in the know, upon the green bloom's reputation as a marker of fraternity for Parisian homosexuals; it also gave Robert S. Hichens the title for his 1894 novel of aestheticism, *The Green Carnation*. And it unquestionably reinforced the point that aestheticism delighted in nature's trumping by artifice.

Yet if from one point of view Stephen's captivation by the badges says that he is a child likely to become an aesthete, from another it says only that he is a child. Given the attraction of the very young to the basic sensory stimuli of shape and color (noted by commentators at least since Locke), we might take Stephen to be like rather than unlike many of his classmates in being more absorbed by the look of the roses than by the math contest. A similar inference seems warranted with respect to the eighth paragraph of the novel, in which the reader is told how Stephen's aunt Dante Riordan "had two brushes in her press. The brush with the maroon velvet back was for Michael Davitt and the brush with the green velvet back was for Parnell" (5). It would be surprising if the very young Stephen had a profound grasp of the political struggles Dante is commemorating, but there is nothing unusual in his being fascinated by the visual contrast between objects to which an adult has imputed obscure significance. This point carrying forward to the math contest, it becomes hard to say whether Stephen's absorption by flowers and colors makes him unusual or typical, just as in Pater's "Child in the House" Florian sometimes seems a special case, sometimes exemplary of children in general. In *Portrait*, this kind of ambiguity is abetted by the sheer reticence of the narrator, who presents Stephen's early experiences without offering generalizations about the subjective life of children—and in this very withholding captures children's tendency to doubt that their feelings are shared by others (particularly where those feelings, as of liking roses better than competitions, deviate from the supposed norm).

However ordinary or unusual Florian and Stephen may be, then, their narratives clearly imply some continuity between the child and the artist or aesthete. If children are artists all in their fascination with the sensuous, it might equally be said that artists are adults who retain the sensuous disposition of childhood—who remain absorbed by the colors of brushes or roses, say, long after they have come to understand Irish nationalism or contention over the English throne. This connection between childhood and genius had been remarked by philosophers well before Joyce (including Arthur Schopenhauer), and modern psychological research would reiterate the point: in his influential 1943 brief for art education, for example, Herbert Read quotes the psychologist E. R. Jaensch's conclusion that "*the closest parallel to the structure of personality of the child is . . . that of the artist*" (quoted in Read 57). Further, almost anyone's recollection of childhood will appear to verify that in early life intense absorption by the immediately sensuous is joined to a certain haziness about the abstractions, such as commerce and politics, that make the world go round. From here, it seems but a short step to presentiments of a basic and necessary opposition between the intense experience associated with art and the routines of modern existence, between the art object and the commodity, between the artist and the bourgeois citizen, between the pursuit of beauty and the pursuit of gain. And this is clearly one reason why the figure of the child could so readily be conscripted for oppositional stances associated with art by Romanticism, aestheticism, and modernism.

For Stephen Dedalus, the pursuit of beauty is especially fraught because it opens a path to practical liberation from his oppressive turn-of-the-century Dublin surroundings. The early chapters of the novel are filled with references to the "vague dissatisfaction," the "unrest and bitter thoughts," his environment inspires (55, 65–66), and at one point he is described as trying "to build a breakwater of order and elegance against the sordid tide of life without him and to dam up, by rules of conduct and active interests and new filial relations, the powerful recurrence of the tides within him" (82). These quasi-aesthetic efforts proving insufficient, Stephen finally chooses the path of the artist as such, so that by the last of the novel's five acts he is telling his friend Davin how he will use art to "fly by" the "nets" of "nationality, language, religion" (171), unleashing upon his friend Lynch a theory in which the aesthetic frees one from the trammels of ordinary desire, and announcing to his friend Cranly his will to express himself "in some mode of life or art as freely as [he] can and as wholly as [he] can," using only the defenses of "silence, exile, and cunning" (208). Within Stephen's life, in other words, (the choice of) aestheticism opposes the naturalist donnée as freedom opposes limitation. Confronted by many of the forces that crush characters in naturalist novels—a family dropping down the socioeconomic ladder, a narrow morality enforced by circumambient busybodies, a restriction of vocational possibility, an urban scene by turns enthralling and poisonous to the spirit—Stephen wields his doctrine of beauty and his determination to become an artist, as though trying to step out of a naturalist *roman expérimental* into a *kunstlerroman* of his own devising.

One of the ironies famously attending his story, however, is that aesthete Stephen can only develop into artist Joyce by becoming a kind of naturalist—by extracting the material for a successful art not from the ether of the Nineties but from the fateful grit of Dublin and its "scrupulous meanness."[4] Stephen is clearly aware of this requirement at some level: although his verses leave doubtful whether he yet has the tools to produce an art aggressively in contact with the life around him ("And still you hold our longing gaze / With languorous look and lavish limb!" [188]), he clearly believes such contact to be necessary. In *Portrait*, he recurs to the artist's struggle to express beauty "from lumps of earth" (159) and fancies himself "a priest of the eternal imagination, transmuting the daily bread of experience into the radiant body of everliving life" (186); in *Stephen Hero*, that earlier version of *Portrait* composed between 1904 and 1906 and of which only a long fragment survives, he tells his mother, "Art is not an escape from life. It's the very opposite. Art, on the contrary, is the very central expression of life" (86).[5]

We clearly lose sight of something crucial, however, if we treat the career of Joyce-Stephen as a straightforward passage from aestheticism to naturalism (or, on the other side, as a simple transcending of lived naturalist squalor through aesthetic self-fashioning). That something is, precisely, the commonality of origin between naturalism and aestheticism that we have just elucidated—their common foundation in a vision of life as a series of physiochemical transactions governed by natural law. For Zola, again, this view of the universe mandated a kind of novel in which scientific inquiry and the social good would be served by careful recording of heredity's interactions with environment; for Pater, it required a representation of experience that would impart a feeling of freedom by stimulating reflection on the forces that rule our lives. Overtly different as these new forms for writing were, however, the understanding that seemed to demand them—the sense of what the world truly is, of how life invariably works—was profoundly shared.

Joyce partakes of this same understanding of human life in the world, and when he or his characters allude to it they often do so in Paterian accents. Expatiating on art and imagination in episode nine of *Ulysses*, for example, Stephen presents as an axiom that "we, or mother Dana"—that is, necessity—"weave and unweave our bodies . . . from day to day"; since corporeal atoms are "shuttled to and fro" constantly, he explains, his body "has been woven of new stuff time after time" even though "the mole on [his] right breast is where it was when [he] was born" (159–60). As many readers have noted, this language evokes directly the "perpetual weaving and unweaving of ourselves" that Pater describes in the conclusion to *The Renaissance*, and it does so with perhaps less irony than might be expected given the archness with which Stephen has been laying out his theories. It might seem that Stephen is essentially parodying Pater, substituting a banal claim about the body for Paterian exhalations anent the soul; but as the conclusion to *The Renaissance* itself makes quite clear, the formation of the soul was a material process for Pater in the same fundamental sense that it was for Joyce. From this point of view, the exchange of an atom in the mole on Stephen's right breast for one initially outside Stephen's body would not be radically different from the experience of gazing upon a particular object: both are transactions between the organism and its environment, and both are grounded in physical events occurring on so small a scale that no eye can perceive them.

Joyce notably alludes to this kind of molecular event late in *Portrait*. When Cranly asks if Stephen refuses the sacrament because he fears that God will damn him for making a communion without real faith, Stephen answers, "I fear more the chemical action which would be set up in my soul by a false homage to a symbol behind which are massed twenty centuries of authority and veneration" (205). The rejoinder is tongue-in-cheek, but it is at the same time true to an understanding that takes the soul's development to be mediated by transformations of matter. Wryly replacing a religious explanation with one compounded of physiology ("chemical action") and sociology ("twenty centuries of authority and veneration"), Stephen moreover captures in exemplary fashion the naturalist view that there can be no sharp demarcation between the biological and psychological realms. He also well captures a point we have remarked several times in relation to what we have been calling the developmental unconscious: that a recognition of the mind's submission to physiological transactions leads to a sense of the limits of volition. In Stephen's telling, the more or less deliberate gesture of accepting the host may have consequences that exceed deliberation because it can set going, and will interact with, events and processes unregistered by consciousness.[6]

In the version of this exchange appearing in *Stephen Hero*, Stephen makes no reference to chemical action when answering Cranly's question about the sacrament. But a still more suggestive passage appears a few pages earlier. At that juncture, Cranly is trying to lure Stephen back to the fold by suggesting that the Church might—within limits—accommodate a certain surface heresy. It might "not be over hasty in condemning . . . even the use of pagan emblems and flourishes," he offers, "so long as her ground rent was paid quarterly in advance." The narrator then continues, "These accommodating business terms, which would have seemed of suspicious piety to more simple souls, were not likely to startle two young men who were fond of tracing even moral phenomena back to the region of their primal cells" (123). Even Cranly, it seems, takes for granted that the life of the soul is governed by the small units of the body, and it is on this basis that he fields his highly pragmatic Catholicism. The ramifications of this kind of assumption were even more serious, of course, for the non-believing or secular modern intellectual: from the ground of the sciences, as Pater puts it in "Coleridge's Writings," the relative spirit had invaded moral philosophy, starting there "a new analysis of the relations of body and mind, good and evil, freedom and necessity."

Of course, Joyce would have encountered this view of the materiality of experience in many places besides the texts of Walter Pater. Debates around the physiology of mind were so much an obsession of the later nineteenth century and the early twentieth that they simply could not have been missed by an intellectual wanting to keep abreast of current trends (as Joyce was), let alone by a person briefly enrolled as a medical student (as Joyce was in 1902). Equally unavoidable would have been the role played by physiological transformations of the organism in evolutionary theories, including the very ambitious ones that sought in evolution a key to all the processes and tendencies of the universe. No English-language writer was more renowned for this kind of undertaking than Herbert Spencer: as we saw in chapter 1, he not only helped make "environment" an essential concept for science but also encouraged thousands of readers to conceive of life as a continuous action and reaction occurring between organisms and their surroundings. The young Oscar Wilde was certainly among those readers,[7] and it is clear that the young Joyce, too, was acquainted with Spencer's ideas. In an article of 1903, he mentions—disparagingly—"the Unknowable of Mr Spencer" (that is, Spencer's attempt to reconcile science and religion by showing how both are concerned with an ultimate that defies comprehension), and years later he would include Spencer in an inventory of his early reading prepared for the biographer Herbert Gorman (*Occasional* 96; Ellmann, *James Joyce* 142). Joyce scholarship has, happily, started to accord Spencer some attention: in his recent *Joyce and Reality*, John Gordon argues suggestively that the narrative trajectories of both *Portrait* and the "Oxen of the Sun" episode in *Ulysses* mime the progress of the Spencerian cosmology, wherein all systems proceed from disorganized homogeneity to organized heterogeneity (8–15).

Especially important for us is Spencer's point that defining life in terms of "the continuous adjustment of internal relations to external relations" must affect our view of the mind as well as the body. "There is," he writes in *First Principles* (1860–62), "a correlation and equivalence between external physical forces and the mental forces generated by them in us under the form of sensations" and between "sensations and those physical forces which, in the shape of bodily actions, result from them" (*First* 221). Afferent and efferent neural processes, in other words, are to be understood in terms of equilibration between the interior and exterior worlds of the organism, and mental events prove, like everything else in the universe, a matter of physics and chemistry governed by a principle of balance: "That no idea or feeling arises, save as a result of some physical force expended in producing it, is fast becoming a common place of science" (225). As the young Wilde faithfully framed matters in his Commonplace Book, "there can be no knowledge of human nature without knowledge of the Laws of Mind, (Psychology) nor of the Laws of Mind without knowledge of the Laws of Life (Biology)" (*Oxford Notebooks* 109).

We might take a moment to notice that in advancing such a claim within the frame of his larger theories, Spencer lent a subtle but powerful Lamarckian frisson to the minute transactions of daily experience. From a strictly Darwinian perspective, adjustments to the environment made by the individual creature over the course of its life are evolutionarily negligible; what is crucial is that advantageous characteristics help the organisms carrying them to survive best and reproduce most over many generations, extinction then being the fate of traits that fail to serve. Under a Lamarckian dispensation, however, any organism can adapt itself to environmental conditions over the course of its life, or even in a moment, and transmit its new characteristics to its offspring. This view, especially as mediated through Spencer's notion of continuous adaptation, puts the Joycean "significance of trivial things" in a curious and interesting light, even if Joyce can scarcely be accused of sharing the allegiance to Spencer exhibited by some of his contemporaries. For it suggests that when we encounter the small transactions between character and world that constitute the fabric as well as the originality of books like *Portrait* and *Ulysses*, we are in some sense meeting versions of the ongoing interaction between environment and organism that constituted life as Spencer understood it, and as it was understood by many educated people in the late nineteenth and early twentieth centuries—perhaps not excluding James Joyce.

This speculation, in turn, supplies an appendix to our point about aestheticism and naturalism's common debt to the problem of human determination by external forces. For it may be that we grasp something new about the relation between naturalism and *modernism* when we see that depicting environments' shaping of human destinies could mean not only tracing the arc of a life over a span of years but also getting down interactions between person and world transpiring in a day, an hour, a minute. From this point of view, the registering of little experiences in Joyce's fictions or protomodernist texts like "The Child in the House" seems less the protest of a detail-privileging modernism against more sweeping accounts of the power of milieu than a contribution to a larger project shared with naturalist narratives. Thinking in these terms, we might credit Lukács with a canny insight in his flagging of the continuity between modernism's details and the "arbitrariness" of naturalist destinies, even if we still reject his charge that modernism and naturalism normalize social dysfunction.

Another authority helping to persuade readers of Joyce's era that the intimate physiology of experience was connected to the irresistible physics of the universe was Hermann von Helmholtz, not only one of the great practicing scientists of the nineteenth century but also a well-known expositor of science for the general public—and the referent of at least one notable Joycean allusion. At what is generally agreed to be the climactic moment of *Finnegans Wake* (1939), the break of dawn after the book's hours of night, Saint Patrick debates the Archdruid of Ireland on the nature of light and vision. Just at this crux, as Donald Theall and others have noted, Joyce encrypts Helmholtz in the word "hemhaltshealing," ambiguously applied either to the Archdruid or to Patrick. To be sure, Joyce may have meant no more, by this, than to work into his text another famous name in the history of optics. But the passage hints that Joyce had more than a glancing acquaintance with Helmholtz inasmuch as Patrick's forensic demolition of the Archdruid resembles in many ways Helmholtz's critique of Goethe's theory of color vision.[8]

Joyce could have come across this critique in Helmholtz's seminal *Treatise on Physiological Optics* of 1867, but he would more likely have encountered it in his *Popular Lectures on Scientific Subjects*, first published in English translation in 1873. Even if Joyce had never read the latter volume, however, he would likely have been familiar with many of the ideas it contains, for much of the material in the *Popular Lectures* was indeed popular by Joyce's early adulthood. Treating of major scientific findings from the middle of the nineteenth century that were widely disseminated in succeeding decades, the book indexes superbly the knowledge that would have been the general property of those aspiring to scientific literacy in Joyce's time.

One of the discoveries presented therein is the principle of conservation of force, which Helmholtz describes as the rule that "Nature as a whole possesses a store of force which cannot in any way be either increased or diminished, and . . . therefore the quantity of force in Nature is just as eternal and unalterable as the quantity of matter" (170). Worked out by several investigators proceeding independently in the 1840s, Helmholtz among them, this law was at the dawn of the twentieth century widely regarded as one of the two most influential discoveries of the nineteenth, the other being natural selection (Martin xii). As Ronald Martin has shown, further, the principle was the basis of a multiply ramifying discourse on force that spread quickly through the scientific community and—with the help, once again, of the ubiquitous Spencer—eventually obtained immense public circulation. Like Spencer, Helmholtz makes clear in the *Popular Lectures* that the human organism cannot be exempt from this rule: conservation of force must "hold good also for the body," since the body depends upon nutritive materials that, after "being passed into the blood, actually undergo a slow combustion, and finally enter into almost the same combinations with the oxygen of the atmosphere that are produced in an open fire" (384, 183). Clearly, the "physical and chemical forces of the material employed in building up the body are in continuous action without intermission and without choice, and . . . *their exact conformity to law never suffers a moment's interruption*" (384).

Nor is it only cells and tissues as such that must abide by this law. For if the body be a machine uninterruptedly subject to physical and chemical forces, then all experience, at least all experience mediated by the organs of sensation and perception, must also be governed by physics and chemistry. We have seen Spencer and Pater revolving this point, but Helmholtz holds a certain priority in this area because another of his great contributions to midcentury science lay in his work on the physiological grounding of perception. Not only did he quantify the speed of neural transmission; he also documented extensively the physiology of color perception, thus helping to cement the shift, described by Jonathan Crary in *Techniques of the Observer*, under which a tendency to conceive of vision in terms of a lucid viewer confronting an orderly reality gave way to pressing awareness of "the constitutive role of the body in the apprehension of the visible world" (Crary 16). Rehearsing the law of specific nerve energies elucidated by Johannes Müller, Helmholtz writes at one point in the *Popular Lectures*:

> [T]he organs of sense do indeed give us information about external effects produced on them, but convey those effects to our consciousness in a totally different form, so that the character of a sensuous perception depends not so much on the properties of the object perceived as on those of the organ by which we receive the information. All that the optic nerve conveys to us, it conveys under the form of a sensation of light, whether it be the rays of the sun, or a blow in the eye, or an electric current passing through it. Again, the auditory nerve translates everything into phenomena of sound, the nerves of the skin into sensations of temperature or touch. (53)

Sensation is not a registering of the world as it really is, then, but a sort of radical leap between modalities: "no kind and no degree of similarity exists between the quality of a sensation and the quality of the agent inducing it, and portrayed by it" (390). Although a perception is materially related to the object perceived, "our sensations are for us only *symbols* of the objects of the external world, and correspond to them only in some such way as written characters or articulate words to the things they denote" (54). In other words, symbolization does not happen at the point in the route of perception that we ordinarily suppose. It is not that our receptors seize from the world a representation (an outline, an image, a figure) of an object in the world; it is that once materially stimulated, our receptors initiate within us the process of constructing such a representation.

In the famous opening of the "Proteus" episode of *Ulysses*, Stephen Dedalus thinks, while standing on the shore, "Ineluctable modality of the visible: at least that if no more, thought through my eyes. Signatures of all things I am here to read, seaspawn and seawrack, the nearing tide, that rusty boot" (31). "Signatures of all things" carries a wealth of philosophical and religious allusions, most prominently to the theologian Jacob Böhme's *Signature of All Things*, but it also evokes, quite strikingly, Helmholtz's description of the relation between objects and our sensations of them, which allies a certain epistemological skepticism not with Cartesian disdain for the body but with intensified attention to the body's vicissitudes. And this attention is a critical and recurrent feature of Joyce's fictions. In another recent book, a study of physiology and literature, Gordon aptly notes that Joyce maintained "a lifelong interest in perception as an environmentally conditioned, somatically coordinated event," as when in the "Lestrygonians" episode of *Ulysses* he leaves a "record of Dublin being seen by a certain mind that is in a certain body while in a state of mild food deprivation and low blood sugar" (*Physiology* 161).[9]

Yet if Stephen's musings in "Proteus" illustrate how we can reflect on our sensations more or less as we experience them, they also remind us that the processes by which we are woven and unwoven more usually occur away from the eye of consciousness. In Joyce as in Bain, Carpenter, Tyndall, Taine, James, Prince, Pater, Wilde, and others, consideration of life as a series of molecular transformations leads readily to concern with the formative power of unregistered experience, a connection Helmholtz highlights in noting that "physiology traces in our sensations the results of mental processes which do not fall within the sphere of consciousness, and must therefore have remained inaccessible to us" (32). Or as Stephen frames it for Cranly: even an action one has consciously performed may unleash unobservable chemical activity in one's soul.

In Joyce's oeuvre, this subjection of the human organism to chemical and physical forces plays out most visibly in the area of sex and sexual desire. In his *Conversations with James Joyce*, Arthur Power reports Joyce as saying that the "modern theme," realized in *Ulysses*, "is the subterranean forces, those hidden tides which govern everything and run humanity counter to the apparent flood: those poisonous subtleties which envelop the soul, the ascending fumes of sex" (64). What matters in the modern novel, therefore, is the "inner construction, the pathological and psychological body which our behaviour and thought depend on. Comprehension is the purpose of literature, but how can we know human beings if we continue to ignore their most vital functions?" (66). Of course,

such phrasing approaches closely the diction of libidinal energies and unconscious processes developed by Freud, a figure whose relation to Joyce
has predictably generated a vast published commentary. Here, however,
we need only take note of the broad point that both writers saw desire's
embedding in the unchosen body of the organism as lending it a claim to
consideration largely rejected by the dominant discourses of the age.

This conclusion undoubtedly bears its most significant Joycean fruit in
*Ulysses*, whose genial sexual frankness so exercised the guardians of morality, but it also informs *Portrait*, where Stephen passes from the belief that
"earthly beauty" in women is "dangerous to look upon" (98) to the recognition that—as he phrases it more pointedly in *Stephen Hero*—"Philosophy, love, art will not disappear from my world because I no longer believe
that by entertaining an emotion of desire for the tenth part of a second I
prepare for myself an eternity of torture" (142). Putting this theory into
practice, the Stephen of that earlier version lobs a frank proposition at his
adored Emma and then, in response to her taking offense, asserts confidently, "It is no insult" (198). Nor, in that version of Stephen's story, does
acknowledgment of the claims of sex seem incompatible with attraction
to so-called higher things: the Lynch of *Stephen Hero* is "very much relieved to find Stephen's estheticism united with a sane and conscienceless
acceptance of the animal needs of young men" (151).

Yet while there appears to be a rapprochement between the call of art
and the call of sex in *Stephen Hero*, in *Portrait* aestheticism and the animal needs of young men seem to come to blows. In the famous closing
scene of chapter 4, Stephen beholds a girl in a rivulet of the strand and
is catapulted into an exhilaration that many critics have treated as a step
in sublimation, the beginning of a transcendence of bodily desire that
will lead to the empyrean of art. "Her image had passed into his soul for
ever and no word had broken the holy silence of his ecstasy" (145), nor
is the silence perturbed by any contact closer than the exchange of a long
look, her turning of her eyes to him "in quiet sufferance of his gaze,
without shame or wantonness" (144). That this encounter initiates a
passage beyond the exactions of sex is further suggested by Stephen's
disquisition on beauty in the following chapter, wherein he propounds
a fundamental opposition between aesthetic experience, on the one
hand, and erotic arousal, on the other:

> As for that, Stephen said . . . , we are all animals. I also am an animal.
> —You are, said Lynch.
> —But we are just now in a mental world, Stephen continued. The desire
> and loathing excited by improper esthetic means are really unesthetic emotions
> not only because they are kinetic in character but also because they are not

more than physical. Our flesh shrinks from what it dreads and responds to the stimulus of what it desires by a purely reflex action of the nervous system. Our eyelid closes before we are aware that the fly is about to enter our eye.

—Not always, said Lynch critically.

—In the same way, said Stephen, your flesh responded to the stimulus of a naked statue but it was, I say, simply a reflex action of the nerves. Beauty expressed by the artist cannot awaken in us an emotion which is kinetic or a sensation which is purely physical. It awakens, or ought to awaken, or induces, or ought to induce, an esthetic stasis, an ideal pity or an ideal terror, a stasis called forth, prolonged and at last dissolved by what I call the rhythm of beauty. (173)

Having earlier extolled sexual desire on the basis of its rootedness in the physiochemical processes of the human organism, Stephen seems now to denigrate it for virtually the same reason. There may be nothing morally problematic about sexual impulses, but in *Portrait* sex comes to seem a hindrance to art, where in *Stephen Hero* impulses to sexual and artistic freedom seem happily and productively connected.

How, then, are we to understand this turn? Has the later Stephen found some strange new attraction in the Victorian imperative of self-control, the continuous domination of the body's urges by a purer mind? Is the allusion to sexual asceticism designed to link the aesthete to the priest, thus confirming in advance Cranly's subsequent jab, "It is a curious thing . . . how your mind is supersaturated with the religion in which you say you disbelieve" (202)? Does Joyce mean to intimate a certain immaturity in Stephen's theory of art? And should we then find in *Ulysses* (with its extraordinary generosity toward so many forms of desire) a testament to Joyce's own passage beyond Stephen's narrower aestheticism? Certainly, scores of critics and scholars have argued that the answer to the last question is yes, and this verdict might imply corresponding affirmatives for the preceding three. Before trying to settle the case, however, we might do well to look a little more closely at Stephen's arguments concerning aesthetics and physiology—which will, as it happens, lead us to some important insights about beauty and environment in Joyce.

## WHY *INTEGRITAS*

In the passage just quoted, Stephen frames Lynch's reaction to a naked statue as a reflex, a response to environmental stimuli occurring apart from the organism's conscious control. In his "Trieste notebook," thought to have been a product of 1907–1909 and thus to have postdated *Stephen Hero*, Joyce had written, under the heading "*Esthetic*":

An enchantment of the heart

 Pornographic and cinematographic images act like those stimuli which produce a reflex action of the nerves through channels which are independent of esthetic perception. (in Scholes, *Workshop* 96)

The entry might be taken to mean that the difference between art and pornography (or cinema) lies in corporeality as such, but this inference is not well supported by the last chapter of *Portrait*. There, Stephen compares the "spiritual state" of "esthetic pleasure" to "that cardiac condition which the Italian physiologist Luigi Galvani . . . called the enchantment of the heart" (179), thus implying that aesthetic experience suffers no loss of dignity if conceived in bodily terms. Further, the notebook entry itself holds that reflex-inducing stimuli act through neural "channels . . . independent of esthetic perception," which hints that aesthetic perception may have channels of its own. The real difference between sexual reflex and aesthetic response seems to be that the former can awaken "a sensation which is *purely* physical" while the latter invariably requires the participation of mind. Putting this together with Stephen's insistence on stasis in the exposition he directs at Lynch, we can hazard that what aesthetic experience involves, in his theory, is a "channel" from stimulus to response that runs through the higher centers (rather than bypassing them, as in the reflex) and thereby permits a mind-governed pause between perception and action—a delay in the relentless course of animal life wherein consciousness would expand and hold sway.[10]

One theorist immediately evoked by this formulation is Schopenhauer, who, as we saw in chapter 1, treats aesthetic contemplation as something like a temporary halt in the physiological circuit, an enlarging of the interval or separation between a motive and the action it elicits. Yet though it may be Schopenhauer whom Stephen approaches most closely here, his thinking clearly falls into step with that of Pater as well. For the early Pater, once again, the essential work of modern consciousness lay in a cool yet impassioned observation of a frankly deterministic world, a world of natural laws beyond our power to change but not beyond our power to assess. And because this close watching attains a special height in aesthetic experience, the enjoyment of beauty and art assumes the aspect of a leverage of mind against the physical grounding by which it is constrained, of an eruption of freedom (or at least a feeling of freedom) in a universe governed by necessity.

That Stephen partakes of something like this view is suggested by the passage in which he first introduces the matter of aesthetic stasis. "The feelings excited by improper art," he tells Lynch (again in a Schopenhauerian vein), "are kinetic, desire or loathing. Desire urges us to possess, to go to something; loathing urges us to abandon, to go from something. These are kinetic emotions. The arts which excite them, pornographical or didactic, are therefore improper arts. The esthetic emotion (I use the general term) is therefore static. The mind is arrested and raised above desire and loathing" (172). Improper arts enmesh one in attraction to, or repulsion from, the things of this world; they impel one either to collapse the distance between oneself and the object or to remove oneself from the object altogether. Aesthetic experience, by contrast, allows one to face the object in a manner free from either compulsion, and in this sense seems to loosen the grip of those forces that Pater represented as constantly playing upon and through the human organism.[11] Indeed if Stephen departs from Pater significantly here, he does so only in hinting that the aesthetic permits a *real* transcendence of mechanistic determination rather than a mere feeling of liberation.

Stephen's disquisition may be too pedantic and abstract for some tastes, but it is worth recalling that he has acquired his insights on desire and freedom at the cost of a good deal of anguish. Back in the third chapter of *Portrait*, his younger self is deeply shaken by a series of sermons given by Father Arnall, whose evocation of the pains of hell takes up what some readers have felt to be a disproportionately long stretch of the novel. Awakened to the peril of his soul, Stephen recalls with horror and astonishment his sexual fantasies and deeds, including visits to prostitutes: "Mad! Mad! Was it possible he had done these things?" (97). Later the same evening, he wonders again, "Could it be that he, Stephen Dedalus, had done those things?" (115–16) and is prompted by a vision of his own evil to seek immediate absolution. Walking the streets in search of a confessional, he reflects:

> He was in mortal sin. Even once was a mortal sin. It could happen in an instant. But how so quickly? By seeing or by thinking of seeing. The eyes see the thing, without having wished first to see. Then *in an instant* it happens. But does that part of the body understand or what? The serpent, the most subtle beast of the field. It must understand when it desires in one instant and then prolongs its own desire instant after instant, sinfully. It feels and understands and desires. What a horrible thing! Who made it to be like that, a bestial part of the body able to understand bestially and desire bestially? Was that then he or an inhuman thing moved by a lower soul than his soul? His soul sickened at the thought of a torpid snaky life feeding itself out of the tender marrow of his life and fattening upon the slime of lust. O why was that so? O why? (117–18)

Because an "eternity of endless agony, of endless bodily and spiritual torment . . . is the terrible punishment decreed for those who die in mortal sin by an almighty and a just God" (111), one must remain continuously alert against the chance of dying in mortal sin. Yet try as he will to remain unblemished in thought, word, and deed, Stephen finds impurity creeping in: it comes in a moment, even when he believes himself most vigilant. And this confrontation with the instantaneousness by which sin enters seems to bring with it the discovery that the self is less than wholly unified. If one desires only to serve God contritely, why should bestial desires ever arise? Does the self really own its basest impulses? Or are these rightly understood as an alien presence, a "torpid snaky life" parasitic upon one's own?

Confronted by such questions, one may feel (as Stephen seems to at this crisis) that the core of one's selfhood has contracted to a vulnerable center ever on guard against this alien desire—a center whose main business, in fact, consists of watching and observing. But it is just here that we find ourselves back at the early Pater, with his claim that the task (and delight) of modern consciousness is to regard the laws of life at work and his intimation that such regarding is the activity that constitutes the truest self. Indeed, in his stress on freedom from desire and loathing in aesthetic experience, Stephen seems to be responding both to his own prior religious obsession and to something like Pater's negotiation with the mechanistic universe revealed by modern thought: "The truth of these relations experience gives us . . . and bids us by a constant clearing of the organs of observation and perfecting of analysis to make what we can of these. To the intellect, the critical spirit, these subtleties of effect are more precious than anything else." The ascetic dimension in Stephen's theory may have its element of residual Christian prudery, but it is grounded in a philosophy (and a knowledge gained through life experience) to which pagans of a Paterian cast would surely be sympathetic. The problem with sexual desire is not that the Catholic Church (institutional or internalized) dislikes it, but that *as* desire it seems to tether one more tightly to circumstances and impinging influences, to lead one to act in ways that might seem, to the more coolly observing self, as curious as any other operation of natural laws.

Not coincidentally, this is one of the preeminent lessons of naturalism. For in the most famous naturalist fictions, desire does not constitute some resistance to environment but environment's very toehold in the soul, the medium by which external forces most insidiously bend the self to their demands. In the world of naturalism—where relentless torrents of stimuli engender ungovernable responses, where vivid deprivations give rise to violent wants, where sordid milieux breed brutality as reliably as gravity brings bodies to the ground—to have desires is not to be confirmed in possession of autonomy, but something like the reverse. As Lee Clark Mitchell observes in his study of determinism in American naturalist fiction, "Naturalist characters . . . will always accede to their strongest desire whatever [else] it is they resolve to do" (9). Or as the anthropologist Charles Letourneau puts it, in a passage Zola transcribed into some early notes toward his monumental series of novels, "Man, constantly solicited by numerous and simultaneous desires, obeys the strongest while being conscious of the others, and *that is why he feels as if he were free*" (quoted in Hecht 96; emphasis Zola's). In this light, Stephen's effort to unloose himself from the trammels of desire reads as yet another aspect of his struggle against his environment and against the naturalist plot. And it makes sense that the weapon he wields against both the importunings of Dublin and the hold of appetitive longing is a schema in which aesthetic experience figures as a pause in the circuit of stimulus and response—a pause of high consciousness, keen observation, and complex contemplation that naturalist characters are usually denied.

For Mitchell, a proneness to accede to their desires is what most particularly sets American naturalism's characters apart from the personae of American high realism. "Realist crises," he writes, "occur typically in scenes of deliberation, which means that individuals are defined through an elaborate process of responsible choice" (xii). Further, the "recurrent solution devised by the realists as the best means of depicting agency was not to show characters freely acting but to show them freely *not* acting" (8), as when in Wharton's *House of Mirth* Lily Bart chooses not to engage in the minor blackmail that would grant her the security she has sought all through the novel (12). Under realism, in other words, the mark of a free being is the capacity to refrain. Mitchell's argument may not be unassailable on all points, but the idea that agency would be associated with a resistance to acting on one's desires clearly speaks to the case of Stephen Dedalus—and to that of many figures in modernist fiction who seem to value observing over doing. It seems, then, that both nineteenth-century realism and modernism, in contradistinction to naturalism, present characters who prove their freedom by not succumbing to desire. But where realism pivots on a mastering of desire through renunciation, modernism would be associated with the maintenance of a particular kind of distance from desire, the distance of observation and of irony.

Yet these conclusions only provoke more questions. For if Joyce shows himself as attuned as any naturalist to environment's profound connection with desire, why does he not, with Zola, look toward a transformation of social environment in which good impulses would be promoted by the right kinds of stimuli? And if his proposal for evading appetitive desire's trap has aesthetic feeling at its liberatory heart, why does he not, like Wilde, propose some wise provision of beautiful surroundings, out of which might emerge beautiful souls?[12]

One answer is implicit in the very phrasing of the latter question. As we can see if we ponder Wilde's disconcertingly sanguine expectation that Individualism will thrive where conditions are properly arranged, the idea of manipulating environments to produce beautiful personalities implies, in its way, a choice of beauty over freedom—a staking of hopes on a future in which people might be said to conform to their (admirably managed) circumstances rather than resisting them. It is very hard to imagine Joyce embracing such a commitment, because, in the vision he elaborates, beauty, happiness, and harmony seem none of them quite as important as freedom. In the end, after all, it is less that Stephen needs to disentangle himself from his circumstances in order to find beauty than that beauty provides him an excellent way of getting free of circumstances. Joyce would surely, therefore, have found Wilde's engineered Individualism fatally contradictory—not a paradox upon which thoughtful work might begin but an oxymoron dooming from the outset any programs it would be alleged to underwrite. This may be part of the reason why, in spite of his clear interest in utopia as an intellectual topic, he so confidently asserted the importance of his art against more direct efforts at social improvement.

Another answer, however, has to do with what beauty itself means for Joyce—with its structural place in *Portrait* and in his thinking generally. To get a handle on how this works, we will need to revisit a topic that has come up in previous chapters of this book but has not loomed large in this one so far: the significance of the moment in human development. Let us return, then, to Stephen in his penitent phrase, when any sinful thought, let alone deed, might result in eternal damnation.

At the judgment of God, Stephen believes, "[e]very sin would . . . come forth from its lurkingplace, . . . the tiniest imperfection and the most heinous atrocity. . . . One single instant was enough for the trial of a man's soul. One single instant after the body's death" (95). As Father Arnall has reminded him, Lucifer had but to think, "*non serviam: I will not serve*" to be condemned for all eternity, and "[t]hat instant was his ruin. He offended the majesty of God by the sinful thought of one instant and God cast him out of heaven into hell for ever" (99). Just as an "instant of rebellious pride of the intellect . . . made Lucifer and a third part of the cohorts of angels fall from their glory," so a single sin, "an instant of folly and weakness, drove Adam and Eve out of Eden and brought death and suffering into the world" (112–13). Indeed "[e]very word of sin is a wound in" Christ's "tender side. Every sinful act is a thorn piercing His head. Every impure thought, deliberately yielded to, is a keen lance transfixing that sacred and loving heart" (112–13). Every moment counts, in other words, in the most literal and appalling way. It is as though Stephen has, with Father Arnall's help, transposed into religious terms the parental and pedagogical anxieties we explored earlier, under which even the briefest passage in the life of the young seems fraught with developmental dangers. And indeed it may be hard to think of anything else in English-language writing that captures so chillingly the anxiety that any instant might be fatal.

In spite of all, Stephen holds to a faith that "he would still be spared; he would repent in his heart and be forgiven; and then those above, those in heaven, would see what he would do to make up for the past: a whole life, every hour of life" (106).[13] Having made his confession, he embarks on a rigorous routine, laying out his "daily life" in "devotional areas," praying relentlessly for remission of the pain of souls in purgatory, driving "his soul daily through an increasing circle of works of supererogation" (124). He even practices a "constant mortification" under which each of his senses is brought "under a rigorous discipline": mortifying sight, for example, he walks with "downcast eyes" and shuns "every encounter with the eyes of women"; mortifying touch, he maintains "the most uncomfortable positions" and "suffer[s] patiently every itch and pain" (126–27). Yet still it proves impossible to control his feelings at every moment: he often discovers himself guilty of "some momentary inattention at prayer, a movement of trivial anger in his soul or a subtle willfulness in speech or act," and senses that a "restless feeling of guilt would always be present with him" (129).

Horrible as this obsession is, we have seen that it does bequeath Stephen one useful discovery: long after his devout phase is over, he seems to retain the insights that appetitive desire is in some way alien to the self and that the self might try to manifest its freedom by undoing desire's hold. Being wary of repeating the deadly repressions enjoined by his Christian guides, however, Stephen would hardly want to embrace another full-throttle asceticism in his own design for living. He would want, surely, to make generous allowance for the play of urges belonging to the body—would want, as the prevailing bonhomie of *Ulysses* seems to confirm, to imagine a liberation from desire not altogether unmoved by desire's claims.

But how to do so? One way might be to look for a far less continuous expression of freedom, a transcendence not sustained by mortification but enjoyed at privileged intervals. And this is exactly what we find in his aesthetic theory. For in chapter 5, Stephen is careful to mark the experience of beauty as a temporary transcendence, a matter of moments rather than long durations.[14] Elaborating on what he names the third and culminating stage of aesthetic apprehension, *claritas*, he tells Lynch that "this supreme quality" is

> felt by the artist when the esthetic image is first conceived in his imagination. The mind in that mysterious instant Shelley likened beautifully to a fading coal. The instant wherein that supreme quality of beauty, the clear radiance of the esthetic image, is apprehended luminously by the mind which has been arrested by its wholeness and fascinated by its harmony is the luminous silent

> stasis of esthetic pleasure, a spiritual state very like to that cardiac condition
> which the Italian physiologist Luigi Galvani, using a phrase almost as beauti-
> ful as Shelley's, called the enchantment of the heart. (179)

Again, significant aesthetic experience is for Stephen an arrest, a pause in
the circuit of stimulus and response. The same is true for Pater; but where
Pater's professed ideal is a life of continuous intensity, Stephen's aesthetic
moment cannot be sustained for long. Its nature and its promise depend
too heavily on a resistance to the usual course of things—a fleeting sepa-
rateness from the ordinary routines, physiological and otherwise, of the
world. In another of the many symmetries or inversions that make *Portrait*
so intricate, then, Joyce offers as Stephen's answer to the instant of sin the
moment of ravishment by beauty, wherein salvation comes not in flight
from the sensuous but in a poised relation between the sensuous object
and the intensely conscious self.[15]

But Stephen's interest in a bounded or contained beauty is not limited
to the temporal dimension. In chapter 1, we saw how, when environment's
influence is at issue, considerations of time have a way of running in parallel with, even morphing into, considerations of space. And so we may not
be surprised to find Stephen referring also to the importance of spatial
distinctness in aesthetic apprehension. Pointing to a "basket which a
butcher's boy had slung inverted on his head," he tells Lynch: "In order
to see that basket . . . your mind first of all separates the basket from the
rest of the visible universe which is not the basket. The first phase of apprehension is a bounding line drawn about the object to be apprehended. . . .
You apprehend it as *one* thing. . . . That is *integritas*" (178). The subsequent phases then prove to be *consonantia*, in which "[h]aving first felt
that it is *one* thing you feel now that it is a *thing*," and the aforementioned
*claritas*, in which you "see that it is that thing which it is and no other
thing. The radiance of which [Thomas Aquinas] speaks is the scholastic
*quidditas*, the *whatness* of a thing" (178–79).[16]

For some readers, the significance of these remarks lies less in their particular content than in their mere existence: the young aesthete has to
have some highfalutin principles to spout, and these exhale enough of "the
true scholastic stink," as Lynch phrases it shortly after, to fill the bill (180).
Even readers who take Stephen's theory seriously may be tempted to pass
over its details, inferring that what really counts here is our arrival at the
radiance of whatness, a striking formulation that speaks to long-running
philosophical debates about the relation between aesthetic objects and
beholding subjects. Yet we are now in a position to see that the first of
Stephen's stages of apprehension—that in which "a bounding line" is
"drawn about the object to be apprehended"—has its place within a complex configuration of ideas about beauty's relation to desire and freedom.

In this scheme, aesthetic experience obtains its full value from its character as a focused and intense interruption, from its capacity to break the continuity of circumstances temporally (by occurring in a moment of heightened consciousness), spatially (by requiring a particularity to disengage itself from a background), and as we might say organismally (by marking a pause or impediment in the animal circuits of existence). Drawing on Pater but discarding Pater's fantasy of a life of ongoing intensity, Joyce positions beauty as a necessarily acute eruption of freedom into a world of determinations, as something that undoes the hold of environment by compromising environment's quality of totality.

With this recognition, we arrive at the other reason why Joyce would have had trouble endorsing Wilde's brief for the cultivation of beautiful souls through beautiful environments. If aesthetic experience draws its meaning from a certain disengaging of the object from its surroundings, as Stephen proposes, then a beautiful environment would seem to be a kind of contradiction in terms. Although eminently alert to children's responsiveness to the sensuous, Joyce does not indicate that immersing them in things commonly thought lovely and removing them from the unlovely would be the way to improve their souls. A butcher's basket will do perfectly well for aesthetic experience, indeed perhaps better than conventionally beautiful objects, because what matters is contrast and intensity. In so suggesting, Joyce does in a way elevate the common items of existence ("trivial things" in another sense), but he also widens the gap between artist and artisan that Morris and Wilde wanted to diminish. The decorator or craftsman, after all, tries to make the world more beautiful by putting intrinsically beautiful articles into it, but it is not clear that from a Joycean perspective this addition would conduce to meaningful aesthetic experience, since amid all lovely things the oppositional quality of beauty could well go missing. For Joyce, it seems, the artist's distinctive work is to make whatever entities might lie about us into temporary objects of aesthetic apprehension, thus allowing that oppositional quality its full play.

We might say, then, that what Joyce wishes very precisely to reject is the "ideological" work performed by the aesthetic in the philosophy examined by Eagleton and in Wilde's more utopian claims for the power of art. The harmonizing of soul with society projected in such programs clearly sorts ill with Joyce's sense of an agon between environment's trammels and beauty's transcendence, just as it sorts ill with the antithetical, disruptive strain predominant in some of Wilde's other statements and in much of the rhetoric of twentieth-century avant-gardes. At the same time, however, we need to keep in mind that beauty in Joyce is not oppositional in any straightforwardly political sense. As an exhilarating stasis, a matter of suspension rather than motion and of observation rather than action, it presents an alternative (and might even be said to harbor an aversion) to more vigorous ways of kicking against the pricks of circumstance. Like many other phenomena of modernism, Joyce's adaptation of aestheticism reminds us that there is no reliable linkage between an antithetical disposition and practical insurrection or, on the other side, between satisfaction and concord with a world untransformed.

Joyce's adaptation also reminds us, however, that there was a way of thinking about the aesthetic that associated it neither with rebellion as such nor with utter apathy to society's flaws. It reminds us that for some inhabitants of the late nineteenth and early twentieth centuries, the meaning of art was associated with the possibility that beauty might shape beneficially the souls of those exposed to it, might usher in a better society by perfecting the persons who would in the most literal sense make it up. Amid such hopes and speculations, Joyce occupies an especially intriguing position. Steeped in the aspirations of Pater and Wilde and Ruskin and Symons, he alludes repeatedly to beauty's solicitation in *Portrait* and elsewhere. But in his scheme this call is so acute a thing, so much a matter of circumscribed freedom emerging against a background not aesthetic until transformed by a certain kind of attention, that there seems small chance of deploying it systematically to engender a better world. From this perspective, what can be undertaken is rather what his version of the modern artist undertakes: the fashioning of antithetical things that draw out the radiance of ordinary ones, and in so doing perhaps make the flashes of aesthetic experience a little more frequent, a little more liberating still.

## CHAPTER FOUR

# Tropisms of Longing

## COMPULSIONS OF THE BODY

For the late nineteenth century, as the preceding pages should have suggested, social and economic determinism was strongly connected to biological and mechanistic determinism. Today, the disciplinary divide between the social and the natural sciences may reinforce the intuition that socioeconomic conditions belong to a different area of inquiry from molecular transactions of the human organism, even where we remain aware that countless practical crossings of this divide occur every day in research, policy-making, and other institutional practices. For writers like Émile Zola and the criminologists quoted in chapter 1, however, the idea that a person's destiny would be shaped by wealth or poverty, by education or its lack, was scarcely separable from the belief that development must be understood as a series of physiochemical interactions, proceeding according to immitigable scientific laws, between the body and the stimuli that impinge on it. Indeed as we have seen, Zola promoted the new fiction of naturalism as a further step in the sciences of the human, declaring that it would build on physiology's insights to show how the human machinery is worked upon by heredity and environment, and how individuals both transform and are transformed by their social conditions.

Among United States writers, none explored the connections between social and biological forces more intrepidly than Theodore Dreiser, whose protagonists are typically driven both by yearning for the goods dangled by capitalism and by eminently physiological attractions of sex and personality. As we noted at the beginning of chapter 3, Dreiser's course in this regard was not inspired by some desire to follow Zola; rather, it emerged from a convergence of living, working, and reading that make him a fascinating epitome of trends in the turn-of-the-century United States. His fictions were partly the fruit of growing up in the Midwest, poor and full of heartache over the things that lack of money and position seemed to preclude; they were also an outgrowth of the spectacle, to which he was led by his work as a reporter, of even more dire poverty in the midst of the Gilded Age affluence of the American city. And they owed a great deal to his acquaintance, readerly and personal, with scientists who insisted that life is neither an intangible entity (as held by metaphysicians) nor a force distinct from all others (as held by vitalists), but a material phenomenon governed wholly by physiochemical mechanisms.

Nearly every critic writing on Dreiser has attended to the sociological side of his vision, and his acquaintance with mechanistic doctrine has also been documented extensively. (Among scholarly treatments of the latter, Ellen Moers's extraordinary 1969 study, *Two Dreisers*, and Louis Zanine's richly thorough book of 1993, *Mechanism and Mysticism*, are indispensable, and both will be cited frequently here.) Dreiser's preoccupation with beauty in life, art, and women has also been widely discussed. Yet little attention has been accorded the interplay of beauty and environment in his imagination, apart from the recognition that contact with beauty tends to inflame those of his characters with whom he strongly identifies. In this chapter, we will see that like Joyce, Dreiser found in the aesthetic a potent disruption of life's physiological and social courses and at times positioned the liberatory promise of beauty against the naturalist plot of environmental determination. But we will also see that because he recognized the longing for beauty itself as a species of desire rooted in biology, he could not maintain faith in the capacity of aesthetic experience to transcend desire's hold.

A good place to begin this exploration is with a series of articles Dreiser wrote for *Ev'ry Month*, a low-priced magazine containing piano music and other features directed to a predominantly female audience. From 1895 to 1897, when he was in his mid-twenties, Dreiser served as this monthly's editor, and in the early days of his tenure especially he was required to write much of its feature copy under various pseudonyms, most prominently "The Prophet." Nothing in Dreiser's early writing matches Pater, Wilde, or Joyce for close attention to the place of the aesthetic in the life of the young, but some of The Prophet's "Reflections" (as the column was called) do take up the environment of schools in a way that bespeaks acquaintance with the upswell of interest in school decoration in 1890s America as well as real concern about larger questions pertaining to beauty, education, and the care of juvenile destinies.

The August 1896 number of *Ev'ry Month*, for example, finds The Prophet insisting on the unmatched importance of provision for young people: while we should "extend a charitably regulating hand" to adults done ill by "early miseries and deprivations," he declares, it is yet more vital that we "go down into the childhood of to-day and do what we can. Neglect the infants much longer we dare not, else we imperil the ultimate life of the race itself" (144). Dreiser's use of "the race itself"—construable, as so often, in terms of either humankind in general or some subset thereof—may call up for us the eugenically inflected anxieties of writers like Ellen Key, but more characteristic of The Prophet is the larger claim (also stressed in Mary Jeune's "Children of a Great City" and countless other period declarations) that the only path to a better world lies through preferential direction of resources to children. Precisely because their individual characters are still malleable, precisely because their destinies are not yet fixed, the young bear the promise of the future.

In the "Reflections" of the following March, The Prophet restricts the scope of legitimate public provision yet more narrowly. Assuming a vigorously Social-Darwinist stance (which in this piece, as in others from every phase of Dreiser's career, combines in unpredictable ways with strong sympathy for the plight of the underprivileged),[1] he now insists that the State owes the unfortunate nothing save the placing of "the means of education within their grasp" (257). But this assistance it owes absolutely, and inferior education is in no way to be countenanced. In his May column, he continues his diatribe:

> The children of Americans are to-day being taught under conditions that are absolutely outrageous when compared with the manner in which other public institutions are looked after. The rooms are largely barren of ornament; their general equipments are short even of the necessary in many cases. There is not room enough for near all the children in the larger cities, and the architecture is not only sullen, gloomy, and forbidding but as a rule it is vile. The children are not enticed and impressed with the conditions which prevail here. They are not inflamed by anything about them with a desire to accumulate knowledge. Their taste for the beautiful is not enhanced by anything in the rooms. Their minds are not imbued with a fine feeling by the architecture, or, if so, the people who talk of these things when a monument is unveiled don't worry over it. Anything is good enough for the children. . . .
>
> . . . Let the schools be vast in structure, ornate and impressive in their architecture, beautiful and useful in every detail. To the dogs with State capitols and monuments. Away with museums. Schools—they are the first! After them, all things! One year of correct training given to a child by kindly teachers amid surroundings of impressive strength and beauty will do more for its future life than a whole prairie full of libraries and monuments will do afterward. The great need is the one year—the first impression. (275–76)

At least two theories with which we are by now quite familiar surface in this admonition. One is that good interiors help make better souls, the other that when it comes to juvenile development, time is incalculably precious. Enticing conditions ignite the desire to learn; good furnishings cultivate a taste for beauty; worthy architecture imbues the mind with fine feeling; and one year of education in the right circumstances is worth a lifetime of remedial public works. In the last sentence, moreover, the imagined year of correct training undergoes a remarkable contraction to a single improving "first impression"—which implies that a poor or inadequate first impression, whatever that might mean, could be correspondingly damaging.[2]

The Prophet returns to the physical environment of education yet again in the next number of *Ev'ry Month*, June 1897. "The school," he writes, "should be architecturally worthy of its purpose. If beautiful architecture is elevating and valuable then the school should in its architectural appearance be ennobling. . . . Its simple beauty and usefulness would be a valuable lesson in life—a lesson that would linger and grow, and drive out from the heart the joy in the trivial and showy, in which use is not involved. . . . The walls should be decorated in fair and inviting colors" (286). Here the Prophet not only picks up on themes dear to advocates for beauty but also shows how modern architectural canons could lie incipient in nineteenth-century views of moral effect. The school's physical excellence administers a lesson that lingers and grows, which is to say, yet again, that surroundings have the power to shape the individual nondiscursively and irremediably. And while the kinds of buildings recommended by The Prophet would hardly exhibit the pared-down functionalism of high modernism, they would—in a sort of a first step toward that aesthetic in which all ornament is gratuitous ornament—avoid the merely showy in favor of the useful, the better to imbue their inhabitants with a care for thrift and authenticity.[3]

Dreiser was certainly not alone in pleading for attention to the aesthetic quality of schools. Ruskinians British and American had been doing so since the middle of the century, and many commentators on educational conditions invoked the susceptibility of children to impressions. In the nearly contemporary *School Sanitation and Decoration: A Practical Study of Health and Beauty in Their Relation to the Public Schools* (1899), for example, Severance Burrage and Henry Turner Bailey observe that while the "modern schoolroom is a workshop" and "a study," it is also "a living room for children extremely sensitive to impression [*sic*]" and "therefore . . . should be as beautiful as a favored home" (83). In a model schoolroom, they note, "[t]here is no crowding, no confusion, no clutter anywhere; the blackboards are utilized with some thought of orderly spacing, the vases of flowers are tastefully arranged, and the effect of the room as a whole is clean, temperate, restful, wholesome. One cannot imagine haphazard, slovenly results from children accustomed to such an atmosphere of order and peace and beauty" (95). In *The School Beautiful*, issued by the State Superintendent of Public Instruction for Wisconsin in 1907, Maud Barnett would recommend that schoolroom walls be colored "[n]ot only for beauty" but also "for the undeniable effect of colors upon the child," since it is "a fact now generally accepted by neurologists and physicians . . . that colors have a considerable influence upon the mental and physical condition of children. In recent years many cases of severe nervous headache and nervous irritation have been traced to the bare or poorly colored walls of schoolrooms" (28).[4]

The aesthetic quality of schools being a prominent topic of discussion in the fin de siècle United States, Dreiser would scarcely have had to consult the primary texts of high aestheticism to make the claims he does in *Ev'ry Month*. Yet as it happens, the name of Walter Pater and a number of phrases from the conclusion to *Studies in the History of the Renaissance* appear in the previous section of the June 1897 column:

> The question of whether experiences, good, bad and indifferent, make the individual who possesses them better or worse is something which stimulates the mind to speculation at times, and one finds that the question is by no means trivial. Walter Pater, the late critic, believed that the object of the youth should be to make his life dramatic—to fill it with sensation. . . . To-morrow may contain nothing, the next day nothing, for all time nothing, and therefore a moment now is everything. Let your moments be as exquisite as possible, then—not the fruit of experience, but experience is the end. . . . To burn always with this desire, to maintain the rarest ecstasy that has ever been attained—that is the chief consideration. (284)[5]

The Prophet goes on to pose against Pater an imagined "religionist" who insists that because much of what one absorbs is dangerous, "experience is the object, but only selected experience"—that "[o]ne should strive to fill the moments with experiences that are elevating in a purposeful direction." And then The Prophet sets against both Pater and the religionist a third commentator, a "spectator of affairs in general," who says that "the finer things do not teach everything," and that the "creature who is going to live rightly" must "go forward, fearing no evil and tasting everything that is" (284–85).

With which of these three, if any, does The Prophet cast his lot? His conclusion offers no clear answer:

> Here, then, is a curious formula for living. . . . You are to hear all that is to be heard, see all that is to be seen, feel all that may be felt, and keep yourself brightly alive with occurrences. There is nothing to be said about moral or immoral, right or wrong, but all is to be trusted to your right tendency. This is like making of a human being a threshing machine, into which wheat and tares are indiscriminately fed. If it has a right apparatus only the grain will be preserved and the chaff cast out. So it may be said of the human beginner that if he has a right heart only the good will be preserved, and that out of the mixed evil of experience he will obtain all that makes for his highest development. (285)

"So it may be said," but does The Prophet mean to accept or contravene such saying? The simile of the threshing machine, coupled with the adjective "curious" in the first sentence, suggests a doubt that people retain the effects of good experience only, and hence a skepticism about encouragements to embrace every adventure. If this is so, then the imaginary speaker The Prophet should find most sympathetic must be the religionist, alert to how much damage bad experience can do.

Such an outcome cannot but look a little strange given Dreiser's bitter resentment of Roman Catholic primary education, which, he never ceased to insist, taught him nothing except the precepts of a religion in which he could not believe. Yet it does square with his take on educational environments in the section of the column quoted earlier, which resists vehemently the suggestion that children might be served well enough by surroundings of just any aesthetic caliber. There is thus a certain aptness to The Prophet's distancing of himself from Pater, who after all believed that the child who lacks "better ministries to its desire of beauty" will manage to find salutary loveliness in humble things. Dreiser, we might say, inclines more to the position of Wilde's lectures, with their call for deliberate and complete aesthetic provision. Indeed the section on school environments closes in tones evocative of Wilde on his lecture tour as well as Mary Jeune and Ellen Key: "If the representatives of the people would only see how impressionable a child is—how the good, the true, the beautiful are received so gladly by the tender young heart; how its every faculty responds to all that tends upward and onward, they would not be slow to give all needful to make the child a good man. . . . It is the child, the child, that is important! It is the beautiful school working upon the impressionable heart of the child that will lift us out of our troubles" (286). One could hardly ask for a more concise rendering of the high hopes reposed on aesthetic environments for the young.

The wide dissemination of such hopes in the late nineteenth century meant that one would not have had to know much about scientific views of environment, any more than one would have to have read Pater, to pen such a peroration. Yet Dreiser was well informed in this area also, above all via the writings of Spencer, whose ideas about evolution, milieu, and the social organism also had their significance for the young Wilde and the young Joyce. Nor was Dreiser alone among Americans in being touched by Spencer's work; as Ronald Martin shows, Spencer's astounding American audience exceeded even his vast European one. In North America, his books sold half a million copies ("an unprecedented sale for a philosopher" [60]), and the idea "that reality was in essence a system of forces," which Spencer more than any other writer helped to disseminate, penetrated "to levels of the American population never before reached by any formal philosophy save Christianity" (60). According to Martin, Spencer's vision of a universe of force manifested itself "not only in the usual media of scientific and philosophical discussion, but in newspapers and novels, in letters and diaries, in speeches, sermons, and boardroom exhortations" (xi).

Given Dreiser's unquenchable curiosity about the meaning and nature of life, it would have been strange if he had not come under Spencer's spell eventually. As it was, he deferred doing so longer than might have been expected. When he departed for Indiana University in 1889, the generous teacher who volunteered to fund his college education, Mildred Fleming, told him, "Read Spencer," and in subsequent years—one at the university, followed by several at Midwestern newspapers—he would be directed by friends and acquaintances to such staples of the secularizing canon as Spencer, Schopenhauer, Voltaire, Huxley, Darwin, and Taine. His conversion, however, seems not to have come until the summer of 1894, when he consumed Huxley, Tyndall, Darwin, Alfred Russel Wallace, and finally Spencer in hours free from his job as a reporter for the *Pittsburgh Dispatch* (Zanine 7, 10–17). Later on, he would recall his encounter with *First Principles*—the 1862 volume, once again, in which Spencer lays the foundation for his multivolume works on psychology, biology, sociology, and ethics—as follows:

> *First Principles* . . . quite blew me to bits intellectually. . . . [T]aking up *First Principles* I discovered that all that I had deemed substantial . . . was questioned and dissolved into other and less understandable things. I was completely thrown down in my conceptions or non-conceptions of life and made very gloomy.
>
> . . . I was still staggered now to find myself . . . an unaccountable wisp of energy or mist or nothing, moving via inexplicable laws and for inexplicable reasons, or none, from nowhere to nowhere. Indeed I was really months in getting over it (I never did wholly)—getting to a place where I could believe in the importance of anything. (*Newspaper Days* 610–11)

"I never did wholly": to the end of his life, in fact, Dreiser sought to understand how the individual life could have meaning in a universe governed by laws whose nature might be disclosed but whose ultimate rationale could never be known. Yet if Spencer's grand scheme could be disheartening, it could also be inspiring, for it seemed to reveal in the universe a magnificent symmetry, an irresistible pattern, an analogy reiterated at every level of existence. From the trajectories of molecules to the behavior of organisms to the currents of the social body to the movements of the solar system and beyond, according to Spencer, the same simple principle governed: force is conserved, but organization evolves. And what does it mean to evolve? "Evolution," Spencer explains, "is an integration of matter and concomitant dissipation of motion; during which the matter passes from an indefinite, incoherent homogeneity to a definite, coherent heterogeneity; and during which the retained motion undergoes a parallel transformation" (*First* 407). (This most fundamental of Spencerian doxa can be illustrated by the history of organic systems, which seem to progress from building-block molecules much like each other but not coherently arranged up through cells and tissues to the highly systematic heterogeneity of the organs of the human body.)

As Martin observes, Dreiser was at once alienated by and strangely at home in such a cosmology: "The universe of force was, in his literary vision of self and desire, a metaphor for that which limited individuality, coerced, determined, and ultimately defeated individual men (and indeed all individual earthly things), yet at the same time produced the richness and color of the earthly welter. The universe of force was deeply actual for him, and he felt toward it, as he felt toward life, a complex mixture of enthusiasm, anguish, and awe" (255). Already by 1896, Dreiser as The Prophet was urging consumers of *Ev'ry Month* to read Cuvier, Huxley, Tyndall, and especially Spencer, as when in the September number he extols having "the whole universe passed in review before you, as Spencer marshals it, showing you how certain beautiful laws exist, and how, by these laws, all animate and inanimate things have developed and arranged themselves; how life has gradually become more and more complicated, more and more beautiful" (167–68). A few months later, he gushes unashamedly, "Our minds belong to the universe which Spencer has united; our thoughts upon its meaning are subject to the laws which he has laid down. . . . All life has been comprehended best by him" (241).

Spencer discloses the nature of this ever more complicated and beautiful life early in *First Principles*, defining it, as he had in *Principles of Psychology*, as "the continuous adjustment of internal relations to external relations," and adding that "the physical and the psychical life are equally comprehended by the definition" (*First* 86). As we saw in the previous chapter, Spencer joined Helmholtz in seeing this continuity of material and mental as premised on the impossibility of any system's evading the principle of conservation of force ("All impressions from moment to moment made on our organs of sense, stand in direct correlation with physical forces existing externally") and held that psychic development consists in chemical modification of the nervous system. In a passage that looks backward to associationism but also forward to texts like (the anti-Spencerian) William James's *Principles of Psychology* and Pavlov's *Conditioned Reflexes*, Spencer writes,

> When two phenomena that have been experienced in a given order, are repeated in the same order, those nerves which before were affected by the transition are again affected; and such molecular modification as they received from the first motion propagated through them, is increased by this second motion along the same route. Each such motion works a structural alteration, which . . . involves a diminution of the resistance to all such motions that afterwards occur. The segregation of these successive motions . . .

thus becomes the cause of, and the measure of, the mental connexion between the impressions which the phenomena produce. ( *First* 488)

As in associationism, perception is a matter of transmission of motion along the nerves; as in James, the physiology of habit building is paradigmatic of all mental development; as in Pavlov, the repeated experience of two events in sequence is critical to the formation of the organism's powers. And as in all three, the organism's development is affected by every one of its experiences, even those scarcely descried in their occurring.

It is hard to imagine Dreiser failing to be arrested by the parts of Spencer's immense panorama that concerned the material basis of the growth of mind. We have seen that he was interested in problems of education early on, and even a year before his pivotal discovery of Spencer he was arguing for the significance of bodily health in the assessment of criminal responsibility. In a newspaper article of 1893, he reported on the case of a man named John Finn, who had tried to kill his two sons and two daughters; noting that "[a]t the time of the tragedy" Finn "had been ill with a kind of bilious fever" inducing spectacular delusions, Dreiser concluded, "Finn is not a murderer. Long illness had weakened him and temporarily affected his brain. A sudden fever seized him and a ruthless vision prompted him with a glamour that made it seem charity to take the lives of his children" (*Journalism* 1: 175–76).[6]

By the turn of the century, Dreiser was clearly fascinated by environments' capacity to induce "molecular modification" of the nerves. In early 1900, as both Moers and Zanine recount, he paid a call on a researcher named Elmer Gates, who, though lacking any formal training in experimental psychology, had used his own money to build a laboratory devoted to the discipline in Chevy Chase, Maryland. Shortly after, Dreiser seems to have read a manuscript that Gates would publish in 1903 as a slim volume, *The Relations and Development of the Mind and Brain* (Moers 165, 167; Zanine 57, 59), among whose revelations is that animals to whom Gates gave "extraordinary and excessive training in one mental faculty—e.g., seeing or hearing," showed on autopsy "a far greater number of brain-cells than any animal of like breed ever possessed" (9). Another was that dogs Gates had rigorously trained in color separation "were able to discriminate between seven shades of red and six or eight of green, besides manifesting in other ways more mental ability than any untrained dog" (9–10). Yet a third was that a child trained in subtle temperature discrimination for its first six weeks of life had twenty-four times the average number of brain cells "in the temperature areas of the brain" (10).

Passing over the gruesome question of how Gates might have measured such a child's brain cells, we can gauge the truthfulness of his report from the facts that dogs have only limited color vision, particularly when it comes to distinguishing green from red, and that neurogenesis in the postnatal brains of animals has been demonstrated only recently, by means of sophisticated techniques unavailable in Gates's day. Still more remarkable than the fervency with which Gates unfolded his fictitious results, however, was the immensity of his claim for his work's significance. In *Relations*, he declares that such discoveries as he cites "open a new epoch in the methods of progress and civilization," since it is "the mind which creates sciences, arts, and institutions. . . . Give to people more mind, and all undertaking will be ameliorated, and better results accomplished. Give them more moral mind, and the evils of society will gradually disappear" (14).

What most attracted Dreiser to Gates's claims, undoubtedly, was their evident demonstration of how positive good could emerge from the mechanistic understanding of life that had earlier blown him to bits intellectually. But it surely did not hurt that Gates, like the *Ev'ry Month* Prophet, believed education, and especially early education, to hold the key to social improvement. In his book, Gates claims that someone desiring to make a major scientific discovery can have his "brain rebuilt with reference to that science," taught "whatever knowledge the human race has acquired concerning that subject" and "trained for several hours a day for several years to apply each of his mental faculties to this data." Even six months of such practice "generally quadruples the mental capacity and more than quadruples the number of ideas gained each day" (21–23), but results will be even more impressive when this kind of training is "commenced with infants" (20); indeed for maximum effect, brain building "should properly begin a few weeks after birth" (10). Further, the improvements that can be effected in this way include moral reform as well as cognitive augmentation. By "the force of brain-building," any evil "motive can be eliminated," as is demonstrated by experiments in which Gates "succeeded in entirely eliminating vicious propensities from children with dispositions toward cruelty, stealing or anger" (11–12).

Gates's ideas might have been of interest to parents and others concerned with juvenile destinies—and were, as it turns out, heard by some of those persons on at least one august occasion. For in 1897, it appears, Gates spoke before the First National Congress of Mothers on "The Art of Rearing Children." The title would suggest that the talk's topic was the proper training of the juvenile organism, and certainly Gates does not fail to work in references to experiments in which he enlarged color discrimination in dogs and gave guinea pigs more mind. But his main point is not that children should be subjected to like regimens; it is rather that experiments on successive generations of animals support the Lamarckian "doctrine that we can transmit acquired characteristics" (243), as long as the characteristics in question are mental ones produced by brain building. Parents, he avers, should consider developing their brain structures before reproducing—and even more important is that maternal emotions be carefully tended when the child is in the womb.

For like many experts around this time, Gates had a theory about the unparalleled consequence of prenatal conditions. "[E]vil and painful emotions," he told the National Congress, "create in a very few minutes poisonous chemicals in the fluids of the body" that "arrest the normal rate of cell multiplication" and "affect also the sperm cell of the male and the egg cell of the female" (246–47). To produce the best possible child, then, parents (but especially mothers) must keep close control over their feelings, retreating to some quiet space for at least an hour a day to call up "desirable emotional conditions to the fullest possible intensity." Drawing to a close, Gates assures his listeners that "[o]ur country demands and your mother love craves such a child," and that if we can produce "great persons . . . all other things follow" (249). Decades earlier, Lydia Maria Child had insisted that the future depends on mothers' smallest turns of mood, and Gates agrees. But in his formulation, as in many from this period, society's destiny hinges less upon postnatal influences than upon the chemistry of feeling during gestation.[7]

On the basis of his 1900 visit with Gates, or his reading of the manuscript of *Relations*, or both, Dreiser drafted an article called "The Training of the Senses" that relayed a number of Gates's startling claims for multiplication of sensory capabilities in human subjects ("Training"; see also Moers 164–65 and Zanine 59–60). The piece was never printed, but one or two theories issuing from "our foremost American investigator" (as Dreiser described Gates to his editor at *Pearson's Magazine* [Moers 160, Zanine 57]), did make their way into Dreiser's first published novel, *Sister Carrie*. Most significant among these, as Moers and Zanine point out, was the theory that bad emotions breed dangerous chemicals that weaken the human organism, while good emotions breed helpful chemicals promoting augmentation of mind (quoted in Moers 166, Zanine 60). In a section of *Carrie* that Dreiser wrote not long after the meeting with Gates, his narrator explains that "it has been shown experimentally that a constantly subdued frame of mind produces certain poisons in the blood, called katastates, just as virtuous feelings of pleasure and delight produce helpful chemicals called anastates." The former—"poisons generated by remorse" that "inveigh against the system, and eventually produce marked physical deterioration"—then come to tell particularly upon the temper of George Hurstwood, who, having stolen money from his employers in Chicago, has fled to New York City with his lover Carrie in tow (302).[8] The disgraced former saloon manager ends up trapped in a vicious circle where depression generates katastates and katastates further intensify depression—a version of the downward spiral dear to the school of Zola, but with a gratifyingly specific bit of science to back it. It is as if Gates's ideas supplied Dreiser a basis for the naturalist trajectory handier and more resonant even than Spencer's sprawling system.

Nor is this the only chemical effect upon Hurstwood registered in the novel. That unfortunate soul is also transformed by the spectacle of New York affluence: "The great create an atmosphere which reacts badly upon the small. . . . It is like a chemical reagent. One day of it, like one drop of the other, will so affect and discolour the views, the aim, the desire of the mind, that it will thereafter remain forever dyed. A day of it to the untried mind is like opium to the untried body. A craving is set up which, if gratified, shall eternally result in dreams and death" (269–70). Read in light of the subsequent passage on katastates, Dreiser's comparison of urban milieu to chemical reagent comes to look rather more than figurative: the atmosphere of the great seems not merely *like* a chemical reagent or opium but a stimulus inducing a devastating cascade of chemical events, which Hurstwood experiences as insatiable craving. (We might think here of Stephen Dedalus's, "I fear more the chemical action which would be set up in my soul by a false homage to a symbol behind which are massed twenty centuries of authority and veneration.") Dreiser then enhances the intimation that social desire is to be understood as the consequence of environmental stimuli impinging on sensitive receptors by means of the felicitous phrase "dreams and death," which in this context evokes the link between opium-generated hallucination and the fragility of the addicted body.

Of course, in succumbing to the poison of the city without either willing or fully understanding what is transpiring, Hurstwood fits quite smoothly into the world of *Sister Carrie*—a novel long deemed noteworthy, indeed a breakthrough in American literature, for the consistency with which it shows characters moved by forces beyond themselves instead of moral impulses that can be called their own.[9] Carrie's first lover, Charles Drouet, ambles through life genially grasping whatever pleasures solicit him; Carrie rises to theatrical fame with no training, minimal effort, and a thirst for success not evidently more robust than that of other girls around her; Hurstwood seems far less to choose his destiny than to be carried along by a combination of accident and desire. This last point is highlighted especially dramatically, as readers have long noted, in the scene of crisis that divides the first part of the book from the second, in which Hurstwood contemplates stealing from his employers, running away with Carrie, and leaving behind a family for which he feels little affection. For while the conflict between dream and responsibility rages within him, the door of the saloon safe simply locks:

After he had all the money in the hand bag, a revulsion of feeling seized him. He would not do it—no! Think of what a scandal it would make. . . . He took out the two boxes and put all the money back. In his excitement he forgot what he was doing, and put the sums in the wrong boxes. . . .

He took them out and straightened the matter, but now the terror had gone. Why be afraid?

While the money was in his hand the lock clicked. It had sprung! Did he do it? He grabbed at the knob and pulled vigorously. It had closed. Heavens! He was in for it now, sure enough. (243)

Thus left to choose between flight and admitting to his employers that he had contemplated theft, Hurstwood chooses flight.

In his biography, Robert H. Elias records that Dreiser struggled with the writing of this scene, indeed ceased work on the novel for several weeks because he could not figure out how to have Hurstwood commit the crime "in such a way as to leave the problem of guilt or moral wrong ambiguous" (107). Moers shows that it was precisely during this hiatus that Dreiser met Gates, and speculates that the encounter helped Dreiser through his block: "Little wonder" that Gates's theory of katastates and anastates "stirred Dreiser's imagination at the time when he faced the task of accounting for the effects of false, depressing, and evil emotions on Hurstwood's material and mental decline. . . . Confident now of his own grasp of the scientific *how* of this phenomenon, Dreiser drew support from Elmer Gates's studies of the interdependence of mental and chemical phenomena" (166–67). To Moers's apt suggestion we might add that the proximity between the visit to Gates and the resolution of the safe scene emblematizes once again how materialist theories of environmental causation implied an altered understanding of responsibility. As participants on every side of the grand nineteenth-century debates on science and theology acknowledged, it is but a short step from the idea that mental life depends on chemical reactions engendered by impinging stimuli to the view that consciousness is an epiphenomenon of molecular processes beyond our control. From this perspective, consciousness may best understand its own nature not when it imagines itself the origin of actions but rather when it draws back to observe events as they unfold. Thus when Hurstwood watches the life-changing event of the theft transpire without his full direction—or when, earlier in the scene, he thinks that he does "not know why he wished to look in" the safe and "his mind [says] to itself, lingering, 'What makes me pause here?'" (239–40)—he allegorizes the true position of consciousness in a universe where what happens is determined by scientific laws set going at the beginning of time and unaffected by human resolves.

This point, of course, returns us to the deep continuities between naturalism and aestheticism that emerged in chapters 2 and 3. We saw there how Pater's and Zola's apparently very different literary modes both negotiated the problem of determinism unleashed by mid-nineteenth-century science; we saw too how Joyce, building on Pater, worked through this problem by conceiving the core self as a self of observation (in chapter 3 of *Portrait*) and then having Stephen propound a theory in which this self achieves freedom through aesthetic experience. It should therefore not surprise us that Hurstwood's perplexity before the safe exhibits some striking similarities to Stephen's third-chapter torments. Just as the saloon manager's mind asks itself, "What makes me pause here?," Stephen regards with horror a desire that seems to come from within himself without being fully his: "The eyes see the thing, without having wished first to see. Then *in an instant* it happens. . . . Was that then he or an inhuman thing moved by a lower soul than his soul? His soul sickened at the thought of a torpid snaky life feeding itself out of the tender marrow of his life and fattening upon the slime of lust."

Examining the scene of Hurstwood and the safe, Lee Mitchell notes astutely that the "inconclusiveness of Hurstwood's reflections, his uncertainty about the source of his intentions, and the wearying length of the process all gradually deny him an integrated self. Indeed, the narrative divides the man so deeply from himself—'He did not know why he . . .'— as to make him seem little more than the intersection of desires: of greed, fear, loneliness, lust, inebriation, and so on." It is as if, Mitchell concludes, "the very process" of attending to the self in this way "somehow dismantled subjectivity, breaking the self apart piece-by-piece and absorbing it into an indifferent world" (17). This analysis seems just as apposite to Stephen's introspective horror in the third chapter of *Portrait*. And as Mitchell intimates, it also suits neatly the other most famous scene of moral failing in Dreiser's oeuvre: the drowning of Roberta Alden, which divides the first part of *An American Tragedy* (1925) from the second.

At that point in the narrative, the protagonist, Clyde Griffiths, has kindled a romance with the moneyed and attractive Sondra Finchley, marriage to whom promises not only a delightful mate but also accession to the social berth of which he has long dreamed. Standing in the way, however, is Roberta, a factory girl threatening to reveal that she is carrying his child unless he marries her. Having taken Roberta to a secluded section of a distant lake with the intention of drowning her, he finds that he lacks the will to do the deed, but as she approaches him in the boat, he strikes at her reflexively with his camera. She reels back; he tries to reach her; the craft capsizes. And then a "voice at his ear" tells him that such an accident is precisely what he needs to fulfill his desires:

Wait—wait—ignore the pity of that appeal. And then—then— But here! Behold. It is over. She is sinking now. You will never, never see her alive any more—ever. . . .

. . . [H]e had not really killed her. No, no. Thank God for that. He had not. And yet (stepping up on the near-by bank and shaking the water from his clothes) had he? Or had he not? For had he not refused to go to her rescue, and when he might have saved her, and when the fault for casting her in the water, however accidentally, was so truly his? And yet—and yet— (514–15)

Dreiser seems led to make the crime half accident, once again, not just by a broad naturalist discomfort with individual agency but also by intense interest in the splitting of self that occurs with the upsurge of dangerous desires. Indeed if Hurstwood and Stephen experience an unsettling cleaving as they reflect on their courses, Clyde's mind seems divided from the first moment he thinks of murder: "He took his straw hat and went out, almost before anyone heard him *think*, as he would have phrased it to himself, such horrible, terrible thoughts. He could not and would not think them from now on. He was no such person. . . . He walked fast, thinking, and perspiring as he did so, as though he were seeking to outwalk and outthink or divert some inner self that preferred to be still and think" (480; see also 482, 483, 486, 491, 494). As in the middle chapter of *Portrait* and the pivotal scene of *Carrie*, one self observes and reacts while another seems to brandish unconscionable possibilities, though in this passage the observing mind curiously designates as "inner" not itself but the other self, the one that would succumb to temptation.

There is also a more telling difference, in this matter of shameful feelings, between Stephen, on the one hand, and Clyde and Hurstwood, on the other. Though the older Stephen who "trac[es] even moral phenomena back to the region of . . . primal cells" might in theory lay his undesirable desiring at the door of biology, the Stephen of chapter three never ventures to blame heredity or environment for his lust. Hurstwood, by contrast, seems freed from much of the guilt that might otherwise plague him by the fact of the lock's clicking on its own and by his fervid sense of oppression by the family life he endured in Chicago. Clyde, for his part, recurs frequently to the circumstances that propelled his fatal passage, as when at the very end of the novel he thinks:

And yet—and yet—. . . he had a feeling in his heart that he was not as guilty as they all seemed to think. After all they had not been tortured as he had by Roberta with her determination that he marry her and thus ruin his whole life. They had not burned with that unquenchable passion for the Sondra of his beautiful dream as he had. They had not been harassed, tortured, mocked by the ill-fate of his early life and training, forced to sing and pray on the streets as he had in such a degrading way, when his whole heart and soul cried out for better things. How could they judge him, these people . . . ? . . . [W]hile at times he felt strongly that he was innocent, at others he felt that he must be guilty. (839; see also 845–48)

Hurstwood and Clyde are far from unique among Dreiser's characters in their readiness to refer their desires and actions at least partly to external forces. In *The Financier* (1912), the womanizing capitalist Frank Cowperwood's philosophy of relationships takes the form of a *"laissez-faire* attitude" according to which "all the little differences of personality that sprang up between people, causing quarrels, bickering, oppositions, and separation . . . could not be helped." In *The "Genius"* (1915), the Dreiser-like protagonist Eugene Witla often reflects that his yearnings come to him unbidden: "If you went astray, overbalanced by your desires, wasn't it after all in the scheme of things? Did we make our desires? Certainly we did not, and if we did not succeed completely in controlling them—well—" (218). Other Dreiserian characters refer to circumstances in exculpating not themselves but relatives, friends, or even strangers, as when in *Jennie Gerhardt* (1911) Senator Brander hears the story of Jennie's brother, caught trying to sneak his desperate family some coal, and thinks, "Here was this boy arrested and fined for what fate was practically driving him to do" (66). Later in the same novel, Jennie excuses the extravagance of her subsequent paramour, Lester Kane, with the protest, "He can't help it, papa. . . . That's the way he was raised" (231).

In *An American Tragedy,* all parties involved in Clyde's trial seem transfixed by the question of how external factors might mitigate his criminality. The defense represents Clyde as "trapped by circumstances" (645), while Clyde's mother appeals to the newspapers "for a correct understanding of the extenuating circumstances surrounding her son's downfall" (842) and the public wonders, with respect to that parent, "if she had remained at home, as a good mother should, and devoted herself to her son, as well as to her other children—their care and education—would this—have happened?" (804). The prosecution too acknowledges the power of circumstances, but tries to use that power against the accused. Attempting to elicit a confession before the trial, the district attorney tells Clyde that there may be "extenuating circumstances, which, if they were related by you now, might throw a slightly different light on all this" (588); during the trial, the same prosecutor puts to the jury the question, "Is he the son of wastrel parents—a product of the slums . . . ?" only to answer in the negative: "On the contrary. His father is of the same strain that has given Lycurgus one of its largest and most constructive industries—the Griffiths Collar & Shirt Company. He was poor—yes—no doubt of that. But not more so than Roberta Alden—and her character appears not to have been affected by her poverty" (674). The point made by the many pages of *An American Tragedy* devoted to Clyde's life before the drowning, of course, is that so broad a reduction of circumstances to socioeconomic categories can never tell the whole story: the reader knows that although Roberta, too, had her dreams, she was never exposed to her social superiors (fatal also to Hurstwood) in the overwhelming fashion Clyde was.

In showing questions about extenuating circumstances arising almost as soon as a perpetrator is identified, Dreiser was unquestionably capturing an obsession of his age. Not only was the general public fascinated by the origins of criminality; it seems that already by the turn of the century delinquents themselves were calling upon theories of heredity and environment drawn from contemporary criminology, sociology, medicine, and law as well as naturalist fictions. In *Adolescence*, Hall refers to a 1903 address in which an expert "protests against the frequent acceptance of hereditary tendencies or fatalism which even the young sometimes now use as an excuse for their bad conduct" (1.306); in his 1925 volume, Burt observes that "perhaps none is so eager to advocate" the view that cinema inspires juvenile criminality "as the young culprit himself, who frequently sees, or thinks he sees, in such a derivation of his deeds a chance to deflect blame and attention from his own moral laxity to that of the producer of films" (137).

Yet though Dreiser often allowed the etiology of antisocial or self-ruining behavior to serve as a tool for lawyers, defendants, and others seeking practical results in his fictions, it remained at the same time a deeply serious philosophical problem for him, a synecdoche of the perplexities of desire, free will, and meaning bequeathed by nineteenth-century science. The chemistry of social ambition that drives Hurstwood and Clyde is in Dreiser a medium of address to the wrenching questions thrown up by Spencer and company; the sexual compulsion that Cowperwood and Witla sometimes name in breezy excuse appears to them at other junctures a disruptively overmastering force, and to their author the face of an endlessly troubling cosmic mystery. This last point is reinforced quite directly by several of the short pieces from the late 1910s that Dreiser collected in the volume *Hey, Rub-a-Dub-Dub: A Book of the Mystery and Wonder and Terror of Life* (1920). "Marriage and Divorce," for instance, dwells on nature's "curs[ing] or endow[ing]" of many of its creatures "with strange and horrible vices, with vast and self-torturing passions, with immeasurable longings and desires, which unfit them for the proper fulfillment of the monogamic conception of the perfect marriage, hence of the care of the ensuing children." Asking therein, "Who is to blame—Nature or man?," Dreiser answers, "certainly man is not to blame, for from the very beginning he has been crucified upon a rood which is not of his devising" (216–17).

Perhaps Dreiser's most fearful rendering of enslavement to bodily desire appears in *The Hand of the Potter*, a play of 1916 centering on a family of Jewish immigrants in New York, one of whose members rapes and murders an eleven-year-old girl. The title of the play—drawn from the *Omar Khayyam* line, "What! Did the Hand then of the Potter shake?"—refers to the problem, revolved by various characters including the murderer himself, of how the impulse to commit so terrible an act could possibly be a constituent of any person's character. In the last of the debates Dreiser stages, reporters discuss the case for hereditary disposition, one trotting out research conducted at Johns Hopkins and Cornell, another drawing on Freud, Kraft-Ebbing, and Havelock Ellis to conclude that the perpetrator is

> no more guilty than other people with a disease. Did ye know, ayther ave ye, that there's something they've called *harmones* which the body manufactures an' which is poured into the blood streams of every waan ave us which excites us to the m'aning ave beauty an' thim things—"sensitizes" is the word they use. Now if a felly is so constituted that he has more ave that an' less ave somethin' else—somethin' which balances him a little an' makes him less sensitive to the beauty of women or girls—he's likely to be like that. He can't help it. There's something that pushes him on in spite of himself. (193)

This disquisition certainly evokes the Greenian compounds that had made their way into *Sister Carrie* as well as the 1893 defense of John Finn, but by the time he wrote *The Hand of the Potter* Dreiser had also acquainted himself with more reliable and specific studies of the chemistry of organisms' inclinations. As Moers and Zanine note, he began to read assiduously in this field in 1915, even requesting a room at the New York Public Library where he might commence, in his words, "investigations . . . in the line of chemistry and physics" (quoted in Zanine 78; see also Moers 246). He also began to contact scientists whose work seemed especially inspiring, among them Jacques Loeb, a German biologist whom G. Stanley Hall had helped lure to the United States and who, after stints at Bryn Mawr, the University of Chicago, and Berkeley, became director of the Rockefeller Institute (Moers 248, Zanine 79). Not only an eminent researcher, Loeb was also a fierce evangelist for the mechanistic worldview, to which he had been introduced years earlier by the botanist Julius Sachs, who had in turn adapted the ideas of mid-nineteenth-century mechanists such as Helmholtz (Zanine 79). How ardently Loeb held his beliefs may be gauged from his fear that the world would return to a "dark ages," as he told Dreiser, should mechanism succumb to the attacks of reactionaries propounding vitalist or metaphysical accounts of life's nature (Zanine 99).

Dreiser's first acquaintance with Loeb probably came through the latter's 1912 volume, *The Mechanistic Conception of Life*; when Dreiser wrote to Loeb a few years later, Loeb recommended two more of his books, *Forced Movements, Tropisms, and Animal Conduct* and *The Organism as a Whole* (Zanine 98). At the factual heart of these texts lies Loeb's experimental demonstration that what looks like instinctive survival behavior in animals can often be shown to consist of chemical reactions as inevitable as those of compounds in a test tube. For example, it might be assumed that newly born caterpillars' tendency to move toward light is driven by an instinct that nourishment will lie in that direction. When Loeb put starving young caterpillars of the species *Porthesia chrysorrhoea* into glass tubes at right angles to a window, however, "the caterpillars went to the window side of the tube and remained there, even if leaves of their food plant were put into the tube directly behind them. Under such conditions the animals actually died from starvation, the light preventing them from turning to the food, which they eagerly ate when the light allowed them do so" (*Mechanistic* 202). Through these and related experiments, Loeb was able to show that movements appearing "to the layman" as "expressions of will and purpose on the part of the animal" are produced by interactions between external stimuli (such as light) and patterns of chemical distribution in the animal's body (such as the doubling in laterally symmetrical organisms). Such movements are thus akin to the tropisms observed in plants (*Forced* 14).

Nor does the point hold only for instinctive behaviors; it also applies to behaviors that appear to be learned. "When a muscle is stimulated several times in succession," Loeb writes in *Forced Movements,* "the effect of the second or third or later stimulation may be greater than that of the first," so that it may seem as if the muscle is learning to react appropriately. What actually happens, however, is that "the hydrogen concentration is raised by the first stimulations to a point where the effect" of subsequent stimulations is inevitably enhanced. We can only really speak of learning, in fact, if an organism is possessed of "associative memory," wherein "a stimulus produces not only the direct effects determined by its nature, but also the effects of entirely different stimuli which at some former period by chance attacked the organism at the same time with the given stimulus" (*Forced* 164–65). Only some higher species seem to have associative memory, Loeb explains, and even here, Pavlov's experiments on "conditioned reflexes" have established "that the influence of an associative memory image is . . . exactly measurable . . . and . . . that what we call a memory image is not a 'spiritual' but a physical agency" (*Forced* 167). Indeed ideas themselves can be comprehended in chemical terms: "'ideas' also can act, much as acids do for the heliotropism of certain animals, namely, to increase the sensitiveness to certain stimuli, and thus can lead to tropism-like movements or actions directed toward a goal" (*Mechanistic* 56).

In Loeb's representation, as in the nineteenth-century treatments of reflex, habit, and instinct that we considered in chapter 1, activities commonly attributed to consciousness come to have a decidedly unconscious quality, their essence lying not in eruptions of will from within the organism but in law-governed responses to stimuli. If human beings still appear to have free will, the reason is not that a vital principle or immaterial essence allows them to resist the laws of chemistry and physics, but rather that the countless causes leading to an action cannot all be apprehended (just as determinism in its 1855 *Oxford Essays* definition holds). "Our conception of the existence of 'free will' in human beings," Loeb observes, "rests on the fact that our knowledge is often not sufficiently complete to account for the orienting forces, especially when we carry out a 'premeditated' act, or when we carry out an act which gives us pain or may lead to our destruction" (*Forced* 171–72).

Moers hazards that Dreiser read more books by Loeb than by any other scientist over the years, and certainly this estimate is supported by the frequency with which Loebian themes surface in his writing after 1915. The problem of free will becomes a problem of chemistry in *The Hand of the Potter*, as we have seen, and several essays included in *Hey, Rub-a-Dub-Dub* exhibit a vocabulary yet more acutely indebted to Loeb: in "Equation Inevitable," for example, Dreiser invokes tropisms when contemplating the apparently moral behavior of animals (172), while in "The Essential Tragedy of Life" he credits chemistry and physics with showing that man "is merely—and what is worse, accidentally so—an evoluted arrangement of attractions and repulsions, arranged by chemicals and forces which desire or cannot escape whorls or epitomes of complicated motions and emotions or attractions which take the odd forms presented by men and animals" (242). In the same essay, he insists that the structure of the human body, wonderful as it may seem, is from the point of view of biology and anthropology "all brought about by the inescapable chemical and physical reactions and compulsions of seemingly blind forces, as Crile and Loeb have shown. . . . [Man's] thoughts also are apparently little more than compelled reactions of one chemical upon another which he can no more escape than can he his form or motions" (247).

But if free will is thus an illusion and every organism at the mercy of its environment and physiology, can anything be done to improve the human lot? For Loeb, as for Zola, the answer is a resounding yes, since it is precisely when we acknowledge that our best impulses emerge from ineluctable "processes in our central nervous system" that we can begin to "create a civilization" that does not "warp and inhibit the inherited instincts" (*Mechanistic* 33). This view is notably shared, indeed rehearsed more extensively, by the scientist Dreiser pairs with Loeb in the foregoing quotation and at numerous other junctures in his writing, George Crile. In texts such as *Man—An Adaptive Mechanism*, which was part of Dreiser's course of reading in the mid-1910s, Crile maintains as Loeb does that "man's claim to a superior place among animals depends less on *different reactions* than upon a *greater number* of reactions compared with the reactions of 'lower' animals. Ability to respond adaptively to more elements in the environment gives a larger dominion, that is all" (*Man* 37–38). In another book Dreiser probably read, *The Origin and Nature of the Emotions* of 1915, Crile asserts, with echoes of Spencer, that "environment has been the actual *creator* of man" and that consciousness must be understood as a "power of response [to stimuli] on the part of the brain," a "reaction to environment" (128, 140).

For Crile, what was most worrisome about the human environments of modernity was their tendency to induce stress; hence what would most benefit modern individuals would be relief from emotional strain. But it was not only that the adult so freed would "rise to a plane of poise and efficiency far above that of his uncontrolled fellows." Crile also asserted that a "full acceptance" of his theories could not "fail to produce in those in whose charge rests the welfare of the young, an overwhelming desire to surround children with those environmental stimuli only which will tend to their highest ultimate development" (*Origin* 153–54).[10] The claim will be familiar enough by now, evoking as it does G. Stanley Hall on the elimination of every cause of arrest, delinquency specialists on the origins of criminality, Elmer Gates on social transformation through brain building, and The Prophet on the physical appearance of schools. Yet that Loeb and Crile impressed still more forcefully on Dreiser the connection between chemical excitation by external stimuli and the fate of the young is suggested by the predicament of the relatively youthful murderer in 1916's *Hand of the Potter*—and by the fact that the single major Dreiser novel in which the dangers of juvenile environment play a leading role is also the one that germinated around the end of the 1910s: *An American Tragedy.*[11]

In *Sister Carrie*, certainly, Dreiser had shown contact with privilege initiating a chemical cascade of desires; in *Jennie Gerhardt*, he had presented straitened circumstances leading young people to ethically and legally dubious expedients; in *The Financier* and *The "Genius,"* he had sketched briefly how early experience can ignite ambition in the unusually gifted. In none of these books, however, does a fatality in the transactions between environment and young organism take center stage. In *Carrie*, the people affected by the spectacle of affluence are adults; in *Jennie Gerhardt*, the partly conscious accession to desire privileged by naturalism is much less consequential than a kind of bowing to moral necessity more usually associated with realism; and in *The Financier* and *The "Genius,"* youthful experience eventuates not in unmitigated disaster but in notoriety and position (if hardly unbounded happiness). *An American Tragedy*, by contrast, can be read as an exploration of the causes and forces leading to a criminal deed, a lengthy refutation or qualification, once again, of the prosecutor's claim that mitigating circumstances can be reduced to a single category as broad as "poverty."

But can we specify a little more closely the problems with Clyde's environment? Doing so will, as it happens, lead us back to the aesthetic, which we may appear to have left for some time.

## INSIDIOUS BEAUTY

In the first pages of *An American Tragedy*, Clyde Griffiths is twelve years old and restless in the life of street preaching and mission work to which his parents have consigned him and his siblings. Believing that God will provide and that the highest calling for their offspring must be to assist the proselytizing enterprise, Clyde's mother and father are eminently "impractical in the matter of the future of their children. They did not understand . . . the essential necessity for some form of practical or professional training for each and every one of their young ones. Instead, being wrapped up in the notion of evangelizing the world, they had neglected to keep their children in school in any one place" (9). Nor do they seem to notice how ill their way of living sorts with Clyde's temperament, though Dreiser makes this friction obvious even to strangers: in the opening scene, a witness to a Griffiths street performance remarks, "That oldest boy don't wanta be here. He feels outa place, I can see that. It ain't right to make a kid like that come out unless he wants to. He can't understand all this stuff, anyhow" (5). Blessed with intelligence and good looks, but unarmed against the allure of roaring urban life's expensive pleasures, the discontented Clyde is soon led into the series of encounters that will end, years later, in his execution for murder.

After Roberta's drowning, as we have seen, the influences bringing Clyde to that pass provide food for thought to many persons of the drama, including Clyde himself, the district attorney, the newspaper-reading public, and Mrs. Griffiths, who resolves to modify her methods in raising her grandson Russell: "She must be kind to him, more liberal with him, not restrain him too much, as maybe, maybe, she had . . ."—that is, as maybe she had restrained Clyde (856). Yet none of the characters interested in Clyde's case—except, and this infrequently, Clyde himself—reflects much on an element mentioned twice in the novel's first chapter and recurrently thereafter: his longing for beauty. "Plainly pagan rather than religious," the narrator tells us in the opening pages, Clyde is thoroughly interested in the life around him, "although as yet he was not fully aware of this. All that could be truly said of him now was that there was no definite appeal in all this [his parents' mission] for him. He was too young, his mind much too responsive to phases of beauty and pleasure which had little, if anything, to do with the remote and cloudy romance which swayed the minds of his mother and father" (3). And then, a few paragraphs later: "The handsome automobiles that sped by, the loitering pedestrians moving off to what interests and comforts he could only surmise; the gay pairs of young people, laughing and jesting and the 'kids' staring, all troubled him with a sense of something different, better, more beautiful than his, or rather their life" (4–5).

Clyde's inclining toward beauty is certainly bound up with a longing for status: subsequent pages describe his envy of other boys' clothing and his humiliation on recognizing that "the calling or profession of his parents" is a "shabby thing . . . in the eyes of others" (8). Yet it would be wrong to reduce his response wholly to anxiety about social position. In the first quotation, his "pagan" impulse seems a broad attraction to the richness of life in this world rather than the next, a gravitation not completely unconnected to the paganism of more voluble lovers of the sensuous such as Walter Pater. In the second passage, he seems dimly to imagine a style of life enviable not just because people envy it but because it would be intrinsically finer than what he has known.

Indeed Dreiser suggests that the most damaging aspect of Clyde's environment may be its lack of beauty in a more specifically aesthetic sense. Calling the "combination home and mission" inhabited by the Griffiths of Kansas City "dreary enough in most of its phases to discourage the average youth or girl of any spirit" (9), the narrator evokes a literature of urban deprivation that includes *The Spirit of Youth and the City Streets* (1909), in which Dreiser's fellow Midwesterner Jane Addams asserts, at one point, that if educators cared to look they would find in "that army of boys and girls who enter industry each year" powerful aesthetic yearnings withering for lack of employment and "many instances of high-spirited young people who suffer a veritable martyrdom in order to satisfy their artistic impulse" (124, 132). The Griffiths domicile consists "of one long stone floor in an old and decidedly colorless and inartistic wooden building" (9), while the neighborhood as a whole is "so dreary and run-down" that Clyde "hate[s] the thought of living in it, let alone being part of a work that require[s] constant appeals for aid" (11). The misery induced by poverty and squalid quarters is for him conjoint, in other words, with a feeling that his family's soliciting is an unbeautiful kind of conduct, a failure of that grace or graciousness in which social interaction acquires an aesthetic luster. In the 1890s, Dreiser as The Prophet had credited "the beautiful school working upon the impressionable heart of the child" with the power to "lift us out of our troubles"; that belief lingers in converse form here, where ugly conditions sow in the child's heart dissatisfaction, resentment, and shame.

Again, to say that Clyde's feeling for beauty is in some sense genuinely aesthetic is not to insist that it can be separated absolutely from longings for wealth and social recognition. A characteristically Dreiserian figure inasmuch as his idea of a beautiful life coalesces around automobiles and happy couples, Clyde seems not to want to serve beauty in the way of Stephen Dedalus and other heroes of the *kunstlerroman*, only to have some share in a loveliness evidently available to the more fortunate. This hard truth is adumbrated as early as the narrator's initial description of Clyde's urban milieu, which leaves uncertain whether its aesthetic inadequacy is to be blamed on commerce's absence or on its residual imprint: the neighborhood "was very faintly and yet not agreeably redolent of a commercial life which had long since moved farther south, if not west" (9).

In other writings, Dreiser proves similarly unwilling to make a sharp distinction between some pure aesthetic feeling and attraction to the affluence bespoken by splendid surroundings. As The Prophet, we might recall, he had demanded not only that schools be "beautiful and useful in every detail" but also that they be "vast in structure, ornate and impressive in their architecture." The continuity between beauty and ostentation is marked especially forthrightly in Dreiser's second volume of autobiography, *Newspaper Days*, where he recounts how, as a newcomer to New York, he was transfixed by a billboard advertising Manhattan Beach on Long Island ("SWEPT BY OCEAN BREEZES / THE GREAT HOTELS" [600]). Duly taken there by his brother, he finds in its "great hotels, its crowds, amusements, music, bathing, dining" an incomparable new world and thinks, "I have never lived at all until now" (602–603). It seems

> all too beautiful. I was so wrought up by it all that I could scarcely eat. . . . Beauty, beauty, beauty. That was the message and the import of it all—the will to and the search for beauty. By the hard processes of trade—this to me very wonderful and entrancing thing had been accomplished. Unimportant to me now how hard some of these people looked or were or had been—or how selfish or vain or indifferent. They had sought and bought and paid for this thing, and it was beautiful. (604–605)

Dreiser is notably at pains to deny that this spectacle's spiritual failings, or even what some would call its aesthetic ones, utterly compromise its claims to beauty. He admits that those who cavorted there could be narrow of soul, even that their clothes were "a little showy" (602), but he also makes clear that this in no way diminished the scene's significance for his younger self. Veraciously in the eye of that beholder, beauty here emerges both in spite of and by means of "the hard processes of trade," just as in Yeats's nearly contemporary poem "Ancestral Houses" (to which we will return in the next chapter) those who "rear in stone / The sweetness that all longed for night and day" are bitter and violent men, not refined and sensitive ones.

The question of what beauty means for Clyde Griffiths is further complicated by the narrator's insistence on its sexual component. A few pages into the novel, we learn that at sixteen "the sex lure or appeal had begun to manifest itself and he was already intensely interested and troubled by the beauty of the opposite sex" (13). This troubling leads, of course, to fatal trouble: Clyde's story simply could not be what it becomes without the physical attractions of Roberta and Sondra, and indeed after the drowning he thinks how strange it is that he can never tell the latter how "because of her, her beauty, his passion for her and all that she had come to mean to him, he had been able to . . . to . . . to . . . well, *attempt* this terrible thing" (554, emphasis Dreiser's). The narrator, meanwhile, stresses the pheromonal basis of sexual desire when describing Roberta's appeal: having mentioned early on the "chemistry and urge toward mating which lies back of all youthful thought and action" (15), he reminds us that Clyde's "was a disposition easily and often intensely inflamed by the chemistry of sex and the formula of beauty" (245). It comes as no surprise, then, that "because so much alone, and furthermore because of so strong a chemic or temperamental pull . . . , he could no longer keep his eyes off" Roberta, nor could she keep hers away from him (262).

That this understanding of sex was rooted in Dreiser's own experience is attested by the first volume of his autobiography, *Dawn*, which he had drafted by 1916 but published only much later. "For the second, third and fourth decades of my life—or from fifteen to thirty-five—" he writes in that memoir,

> there appeared to be a toxic something in form itself—that of the female of the species where beautiful—that could effect veritable paroxysms of emotion and desire in me, and that over distances of time and space. The mystery! The subtleties of physics and chemistry behind it! . . .
>
> Let us say that my blood has been either ill or well compounded, as you will. But because of this pre-arranged system . . . I have thrilled again and again from head to toe, the sight of this particular formula (female) resulting in the invasion of homes, the destruction of happy arrangements among others, lies, persuasions, this, that. (167–68)

In referring such disruptions and dishonesty not to acts of will but to a "pre-arranged system" of hereditary "compound[ing]" that reacts disastrously with environmental stimuli, of course, Dreiser engages in a form of self-exculpation dear also to some of his characters. It might be inferred, then, that he reaches for the mechanistic vision primarily out of a need to defend his real-life infidelities. Yet it is important to recognize, at the same time, that Dreiser's very belief in mechanism was solidified by his experience of being overwhelmed by desire—that his never slackening interest in how people are propelled by chemistry instead of conscience was driven above all by wonder at his own sexual tumult. Not surprisingly, his semi-autobiographical novel *The "Genius"* also represents the fatality of beauty as physiochemical: "so powerful was the illusion of desire, the sheer animal magnetism of beauty, that when it came near him in the form of a lovely girl of [Witla's] own temperamental inclinations he could not resist it. . . . It was as though the very form of the face, without will or intention on the part of the possessor, acted hypnotically upon its beholder" (274).

Surpassing even Clyde, Witla, and Dreiser himself in the starkness with which he unites the craving for beauty with attractions to money and sex is Frank Cowperwood, the arch-capitalist whose story is told in the "Trilogy of Desire" formed by *The Financier*, *The Titan* (1914), and *The Stoic* (1947). Relentlessly acquisitive of wealth and power, Cowperwood is also captivated, from an early age, by the beauty of women and the beauty of art—so much so that his first real romance incorporates a finicky impulse to put the object of his affections in a suitable setting: "The interior of the house was not as pleasing as he would have had it. Artistic impressiveness, as to the furniture at least, was wanting, although it was new and good. . . . The china was good—of a delicate pattern. The carpets and wall-paper were too high in key. So it went. Still, the personality of Lillian Semple was worth something, for she was really pleasing to look upon, making a picture wherever she stood or sat" (43). A few pages later, Cowperwood thinks "how attractive he could make" Lillian look "in other surroundings" (52); commencing his affair with Aileen Butler further on in the novel, he grows similarly absorbed by the need to compose an artistically satisfying love nest. And when he finally meets the right woman, late in *The Titan*, what seals Berenice Fleming's perfection (on top of her striking beauty and unearthly wisdom) is her artistic discernment. Dreiser clearly means for Cowperwood's appreciation of Berenice's gifts to transcend—and so, somehow, validate—his attraction to the women with whom he had previously been involved, just as he means for Cowperwood's more grossly acquisitive drives to be redeemed by his aesthetic feeling.[12]

Critical to this redemption is that the financier's attraction to beauty, especially on the romantic side, comes to blows with some of his other ambitions—above all by leading him to affairs inimical to his social climb and, at times, his financial interests. Nor is it only in Cowperwood's narrative that aesthetic feeling proves at once sincere, inextricable from an appetite for wealth and eminence, and perilous to that appetite's sustained satisfaction. In *The "Genius,"* Dreiser transforms his youthful raptures over Manhattan Beach into a scheme by which Eugene Witla aims to bring something opulent and fine into the world, but whose upshot proves utterly disastrous. Impelled by "an idea of beauty" (496), a conviction that "[n]othing interested him quite so much as beauty and luxury in some artistic combination" (512), Witla invests in and largely designs a massive resort development called Blue Sea—which slow-moving project requires repeated infusions of cash and thus leaves him, at the climax of the novel, bereft of liquid assets just when he needs them most. In *Newspaper Days* itself, Dreiser observes that in the years since his dazzling by Manhattan Beach he has "had at least some of the things which [his] soul at that time most eagerly craved," yet still finds himself wondering whether his or "or any other heart" is ever "really satisfied" (606). A similar insatiability rules Carrie Meeber in *Sister Carrie*, to whom we will return in just a moment. And in *An American Tragedy*, Clyde conceives his homicidal plan by way of holding on to the beauty of a world that he has, against all odds, entered on Sondra's arm. Her own attractiveness, however immense, does not seem quite enough to inspire his desperate resolution; what surely turns the scale is the chance to leave forever the ugliness amid which he grew up.

Beauty in Dreiser thus seems to bear a tension or contradiction not unlike that borne by aestheticism writ large, which was rendered the more perversely commodifiable by its very protest against society's enslavement to material gain. On the one hand, Dreiser rehearses how beauty is often to be found in the company of wealth and ease; on the other, he presents it as a call to swerve from the practical, and thus precisely the sort of reproof to a world dominated by commerce that it had been for many artists since the Romantics.[13] These alternatives cohabit nowhere more strikingly, perhaps, than in Clyde's plan to murder Roberta, which can be read as a calculating grab at affluence but also—especially given Clyde's mental instability during the plotting and the proliferation of mistakes that lead to his prompt capture—as a self-destructive, beauty-induced departure from more prudent paths (such as marrying Roberta or leaving town). Just before the drowning, Clyde himself conjures a kind of metaphor for the fatal allure of Sondra's world: of the secluded spot where he plans to kill Roberta, he thinks, "The insidious beauty of this place! Truly, it seemed to mock him. . . . And Clyde was alone, so very much alone and forlorn, in this somber, beautiful realm to which apparently he had been led, and then deserted. Also he felt strangely cold—the spell of this strange beauty overwhelming him with a kind of chill" (510).

But is it the case that for Dreiser this tension in the beautiful arises from the lamentable commodifiability of an aesthetic whose essence nonetheless lies in disinterested contemplation? Or is it rather that Dreiser's work is to demystify aesthetic ideology, revealing how the real aspiration in talk of beauty is to maintain social hierarchies, to find kinder names for acquisition, to ensure that people climb individually instead of revolting en masse? There are at least two reasons to resist both of these framings. One, which may sound crude but whose virtues will shortly appear, is that in privileging Dreiser's interest in capitalism to the exclusion of his interest in science, such approaches miss the important ways in which these interests shape each other—and shape Dreiser's approach to the aesthetic as well. The second reason is that adhering to these constructions may distract us from another tension in beauty's operation, a tension that Dreiser may have regarded as more fundamental and that links him to, even as it distinguishes him from, the other authors visited in this book. To see how these points work out in detail, we might begin by returning for a moment to the Dreiserian fiction most persistently examined in terms of the culture of commodities, *Sister Carrie*.

## ONWARD, ONWARD

Near the beginning of that narrative, Carrie Meeber is entranced by her first visit to a department store: in a passage that has lately become one of the most cited in American fiction, she "passe[s] along the busy aisles, much affected by the remarkable displays of trinkets, dress goods, stationery, and jewelry"; she cannot "help feeling the claim of each trinket and valuable upon her personally" (20). Later on, visiting the better neighborhoods of 1890s Chicago, she imagines "that across these richly carved entranceways, where the globed and crystalled lamps shone upon panelled doors set with stained and designed panes of glass, was neither care nor unsatisfied desire. She was perfectly certain that here was happiness" (108). Eventually, she acquires the means to possess such things: having accompanied Hurstwood to New York, she rises to wealth and renown through a series of small and then large theatrical successes.

Less assuredly within her grasp until the end of the novel (and possibly even then), however, is another kind of attainment: a certain cultural facility represented by Bob Ames, a young man "connected with an electrical company" in Indianapolis yet devoted to the arts as no one among Carrie's New York acquaintance seems to be (293). When she first meets him, Carrie senses that Ames is "better educated than she was—that his mind was better," and "for the first time" in her life feels "the pain of not understanding" (297). When she thinks of him later, her mind "halt[s]. It was a strong, clean vision. He liked better books than she read, better people than she associated with. His ideals burned in her heart" (366). Her "new desire" is to meet him at his level (443), and by the closing pages, she can indeed be found reading *Père Goriot* on his recommendation, catching "nearly the full sympathetic significance of" Balzac's text: "[f]or the first time, it was being borne in upon her how silly and worthless had been her earlier reading." Yet in the next sentence, she grows weary, yawns, and looks out the window at the "winding procession of carriages rolling up Fifth Avenue" (453).

It is not clear whether the yawn signals the incapacity even of art to deliver the happiness for which she longs or only Carrie's inability to bestow on art the attention it requires. What is clear is that in the vicinity of Ames, she is piqued by the culture of fin de siècle aestheticism, wherein the capacity to appreciate certain manifestations of the beautiful and artistic is itself a desirable acquisition. Aestheticism's rhetoric does not figure into Clyde Griffiths's strivings, of course, yet Carrie's story is clearly at one with his (as with those of Cowperwood, Witla, and Theodore Dreiser) inasmuch as it prompts questions about the relations among love of beauty, desire for status, and chances at happiness in a world that seems governed by endless wanting. For Amy Kaplan in *The Social Construction of American Realism*, Ames's influence does not prod Carrie to action but "only makes her more acutely conscious of her lack of the 'better thing' which Ames represents"; when confronted by Balzac and high art as when confronted by department-store merchandise, "Carrie desires things not for their own qualities or for the pleasures they afford, but for the new self-image they seem to offer" (144). Writing on *Sister Carrie* in *Hard Facts: Setting and Form in the American Novel*, Philip Fisher notes how in the modern city one's relation to things and even persons shifts "from that of caring for things that one has . . . to buying things one hasn't," with the consequence that the self may be said to reside not in one's body but in one's environment (133–34). In *The Gold Standard and the Logic of Naturalism*, Walter Benn Michaels too fixes on the endlessness of desire in Dreiser's novels, but in his reading the insatiability confirmed by Carrie's reaching toward Ames is the very sign of life. In this text, "[w]hat you are is what you want, in other words, what you aren't. The ideal that Ames represents to Carrie is thus an ideal of dissatisfaction, of perpetual desire. And in fact, in *Sister Carrie*, satisfaction itself is never desirable; it is instead the sign of incipient failure, decay, and finally death" (Michaels 42).

Readings focusing on Carrie's dissatisfaction draw much of their force from the three-page finale of the novel, which describes both her past and her future in terms of unceasing longing.[14] Unremarked in major critical treatments of her desiring, however, is the prominence of the word "beauty," which Dreiser uses nine times in that conclusion (as he uses it twice in his opening description of Clyde's predicament). The narrator first remarks that although Carrie has attained "[b]eauty—her type of loveliness," she remains lonely for all that; he then evokes the figure of the dreamer, "[e]ver hearkening to the sound of beauty, straining for the flash of its distant wings, . . . wearying his feet in travelling. So watched Carrie, so followed, rocking and singing" (458). Next, he asks "who shall cast the first stone" at those who, like Carrie, make their way partly by means other than "honest labour," if "honest labour be unremunerative and difficult to endure; if it be the long, long road which never reaches beauty, but wearies the feet and the heart; if the drag to follow beauty be such that one abandons the admired way, taking rather the despised path leading to her dreams quickly" (459).

Succeeding these four appearances of the word comes the note that Carrie, her purse now "open to him whose need was greatest," no longer thinks of the elegance of wealthy women promenading on Broadway; only "[h]ad they more of that peace and beauty which glimmered afar off" would she envy their lives (459). A counterfactual hypothesis about what would happen could Hurstwood return "in his original beauty" (460) follows, and after that a triad of invocations of "beauty" in the last two paragraphs:

> Sitting alone, she was now an illustration of the envious ways by which one who feels, rather than reasons, may be led in the pursuit of beauty. Though often disillusioned, she was still waiting for that halcyon day when she should be led forth among dreams become real. Ames had pointed out a farther step, but on and on beyond that, if accomplished, would lie others for her. It was forever to be the pursuit of that radiance of delight which tints the distant hilltops of the world.
>
>     Oh, Carrie, Carrie! Oh, blind strivings of the human heart! Onward, onward, it saith, and where beauty leads, there it follows. Whether it be the tinkle of a lone sheep bell o'er some quiet landscape, or the glimmer of beauty in sylvan places, or the show of soul in some passing eye, the heart knows and makes answer, following. It is when the feet weary and hope seems vain that the heartaches and the longings arise. Know, then, that for you is neither surfeit nor content. In your rocking-chair, by your window dreaming, shall you long, alone. In your rocking-chair, by your window, shall you dream such happiness as you may never feel. (460)

The narrator's invocations of beauty in these closing pages seem, on inspection, to divide into two types. In the references to Carrie's physical loveliness, Hurstwood's lost looks, and (arguably) what glimmers in sylvan places, beauty is something materially present in this world; in the other instances, it takes the form of an ideal ever elusive of capture by the heart it nonetheless compels to follow. The ending thus faithfully abstracts the action of the novel as a whole (and of Dreiser's other long fictions), in which beauty maintains its grip by appearing and withdrawing, extending just enough of itself into the tangible immediate to keep its devotee in hopes of some fully satisfying consummation to come. In Dreiser's world, every gift of beauty seems punctuated by irony, the pleasure of having tasted being predicated on the pain of not having won.

But what, according to *Sister Carrie*, might it feel like to catch beauty at last, to be led forth among dreams become real? What condition of mind would accompany this radically impossible possession? Dreiser offers a hint in Carrie's thought that she would envy other beautiful, affluent women only if they had "more of that peace and beauty which glimmered afar off." What she and other Dreiserian seekers seem to imagine for the end of the journey is a stilling of the pulsations of desire, an enduring serenity of which the experience of beauty in this world would give a (paradoxically unsettling) foretaste. Such an intuition of conclusive repose echoes a number of aesthetic philosophers from Edmund Burke to Stephen Dedalus, who note that the experience of beauty can include a feeling of calm or tranquility, even a melting or relaxing that may or may not complement a more energizing kind of pleasure.

Even apart from this tradition, however, it seems clear that Michaels's sweeping claim—that desire is always the sign of life in *Sister Carrie*—requires qualification. For in making a beauty affiliated with serenity his characters' ultimate wish, Dreiser suggests that their authentic dream is one of escape from the endless cycle of longing—even if, in practice, this very dream of rest perpetuates restlessness. The salience of such a movement toward stilling is eloquently confirmed by the ending of *The Stoic*, on which Dreiser was working at his death in 1945: there, Berenice, who has already followed Carrie in opening her purse to the disadvantaged, seeks through years of Yoga discipline to—as her Guru puts it—"lose the suffering that comes from desire" (312).

It is worth noting, in this regard, that the beauty associated with affluence and culture is not the only kind that works by offering a taste of a serenity it then withholds. The beauty of persons also seems to operate this way in Dreiser's fictions, inasmuch as his male protagonists' serial infatuations all seem propelled by intimations of some perfect relationship shimmering through the charm of each adored but finally inadequate woman. (Cowperwood's attainment of something like perfection with Berenice at the end of the Trilogy of Desire seems the vivid exception that only confirms this rule.) We can also discern a structure of giving and withholding in Dreiserian sexual attraction, which however hot in its transpiring emanates from, and orients itself toward, the cooler precincts of form: "there appeared to be a toxic something in form itself—that of the female of the species where beautiful—that could effect veritable paroxysms of emotion and desire in me, and that over distances of time and space." The Kantian tradition in aesthetics relies on the point that form, unlike matter, resists incorporation; to remain form, it has to retain a certain autonomy and integrity, which means that to speak of beautiful form is always in a sense to mark the gap between the beautiful thing and its beholder. But one does not need this tradition, either, to see that in tracing the power of feminine beauty back to form as such, Dreiser embeds a certain unbridgeable distance, an irremediable block to consummation, in the relation between desirer and desired.

Moreover, it seems that Dreiser saw even natural beauty as working by means of a tantalizing and withdrawing. In an 1896 number of *Ev'ry Month*, he writes, "The 'why' for which we stroll out on a beautiful day is that its beauty is hypnotic and magnetic, draws us on and on, until we cannot rest, but must roam the fields and lanes, and drink in its grandeur. The reason for gazing dreamily into the placid surface of a glassy pool is that it fascinates, and our mind is too weak before its influence to resist" (55). Through the lens of Dreiser's later writings, especially, we can discern among these platitudes an unexpectedly unsettling claim: that our response to natural beauty betokens not intensified consciousness but a kind of dissipation of the will, a mechanical submission to forces beyond our control. The passage thus obviously anticipates the failures of volition that would help make Dreiser's yearning characters recognizably naturalist, but it also looks forward strikingly to the figurative landscape across which Carrie will make her way at the end of her novel. In this passage we have, then, an early and quite concrete exposition of how beauty disquiets through its very adumbrations of placidity.

Before considering what else this *Ev'ry Month* piece reveals, we should no doubt acknowledge that beauty's baiting of its victims with serenity might be understood as yet another figure for the culture of consumption's way of practicing upon its servants. It can certainly be argued, after all, that the ultimate lure of this culture is not wealth or status but a kind of final peacefulness, that the modern individual is driven less by the pleasure to be obtained from possessions or position than by the prospect of relief from the pain of lacking these things. Such a reading would then fit into a broader take on Dreiser, adopted by a number of critics over the years, according to which his relentless exposure of capitalism's dependence on its subjects' discontent did not quite free him of the false consciousness he illuminates—did not enable him to see that he was mistaking a systemically enjoined restlessness for an immutable aspect of the human condition, or that the dissatisfaction engendered by economic arrangements was not merely one of his topics but the great theme of all his work.

However Dreiser himself might have reacted to such an assessment, he would surely have agreed that the largest frame in which he interpreted beauty's elusiveness was that of the human condition—or, more exactly, the cosmic condition. This is well illustrated by the *Ev'ry Month* piece, in which he goes on to suggest that the experience of thralldom before natural beauty actually imparts a certain comfort:

And yet, being human and subject to earthly conditions, what better can we wish for than to be influenced, hypnotized, if you will, by the grandeurs of creation? If we cannot see the beauties of our allotted home without being abjectly controlled by them, what better than to be charmed and fascinated by them—compelled to perceive and to relinquish our self-control to them? It proves that we are influenced by a soul without—that we are not of our own making, but guided and swayed, and seldom injured save by our own folly. (55)

The awareness that we are abjectly controlled, aroused in us by natural beauty, thus offers a certain recompense for that very controlling, in its intimation that the powers moving us are generally benign. This suggestion looks backward to Christian and pantheistic forms of solace that Dreiser largely rejected (though many of his *Ev'ry Month* readers no doubt embraced them), but it also looks forward to an idea increasingly important to him in later years: that some sort of cosmic soul might be expressed in natural laws themselves, which however ambient had also produced marvels of design such as the human being.[15]

In thus placing beauty at the juncture between the unattainable and the immediate, Dreiser seems to be trying to manage, if not exactly to answer, the question that tormented him from his first acceptance of the mechanistic vision to the end of his life: What can it all be for? In the passage at hand, experience of the obvious positivity of beauty (its capacity to give pleasure) combines with a sense of its power over us to suggest that the forces by which we are swayed operate for our good, even if we cannot precisely articulate in what an ultimate goodness would consist. His later writings make clear, however, that such a resolution could not satisfy Dreiser for long. In most of his major work, as we have seen, beauty has much more mixed effects on those it seduces, as though Dreiser remained torn between the urge to find sufficient comfort in the loveliness of the world and an inability to be consoled.

But why so? Other writers of the period, after all, enjoyed notable success in deploying the aesthetic to assuage worries about meaning in human existence. Pater, Wilde, and Joyce were able to conclude with much less wavering that significance must inhere in spirited contemplation of the world as we find it, and similar approaches to the problem of meaning after God inform the work of other modernists such as Wallace Stevens and William Carlos Williams. Why did this kind of solution work so much less effectively for Dreiser?

One reason is indicated by a passage from *Dawn* in which he remembers being fascinated, "in the earliest days of [his] unfolding sensory faculties . . . by strange impressions in connection with them. Life moved before me then as little more than form, sound, color, odor." From such a beginning, a more thoroughly Paterian writer might have gone on to trace the maturing of the sensory faculties in the sensitive soul, but Dreiser heads in a different direction, one more reminiscent of the science-entranced Wilde of the Oxford notebooks:

> I have often wondered as to the primary condition of the energy or force we call life before it proceeds to construct the piece of machinery that is the human body, by which, through which, in which, it is to function and receive experiences from this early state. Sight! What is that? And how comes it to be achieved out of gases, solids, electrons, protons, quantums? And hearing! The ear! How does ultimate energy—atoms, electrons, ergs—go about the work of building an ear? And the senses—touch, smell, the nervous system! And all for what? The very, very temporary enjoyment of such forms, motions, colors, odors, sounds, taste and feelings we find here and so soon leave? And without one word as to the meaning of it all. (11)

For Dreiser, perhaps, nothing so transient as the "very, very temporary enjoyment" of the sensuous could ever supply a firm grounding for human meaning, even were the category of such enjoyment enlarged (as it often was in aestheticism) to admit the deepening of immediate experience in memory and thought.[16] But it was not just its transience that made experience seem to him a less than perfect remedy for existential dilemmas. More fundamentally problematic, this passage suggests, was a kind of bleakness in the idea that the culminating activity of human consciousness—that summit of design achieved over millions of years by the slow processes of the Spencerian universe—is nothing more than a gazing back upon the forces that produced it. As he would write in one of the hundreds of ruminations published posthumously as *Notes on Life*, "Exhibitionism—setting things forth to be seen, one thing materially impressing another—is the eternal law of what we call evolution. All existence is toward more and more of that—the universe mirroring itself to itself" (16).[17] So avowing, Dreiser eliminates the very foundation for Pater's idea that intense perceiving opens a way to freedom and meaning in a mechanistic cosmos. Against Pater's "Natural laws we shall never modify . . . but there is still something in the nobler or less noble attitude with which we watch their fatal combinations," he wonders where the nobility can be if nature's great achievement is mere self-regard, forms coalescing over the ages just to make beholders of form, molecules organizing into complex systems only to permit impressions of motion and color.

Dreiser's quandary on this front was magnified incalculably by his unflinching recognition that aesthetic feeling is itself a phenomenon of physiology. As the *Ev'ry Month* piece indicates, he believed from early on that responsiveness to beauty is hard-wired in the human organism, and he maintained this belief through the later phases of his career. We have seen how in *The "Genius"* Witla finds "the very form of the face" of a lovely girl acting hypnotically upon him and how in *Dawn* Dreiser finds "a toxic something in form itself—that of the female of the species where beautiful." In both cases, an external stimulus initiates a chemical reaction in the body, just as light falling on receptors does in Loeb's investigations and a false homage does in Stephen Dedalus's remark to Cranly. What is unusual about Dreiser's version of this molecular event is that in it formal beauty and erotic allure are one. In other words, just where Stephen Dedalus and others working from a Kantian or Schopenhauerian aesthetics would insist on a disjunction—that is, between the aesthetic and sexual domains—Dreiser locates a charged continuity.

Passages from *Hey-Rub-a-Dub-Dub*, *The Hand of the Potter* ("harmones" excite us "to the m'aning ave beauty an' thim things"), and *An American Tragedy* confirm that Dreiser continued to be occupied by the physiology of responses to beauty, and so does the testimony of biography. On one occasion in the mid-1930s, he appears to have asked his research assistant Esther McCoy to locate a copy of George Santayana's *Sense of Beauty*, instructing her, "See if he interprets beauty mechanistically & give me some exact quotations—if any";[18] a few months later, he had her research the scientific relation of color to the emotions (Zanine 172). In one of the jottings from his *Notes on Life*, he posits that the child admires sun, moon, stars, rippling water, leaves, and grass "automatically, instinctively. Warmth and a bright day comfort you, but no previous instruction on the part of anyone . . . brings that about. The mystical and chemical structure of your body, with the production of which you had nothing to do, brings that about" (64). In another of those notes, he reflects on the "hunger" that leads the artist to "express the beauty and the drama or arrangement which have . . . assailed his internalized sensory equipment and caused that to react—that is to register the beauty or drama or both that is affecting him stimuli-wise. Not only that but he depends upon a relatively sensitive public to verify the accuracy of his reactions. In other words, they too, in a lesser measure maybe, react to the same stimuli that he does, and so automatically verify his" (110). Dreiser then describes "seeing clearly, feeling and understanding and desiring to write what one sees, feels, thinks or registers" as "environmentally compelled reactions" (110).

Such attention to the corporeality of aesthetic response exacerbates the problem of meaning, of course, because it undermines the distinction between mental life and the mechanical operations of natural law. Pater's suggestion that heightened consciousness opens the door to a sense of freedom owes much of its traction, undoubtedly, to a feeling (often stressed by nineteenth-century interpreters of science such as John Tyndall) that there is a radical qualitative difference between subjective experience and the objective material processes that sustain it—that no imaginable mediation can help us make the leap from the modality of nonsentient molecules to that of the mental life such molecules somehow engender. In Wilde, neither physiochemical determinism nor the social determinism that follows from it is terminally worrisome because in a perfectly arranged society the outcome of determinations would be Individualism, experienced as consummate freedom whether or not free according to the most rigorous standards of ontology. For Joyce, aesthetic experience provides an opening for freedom in a world of constraints not only because our ability to reflect on the material world implies a transcending of material forces (as in Pater) but also because such experience offers a respite from the relentless desiring by which our environments and bodies prove their command over us (as in Schopenhauer). Dreiser does see how the feeling for beauty holds out a possibility of transcendence, but because he recurs to the point that this feeling is itself a form of corporeal desire, he is less able to find in it the glimmer of freedom that might ease anxiety about the aimlessness of a universe of blind forces. What emerges is not a proto-Sartrean division between the world governed by natural laws, on the one hand, and the mind that might contemplate those laws, on the other, but rather what we have seen Dreiser calling in *Notes on Life* "[e]xhibitionism . . . the universe mirroring itself to itself."

There was, however, yet one more key reason why Dreiser was less sanguine about aesthetic consolation than Pater, Wilde, and Joyce: his insight that the human organism can be affected as powerfully by a sense of beauty's *absence* from its surroundings as by the enjoyment of its presence. To be sure, Wilde, Ouida, and other aesthetes worried about the dispiriting effects of ugliness, and Stephen Dedalus's great struggle is to achieve a beauty that Dublin does not evidently furnish on its own. Yet the philosophical problems raised by these representations of a more or less remediable lack are clearly less intractable than those posed by Dreiser's interest in the effects (and not just on artists) of the belief that beauty waits just out of reach—that it lies past the next turn on life's road, that it will issue forth upon acquisition of the right property or companion or social position, or (most insidiously) that it thrives in the world of the present but only among other, luckier people. The tale told in the careers of Clyde, Carrie, Hurstwood, and Dreiser's other discontented seekers is indeed that of the human organism in its material environment, as construed with the help of expositors such as Gates, Loeb, and Crile. In Dreiser's version, however, the most consequential stimuli are not those the body receives in plenitude but those it receives insufficiently, those that tease with the prospect of more: "The great create an atmosphere which reacts badly upon the small. . . . A day of it to the untried mind is like opium to the untried body. A craving is set up which, if gratified, shall eternally result in dreams and death."

These points bear significantly, of course, on Dreiser's address to beauty's influence over the young. That he was no less interested than Pater, Wilde, and Joyce in the formative power of the aesthetic is indicated by his early polemics on school architecture, by his fictional renderings of beauty's call to the heart, and by his remembrances of his own youthful response to that call. It is impossible to doubt that he believed young people should have ample aesthetic stimulation. Yet his conviction that beauty operates by withholding rather than satisfying would surely have made it difficult for him to imagine a future truly perfected by means of aesthetically sound juvenile environments. In Pater, Wilde, and Joyce, the soul that responds to beauty is usually a calmer, finer, more lucid soul, but in Dreiser that soul tends to be less settled and more confused. It might be possible to imagine a world where beauty would be so complete as to still the pulsations of longing, but to trust such imagining would surely be, for Dreiser, to succumb to a lure very like the one that leads his characters on.

Moreover, Dreiser would almost certainly have been ambivalent about the virtues of such a world even could he conceive of its materializing. For while the soul unsettled by beauty's teasing may suffer, such a soul may also be more active, more determined, more aggressive—and hence more attractive from a certain point of view. Often outraged by the economic inequality he saw around him (and indeed lived through), Dreiser also admired fervently the entrepreneurial, dominating type represented by speculators like Frank Cowperwood; for him, a world without exploitation seemed an incontestable good, but so did a world in which those able to exploit rose to their appropriate station. This contradiction, never resolved over his many years of writing, is another variant of his more central dilemma anent the nature and direction of the universe: sometimes repelled by the thought of a cosmos built on the constant subjugation of weak entities by strong, he was also captivated by the Spencerian grand narrative in which continuous paring away of the less effective makes for a continuous evolutionary ascent. In other words, he could accept neither a privileging of the desire that seemed to drive organisms endlessly through brutal trials nor a clear dismissal of desire so understood. This essential irresolution clearly sets him apart from Pater, Wilde, and Joyce—who, though more complex in a hundred other ways, do not exhibit so fundamental a conflict in their basic philosophies. And it implies, too, that while Dreiser might have counted as ultimately good the glimmering beauty that draws its creatures on, he could not have been perfectly easy about an encompassing beauty whose consequence would be untroubled peace.

This irresolution can, of course, be traced to aspects of Dreiser's own juvenile environment. Coming of age in a country that worshiped the daring of the businessman and registered less ambivalence than Europe about the ceaseless pursuit of wealth, Dreiser was the less able to separate beauty's allure from the acquisitive impulse, the pursuit of mastery, the drive toward progress as such. But the difference between a United States in love with entrepreneurs and a Europe that often disdained them could not have been the only difference that pertained. After all, in the decades of Dreiser's coming of age there were scores of American aesthetic societies, American treatises on beauty, and American polemics on behalf of art education, all contesting the idea that the beautiful should be subordinated to other ideals.

Perhaps the difference that mattered most in Dreiser's case was a difference of educational milieu. Pater, Wilde, and Joyce were all shaped by university communities in which ideals enjoyed what we might call an intense reality—in which abstractions and categories such as beauty were so consecrated by tradition and daily discourse as to become, in effect, familiar presences. This being so, there could be no disputing beauty's claim to attention, at least not in the age of aestheticism: though upon philosophical reflection or utilitarian calculation it might have to give way to other priorities, it had no need to prove that it was as actual and imperative as the conduct of practical existence. For an American not born among enthusiasts of culture and to a high degree self-educated, however, the aesthetic could hardly have presented so unembarrassed a claim; on the contrary, it would have had to fight for its place among many paths and values. No wonder, then, that beauty installed itself in Dreiser's imagination as an incitement to struggle as well as a promise of repose. For Dreiser, to have disdained such struggle would, in a sense, have been to repudiate his own youth.

## CHAPTER FIVE

# Great House and Super-Cortex

## WEST'S ANCESTRAL ENCLOSURES

For those wrestling with the dangers besetting the young, as we have seen, one benefit of thinking in terms of environment was that it could make the complete safeguarding of juvenile experience appear more nearly possible. Where one might have trouble imagining the entire temporal span of a young person's life kept free from shock, vice, and temptation, one might yet have hopes of maintaining a perfectly secure environment, especially since the examples of home, school, and prison seemed to confirm the achievability of protection when spatially conceived. In chapter 2, we saw Wilde giving this conception some specificity by conjuring aesthetic spaces where stimuli impinging on the young might be orchestrated by careful guardians; yet we also saw how this program would encounter a certain limit in the practical experience of the less affluent and of urbanites of any class. Despite Wilde's insistence that beautiful things could be had without great expense, there were obviously many people still too poor to purge their surroundings of everything not adequately comely. And any city-dwelling young person would confront ugliness unless confined utterly to the home, for (as Ouida tirelessly complained) aesthetic evil lurked in every street. Was there, then, any place in the sublunary world where a child might be enfolded in unbroken loveliness? Was there an actual environment secure enough to resist irruptions of ugliness from without, various enough to stimulate the senses without monotony, and removed enough from the city to neutralize its aesthetic threat?

In the British context, there was at least one kind of place that might be thought to fill the bill: the great country house, also known as the big house or the ancestral house. As a social institution, the great house had been potent for centuries in the British imagination, but it grew especially fraught in the late Victorian, Edwardian, and early Georgian years because it embodied a crisis in the very notion of inherited privilege. A material testament to aristocratic continuity (and, in Ireland, to English colonialism), it could seem, to those interested in democratic reforms, the very incarnation of distributive injustice; for those who worried about the vanishing of old stabilities, however, it could emblematize everything tragically on the verge of passing away. As Raymond Williams points out in *The Country and the City*, ancestral houses became in this period focuses of nostalgia for the limited, the local, and the self-sustaining, even though they had in actuality become embedded in commercial networks extending to the financial city and the imperial periphery beyond.[1] What has not been much remarked of the great house at this time is that it could also function, at least in idea, as a testing ground for the proposition that a beautiful environment will produce a beautiful soul.

One literary site at which something like this testing takes place is "Ancestral Houses," the 1923 poem that opens W. B. Yeats's sequence, *Meditations in Time of Civil War*. In the third of his five stanzas, Yeats approaches the question of what beautiful places do for those raised within them by observing (as had writers of much earlier country-house poems such as Andrew Marvell, in "Upon Appleton House," and John Langhorne, in "The Country Justice")[2] that the hereditary heir of a great estate may retain little of the original builder's character:

> Some violent bitter man, some powerful man
> Called architect and artist in, that they,
> Bitter and violent men, might rear in stone
> The sweetness that all longed for night and day,
> The gentleness none there had ever known;
> But when the master's buried mice can play,
> And maybe the great-grandson of that house,
> For all its bronze and marble, 's but a mouse. (200)

Whether a beautiful place might produce a beautiful soul, Yeats does not yet say, but he does answer—with a negative—the question of whether an impressive place must produce an impressive one. Aristocracy will not necessarily sink into decadence, but it can: maybe the great-grandson will not prove a mouse, but maybe he will.

Yeats continues to ponder the effects of the beautiful estate in the remaining two stanzas. The fourth ends:

> O what if levelled lawns and gravelled ways
> Where slippered Contemplation finds his ease
> And Childhood a delight for every sense,
> But take our greatness with our violence? (201)

The ambiguity of the poem as a whole reposes on the ambiguity of "take" as used here and in the next stanza. Yeats may be suggesting that what seems the softer mode of the present is also permeated by violence ("take" our greatness and violence in the sense of absorbing these qualities), but an implication more in line with stanza three is that beautiful surroundings sap greatness by draining away the violent energies that get things built ("take" in the sense of "remove"). Whatever its faults, however, the estate does exude the sweetness once longed for and does provide a haven for contemplation—contributions of no small moment, perhaps, in a time of civil war.[3]

Notably sharing an initially capitalized "c" with "Contemplation," here, is "Childhood," which like contemplation seems to benefit from (sonically as well as topographically harmonious) "levelled lawns" and "gravelled ways," to thrive where tranquility reigns and the path is smooth and tended. Specifically, childhood finds "a delight for every sense," which is to say that it receives in the aristocratic demesne just what those concerned with the proper development of the faculties had for decades been saying it needs. Some of Yeats's readers might have felt a vibration of his adored Pater in these lines, but one did not have to know "The Child in the House" to believe that children require ample sensory stimulation without excessive distraction: if the point was not popular wisdom when the ancestral houses were raised, it had been pressed often enough by Pestalozzi, Spencer, the object-lesson-promoting Mayos, and other educators to have become so by the end of the nineteenth century. As a counterweight to the image of the great-grandson as mouse, then, Yeats puts into stanza four an economical evocation of what a healthy childhood should be, thereby reinforcing the tension between losses and gains, costs and benefits, that he finds in the great house's complacent splendor.[4]

Yeats was not the only writer to conceive of the country house as an environment whose beauty might have powerful effects. Virginia Woolf conducted an implicit meditation on this possibility, from the late 1920s to the end of her career, in a series of essays on the material circumstances of the artist (*A Room of One's Own* and "The Leaning Tower," for example) that enter into a kind of dialogue with fictions of hereditary estates (*Orlando* and *Between the Acts*). The matter was also taken up in various ways by novelists such as H. G. Wells in *Tono-Bungay*, Aldous Huxley in *Crome Yellow*, Evelyn Waugh in *Brideshead Revisited*, and, though his eponymous property is not a large house, E. M. Forster in *Howards End*. Perhaps the most fascinating address to the question of what the great house nurtures, however, appears in a book published five years prior to "Ancestral Houses," *The Return of the Soldier*. The first and still the best-known novel by the critic, journalist, and fiction writer Rebecca West, *Return* is narrated by a great-house inhabitant who makes the relation between fine surroundings and fine souls an inescapably central theme. It also belongs to an oeuvre that includes a series of fictions in which much is staked on characters' aesthetic sensitivity, as well as several explicit indictments of ancestral house culture, an essayistic attempt to found a theory of art on research into conditioned reflexes, and a defense of patriotism grounded in the human organism's ceaseless struggle with its milieu. In West's body of writing, in other words, we find an unusually complex appearance of that constellation in which aesthetics, psychology, physiology, educational theory, and social analysis meet on the ground of interest in environment, and we will examine this convergence in various ways over the course of this chapter. But let us begin with the plot of *Return*.

In that novel, Chris Baldry, the wealthy master of a great house named Baldry Court, suffers shell shock and amnesia while fighting in Flanders in 1916; he can therefore remember nothing of the years since 1901, when as a youth of twenty-one he had enjoyed a brief romance with a woman of far lower social standing, an innkeeper's daughter named Margaret Allington. Indeed his memory halts precisely at the moment when he and Margaret had consummated their tender, slightly shy, and thoroughly beautiful courtship—a moment soon followed by a quarrel and a series of other events that parted them. In the fifteen years since, Chris has married a fashionable woman of his own class, Kitty, who has presided over a magnificent renovation of Baldry Court with the assistance of the tale's narrator, Chris's cousin Jenny. Sent home to recover from his injury, Chris is appalled to find his house altered and himself married not to Margaret but to a woman he does not know. He demands that Margaret be brought to Baldry Court.

Jenny has already met Margaret, who seems—after years of life in a dreary suburb with a dull husband of roughly her own social level—as weathered as she is unfashionable. Not unreasonably, perhaps, Jenny forecasts heartbreak in Margaret's reunion with her wealthy and handsome former lover, sees in her mind's eye Chris's revulsion and the anguish that will consume Margaret on being rejected. But the actual reunion defies this expectation. Bound by a love so pure that it remains indifferent to externals, Chris and Margaret resume the thread of their romance over weeks during which Kitty rages and frets and Jenny finally sides with true love, delirious happiness, and Margaret. Eventually, however, an expert on mental disorders (located by Kitty) prompts Margaret to the insight that Chris could be brought back to the present were she to confront him with some visible reminder of the tragedy no one has told him about since his return: the death five years before of his little son, Oliver. At first, she and Jenny conspire to withhold the revelation; but after seeing Kitty in her misery, they agree that Margaret must show Chris the belongings of his dead child. In the last paragraphs of the novel, Jenny watches Chris returning from this exhibition, which has restored his memory and ended his happiness, while Kitty exults that he has been cured.

So summarized, *The Return of the Soldier* seems to say very little about aesthetic environments' effects on human development. Its plot—which in its bare bones seems so long on romance and so short on realism—is nothing like that of the bildungsroman, nor does it feature anywhere the intimate experiences of a child or an adolescent. As we have seen, however, novels of this period could say as much about development by disrupting the bildungsroman's familiar progression as by adhering to it, as when *Dorian Gray* unleashes a protagonist who fails to mature, or when *A Portrait of the Artist* counterposes to socialization through experience a kind of experience that bids to negate social determination. *The Return of the Soldier* might be seen as inverting or dismantling the novel of formation in another way, namely, by telling a story in which fifteen years' worth of experience is lost—and this under the pressure of a kind of experience, the traumatic event, whose very intensity forbids its retention in consciousness.

We will return to Chris's loss of experience shortly, but first we will do well to visit in more detail this novel's devotion to interiors and personalities. Just a few pages in, Jenny reflects, as if answering in anticipation the third stanza of "Ancestral Houses," that she and Kitty had proved themselves "worthy of the past generation that had set the old house on this sunny ledge, overhanging and overhung by beauty," by renovating it so splendidly (6). Always, she says, she can send her mind "creeping from room to room like a purring cat"; she can bask

> in the colour that glowed from all our solemnly chosen fabrics with such pure intensity that it seemed to shed warmth like sunshine. Even now, when spending seemed a little disgraceful, I could think of that beauty with nothing but pride. I was sure that we were preserved from the reproach of luxury because we had made a fine place for Chris, one little part of the world that was, so far as surfaces could make it so, good enough for his amazing goodness. (6)

She and Kitty, she continues, have "made happiness inevitable for him," and he has given "innumerable proofs" of their success: sometimes "in the midst of entertaining a great company, he would smile secretly to us, as though he knew we would not cease in our task of refreshing him" (6).

A few paragraphs later, however, Jenny is already beginning to withdraw these assurances. She recalls that as Chris emerged from boyhood, he came to treasure a hope that he would someday have a great adventure, "an experience that would act on his life like alchemy, turning to gold all the dark metals of events," but that this was not to be. On his father's death, he was obliged to take over the family business; then there was the need to provide for Kitty and her expensive tastes; then there was the death of his son (8). As Jenny says, "there wasn't room to swing a revelation in his crowded life," so that what she and Kitty are really doing in "arranging him a gracious life" is "compensat[ing] him for his lack of free adventure" (8). The house thus starts to look like a burden as much as a blessing quite early, and things only get worse as the narrative goes on. For though his kindness prevents him from saying so outright, it is clear that the amnesiac Chris dislikes the remodeled house as much as he dislikes the usurping presences of Kitty and seignorial responsibility. One of his favorite places, a "little room in the south wing with . . . fishing-rods and . . . old books," has disappeared "in the rebuilding, absorbed by the black and white magnificence that is Kitty's bedroom" (25); the one spot on the grounds that retains his affection is the one bearing no "marks of Kitty's genius" (43).

These revelations demand, of course, that Jenny's assessment of what she and Kitty have achieved be reinterpreted. In their additional light, the phrase "so far as surfaces could make it so" suggests falsity rather than mere limitation, Jenny's mental "creeping" from room to room intimates guilt rather than comfort, and it becomes easier to make sense of the (at first faintly jarring) statement that "when Chris rebuilt Baldry Court after his marriage, he handed it over to architects who had not so much the wild eye of the artist as the knowing wink of the manicurist, and between them they massaged the dear old place into matter for innumerable photographs in the illustrated papers" (4). Compounding the unsavoriness of the new Baldry Court is that a return to its responsibilities means for Chris a return to the battlefield: when near the finale Jenny sees him walking away from Margaret with "the soldier's hard tread upon the heel," she reflects that bad as she and Kitty are, "we were yet not the worst circumstances of his return. When we had lifted the yoke of our embraces from his shoulders he would go back to that flooded trench in Flanders under that sky more full of flying death than clouds" (90).

Opposing Baldry Court, the dangers of combat, and Kitty are the sweetness of love, protection from violent death, and Margaret. Of the last, Jenny theorizes,

> What she had done in leading him into this quiet magic circle out of our life, out of the splendid house which was not so much a house as a vast piece of space partitioned off from the universe and decorated partly for beauty and partly to make our privacy more insolent . . . , may be judged from my anguish in being left there alone. . . . [A]t her touch our lives had at last fallen into a pattern; she was the sober thread whose interweaving with our scattered magnificences had somehow achieved the design that otherwise would not appear. Perhaps even her dinginess was part of her generosity, for in order to fit into the pattern one sometimes has to forgo something of one's individual beauty. . . . While her spell endured they could not send him back into the hell of war. This wonderful kind woman held his body as safely as she held his soul. (70–71)

Jenny is careful to stress that however dreamlike Chris's happiness with Margaret may be, it also has an authenticity that his life with Kitty lacks, and that this authenticity is associated with a beauty of depth rather than surface. Indeed she concludes that Chris's return to Margaret—his "choice of what was to him reality out of all the appearances so copiously presented by the world, this adroit recovery of the dropped pearl of beauty"—is "the act of genius" she "had always expected from him" (65).

Yet relentlessly as Jenny returns to the old moral that beauty of spirit need not be accompanied by beauty of person, she never comes close to disavowing the aesthetic or its pleasures. In the passage just quoted, Margaret's "dinginess" does not challenge compositional beauty's validity but completes it, permitting "scattered magnificences" to fall into a "design." Moreover, the novel is filled with expressions of real joy in comely rooms and objects—many of them uttered by Margaret, whose appreciation seems a natural outflowing from her luminous soul. Moved repeatedly by Kitty's elegance and the fine things at Baldry Court, Margaret even maintains her responsiveness through the moment of crisis:

> She followed me upstairs and along the corridors very slowly, like a child paddling in a summer sea; she enjoyed the feeling of the thick carpet underfoot, she looked lingeringly at the pictures on the wall, occasionally she put a finger to touch a vase as if by that she made its preciousness more her own. Her spirit, I could see, was as deeply concerned about Chris as was mine but she had such faith in life that she retained serenity enough to enjoy what beauty she came across during her period of waiting. Even her enjoyment was indirectly generous; when she came into my room the backward fling of her head and her deep "Oh!" recalled to me what I had long forgotten, how fine were its proportions, how clever the grooved arch above the window, how like evening sky my blue curtains. (75–76)

Margaret's feeling for beauty is thus as genuine and ingenuous as a child's, and when she arrives in the late Oliver's nursery her pleasure is, appropriately, aesthetic above all: "She moved forward slowly, tremulous and responsive and pleased, as though the room's loveliness was a gift to her" (83).[5]

West could have written the novel differently, of course, leaving Margaret cold to the call of beautiful things and requiring Jenny to learn that moral excellence can flourish in the absence of aesthetic receptivity. Yet West herself seems to have believed that the two reliably go together, for nearly all of her fictions exhibit a sharp division between admirable characters having a strong feeling for beauty and the less admirable rest of the world. The separation is perhaps most striking in the late, partly autobiographical trilogy of *The Fountain Overflows*, *This Real Night*, and *Cousin Rosamund*, where the disagreeable oldest of three sisters is set apart from her family by her lack of taste, where the possession of artistic gifts differentiates the rest of that family from the bland run of common humanity, and where the moral gulf between a wonderful friend and his odious wife is confirmed by the latter's obtuseness about paintings. But the distinction also surfaces in *The Judge* (1922), in which good characters are attuned to loveliness and bad characters aggressively vulgar; in *Sunflower* (written in the mid-1920s), whose protagonist wonders repeatedly whether a fine soul can live indifferent to its ugly surroundings; and in the nonfictional *Black Lamb and Grey Falcon: A Journey through Yugoslavia* (1941), where West implies that she is able to grasp that country's essence by virtue of her singular sensitivity to the resonances of its costumes, decorations, and works of art. Indeed there may be no modern writer who more consistently associated moral inadequacy with aesthetic insensitivity than West, though this point can be easy to miss because her novels tend not to dwell on large-scale conflicts between artists and philistines.

Some of her nonfiction does treat failures of taste on a superindividual level, however, and *Black Lamb* in particular recurs to a connection between political iniquities and aesthetic impoverishment. Especially noteworthy for our purposes is a passage 950 pages into that long volume in which West uses some reflections on Old Serbia as the springboard for a critique of the great houses of England. "[T]he men and women of Trepcha" in northern Kosovo, she observes, "know better than those above them . . . that it is good for a man to be temperate and precise and to respect the quality of others. But the people who determine the fate of England have not quite learned that lesson; for we are still governed by our great houses" (948). The problem, as West tells it, is that the inhabitants of those ancestral halls have come to care only about the size of their estates, not their beauty—to "exult in the number and magnitude of their rooms" rather than their quality.[6] "It is rarely the harmonious proportions of their homes that please them," she continues,

> and there indeed lies their true destruction. For they have lost their taste, which left them during the nineteenth century. . . . The eye has lost its acuteness because the well-being of the whole organism does not depend on sight or any other of its senses. These people would eat well, if they were blind and deaf and dumb, because the Industrial Revolution and colonial expansion had in the past combined to drop food in their mouths.
>
> Having lost their taste, they lost their souls. . . . [A] quantity of possessions, on the scale that they have learned to enjoy them, can only be the massed result of past achievements. They cannot have any relation to present achievement. Therefore these people turn away from life. (948–49)

As West has it, aesthetic discrimination is no luxury but a faculty supporting raw survival. Care for the quality of things disappears when the "organism" no longer needs to take care of itself, as when industry and empire conspire to provide it food; but such a loss will clearly prove perilous should unearned provision cease or other factors requiring "acuteness" impinge on the organism's existence. West then goes on to remark that in losing their thirst for achievement, the masters of the great houses lost also the "general good sense that often follows from the practice of a craft" (949)—which is to say that if for Wilde those most in need of artisanal occupation were potential juvenile delinquents of the lower orders, for West the people most notably lacking in capacities nurtured by labor are the leaders of the age.

What makes the great houses' fixation on ancestral accomplishments especially hazardous, in West's view, is a late change in political conditions. For though the twentieth century witnessed a dramatic shift in the relative power of nations, the leaders of England remained "in the nineteenth century and could not believe that English authority was not absolute the whole world over, and English capital inviolably safe. This governing class meant death for England, however well scattered Englishmen might serve life" (949–50). Two hundred pages later, near the very close of *Black Lamb*, West effectively completes this thought, writing of those who carried on a "strange propaganda against the Treaty of Versailles,"

> They had lost all sense that it is sometimes necessary to fight for one's life; and many children born in the decade after the Great War can never have heard a word from their parents and teachers which suggested that their country had or could have been actuated by any motive except stupid and credulous jingoism in taking up arms in 1914. The idea of self-preservation was as jealously hidden from the young as the facts of sex had been in earlier ages. Thus England, not a perverse left-wing England . . . but conservative, mediocre England, put itself in a position of insecurity unique in history by raising a generation of young men to whom the idea of defending their nation was repugnant . . . because they could not believe it would in any circumstances be necessary. Since every day Germany and Italy were formulating in more definite and vehement terms that they meant to vanquish and annihilate England, it was amazing that it should have been possible to enclose them in the magic sphere of this illusion. (1122)

West is not referring only to members of the ancestral estate class here, but the strong continuities between this passage and the one just quoted, along with the reference to "conservative, mediocre England," suggest that those she is faulting at this juncture overlap substantially with the heirs to the great houses. Whatever this group's membership, its loss of contact with the present has led, in her view, to a pacifism that the interwar years have shown to be a disastrous practical mistake—as well as a kind of moral error, since to lose the ability to respond to the world's dangers is for West veritably to lose one's soul. West resembles many writers before her in connecting aesthetic sensitivity with virtue, then, but the nature of the connection she draws is surprising, lying as it does in an alertness of the organism to its dangers and a readiness to defend itself against them.

For herself, West required no world wars to highlight the need of such alertness; biography suggests that she perceived the world as essentially replete with threat even before the outbreak of hostilities in 1914. Still, the Great War seems to have offered both a confirmation of her unease and an object on which that anxiety might profitably fix. In her prologue to *Black Lamb*, she states forthrightly that her original motive in undertaking her journey was not interest in Yugoslavia for its own sake, but a desire to address the Balkans' threat to her existence—a threat disclosed to her in the flash of the Archduke Francis Ferdinand's assassination. "I had to admit," she writes, "that I quite simply and flatly knew nothing at all about the south-eastern corner of Europe; and since there proceeds steadily from that place a stream of events which are a source of danger to me, which indeed for four years threatened my safety and during that time deprived me for ever of many benefits, that is to say I know nothing of my own destiny. That is a calamity" (21). Like another plague, peril flows toward West (and the West) from the East; for her, meeting the Balkans and their people means confronting her fate, here conceived (as so often in her work) as an external threat.

It is thus not surprising to find *Return*, the first major fruit of West's reaction to the Great War, dominated by the motif of protective enclosures compromised from without. This compromising begins in the opening pages, when Jenny and Kitty behold with dismay the address on Margaret's visiting card, which denotes a "red suburban stain which fouls the fields three miles nearer London than Harrowweald. One cannot now protect one's environment as one could in the old days" (9). Jenny here reiterates a familiar anxiety about the encroachment of the city upon country preserves: the suburb is a stain, and Margaret at this point seems its emissary—breaking, as Kitty puts it, "into one's nice quiet day" (9). But this irruption of the ugly and common proves only a tatty premonition of more devastating incursions to come. It will shortly be revealed that the violence of war has broken into Chris's psyche, and then his amnesia will break into the tranquility of Baldry Court, carrying with it Margaret as, once again, a human embodiment of rending. Shortly thereafter Jenny's sympathies will reverse, but her taking of Margaret's part will by no means dispel her fears about enclosures' breaching. On the contrary, succeeding pages find her worrying—presciently, as it turns out—about threats to the fortress of forgetfulness Chris and Margaret inhabit. Just before the meeting with the specialist, a lapse in Margaret's usual serenity leads Jenny to think, "I had of late been underestimating the cruelty of the order of things. Lovers are frustrated; children are not begotten that should have had the loveliest life, the pale usurpers of their birth die young. Such a world will not suffer magic circles to endure" (78).

At this point in *Return*, Jenny's take on the magic circle Margaret conjures seems quite unlike West's view of the "magic sphere of illusion" described in *Black Lamb*, where the one is to be treasured, the other is to be reprehended. Yet by the end of the novel, Jenny and Margaret will conclude that the circle of amnesia—beautiful though it is, suitable as it might be in a kinder universe—cannot be maintained. Suffered to remain in forgetfulness, Chris might be happy, but his "delusion" would turn to "senile idiocy," and those on the outside of the charmed enclosure would no longer respect him: "He who was as a flag flying from our tower would become a queer-shaped patch of eccentricity on the countryside, the stately music of his being would become a witless piping in the bushes. He would not be quite a man" (88). And as the contrasting figures of the flying flag and the patch of eccentricity on the countryside imply, this failure of manhood has as much to do with failure to defend the endangered nation as does the sphere of illusion described in *Black Lamb*. To allow Chris to roam the grounds instead of returning to the fight would be to ignore how the country house and the country-as-house exert like claims to protection—to evade the hard fact that both of these nurturing structures themselves require safeguarding from outside threats. This truth of vulnerability, West suggests, is moreover universal: no imagined realm, no wished-for sphere, no notionally delimited environment can be fundamentally secure, for there will always be some outside force bent on breaking the enclosure apart.

In *Black Lamb*, as we have seen, West associates the dangerous circle of illusion not with surrounding by beauty but with a loss of aesthetic sensitivity: the children of the great houses go wrong not because too much refinement has softened them (per Yeats's concern in "Ancestral Houses") but because they have lost the ability to appreciate the loveliness they possess. We might take a moment to notice here that this account likely owes much to West's own positioning outside the globe of affluence. Like Joyce and Dreiser, she grew up in a household with notably artistic members but little money; more, her parents' own childhoods had been marked by economic and social decline. The family of West's pianist mother Isabella Mackenzie had been forced to decamp from its home on the best street in Edinburgh when it was discovered that the lace shop belonging to its widowed matriarch had been fatally mismanaged, and West's father's slippage was even more dramatic. Having spent part of his childhood in an ancestral house that he came to regard "as his natural domain," in the words of West's biographer (Rollyson 18), Charles Fairfield was removed from it by law at the age of twelve, on the death of his father. Cicily Fairfield, who adopted the pen name Rebecca West at the age of nineteen, was evidently made to feel her father's pride in the great house in which he had been raised (Rollyson 23); she was no doubt made aware, too, of the injustice of his disenfranchisement.

Given these precedents, it is not surprising that West sometimes fashioned herself an aesthetic aristocrat debarred from what should naturally be hers (to appreciate), or that she imputed to the actually wealthy an insensitivity that rendered them unworthy of their exquisite possessions. This animus emerges most fascinatingly in a letter to George Bernard Shaw of 1917 or 1918, wherein she extrapolates the truth about Wilde from the case of Charles Fairfield:

> Those Protestant Irish of the governing class who were reared up with the understanding that they had been born kings and that it was their duty to hate the rest of the world, and so acquired a lifelong incapacity for love, are the most beastly of human beings. My father also was a "Dublin snob" and the circumstances of his upbringing {were exactly similar to those} of Wilde, even to the home in Merrion Square, and it has been interesting to me to note how everything you say of Wilde was true of my father. . . . He had the maddening charlatan attitude to art that you complain of in Wilde; he always talked about any piece of art with condescension and an insolent refusal to take the slightest trouble to find out what it was up to, as if it had been a snuff-box his mother had bought for the silver-table in Merrion Square from some improvident Catholic. (*Letters* 38)[7]

West's opinion had softened considerably by 1960: to Wilde's son Vyvyan Holland, she wrote (regarding the obsession with scandal that always threatened to obscure Wilde's literary legacy), "Your poor father. He *also* wrote, didn't he? Sometimes one would never guess it" (*Letters* 357). Two years later, having read Wilde's published correspondence, she told Holland, "He was a sweet and delightful person and the letters show it" (*Letters* 378). In the 1910s, however, the intensity of West's need to separate the aristocracy of art from the world of hereditary privilege was dramatically attested by her attribution of philistinism to the apostle of beauty. And it informed also the writing of *Return*, where the character whose structural relation to beautiful things most resembles West's is finally Margaret, a woman naturally attuned to loveliness but deprived of access to it by circumstances of birth.

Meanwhile, the high-born Kitty's renovation of Baldry Court is an affair of surfaces, even at times vulgarity, and Kitty herself comes to looks more and more spiritually vulgar as the novel progresses. Were Kitty the single representative of her class in *Return*, and were she absolutely insensitive to beauty, the novel could then be taken to dramatize undeviatingly what *Black Lamb* declares to be the case: that in the modern era, those whose suffer the severest dulling of aesthetic feeling are those raised in the handsomest surroundings. Yet Kitty is by no means completely hapless on the aesthetic front, nor is she the only character in the novel who has been born to wealth. Jenny, sensitive to both the loveliness of things and the nuances of human relations, has spent some or all of her youth at Baldry Court (7, 26, 52), and Chris, who has grown up there too, is by Jenny's account as sterling a soul as can be imagined. Given this diversity of result, it may seem that the novel is very far from saying anything decisive about the effects of beautiful surroundings on the maturing being. Nor are matters helped by the absence, apart from a few words about Chris's past, of any tracing of individuals' courses of development. The only child of this house is a dead child, and we will never know for sure what the beauty of the place might or might not have done for him.

Yet if West withholds direct commentary on this front, she also invites her reader to a number of relevant surmises—most notably through references to the nursery at Baldry Court, whose childish furnishings have been preserved even after the death of the young heir and some diagnosis or decision that Kitty can have no more children ("I wish," she says, "Chris wouldn't have it kept as a nursery when there's no chance—" [4]). The first scene of the quite playlike *Return*, which was in fact adapted for the stage in 1928 and for film in 1981, takes place in this nursery, as does the moral climax in which Margaret decides to bring Chris back to the present; and it is from the vantage of this room that Jenny and Kitty watch Chris returning from his meeting with Margaret at the novel's close. In Jenny's telling of the tale of Chris's amnesia, in other words, this chamber dedicated to memory becomes the most important place in Baldry Court, which is to say that the ghost of little Oliver haunts the story even before his summoning by Margaret restores the fifteen years his father had lost.

Lingering in the nursery does not only mean meditating on the child's death, however. It also means recalling the plans and arrangements that were to give him a successful childhood, as when Margaret, brought to the room by Jenny, ponders "all the exquisite devices of our nursery to rivet health and amusement on our reluctant little visitor" (83). The diction here is noteworthy, "rivet" seeming to gesture sardonically to the will to control that had become a staple in thinking about the raising of the young, "exquisite" evoking the attention to detail and aesthetic solicitude that seem to follow from concern with impinging stimuli. In a subsequent question, Margaret gives vent to another familiar anxiety, that pushing children too hard can be dangerous in its own way. "Why did he die! You didn't overtax his brain? He wasn't taught his letters too soon?"— to which Jenny replies, "Oh, no. . . . The only thing that taxed his little brain were the prayers his Scotch nurse taught him and he didn't bother much over them" (84).

By the time she wrote *Return*, West was a single parent herself: her child with H. G. Wells, Anthony Panther West, had been born on 4 August

1914, the day England declared war on Germany. West was not, by any account, an attentive mother in practice, but she does seem to have been up to date in her theories about proper environments for the young. In a 1912 article on the Reports of the Royal Commission on the Divorce Law, she had already written, "Childhood needs rest and placidity more than it wants the benefit of being brought up in a Christian marriage. It is more important that a child's nervous system should not be jaded than that its father should remain with a drunken mother in order to please the Archbishop of York" (*Young* 126). According to her biographer, Carl Rollyson, West was a believer in the Montessori method and placed Anthony in a Montessori school in 1917 (66–67); in a letter from shortly after, she tells a correspondent that Anthony is particularly nice "now that he's been Montessoried" (quoted in Rollyson 69). Rollyson mentions as distinguishing features of Montessori its recognition that children suffer "continual agonies from the frustration of their will to power" and its accordant effort to guide them "to maturity and to a sense of their own power" (67–68), but a feature that might have attracted West no less strongly was its emphasis on the education of the senses, its careful gearing of lessons toward stimuli that would make children more flexible and responsive. This aspect would certainly have jibed well with her tendency to conceive of human existence in terms of organismal adaptation to environment.

But where did she acquire this tendency? A highly likely source was her father. For Charles Fairfield was not only a journalist, an amateur craftsman, an exile from a great estate, and a black-eyed charmer who abandoned his family when Cicily/Rebecca was eight. He was also an ardent disciple of Herbert Spencer, that man of letters who meant so much to Wilde, Dreiser, and possibly Joyce; who put adaptation at the center of his sprawling cosmology; and who, in his own book on education, joined the chorus of proponents of early and various stimulation of the senses. Referring for support to Pestalozzi, whose belief in the importance of sense impressions had been promoted in England since the 1820s, Spencer recommends in *Education: Intellectual, Moral, and Physical* (1861) that deliberate education commence with exposure of infants to objects of various tactile and visible qualities and a range of sounds. "[B]oth temper and health," he certifies, "will be improved by the continual gratification resulting from a due supply of these impressions which every child so greedily assimilates" (82).

That West understood the provision of vivid stimuli to be important in the riveting of health is suggested by the second paragraph of the novel, where Jenny describes herself as lingering to look in at the nursery,

> so full of whiteness and clear colours, so unendurably gay and familiar, which
> is kept in all respects as though there were still a child in the house. It was
> the first lavish day of spring, and the sunlight was pouring through the tall

arched windows and the flowered curtains so brightly that in the old days a
fat fist would certainly have been raised to point out the new translucent
glories of the rose-buds; . . . and it threw dancing beams, that should have
been gravely watched for hours, on the white paint and the blue distempered
walls. (3)

More directly evoked in these lines than Spencer, of course, is another
nineteenth-century writer concerned with the child's molding by sensory experience. Placing the phrase "child in the house" just before Oliver's reactions to light and color, West gestures toward that semifictional
memoir in which Walter Pater recalls how indelible are "the influences
of the sensible things which are tossed and fall and lie about us . . . in
the environment of early childhood"; how our "susceptibilities, the discovery of our powers, manifold experiences . . . belong to this or the
other well-remembered place in the material habitation—that little white
room with the window across which the heavy blossoms could beat so
peevishly in the wind"; and how, "irresistibly, little shapes, voices, accidents—the angle at which the sun in the morning fell on the pillow—
become parts of the great chain wherewith we are bound." The white-
ness, sunlight, colors, and flowers that irradiate "Child" are all here,
which is to say that in *The Return of the Soldier*, as in so many texts of
British modernism, one of the principal literary ghosts is a Paterian one.
In this case, the ghost is Florian Deleal.

Significantly, the grave watching of sunbeams that Oliver might continue to practice had he lived is echoed in a later passage of the novel.
Imagining herself sharing enjoyment of the beginning of spring with
Chris and Margaret, Jenny thinks how Chris would have talked through
large ideas while Margaret "gravely watched the argument from the
shadow of her broad hat to see that it kept true, like a housewife watching
a saucepan of milk lest it should boil over. They were naturally my friends,
these gentle speculative people" (63). The dignity of this grave observation and these gentle people suggests that we should not take too ironi-
cally the pains to rivet health and amusement memorialized by the nursery: duplicating Oliver's watching in Margaret's, West intimates that the
beauties of the fine, sunlit room might have helped make of him another
gentle, speculative soul—perhaps one as loveable as Margaret or Chris.

Yet not a weak soul. As we have seen, West did not hold with the view
that immersion in beauty produces oversoft people (though she did believe
that habituation to unearned luxury could be detrimental); here, she com-
bats this view with the image of a "fat fist . . . raised to point out the new
translucent glories of the rose-buds." Beauty is gestured to in this vision
not by a slender, effete little finger but by the fist of a male child who,
though sickly, was not effeminate—who was, as Margaret will deduce later
on, a "man from the first" (85). In that same climactic scene, Margaret

will praise the nursery in various terms and, under the spell of this admiration, reveal her own great loss. For she too had given birth to a child in 1909 and she too had endured her child's death in 1911. Confronted by the beautiful nursery at Baldry Court, she confesses, "I thought perhaps my baby had left me because I had so little to give him. But if a baby could leave all this—" (85).

If a baby could leave all this: the problem with the nursery turns out to lie not in its beauty but in its inability to keep death at bay. And this means that whether or not West was wise to risk melodrama in giving Margaret a dead child of her own, the device does furnish a certain theoretical benefit. For it allows West to retain the wisdom that lovely surroundings can make a lovelier soul while subordinating this wisdom to a yet more urgent point: that any environment is subject to rupture from without, that indeed it may be fatal to conceive of anything smaller than the whole world as an environment. In *Return*, the nursery and Margaret's home (with its own dead child) become two more of the tale's breached enclosures, joining Baldry Court, Chris's mind, the charmed circle of Margaret's love, and Britain itself.

We noted earlier that though the Great War was not the source of West's obsession with external threat, it would inevitably have enhanced that obsession's credibility. We need now to notice that the War also altered the terms on which the British, and Europeans generally, could conceive of *Bildung*. It did not do so merely by introducing mortality as a vivid subject of rumination, of course: nineteenth-century life and fiction were full of untimely deaths, from Prince Albert on down, or on up, to Dickens's Little Nell. What changed things was rather the War's prizing apart of the whole framework in which the continuities of life had hitherto been placed—a disruption whose difference from nineteenth-century reversals is marked in *Return* precisely by the series of compromised environments, from nursery to nation, that we have just observed. The late Victorians and Edwardians knew that Britain's military and economic competitors were powerful; losses in the Boer War had only heightened alarm on this score; and history suggested that no empire is forever. But the country's long freedom from immediate military peril, along with the evolutionary tenor of nineteenth-century thought, still made plausible the assumption that stable institutions and borders would be the order of the future. Sustained by such a conviction, one might well repose one's hopes for social renovation upon the careful management of juvenile environments. But no scheme of this kind could remain as promising in a nation whose own fate was uncertain.

Moreover, if *Bildung* had to be reconceived after 1914, so too did the bildungsroman. "[W]hen a world enjoys a Hundred Years' Peace (as Polanyi defined European history between 1815 and 1914)," writes Moretti, neutralized spaces—that is, "areas where people may meet without fear under the protection of clear, unchallenged rules"—tend to "increase in number and to occupy a growing portion of social existence: the *Bildungs-roman*, for instance, took place almost entirely within their boundaries— and understandably so, because in such areas individual growth is shel- tered, and easier, and less painful" (239). Again, the central problem treated by the classical bildungsroman was (as Moretti notes, and as read- ers since the age of Goethe were more or less aware) that of how the maturing individual comes to terms with the society into which he or she is born. But what happens when society itself appears in danger of dismantling? This new uncertainty—about what experience could even mean at a time when no life trajectory was exactly probable—is registered in *The Return of the Soldier* as both a loss of life experience (Chris's amne- sia) and a life experience that should have been but never was (Oliver's).

Registering uncertainty is not the same as being uncertain, of course, and like most of West's writings this novel seems strikingly definite on a number of points, among them that failure to admit the dangerousness of the world is the most dangerous of mistakes. Readers gripped by the beauty of Chris and Margaret's romance, or less prone to a sense of unre- mitting threat than West, may read Chris's resumption of his soldier's role as sheer tragedy. But West's other writings, including *Black Lamb*, make clear that for her this return of the soldier is as necessary as it is sad. In a universe whose essence is struggle, magic circles not only will not endure, but should not; lamentable as Chris's return may be for its present misery, it must also be esteemed, from West's point of view, for its action against future disaster. The last two words of the novel, which are uttered by Kitty, are thus less ironic than they may initially seem—or, we might say, less ironic for West herself than for her sorrowing narrator:

> "Is he coming back?"
> "He's coming back."
> "Jenny, Jenny! How does he look?" "Oh . . ." How could I say it? "Every inch a soldier."
> She crept behind me to the window, peered over my shoulder and saw.
> I heard her suck her breath with satisfaction. "He's cured!" she whispered slowly. "He's cured!" (90)

## EXCITATORY COMPLEXES

For the rest of her publishing career, West would hew to her vision of human life as, at its most fundamental, the struggle of the organism against an environment by no means disposed to help it. In the final sec- tion of this chapter, we will see how this vision grounds her most controversial writing, the study of treason that she published in 1947 and updated in 1964, and which contains a defense of patriotism as fascinating as it is dubious. To gain a full sense of what is at stake in the later work, however, we must first stop with a text that falls between *The Return of the Soldier* and *Black Lamb and Grey Falcon*: the 200-page critical essay that West called "The Strange Necessity" and published, along with a few other critical pieces, in a volume of the same name in 1928.

"The Strange Necessity" begins with West exiting Sylvia Beach's famous Paris bookshop on a lovely fall day, wondering why she has been pleased to find a rather bad, sentimental poem in the volume *Pomes Penyeach*, by the author of the undoubted masterpiece *Ulysses*. From there, a train of associations takes her to the question of what art is, that even its poorer specimens should compel her so: "Why could I not give the whole of my psychic energy to Paris, on which autumn was lying like very fine eighteenth-century gilt . . . ? Yet the soul knows best. There must have been something in *Ulysses*, something about James Joyce, the understanding of which was more essential to me than anything of these things. What could it conceivably have been?" (52). And why, when she might have taken a trip to Versailles, which she would have enjoyed very much, did she feel that she must instead visit the Louvres and gaze at a particular portrait by Ingres? "[W]hat," she asks, "is the necessity that is served in me by the contemplation alike of a young man with damp dark curls and a snuff-coloured coat and of a Dublin slut [Joyce's Molly Bloom]? What is the meaning of this mystery of mysteries? Why does art matter? And why does it matter so much? What is this strange necessity?" (58).

West endeavors to answer the question with the help of another text, some of whose insights we have seen alluded to by Morton Prince and Jacques Loeb: Ivan Petrovich Pavlov's *Conditioned Reflexes*, first published in English in 1927. That book, which brought Pavlov international renown, relates an extensive series of experiments in which dogs were presented auditory and visual stimuli at various intervals before and after they were shown food (or before and after a mildly aversive acid solution was placed in their mouths) and in which the intensity of their responses was measured in the drops of saliva they produced. What Pavlov and his team sought to understand was how instinctive learning emerges, which is to say that they attacked from another angle the problem of how environment shapes an organism apart from that organism's conscious direction. As we have seen, nineteenth-century science associated this question with phenomena like suggestibility, instinct, and habit, and indeed Pavlov writes that we recognize conditioned reflexes "in ourselves and in other people or animals under such names as 'education,' 'habits,' and 'training;' [*sic*] and all of these are really nothing more than the results of an

Figure 5.1. Jean Auguste Dominique Ingres, *Portrait of M. Philibert Rivière*, 1805. Courtesy Réunion des Musées Nationaux/Art Resource, New York.

establishment of new nervous connections during the post-natal existence of the organism" (Pavlov 26).

Just a few pages in, Pavlov also writes of being indebted to "the English philosopher, Herbert Spencer" for "the suggestion that instinctive reactions are reflexes" (Pavlov 9). Given West's probable absorption of a good deal of Spencer from her father, it is not surprising that she alludes to this debt when introducing *Conditioned Reflexes* into "The Strange Necessity":

> For about twenty-five years Professor Pavlov and his assistants carried on a
> series of experiments on dogs which were designed to study their condi-

> tioned reflexes, that is to say, to study their reactions to the same kind of
> confusion as life; for a conditioned reflex is an acquired reaction of the
> nervous system to the stimuli which the environment thrusts on it. The
> basis of all behaviour is, of course, the simple reflexes. . . . Professor Pavlov,
> following up a suggestion dropped by Herbert Spencer, identifies reflexes
> . . . that have to do with reactions of the organism as a whole . . . as the
> instincts. . . .
>      . . . [T]hese instincts are fundamental things. They persist in animals that
> have had their brains removed. They are demands ingrained in the flesh.
> (73–74)

Like Pavlov and other writers we have examined, West is much interested
in changes to the organism happening away from the eye of consciousness.
And like them, she approaches the problem in ways that often have relatively little to do with the restricted sense of the unconscious articulated
in Freud. What attracts her notice here is how even an animal without a
cerebral cortex can respond to its circumstances, how the demands of the
flesh are larger than the demands of the brain, let alone the mind.

Yet although "instincts . . . persist in animals that have had their brains
removed," a decorticated animal will not long survive without the assistance of the laboratory. The only stimuli that will still elicit reactions
from it are, in Pavlov's own words, "of an elemental, generalized nature,
and act at a very short range"; in such an animal, Pavlov notes with an
echo of Spencer, "the dynamic equilibrium between the inner forces of
the animal system and the external forces in its environment has become
elemental as compared with the exquisite adaptability of the normal animal, and the simpler balance is obviously inadequate to life" (Pavlov 13).
But what permits the exquisite adaptability of the normal animal in the
real world? How does it acquire the ability to discern which stimuli,
among the torrents continuously bombarding it, bear on its survival?
Pavlov's answer comes via the experimental demonstration that if a stimulus is not positively reinforced by being quickly followed with an object
of interest (such as food), it will eventually cease to elicit a response (such
as salivation). The "animal at first generalizes any definite individual
stimulus of the outer world," but with "repetition the stimulus becomes
more and more specialized as a result of the development of an inhibitory
process (differentiation)" (Pavlov 131). That is, the animal's ability to
select relevant stimuli from the confusing total field—its exquisite discernment—is a result of conditioning.

Yet it is not enough for the animal to be able to filter and select from the
stimuli that assault it: survival requires that its analytical or differentiating
capacity be complemented by a synthetic counterpart. "The nervous system," Pavlov argues, "possesses on the one hand a definite analysing

mechanism, by means of which it selects out of the whole complexity of the environment those units which are of significance, and, on the other hand, a synthesizing mechanism by means of which individual units can be integrated into an excitatory complex" (Pavlov 110). In other words, once the brain has determined which sensations and perceptions are important to the animal's well-being, it synthesizes the stimuli it deems important into stimulatory complexes eliciting behaviors that help the animal to live. For West, this is the essence of Pavlov's research, and it becomes the foundation on which she will build her own theory about the function of art.

West unfolds this theory as follows. First, she speculates that in humans, the excitatory complexes produced by the cortex are themselves so numerous that some further sorting will be required if the organism is to function efficiently in the world. Bringing this speculation together with her reflections on Joyce, Ingres, and company, she then hazards that the artist's work is to perform a *secondary* analysis and synthesis on the complexes the cortex has produced. Art is the product of this additional set of operations, an organization of the complexes generated by the cortex that might be thought of as a kind of external and collective "super-cortex."[8] Art and the cerebral cortex both attempt

> to select out of the whole complexity of the universe these units which are of significance to the organism, and to integrate those units into what excites to further living. Surely the main differences between them are that the cortex keeps its findings within the head and art stores them outside; that the cortex is an individual possession and that art, though the product of individual effort, is virtually the property of as many people as are aware of it; and that art deals with experience from the point where the cortex finishes with it. (127–28)

What does West mean when she says that art helps assemble "what excites to further living"? One explanation will come at the very end of "The Strange Necessity," where she credits art with enhancing our desire to live, but at this point excitement to further living has less to do with the wish to persist than with the ability to do so in a refractory universe. Distantly recalling Vernon Lee and Grant Allen on the adaptive advantage conferred by aesthetic sensitivity, West proposes that the selection and recombination of stimuli performed by art increase our chances of survival: "What the physiologists make lay people like myself see is a progressive resourcefulness of life. . . . On experiencing the extreme coyness and impurity of the universe, on finding that perfect forms of nourishment do not leap forward to offer themselves to the organism but, on the contrary, may often maintain themselves . . . in as inaccessible positions as may be . . . life so arranged matters that the brain made itself" (125–26). And Pavlov's description of the function of this brain expresses just as neatly the "function that must be fulfilled by any work of art" (126).

In *Black Lamb*, as we noted earlier, West represents aesthetic discrimination as so critical to survival that the loss of it in a governing class can imperil an entire nation. We can now see that she had effectively laid out the theory behind this claim in "The Strange Necessity." Upon Pavlov's point that an animal cannot live if it cannot select the most relevant stimuli from the plenum that confronts it, West builds a model in which the work of art helps organisms to survive not only by requiring them to exercise their powers of selection (in decisions of taste) but also by providing particular excitatory complexes—products of the artist's selection and synthesis—that enhance their ability to meet their environments' challenges. Herein lies not only her rationale for according aesthetic sensitivity so much weight in *Black Lamb* but also her basis for insisting, in texts like *The Fountain Overflows*, that artistic people are the ones most firmly grounded in reality, whatever their putative eccentricities may suggest. "Never," she writes toward the close of "The Strange Necessity," "am I a more healthy, sane, non-neurotic animal than when I let art dictate my reactions. . . . [S]o large a part of man's knowledge and control of his environment is derived from the perception and handling of form and colour that any sensitiveness of the nerves which makes him take pleasure in them is of the greatest practical use to him and is bound to be highly developed" (186). Form, color, sensitive nerves, and aesthetic pleasure bring us back to Pater and Wilde, of course. But if for aestheticism the ability to make discriminations means having the chance to live as finely as possible, for West it seems to furnish a crucial edge in the struggle to survive at all.[9]

West also shares with aestheticism an interest in art's connection to developmental transactions that remain obscure to consciousness. In "The Strange Necessity," she quotes Pavlov's observation that the actual process of synthesizing need not occur within "our field of consciousness"—that the product of synthesis may instead enter that field "as a link already formed, seeming to originate spontaneously" (quoted at 83)—and then elaborates in her own voice:

> Mysterious choices appear, manifested in differences of general behaviour, or more subtly and with more amazing significance, differences in sensitivity towards matters in which there is no logical ground for the existence of any such discrimination. One dog will have a marked preference for visual stimuli; another of apparently identical physical characteristics is far more willing to react to auditory stimuli. Fido and Rover are partaking of a mystery of which, further up the table, Cézanne and Beethoven are participants also. (83)

As in Pater and Wilde, consciousness is incapable of discerning all the factors that have conspired to fashion a particular person's nervous apparatus in a particular way, and this is so both because those factors will be numerous beyond counting and because there is much in experience that consciousness does not register even when it occurs. What West adds in "The Strange Necessity" is that the unregistered transactions modifying the apparatus and leading to particular behaviors involve a continuous reinforcement or inhibition of responses to stimuli. The process of conditioning is thus highly evocative of suggestion, and indeed Pavlov argues that his theory helps to explain suggestibility in the hypnotic state. In hypnosis, "activities based on 'imitation' are accentuated and we see revealed the long-submerged reflex which in all of us in childhood forms and develops . . . individual and social behaviour" (Pavlov 406). Suggestion can then be regarded "as the most simple form of a typical conditioned reflex in man. The command of the hypnotist . . . concentrates the excitation in the cortex of the subject . . . in some definite narrow region, at the same time intensifying . . . the inhibition in the rest of the cortex and so abolishing all competing effects of contemporary stimuli and of traces left by previously received ones" (Pavlov 407). The hypnotist seizes control of the conditioning to which we are always subject, in other words, and the behaviors elicited under this seizing (like all behaviors) have their basis in material changes in the brain.[10]

Though Pavlov was interested in the inside of the head in a physiological sense, however, he famously disdained investigation into subjective states: in his view, the science of mind could do without psychology or—what amounts to the same thing—would do well to remake psychology so as to exclude inferences from data not susceptible to objective measurement.[11] This view had important repercussions in the English-speaking world well before publication of the English translation of *Conditioned Reflexes*, because it became one of the axioms of behaviorist theory and practice. In a 1914 brief, behaviorism's leading evangelist, John B. Watson, declared that it is possible to define psychology as the science of behavior "and never go back upon the definition: never to use the terms consciousness, mental states, mind, content, will, imagery, and the like. . . . It can be done in terms of stimulus and response, in terms of habit formation, habit integration, and the like" (*Behavior* 9). Or as he framed matters in 1924: "Behaviorism . . . holds that the subject matter of human psychology is the *behavior or activities of the human being.* Behaviorism claims that 'consciousness' is neither a definable nor a usable concept; that it is merely another word for the 'soul' of more ancient times" (*Behaviorism* 3).

More even than "the subject matter of human psychology" as a discipline was at issue for behaviorism, however. In the publications of Watson and his party, what started out as a delimitation of the parameters of a science's inquiry soon turned into a claim about the very nature of experience. The premise that we can have scientific knowledge only of what stimuli impinge on the organism and what behaviors it performs, not of mental states, modulated with astonishing rapidity into the dogma that nothing originating with the organism is not behavior. Watson's need to bracket consciousness even led him to the extraordinary claim that thought itself is nothing but an internal version of one kind of behavior, namely, speech: "The behaviorist advances the view that *what the psychologists have hitherto called thought is in short nothing but talking to ourselves.* The evidence for this view is admittedly largely theoretical but it is the one theory so far advanced which explains thought in terms of natural science" (*Behaviorism* 191).

It is hardly surprising to find West, who devoted so many words to nuanced renderings of internal life, announcing her opposition to behaviorism pushed so far. At one point in "The Strange Necessity," she explicitly dismisses the view that thinking is "what Dr. John Watson, the apostle of Behaviorism, alleges it to be, a matter of 'tracing paths for action' in the crudest sense" (59); nor would one know from her essay alone that behaviorism and her admired Pavlov enjoyed strong affiliations. Yet West did come close to Watson and company in one respect, as we can see if we turn to her other allusion to behaviorism in "The Strange Necessity." For although that reference falls in the midst of an attempt to defend subjectivity from behaviorist skepticism, the attempt itself leads West to describe consciousness in a way that resonates with behaviorism's questioning of the priority of subjective mental states. It will be worth our while to attend to this description, not only for itself but also because it figures into a larger set of ideas subtending West's most notorious claims about society and the duties of citizens.

Having argued that art resembles Pavlov's experiments (and science in general) in that it too throws light on the conditions of our existence, West goes on to confront something like the doubt engendered by Zola's claim for naturalist scientificity in "The Experimental Novel": is this assertion of likeness between artistic and scientific explorations not undercut by the point that Pavlov's dogs are real while fictional characters are not? If characters are "fantasies," are "just what their authors chose to make them" and therefore not subject to actual testing (99), how can literary art (paradigmatic for all the arts in much of "The Strange Necessity") purport to extract any rigorous truth about the world in which we live?

West begins her answer with a turn to somatic awareness. Clearly, she writes, we each have a "body-consciousness that packs away a great deal of latent information about how we feel when we move, and also gives us a working knowledge of what we can do with our muscles and our nerves and all other physical possessions." Therefore, she reasons, when others make similar movements, we can imagine what it is like to make them even if we cannot quite make them ourselves: the dancer, for example, "has only the same muscles that we have, though hers are in a different state of development. On the foundation of our experience we are able to penetrate imaginatively into the experience of others" (99–100).

If we accept this much, West then observes (and it is here that the second reference to behaviorism appears), we have to acknowledge the probability that we also

> have a mind-consciousness which tells us as fully about other people's minds as our body-consciousness tells us about other people's bodies. It may be objected that although such a mind-consciousness undoubtedly exists whatever the behaviourists may say (for otherwise we would have no knowledge of other people whatever) it acts less powerfully than the body consciousness. . . . But the difference in human beings is probably not so great as we suppose from the surfaces they offer us. . . . The fundamental groundwork of every human being's character lies in its handling of instincts (and these are so purely the product of the relations between the body and the environment that it is not conceivable that organisms having the same sort of bodies should not have the same instincts). (101–102)

A person may, then, use "in fantasy psychological mechanisms which he does not use in real life." And because these mechanisms will be shared by "all other human beings," an artist deploying them will be able to fashion "a guide to the understanding of real people in the real world" that is as sound a guide as "the record of the behaviour of real dogs in a laboratory is to the understanding of real dogs outside a laboratory" (117–18).

In trying to show how art can impart reliable information, then, West comes to privilege an awareness or alertness that is not of the mind but of the body. She does oppose the behaviorists, to be sure, in insisting that we have a mind-consciousness, or what one might call a conscious consciousness; but in making this claim she has not simply come back to the commonsense view that mind-consciousness is our primary vehicle of understanding and any sort of bodily "learning" a weaker or subordinate process. On the contrary: in her formulation, the fundamental or general relation we animals bear to our environments is body-consciousness, of which mind-consciousness is a kind of special case. In this, West performs a certain updating of nineteenth-century representations (Taine, Hamilton, Fechner) in which conscious life appears as a small center of light amid a vast unconscious dark. At the same time, she indicates that what makes it possible for a work of art produced by one person to be of use to another is not a mystical or metaphysical connection between the two but a commonality in bodily construction coupled with a likeness of environment. Together, these make it probable that artist and audience (or two members of an audience) will have a similar complement of conditioned reflexes—in other words, that when exposed to like stimuli they will respond in like fashion.

But if similarity of environment and bodily organization makes for similarity of response between individuals, what are the sources of unlikeness or variation? West names two: *differences* in environment, and the mysterious element of soul. "It may be admitted that every human being is as unique psychically as physically," she writes,

> but that is the result partly of the inevitable unique circumstances of his life (nobody can occupy exactly the same position in the space-time system that he does, and even if he is one of twenty clerks working in a whitewashed room with a steel-framed window he must see the angle of the walls and the chimneys outside as nobody else does), and partly to [*sic*] that mysterious particle of the soul which dictates the fantasy and chooses what the soul shall do. . . . It may be doubted if there is much else working for uniqueness. (101)

In the reference to the twenty clerks, we may hear an echo of Léonce Manouvrier's remark that no two people belong to the same environment, properly speaking, because anyone's milieu can be altered by a single word, gesture, or look. But West clearly cannot make *too* much of such small differences in environment (or of the mysterious particle of soul) lest she imperil her theory of art. The record of a person's experience would have little meaning for anyone else if the differentiating power of small variations in circumstances were too strong.

West will go on to indicate, however, that *large* differences of milieu obtaining between artist and audience nullify much of the benefit of art. Where environment is basically shared, artist and audience will tend to confront the same predicaments, which means that the former's selection and synthesis of stimuli will be of great help to the latter in the struggle against a recalcitrant and dangerous world. Where environments differ, however, the excitatory complexes provided by the work will not be the ones the audience needs. We should therefore not be surprised, West suggests, to find works of art (and cultural forms more generally) doing their meaningful work *within* cultures—among people "living at the same time or within the orbit of the same civilization" (104)—rather than *between* cultures. The antiuniversalism of this theory of art may be disconcerting, but even more so are the further ideas about nation and culture that West took it to sponsor—ideas that furnish, in turn, the forgotten premises of texts much more widely read, and much more controversial, than "The Strange Necessity."

## CULTIVATING TREASON

Perhaps no segment of "The Strange Necessity" is more curious than the fifth of its seven parts. Beginning with Dostoevsky's assertion of, in West's words, "the necessity for every human being to remain embedded, physically and mentally, in the life of the country in which he was born," this section passes quickly into a disquisition on why emigrant groups run to both philistinism and criminality. The "stock that has left its base" deteriorates "compared with the stock that stayed at home"(141), West avers, because a person who has emigrated from a cultural center to some periphery, or who has descended from such emigrants, is deprived of the full assistance of the home culture. The excitatory complexes furnished by the old art or literature or ritual will not reliably assist in the new situation; valid ways of conducting the struggle with environment will have to be devised from scratch. And thus a "man who goes out from his people cannot attain his full growth" (140).

In support of this far-reaching claim, West offers two principal pieces of evidence.[12] One of these is the culture of the Anglo-Irish Ascendancy, her antipathy to which has already been noted. In her telling, the patent weakness of the literary art produced by that group owes something to Anglo-Irish society's convention-bound hostility to aesthetic innovation, but it owes far more to its members' lack of direct connection to the living English tradition. Enjoying such a link, Anglo-Irish authors would not have needed to build everything from the ground up; but conditions being what they have been, writers like Yeats and George Moore seem to know "nothing of life except what they have found out for themselves. Their power of analysing and synthesizing their own experiences is unequalled, but they seem to be cloistered from the knowledge of anybody else's analyses and syntheses" (154). Lucky the artist who has a tradition "formed and offered him," for that tradition will enrich his experience and may be enriched by his work in turn. But if the artist's "own experience relates to a distant and different civilization it will be of no use to him. It will not show him what the ultimate significance of that experience is; it will not show it to him in relation to the experiences of others that impinge on it. He is left isolated; it is no wonder he is panic-stricken" (172).

West's other main piece of evidence, which concerns not artistic inadequacy but criminal behavior, is drawn from the world of Italian and Jewish immigrants to the United States. West may have come to identify these communities with utter lawlessness after a disconcerting encounter, several years earlier, with Chicago bootleggers who "bragged about bribing public officials" (Rollyson 96), but whatever the source of her associations, "The Strange Necessity" presents life within the mafia as typical of immigrant existence generally. "Scarface Capone" and his fellow gangsters, West affirms, have discovered that the "experience of living by merciless murder in perpetual danger of being mercilessly murdered is not one that humanity can endure." But they would "not have needed to learn this for themselves if they had stayed in their own country. In a thousand million ways their country would have taught it to them, from the day they were born." For in Italy, "there would have been a religion for teacher" (159–60).

This may sound off topic at first, but West goes on to explain that religion is in fact a work of art "unsurpassed as an analysis and synthesis of what is the core of a continent's experience" and that a "child brought up within the zone dominated by this work of art, who therefore never hears or reads a word that is not the product of a mind equally dominated by it, must receive an impression of the excitatory complex which is the result of its analysis and synthesis. That must involve a suggestion of the profound undesirability of committing murder" (162–63). Further, Italian folk songs play their part in rendering criminal behavior unappealing, for they tell "by a slant in the time, a sliding of the voice as insolent as the wheel of a shoulder can be, what honest men think of the thief's corpse." Alas, then, "for Jane Addams and Hull House," alas for all attempts to counsel the immigrant poor in moral rectitude. For it

> was not a settlement that Capone and his like needed, it was only a bar of music. That would have broken up the gang, before they were founded. On one condition: that the bar of music [was one] sung and heard by these whose thousand forefathers were used to sing and hear sequences of notes with that same meaning. Then, in a society interpenetrated with knowledge of this common worship and these folk-songs, no man would find himself anywhere which was not stamped with this conviction of the sacredness of life and the disagreeable mortality of the murdered. . . .
>
> . . . A prohibition which is merely a prohibition, which is not a suggestion made by art, exerts no binding force. (166)

Evoking the connection between suggestion and art adumbrated in many of the texts we have visited (and most explicitly discussed by Henri Bergson and Paul Souriau), West here imagines a source of morality that would not depend on the explicit inculcation of morals. How does art dissuade people from (for instance) murder? In West's formulation, it operates through what we have been calling the developmental unconscious, through a subtle penetration that binds in ways no "prohibition" ever manages. Yet this penetration is not quite the contagious effect sometimes represented by Pater and Wilde, in which the touch of beauty renders the soul beautiful. It seems, rather, to depend upon a convergence between the sensuous stealth of aesthetic influence and a certain literary or narrative quality of moral instruction—a process that we can recognize, in the context of the other theories advanced in "The Strange Necessity," as a continuous conditioning. If the traditional Italian song makes its hearer feel that one will suffer if one kills, it does so as an excitatory complex akin to those described in *Conditioned Reflexes*, and by means of a reiteration not unlike the repeated pairings of stimuli Pavlov deployed in his laboratory. In her adaptation of Pavlov, then, West has evolved a theory according to which guidelines for conduct and exemplary narratives do assume a strong role in moral development yet do not require the participation of consciousness as we normally conceive it.

One could, of course, devote a great deal of space to the absurdities and inconsistencies in West's argument—from her failure to acknowledge organized crime's decades-old tenure in Italy to the presumptuousness with which she sites meaningful culture in the metropole; from her neglect of the point that not every immigrant family produced Capones to her hurry, at this late stage in the essay, to identify folk songs and popular Italian Catholicism as typical works of art. A problem that appears particularly telling, however, is that West proves inconsistent on what finally counts as an environment. At one point in section five of "The Strange Necessity," as we have seen, she stakes a great deal on the assertion that the Anglo-Irish are simply not part of the same milieu as the English living in England, yet she later credits Catholicism with distilling "the core of a continent's experience." At the end of the essay, she will again invoke the continental delimitation, insisting that she (of English and Scottish descent, raised in England and Scotland) can benefit fully from the art of the Irish Joyce and the French Ingres because, like them, she is a citizen of Europe. Of herself and Joyce, in particular, she writes:

> We both live in Europe, we have been exposed to the same philosophy, the same physics, the same pictures, the same books, the same music, and, what is fully as important, we have lived all our lives among people who were similarly children of Europe, who were imprinted by a like science and art. Now since we have such similar individualities, and are the subjects of so nearly identical a stream of excitatory complexes acting on our individualities, our experiences are bound to be very much the same.
>
> It is therefore as certain as may be that I have among my experiences one that bears a strong resemblance to James Joyce's experience which made him write *Ulysses*. (180)

As it turns out, West's Europeanness connotes even more than that she shares many experiences with the author of *Ulysses*. For to live in Europe also means to inhabit a place where many people have read *Ulysses* (if not, though West omits this complication, where many people have viewed Ingres's portrait of the young man in the snuff-colored coat):

I have got to live in a world where a large number of people are to varying degrees conditioned by a knowledge of *Ulysses*. I shall not be able to analyse any experience of mine in which they take part unless I can fully comprehend their conditioning in this respect. Moreover, I shall find it easier to analyse my experiences with people who have not read *Ulysses* if I can put my finger on the differences in them which are due to this abstinence. Obviously it is imperative if I am to get on with my biological job of adapting myself to my environment that I should read *Ulysses*: as also that I should contemplate Ingres' portrait of a young man in a snuff-coloured coat. . . . No wonder a human being that cuts itself off from art blunders round the world hitting against things as a decorticated dog blunders round in a laboratory. (180–81)

West's invocation of Europe and tradition in this part of "The Strange Necessity" bears comparison to T. S. Eliot's use of these terms, beginning around the same time, in arguments for the need of an institutional church. In both cases, the notion of a common culture, where "culture" retains a close association with the carefully tended *Bildung* of the individual, looms large in the author's social vision. But where Eliot treats a common culture as both the foundation and the ambition of an ecclesiastical Europe, West's ultimate term is not culture but survival in a hostile universe, the work of organismal adaptation.

"Obviously it is imperative if I am to get on with my biological job of adapting myself to my environment that I should read *Ulysses*": did West truly believe everything she put into "The Strange Necessity"? At times, certainly, the essay can seem driven less by deep conviction than by unchecked ingenuity; over its length, West adduces many more connections between Pavlov and the promptings of Joyce and Ingres on a fine Paris day than have been recounted here, and not all of these fit happily into a single theory. Still, there are several reasons to think that West did, at least at some level, subscribe to most of the ideas she advances. For one thing, her oeuvre is virtually bare of evidence that she enjoyed dissimulation or approved of rhetorical posturing; like most of her fellow British modernists, she maintained a veritably Victorian uprightness on the question of whether one must speak only what one believes. For another, she preserved throughout her career a Spencerian sense that life's essence lies in the struggle of organisms to adapt to their environments, so that for her there would have been neither absurdity nor denigration in justifying art as a biological imperative. For a third, her letters to her publisher suggest that she took the essay and the book that contained it very seriously, even if we allow a fair margin for the need to project integrity in such communications. Introducing the text to Jonathan Cape in December 1927, she wrote, "It begins with a discussion of James Joyce's *Ulysses* which is probably the first estimate to be done neither praying nor vomiting. . . . I go on to discuss what is this 'strange necessity, art'" (*Letters* 98). A few months later, she wrote Cape again: "*The Strange Necessity*—can you see to it that it's treated as a *technical, highbrow* book? Reviewable really as a *book on psychology*" (*Letters* 99).

Whatever her depth of conviction anent other strands of the essay, West clearly thought enough of her theories of cultural environment to make them the (unadvertised) foundation for her subsequent treatments of nationalism, patriotism, and espionage. Published in *The Meaning of Treason* of 1947 and *The New Meaning of Treason* of 1964, these analyses merit our attention in part because they reveal how attunement to human beings' formation by stealthy transactions could end up underwriting a preference—shared by other writers such as W. H. Auden—for what we might call organic juvenile environments (operating obscurely) as against more deliberately arranged juvenile environments (operating, as it might seem, dishonestly). But another reason to take up these inquiries is that they brought West unprecedented notoriety, and in this stand as an unusually widely disseminated legacy of the developmental preoccupations we have been charting throughout this study.

When near the beginning of section five of "The Strange Necessity" West recalls Dostoevsky's exhortation to fidelity to country, she refers in particular to the claim of his character Shatov, in *The Possessed*, that a great nation must "believe that the truth is only to be found in itself alone." There has, West insists, "been piling up all through the later nineteenth and the early twentieth centuries an immense body of evidence" proving that this view is "as sound as Euclid" (139–41); and in *Black Lamb*, begun only a few years later, she would record her discovery of additional testimony on this score. One such piece of evidence she finds in a patriotic recital by two boys at a Kosovo orphanage:

> Here was the nationalism which the intellectuals of my age agreed to consider a vice and the origin of the world's misfortunes. I cannot imagine why. Every human being is of sublime value, because his experience, which must be in some measure unique, gives him a unique view of reality, and the sum of such views should go far to giving us the complete picture of reality, which the human race must attain if it is ever to comprehend its destiny. Therefore every human being must be encouraged to cultivate his consciousness to the fullest degree. It follows that every nation, being an association of human beings who have been drawn together by common experience, has also its unique view of reality, which must contribute to our deliverance, and should therefore be allowed a like encouragement to its consciousness. Let people, then, hold to their own language, their own customs, their own beliefs, even if this inconveniences the tourist. There is not the smallest reason for confounding national-

ism, which is the desire of a people to be itself, with imperialism, which is the desire of a people to prevent other peoples from being themselves. (842–43)

The counterintuitive argument West advances here might be described as a cosmopolitan justification of nationalism, since by its lights "our" deliverance, which seems to mean deliverance of the whole of humanity from the power of an uncooperative universe, depends upon nationalist consciousness. To get a complete picture of human reality, we need to assemble as many individual pictures as possible; from this it follows that we need also as many national pictures as possible.

West's assumption that it is in any instance possible to distill a substantive national "consciousness" is, of course, as questionable as her leap to the claim that a nation therefore has the same "sublime value" as a human being. Perhaps more interestingly problematic, however, is her use of "nationalism" to name something that we would more usually call "culture." West presents "nationalism" not as a project or set of policies requiring active maintenance and having practical consequences for inhabitants of other nation-states, but rather as a perspective emerging from "common experience" in the form of "customs" and "beliefs"—a natural and essentially benign set of attitudes shared by people who live together. But her aim is not exactly to replace the first meaning with the second; it is rather to legitimate nationalism as a program by demanding that it be evaluated as if it were a perspective, the "unique view of reality" held by "every nation, being an association of human beings who have been drawn together by common experience." One might ask, of course, why the boundaries of *nation* should be so privileged—why Europe (or Sussex or Manchester or Mayfair) may not be thought as likely as England to hold a meaningfully singular and unitary view of reality. But West does not go into her reasoning on this point.

She will, however, use this argument from experiential proximity in her defense of patriotism in *The Meaning of Treason*. Many passages from that later book might be cited in this regard, but surely the most illuminating is the seven-page epilogue, wherein West not only gives this defense its fullest exposition but also brings to bear theories about environment and formation that we have seen evolving through her work. In the main part of *Meaning*, West describes the treason trials of two Englishmen who collaborated with the Nazis, interweaving with this reportage speculations on the forces and motives that led them to their actions as well as notes on other traitors of the period. The epilogue then begins as follows:

The trouble about man is twofold. He cannot learn truths which are too complicated; he forgets truths which are too simple.

Today we have forgotten that we live outwards from the centre of a circle and that what is nearest to the centre is most real to us. If a man cut his hand, it hurts him more than if he cut some other man's hand. . . . Even if he spend his whole life in teaching himself that we are all of one body, and that therefore his neighbour's pain is his also, he will still suffer more when his own hand is hurt, for the message then runs straight from his palm and fingers to his brain, travelling at a speed faster than light or sound, which bear the news of others' accidents. Throughout his life it remains true that what is nearest to his body is of greatest interest to his mind. (301)

Similarly, she continues, a baby cared for by a certain woman will "feel a closer concern for her than for other women of her generation," and a man living with a certain woman will come to behave, barring "disagreeable circumstances," as though "there were a complete community of interest between them" (301). And so on up through houses, regions, and countries: "Born and bred in England, he will find it easier to understand the English than the rest of men, not for any mystical reason, but because their language is his, because he is fully acquainted with their customs, and because he is the product of their common history" (302). And thence up further to continents and worlds: "even those who profess the closest familiarity with the next world speak with more robust certainty of this world and seem not to want to leave it" (302).

Yet though a "child knows that what is near is easier for him to handle than what is far," this simple point has been forgotten by many modern people. Why? The blame, says West, belongs to urban intellectuals who lost touch with the "long memory and the omniscient gossip enjoyed by the village" and thus came to ignore "the metabolism of human nature, by which experiences are absorbed into the mind and magically converted into personality" (303). Under the "new and rationalist philosophy" promoted by this group,

> Children were to grow up straight striplings of light, undeformed by repression, unscarred by conflicts, because their parents would hand them over in their earliest years to the care of pedagogic experts. . . . Furthermore—and this was considered as the sanest adjustment of all—the ardours of patriotism were to be abandoned, and replaced by a cool resolution to place one's country on a level with all others in one's affections and to hand it over without concern to the dominion of any other power which could offer it greater material benefits. . . .
>
> But the five senses had evidently not been rightly understood. Such children as were surrendered by their parents to expert treatment, complained against that surrender as if it had been any other kind of abandonment. . . . Nor, as patriotism was discredited, did peace come nearer. Indeed, the certainty of war now arched over the earth like a second sky, inimical to the first. . . . The men who . . . threw the husband and wife into the gas chamber while the children travelled by train to an unknown destination, had themselves been brought up to contemn their own ties of blood. (304–306)

Certainly, West declares, "[a]ll men should have a drop or two of treason
in their veins, if the nations are not to go soft like so many sleepy pears."
Yet it is also miserable to be a traitor. Of those whose stories she has told—
alienated figures who "needed a nation which was also a hearth"—she
remarks in conclusion, "It was sad to see them, chilled to the bones of
their souls, because the intellectual leaders of their time had professed
a philosophy which was scarcely more than a lapse of memory, and had
forgotten, among much else, that a hearth gives out warmth" (306–307).

Once again, West makes a number of troubling moves, among which
the most stunning and pivotal is to assert that those who "threw the husband and wife into the gas chamber" were those most distanced from
patriotism—as if the servants of the Nazi regime had been driven by inter-
nationalist contempt for the fatherland and the family rather than a mur-
derous loyalty to the near and like. *The Meaning of Treason*, along with
the new recognition it helped bring West (she appeared on the cover of
the 8 December 1947 issue of *Time*), is therefore symptomatic of the way
possible lessons about the benefits of internationalism were conspicuously
*not* learned after the Second World War—the prehistory of which could
be chalked up to the naïveté of internationalists and pacifists, the Allies'
conduct of which was energized more by a sense of national insecurity
than by cosmopolitan aspirations, and the aftermath of which saw the
emergence of a new enemy in a Communism with avowedly international-
ist ambitions. The epilogue is especially revealing for us, however, in the
directness with which it deploys environmental determination to justify
patriotism, and in the earnestness with which it connects antipatriotic
impulses to a "new and rationalist philosophy" dictating new methods of
rearing children.

With respect to the first, we might note that West explicitly eschews
"mystical" rationales for patriotism in favor of sociological and biological
ones. On the sociological side, the nub of the matter is just what village
culture well grasps but intellectuals miss: that people close to one are easier
to understand than people speaking other languages, practicing other customs, and steeped in other histories. Out of this easier relation, West implies, loyalty should naturally emerge. On the side of biology, West advances an argument from nature that begins with an opposition between
the hurt in a person's hand and a lifetime of moral self-educating: "Even
if he spend his whole life in teaching himself that . . . his neighbour's pain
is his also, he will still suffer more when his own hand is hurt, for the
message then runs straight from his palm and fingers to his brain." As in
"The Strange Necessity," a claim about how things are with the organism
becomes a claim about how things should stand with a moral being; here,
however, West's circumventing of conscious ethical training in favor of
something more like the material processes of the developmental uncon-

scious is marshaled against a certain exercise of reason itself, epitomized by the "new and rationalist philosophy" of urban intellectuals.

According to West, that dangerous philosophy mandates entrusting children to "pedagogic experts" instead of instinctive parents and calls for a "cool resolution to place one's country on a level with all others" instead of patriotism. And here we come to the second key dimension of the epilogue. For what most immediately links nonparental care of children with internationalism, as this formulation indicates, is that both forswear a more immediate environment apparently provided by nature: both aspire, broadly speaking, to transcend the claims of the flesh. For West, such an effort implies a naive and perilous faith that one (or one's children) will be well cared for by whatever one chooses in preference to this immediate milieu; it also implies a shaking off of the obligation to protect that milieu should it come to require protection (as England and Baldry Court do in *The Return of the Soldier*). Moving by analogical steps from the nurturing mother (herself the second element in a sequence that begins with one's own body) to the circumambient nation, West reinforces the claim that there can be no valid affection for another country by aligning it with the assumption there can be no affection in child rearing by nonparental experts.

In the interwar years, the case for entrusting child rearing to professionals, or to parents so professionalized as scarcely to resemble the parents of yore, was made most stridently by Watson and his fellow behaviorists. But such success as behaviorism enjoyed was short-lived. Never making much headway in Great Britain, behaviorist methods were initially embraced in the United States as a triumph of American ingenuity, only to fall out of favor under the troubled conditions of the 1930s. By the Second World War, they were being denounced as contrary to democratic principles, their American credibility scarcely helped by the Soviet Union's establishment of Pavlovian science as the preeminent, indeed the only approved, psychology of the Communist state.[13] In aligning nonparental child rearing with both internationalism and authoritarianism in *The Meaning of Treason*, then, West was fully in step with mainstream opinion at the time, though as we have seen, she had some years before coupled her rejection of behaviorism to an approbation of the Pavlovian experiments that helped inspire it. In "The Strange Necessity," research into conditioning is valuable because it discloses processes occurring in the messy world as it is, not because it might help revolutionize the nurture of the young.

West's several arguments about children, environment, and national security then attain a culmination of sorts in *The New Meaning of Treason*, where the subject is still betrayal of country but the political affiliations of noteworthy traitors are significantly different. In the 1947 text, those working against the interests of the British government were agents of

Fascist powers, figures whose connection to the antithetical politics of the Left had to be argued with some ingenuity (indeed, some might say, with a certain disingenuousness). By contrast, "The New Phase," as West titles the second section of *The New Meaning*, was dominated by confederates of Communist regimes, whose histories seemed to provide much less tangled confirmation of her views on what happens when children are raised by educated people out of touch with reality.

By way of beginning her indictment in "The New Phase," West observes that while it is "the function of intellectuals to enable society to adapt itself to changing conditions," a "lazy intellectual, or an intellectual who has adopted the vocation with insufficient equipment, can pretend that he is discharging that function simply by attacking the status quo, without giving any indication of what he proposes to substitute for it" (142–43). Sketching next the sources of discontent that motivated figures like Beatrice Webb, Bernard Shaw, and her former lover Wells ("His mother was the housekeeper in a great house, and he knew the agreeable life from which those without property were excluded" [146]), West goes on to charge that the Left saw "nothing in the existing structure of society which did not deserve to be razed to the ground." This being so, the

> condition of these people's children was paradoxical. They were brought up in a state of complete immunity from any form of physical want. . . . The children were, in fact, more fortunate than any groups which had ever existed previously, save certain scattered patricians. . . . Yet they were taught and believed that they were living in the worst of all possible worlds but that they need not despair, as it would be the easiest thing they and their parents ever did to tear it down and make a better one.
>
> The homes where these children were reared were cheerful; Victorian frowstiness had been turned out of doors. The walls were distempered in light colours, the furniture was made of unstained wood. . . . Behind this simplicity there was an ideological complexity. The furnishing annulled the eighteenth and nineteenth centuries; it cancelled the immediate past which had produced the people who were using it. It had gone back to peasant art, because it was held that all that was true and beautiful lay so near the surface that primitive peoples had possessed it completely and it was only our wicked recent civilization which had perversely lost it. (148–49)

West then turns to the polemical "books lying about" the homes of these people, which, she says, were treated as battlefields whereon most traditional values were duly slaughtered. Among the victims, patriotism "was the first to get its dismissal." For it was held "naïve for a man to feel any conviction that his own country was the best, or even as good as any other country; just as it was naïve to believe that the soldier of any foreign army committed atrocities or to doubt that any English soldier or sailor or colonial administrator failed to do so" (149). Thus ludicrously "sealed in fantasy," the children of these homes were at a loss whenever they found themselves in a position other than the easy one of pure opposition. And such minds, "at once fantasy-bound and literal, will turn happily to communism," for "Communism offers a haven to the infantalist" (150–52).

The sealed sphere of fantasy; the adoration of the distant; the aversion to the near; the failure to come to grips with reality and the political immaturity that results: it is not hard to see why these familiar Westian motifs should reappear in the genealogy of the Communist informant. What may seem a bit odder, at first, is her depiction of the homes of the children of the Left, with its distant echo of the "white paint and the blue distempered walls" of the nursery at Baldry Court. A little reflection reveals, however, that these references to "cheerful" habitations, to walls "distempered in light colours," to furniture "made of unstained wood" draw on the same assumptions about the effects of fine surroundings that intensified the pathos of young Oliver's loss—and that like the tale of Oliver, Chris, Margaret, Jenny, and Kitty, they support a moral about the fragility and significance of boundaries.

As West frames matters here, the children of the Left lived in happy homes where nothing could be wanting (the homes were thus very good) yet the motives governing the decoration of these homes were inimical to civilization (the homes were thus very bad). Rebelling against their milieu, the leftist children may be accused of the most heinous ingratitude (the homes represented prosperous, tolerant, cheerful Britain), yet the children also absorbed through the things surrounding them the terrible prejudices of their parents (the homes implanted the anti-British, naively primitivist sentiments of certain intellectuals). The privileged children who became traitorous adults are thus marked by a deep abnormality (all these usually health-inspiring beauties could do nothing for these anomalous souls), and yet they remained enslaved to their parents' fatal doctrines (all those subtly polemical furnishings had too great an effect by far). The note that "[b]ehind this simplicity there was an ideological complexity" thus turns out to fit West's rhetoric as neatly as it does the subject of her discourse. Enlisting the wisdom that domestic furnishings potently shape the growing soul, she is able to argue that the relation between the children of the Left and their environments was at once perfectly explicable as a matter of nature and wholly unnatural in a moral sense.

In West's analysis, the great sin of the children of the Left (in which they were encouraged by their parents) was that of questioning the eminent rightness of what surrounded them—a move of the most willful self-deception because, as any unprejudiced eye could see, those surroundings were gentle and lovely. What West does not allow, of course, is that this questioning could have been predicated not on a blindness to the loveliness of immediate circumstances but on a sense that this loveliness was bought at the price of unsatisfactory conditions for the less fortunate. As a young journalist, West had repeatedly called attention to the position of the poor, repeatedly tried to convince her more or less privileged readers that the privileged should not be counted representative of society as a whole. In this late work, by contrast, she intimates that those who find themselves comfortably settled should endorse the society that has provided for them, whatever it may have dispensed to or withheld from others.

In thus charging the intellectual Left with an essential perversity, West again renders suspect those leaps of imagination by which one might try to understand what happens outside one's own environment. As in the epilogue to *The Meaning of Treason*, one must keep faith with one's immediate milieu because that is what one knows—and, more, because that is what has made one who one is. In *The New Meaning*, this position evolves further, into something like an epistemologically grounded politics: since one cannot know conditions other than one's own, impulses toward social change coming from the comfortable will in all likelihood prove ill-conceived and illegitimate. When those who do not suffer from want set about reorganizing society, they are predicating action on knowledge they cannot have—and, in a sense, taking sides with people they can never be, not having been formed by the same environmental conditions. West's brief of 1964 thus harks back to identity-centered critiques of upper-class Leftists such as George Orwell's *Road to Wigan Pier* and Wyndham Lewis's *Revenge for Love* (both 1937). But it also looks forward to the persistence of a rhetoric, now evidently more vigorous in the United States than in Europe, that encourages the less affluent to respect the rich who remain loyal to wealth while mistrusting those who denounce economic inequality.

In fairness to West, it must be stressed that her animus in this period was directed principally against dreams of outright revolution; it did not extend to liberal social reform, which also requires a leap of imagination across the boundaries of milieu.[14] Nonetheless, we can learn something important from the way her long-nurtured ideas about development get translated into political terms for *The New Meaning of Treason*. Like other writers we have examined, West incorporated into all her programs and theories the assumption that life is a matter of transactions in which the human organism is shaped continuously by the minutest phenomena of its environment. But where this understanding led some of those others to utopian premonitions, briefs for social engineering, or olympian privilegings of the aesthetic, it led her to a defense of parochialism that could in principal sponsor (even if it did not go so far in her own case) a radical closing off to the claims of the distant and unlike, a repudiation of altruism beyond the narrowest of limits. It seems, then, that a vivid sense of developmental environments' power need not lead to any one particular political position, and further that the position to which it does bring one will be determined by more than the intensity of one's faith that environments can be managed. It will also be affected by one's belief in, or skepticism about, the proposition that a person's native environment exerts claims to protection simply because native. And it will depend, too, on whether one holds that the formative power of milieu can be in certain ways inimical to imagination, in certain ways at odds with speculation about what lies outside the environment one has been given.

## CHAPTER SIX

# Growing Up Awry

## AUDEN'S HOTHOUSE PLANTS

Published in the crisis year of 1939, *I Believe: The Personal Philosophies of Certain Eminent Men and Women of Our Time* assembled views about the nature of the world and the desiderata of life from twenty-one intellectual luminaries, including Franz Boas, Pearl Buck, Albert Einstein, Havelock Ellis, Harold Laski, and George Santayana. Though the volume itself is not much remembered, some of the statements that were part of it— E. M. Forster's, for example—continue to be regarded as crucial windows into the thinking of their authors. The poet, critic, and dramatist W. H. Auden begins his credo (which happens to appear first in the book, because contributions are arranged alphabetically by author surname) with the not un-Spencerian assertion that "any thing or creature is good which is . . . using its powers to the fullest extent permitted by its environment and its own nature." He soon goes on to explain that the "history of life on this planet is the history of the ways in which life has gained control over and freedom within its environment" and that the "distinguishing mark of man as an animal is his plastic . . . nature. . . . He has the widest choice of environment, and, in return, changes in environment, either changes in nature or his social life, have the greatest effect on him" (*English* 372–73 / *Prose 1* 477–79 / *I Believe* 3–5).[1]

These sentiments would undoubtedly have been endorsed by another of the contributors to *I Believe*, Rebecca West. The daughter of a disciple of Spencer, West too understood life's essence to lie in a struggle between organism and milieu, as we saw in the previous chapter, and she would surely have concurred with Auden's further point that the plasticity of human beings arises from their brains' unparalleled ability to organize stimuli: "In contrast to his greatest rivals for biological supremacy, the insects, man has a specialised and concentrated central nervous system, and unspecialised peripheral organs, i.e., the stimuli he receives are collected and pooled in one organ. Intelligence and choice can only arise when more than one stimulus is presented at the same time in the same place" (*English* 373 / *Prose 1* 479 / *I Believe* 5). Auden's exposition here notably dovetails with West's rehearsal, in "The Strange Necessity," of a key conclusion from Pavlov: that the functions of that crowning evolutionary development known as the human cerebral cortex are, first, to select from the undifferentiated mass of stimuli bombarding the sense organs those most pertinent to survival and, second, to synthesize the selected stimuli into excitatory complexes that usefully engage the organism as a whole.

In her own *I Believe* entry, West writes of finding "an ultimate value in the efforts of human beings to do more than merely exist, to choose and analyze their experiences and by the findings of that analysis help themselves to further experiences which are of a more pleasurable kind." And she goes on to explain how, in her view, pleasure is worthwhile in itself but also "serves the purpose of furnishing each human soul with access to the avenue along which it can advance farthest toward the comprehension and mastery of life. Pleasure . . . is the sign by which the human organization shows that it is performing a function which it finds appropriate to its means and ends" (322–23). For both writers, choosing is of the utmost centrality to human meaning, but where for West the accent is on pleasure as the sign of a sound choice of experience, for Auden what matters most is the moral freedom signified by a good choice (or, for that matter, a bad choice) of action. Indeed he arrives at the heart of his convictions when he observes that since "voluntary action always turns, with repetition, into habit, morality is only possible in a world which is constantly changing and presenting a fresh series of choices" (*English* 375 / *Prose 1* 481 / *I Believe* 8).

How his *I Believe* statement distills Auden's major concerns (in this period and across his career) will become clearer in the pages that follow. Yet it should be evident even from the few remarks just quoted that Auden offers a distinctive address to a science-engendered question with which we are by now quite familiar: that of how human beings can wield meaningful freedom when their actions are determined by natural laws and the array of influences that make up environment. For Pater and Joyce, as we have seen, the lock of such laws and influences might be subverted, at least in feeling, by keen observation of their ways of working upon us; for Zola and Wilde (as well as Léonce Manouvrier, Jacques Loeb, George Crile, and others), knowledge of the hold of circumstances might be exploited for humanity's benefit through efforts to improve social conditions. For Dreiser, the power of environment might ultimately constrain action but could by the same token furnish exculpation for those driven to unsanctioned courses, while in West, a training of attention on the agon between organism and visibly uncooperative milieu makes that milieu's ability to conform the soul to itself in stealthy ways seem a less pressing concern. Auden's contribution, which might be said to answer determinist anxieties by returning to certain commonsense assumptions about volition, is that the human organism's active response to its environment should be seen not as at odds with free will but as veritably at one with free will—at least in a milieu that changes frequently enough to prevent virtue from declining into the automatism of habit.

This proposal is not without its difficulties, of course, among them that it was no more possible for Auden than for any of the others to disregard the evidence that our deeds, not to say our selves, are in various ways enjoined upon us by our situations. Indeed it was almost certainly *less* possible for Auden to ignore this point than it was for Victorians like Pater, since for decades anthropologists, criminologists, physicians, educators, psychologists, bureaucrats, and even everyday opinion had been urging that a just assessment of responsibility for any action, good or bad, requires appreciation of the circumstances that fashioned its perpetrator. Auden's writings are full of references to the ways juvenile experience shapes the maturing person, and indeed few poets have found more compelling the drama of the developmental unconscious, of that latency in which apparently trivial events in early life have incalculable effects on subsequent growth.

In a poem of 1934, for example, he writes emblematically,

> Certain it became, while we were still incomplete
> There were certain prizes for which we would never compete;
> A choice was killed by every childish illness,
> The boiling tears among the hothouse plants,
> The rigid promise fractured in the garden,
>     And the long aunts. (*English* 153)

Especially noteworthy here is Auden's acknowledgment that one cannot simply select one's path in life from an infinite array of possibilities; on the contrary, he insists, every childhood distress extinguishes another option. In his elegy for Ernst Toller, the Expressionist playwright who committed suicide in 1939, a few years after his expulsion from Nazi Germany, Auden wonders in a similar vein, "What was it, Ernst, that your shadow unwittingly said? / Did the small child see something horrid in the woodshed / Long ago?" (*Collected* 249).[2] In both cases, the implication is that any child—whether nurtured as carefully as a hothouse plant or allowed to wander toward primal horrors—is likely to have experiences leading to later troubling of mind. In both cases, Auden marks the critical moment's power to set a destiny as succinctly as Ellen Key does when she warns that the smallest unkindness can leave lifelong wounds in the child's soul. And in both cases, the reader is encouraged to feel compassion for the victim of psychic injury.

Yet though Auden repeatedly acknowledged the power of circumstances, he also tended—sometimes genially, sometimes harshly—to dismiss the idea that such acknowledgment must affect our ability to hold people accountable for what they do. At an extreme of geniality, we might place a comment of 1962, in which he allows that some situations seem naturally to invite efforts to trace the causes of malfeasance: "If a stranger forges my name to a check, I do not ask if he had an unhappy childhood, I call the police; if a friend does the same thing, I ask myself what can be the matter with him and the matter with me, that he should so violate our friendship" (*Dyer's* 324).[3] At an extreme of antipathy, we might place his 1940 address to the students of Smith College, in which he insists that "when we say, 'I can't be expected to behave well. I had an unhappy childhood,' or 'I can't be expected to work hard. I come from an oppressed class (or a decaying class)' . . . we are every whit the enemies of democracy as those who speak of German science or Fascist justice" (*Prose* 2 68). Like the roughly contemporaneous *Meaning of Treason*, Auden's latter statement recalls the period view that behavioristic approaches to the making of personality are of a piece with totalitarianism; for him, as for many others at this time, strong claims that environmental factors mitigate responsibility could seem the tip of a slippery slope at whose bottom lay legitimation of states' attempts to control their subjects through conditioning.[4]

The tension between awareness of passing experiences' potentially enormous formative consequences and reluctance to give this awareness a lot of weight in evaluating behavior emerges vividly in some notes for an unpublished book that Auden made in 1939. "The neurotic," he writes there, "is someone who draws a false general conclusion from a particular instance. X was once slapped unjustly by his papa and goes through life thinking that the world must always treat him unjustly" (*English* 395 / *Prose* 2 412). At first blush, it may seem that Auden is thoroughly rejecting inquiry into the etiology of personality: X is, after all, wrong in assuming that this single event is predictive of later ones, and Auden's tone discourages us from entertaining too generously any complaint X might tender. Yet the example actually upholds the claim that juvenile incidents can have immense repercussions. The paternal slap *does* lead X to think that the world will treat him unjustly, which means that his father could indeed be said to bear some responsibility for his subsequent attitude, and that our judgment of how much responsibility X bears might depend on our willingness to treat a mistaken generalization as a moral failing.

Auden's *I Believe* statement itself is informed by a kind of tension between acknowledgment that conditions shape behavior and anxiety about the undermining of moral free will that can seem to proceed from such an admission. Shortly after declaring that "morality is only possible in a world which is constantly changing and presenting a fresh series of choices," Auden says that he inclines to a certain optimism, aligned with "belief in some sort of democracy," that "bad environment is the chief cause of badness in individuals, and that the environment can be changed"

(*English* 375 / *Prose 1* 481 / *I Believe* 9). Where the first statement, that moral exercise requires a changing world, might intimate a serious spiritual and ethical peril in efforts to engineer environment, the subsequent profession evokes the high hopes Zola and Loeb reposed on just such engineering. If there is a consistent principle to be drawn from Auden's comments, then, it seems to be that society should be fashioned so as to encourage morally sound choices, but not so perfectly managed that right behavior would cease to *be* a choice.[5]

Whether this position is finally coherent or contradictory, it is clear that the pull of milieu was never far from Auden's mind, and that he never ceased to conceive of the human being as, foundationally, "an organism with certain desires existing in an environment which fails to satisfy them fully" (as he puts it in a statement of 1935 [*English* 342 / *Prose 1* 109]). Neither his return to the Christianity of his parents in late 1939 nor any subsequent events led him to revise this conviction, nor did he ever doubt that juvenile experiences, even the least remembered, could shape potently the grown-up the young person would later become. But where did Auden come by these views?

One source, beyond question, was Freud. Auden was already reading Freud and Jung and intending to become a psychologist in his midteens (Osborne 29; Mendelson *Early* 41; Davenport-Hines 24), and when he became a poet instead, he was received as the voice of a new generation partly on the basis of his apparent readiness to apply psychoanalysis (as well as Marxist analysis) to social problems. It was certainly Freud whom he associated most closely with the recognition that small early events could have lasting psychological impact. "In Memory of Sigmund Freud," perhaps the finest of the great elegies he wrote in 1939 and 1940, finds him describing how, in the warm radiance of that doctor's teaching, lost things are recovered

> as they lie in the grass of our neglect,
>    so many long-forgotten objects
> revealed by his undiscouraged shining
>
> are returned to us and made precious again;
> games we had thought we must drop as we grew up,
>    little noises we dared not laugh at,
>    faces we made when no one was looking. (*Collected* 275)

The alluring but momentarily puzzling syntax of the first four lines giving way to the clarity of three symmetrical noun phrases allotted exactly one line each, this passage itself enacts something like the recovery and making-precious it describes. In this remarkable rendering, it is not only that Freud's process allows a disinterring of what had been hidden; it is also that his insistence on the power of apparently trivial elements of childhood justifies our affection for those elements. We wish such things could be dignified, and Freud sanctions their dignifying on the ground of their latent consequence.

But Freud was not the only figure to whom Auden was indebted for his ideas about the power of experience and environment. Another, as scholars have shown, was the American Homer Lane, who had run reformatories for juvenile offenders in the United States and England and proclaimed that the chief cause of disease and suffering lay in the repression of basic urges. A third was D. H. Lawrence, who unfolded similar theories in his 1922 *Fantasia of the Unconscious.* Surely the earliest source of Auden's interest in the psychic development of the human organism, however, was a person who, in spite of his singular proximity to the poet, has so far received scant attention in Auden scholarship:[6] a distinguished physician who was also the first school medical officer of the city of Birmingham, a lecturer in public health at Birmingham's university, the author of book-length surveys of the history and geography of Birmingham and York, and a translator of volumes on the preservation of antiquities and the prehistoric collections of the Danish national museum. This multiply capable person was the poet's father, George Augustus Auden.

The foregoing list does not even exhaust the elder Auden's accomplishments, which also included, evidently, selfless parenting: in a 1945 piece, Wystan Hugh wrote that his parents "amazed and frightened" him "by their sacrifice of themselves" to him and his siblings, and that as a child he wondered, "How *can* they be so unselfish?" (*Prose 2* 249–50). (W. H.'s biographers agree that the Auden family circle, though not without its tensions, provided the children ample comfort and security.) But the legacy of George Auden most relevant to our concerns here lies in his contributions to publications such as *The Journal of Mental Science* and *The Lancet.* These writings treat a wide variety of topics, from behavioral changes following encephalitis to the madness of Ajax, from infection by tuberculosis to education for the partially deaf, from the effects of plague on social institutions in Europe since antiquity to malnutrition among British schoolchildren. Yet diverse as they are, virtually all can be said to address in some way a social problem that would also greatly interest his poet son: that of how to conceive of personal responsibility—how to separate culpability from disability, how to demarcate the boundary between criminality and illness—given science's ever greater proficiency at tracing actions to causes beyond their performers' control.

As we saw in chapter 1, European and American legal systems were, from the late nineteenth century on, increasingly charged with meting out diagnosis and treatment as well as guilt and punishment: particularly where the offenders were juveniles, verdicts were coming increasingly to focus on questions about which institutions or therapies would likeliest promote a given offender's reform. Experts on pathologies of the young were of course essential to this new aspect of justice, as they were in other convergences of medicine, education, and law such as the use of schools for psychological screening. George Auden's career largely transpired at just such emblematically Foucaultian loci, much of his writing as well as his day-to-day work turning on how knowledge of juvenile function and dysfunction might be deployed in judicial and, more especially, pedagogical theaters. In a review of the 1922–23 annual report of the British Commissioners of Prisons (for the *Journal of Mental Science*), for example, he predicts characteristically that the "[m]edical inspection of all children in elementary schools" and the "provision of opportunities for the ascertainment of actual mental defect" should "be a great aid as a preliminary sifting of those who show neuropathic or psychopathic tendencies" (120).

Elsewhere in the same review, Auden senior insists on the need for careful case-by-case diagnosis (impossible, he complains, without better staffing and funding); on the importance of placing people suffering from mental "abnormalities" in facilities other than prisons; and on the potent role of early events in the formation of adult personality traits. "Much is to be expected," he writes, "from the foundation of psychological clinics, linked up with the school medical service, and the children's courts, for 'the child is the father of the man,' and it is in childhood that the seeds are sown which in later years produce the juvenile offender and delinquent" (120). In a review of the Commissioners' report of the following year, he complements this call for proactive diagnosis with a word on "the importance of probing behind the actual offence for predisposing or determining factors. In England we are . . . forgetful of the fact that juvenile delinquency is but one aspect of a many-facetted [*sic*] problem, and that feeblemindedness, crippledom, neglect, cruelty, and social environment are other factors in the same protean problem of adolescence" (314). This plea clearly chimes with the recommendations of texts like Cyril Burt's *Young Delinquent*, which was published shortly after and which includes George Auden among the experts it cites.

In other articles, the elder Auden would take up at greater length the "predisposing or determining factors" in antisocial behavior, folding together two claims about the etiology of delinquency that might at first seem to sit uneasily with each other. The first is that delinquency is constituted not by any particular action or point of view but by a mismatch between one's own tendencies, whatever they may be, and those that happen to be valued by the society into which one is born. In the most extensive of his articles to appear in *The Journal of Mental Science*, "On Endogenous and Exogenous Factors in Character Formation" (1926), for example, he observes that the "affective tone of our relations with the other members of the social group to which we belong depends upon the degree of coincidence between these relations and the ideal schema which we have constructed for ourselves. . . . [D]elinquency may be but the repercussion of the state of conflict which may arise between the ego-schema and the environmental circumstances in which it is placed" (20–21). In the years in which Auden senior did most of his writing, this kind of point was laid before the general reading public most vividly, perhaps, by anthropological best sellers such as *Coming of Age in Samoa* (Margaret Mead, 1928), *Middletown* (Robert and Helen Lynd, 1929), and *Patterns of Culture* (Ruth Benedict, 1934).[7] But it was also disseminated, as here, by psychologies Freudian and non-Freudian that pitted the prestige of science's impartial eye against any moral system's claim to absolute authority.

George Auden's other key claim about delinquency, however, was that it was not *only* a matter of cultural mismatch. For, he argued, an individual's inability to adapt to social norms will often be found to arise from a physiological problem—specifically, a form of regression in which an evolutionarily prior neural system escapes the control of the evolutionarily later one that normally holds it in check. In a 1925 article on the sequelae of encephalitis lethargica in children, for example, he refers to "a definite causal relationship between the physical conditions induced by the infection and . . . subsequent aberrations of conduct" and observes that these character changes raise the important question "of the relation of volition and moral responsibility to morbid physical states" ("Encephalitis" 649–50).[8] He then goes on to sketch a "theory of the evolution of the nervous system" developed by the psychiatrist W.H.R. Rivers from findings by Henry Head and published in Rivers's 1920 *Instinct and the Unconscious*:

> [T]hese observers . . . have concluded that there are two distinct stages in the evolution of the nervous system, *viz.*, the primitive protopathic stage, with its pronounced affective tone and its resulting "all-or-none" reactions, and the later-developed epicritic stage . . . which enables more complex and discriminative response to stimuli, with corresponding modifications of behaviour. . . . Rivers . . . regarded the ordinary healthy mental state as one of equilibrium between the protopathic instinctive tendencies and the epicritic powers whereby they are controlled. His experience of war neuroses led him to see in these a suppression, or a removal, of the control exercised by the more recently developed epicritic capacities over the primitive protopathic characters. Now the child is primarily, and essentially, an individualist, or to use Lloyd Morgan's phrase, "a self of enjoyment," and it is only as he grows that the ceaseless stream of suggestions of social import raises in him a predisposition towards conduct, which is in conformity with the inhibitions and sanctions of the community in which he dwells. He only gradually becomes, in Aristotle's phrase, a "social animal," and learns to subordinate or suppress his individual wishes and desires in conformity with the demands of his group. . . .

Now, experience in juvenile delinquency teaches that in many of the cases the basic causal factor is a regression to an earlier period of childhood, whereby a mental conflict is solved. There is, in other words, a suppression of epicritic control. (656–57)

In the refractory postencephalitic child, then, behavioral changes can result when the phylogenetically and ontogenetically later epicritic system loses its power to inhibit the earlier protopathic system, which governs cruder, less nuanced reactions of the organism. And so it is with delinquent behavior generally.[9]

Rivers's theory, in which the epicritic system "enables more complex and discriminative response to stimuli," clearly has affinities with the Pavlovian model West adapts in "The Strange Necessity": in both, the mark of advanced evolution is fine-tuning. But Rivers's ideas also percolate through *The Return of the Soldier*, where the cure for Chris Baldry's amnesia involves a confrontation with a painful event from the past. Not only did Rivers put the restoration of repressed narratives at the center of his therapy for shell-shocked soldiers, he also directed the major clinical polemic of *Instinct* against the view that the horror of precipitating events should be kept away from the consciousness of the traumatized (167). Still more germane to our present concerns is that Chris's illness involves, in addition to a loss of memory, a loss of ordinary checks on the pursuit of gratification. With its dramatic privileging of love over responsibility, Chris's amnesia is utterly brazen in its selfishness (even if it is also affectingly beautiful, in Jenny's telling), and thus neatly exemplifies what Rivers and Auden would call a loss of epicritic control. Indeed we might say that Chris's behavior is prevented from being classed as delinquency only by the practical congruence between his environment and his impulses—by the wealth and status that allow him to pursue his desires without immediate impediment.[10]

For Rivers and Auden, what mattered most about epicritic functioning was, precisely, duty to others. Not much attracted by the idea of social conformity for its own sake, they rather saw as the great virtue of mental health its enabling of a governing unselfishness, a socially conscious altruism emblematized by the Victorian and Edwardian ethic of professional service that underwrote their own strikingly productive lives. In *Instinct*, Rivers avers that education ought to consist "in the direction of innate or instinctive tendencies towards an end in harmony with the highest good of the society of which the child is to be an active member" (157), while in a *Lancet* article of 1928 (where he again rehearses Rivers's theories), George Auden writes that "the purpose of our educational efforts is . . . to give, . . . in the words of Plato, 'that education in virtue from youth upwards, which makes a man eagerly pursue the ideal perfection of citizenship and teaches him how rightly to rule and how to obey'" ("Border-lands" 644). Or as the elder Auden put it in a 1931 article on "The Maladjusted Child" (which yet again promotes the epicritic-protopathic model), "if the cohesion and compactness of the society in which" man moves "is to be preserved, he must subordinate his own individual interests and desires to the demands of the community as a whole. In other words, his own individualist outlook must be sublimated to one of altruism" (269).

In stressing the greater phylogenetic age of the protopathic system, Rivers and Auden pére were, of course, grounding morality the more firmly in biology—indicating that sacrifice of one's personal interests for group benefit is the highest of behaviors, evolutionarily speaking. This being so, we might further expect them to align sociability with consciousness and higher reason. Yet it turns out that what they regarded as most forcefully subtending social feeling was not clear thinking but suggestibility, the mysterious phenomenon that held so much educational promise in the view of commentators like Frederic Myers, Boris Sidis, and (less emphatically) Rebecca West, even as it provoked anxiety, in Gustav Le Bon and others, about the manipulability of social bodies such as crowds. Borrowing language from his own earlier encephalitis piece, Auden senior argues in "Endogenous and Exogenous Factors" that

> in the earliest years of his life the child is essentially individualist. . . . But . . . [f]rom the first days of his life the child is subjected to a ceaseless stream of suggestions of social import from his immediate environment, which stamp upon the malleable material of his innate mental make-up an impression which grows ever stronger with his increasing years. It is this suggestibility which gives to environment its supreme significance. . . . Rivers . . . regarded suggestion as essentially a process of the unconscious, "whereby the mind of one member of a group of animals or human beings acts upon another or others unwittingly to produce in both or all a common content, or a content so similar that both or all will act with complete harmony towards some common end." (11–12)

"It is this suggestibility which gives to environment its supreme significance": the sentence furnishes yet further testimony, if we require it, that attention to the workings of the developmental unconscious, to the human organism's molding by manifold scarcely registered experiences, tends to be accompanied by solicitude about environment so named. But the passage as a whole is also important because it points to an empirical and theoretical problem raised for Rivers and Auden senior by suggestibility itself. Having in earlier years helped to conduct psychoanthropological research in the south Pacific, Rivers was sure that "primitives" possessed a group mind, a form of shared consciousness, that people in "advanced" societies did not seem to have. In a chapter of *Instinct* on "Suggestion," he remarks that the social system of the Melanesian "is on a communistic basis, and communistic principles work throughout the whole of his society with a harmony which is only present in certain aspects of the activity of our own society." Of the native crew of a schooner in the Solomon Islands in 1908, he reports particularly (in a passage that, as we will see, W. H. Auden would paraphrase):

> As soon as we announced our intention to go ashore, five of the crew would at once separate from the rest and man the boat; one would go to the steer-oar and the others to the four thwarts. Never once was there any sign of disagreement or doubt which of the ship's company should man the boat, nor was there ever any hesitation who should take the steer-oar. . . . It is possible that there was some understanding by which the members of the crew arranged who should undertake the different kinds of work, but we could discover no evidence whatever of any such arrangement. The harmony seems to have been due to such delicacy of social adjustment that the intention of five of the members of the crew to man the boat and of one to take the steer-oar was at once intuited by the rest. Such an explanation of the harmony is in agreement with many other aspects of the social behaviour of Melanesian or other lowly peoples. . . . (95)

If suggestibility operates more strongly among putatively less evolved human beings than among more evolved ones, so also, it would appear, does cooperation. And there seemed much additional ethnographic evidence that "lowly peoples" more readily subordinate individual impulses to the desiderata of the group.

We might say that what Rivers and George Auden confront here is a problem also confronted by Oscar Wilde in "The Soul of Man under Socialism," Rebecca West in "The Strange Necessity," and Herbert Spencer throughout his massive oeuvre, a conundrum in which the old liberal dilemma of how to balance social concord with individuality gets projected across the evolutionary schemas of the nineteenth century. Complex, beautiful, difficult Individualism, everything seemed to declare, must be higher than subordination to a group mind; yet at the same time it can hardly be thought that altruism is of a lower order of mind than selfishness. Civilized persons are undoubtedly more advanced than highly suggestible primitives; yet the elegant cooperation exhibited by "lowly peoples" would seem to trump cleanly the competition-induced disarray of civilized social relations. How could this contradiction be resolved?

As we have seen, Spencer dealt with it by forecasting that the ultimately evolved man would be the one "who in *spontaneously* fulfilling his own nature, *incidentally* performs the function of a social unit"; in "The Soul of Man under Socialism," Wilde tacitly followed Spencer's lead; and West may be said to have managed the matter by implying that *Ulysses* or a painting by Ingres work upon cosmopolites in much the same way that old Catholic traditions and local folk songs do upon untutored Italian laborers. Rivers, for his part, posited a fork in human history, arguing that where primitive societies (on one tine) are governed by suggestion and intuition, advanced societies (on the other) make use of suggestion and intuition but possess in addition a significant capacity to be guided by intellect and reason.

George Auden largely adopted Rivers's position, writing in the "Endogenous and Exogenous Factors" piece, for instance, that though the relative strength of pulls toward the protopathic-individualist and the epicritic-altruist in each of us "will depend to a large extent upon the nature of the suggestions which pour in upon us from our environment," it will also be affected by "general intellectual capacity," since "the epicritic capacity for forming judgments and for reason . . . will be able to influence either by augmentation or inhibition the social or dis-social trends" (12, 10–11). Nonetheless, these resolutions remain haunted by questions. Ought one really to prize individuality if the telos of evolution is toward a sacrifice of individual satisfactions? Does the high esteem in which duty and altruism are commonly held not indicate that the best and most advanced society will be one in which the group's interests are understood to be paramount? And what would answers on these fronts imply, prescriptively, about the environments in which human beings mature?

## Evolution and Individuation

That George Auden's son Wystan was early interested in such questions, and familiar with his father's approach to them, is attested by one of his first publications, an April 1930 review appearing in no less distinguished a periodical than T. S. Eliot's *Criterion*. Reporting on a book called *Instinct and Intuition: A Study in Mental Duality* by George Binney Dibblee, the twenty-three-year-old W. H. not only writes knowingly of the "Rivers-Head experiments on protopathic and epicritic sensibility" but also presumes to take issue with the interpretation of those experiments favored by his father and the experimenters themselves. "Dual conceptions, of a higher and lower self, of instinct and reason," he writes in his magisterial finale, "are only too apt to lead to the inhibition rather than the development of desires, to their underground survival in immature forms, the cause of disease, crime, and permanent fatigue. The only duality is that between the whole self at different stages of development— e.g. a man before and after a religious conversion. The old life must die in giving birth to the new" (*English* 301–302 / *Prose 1* 7).

For some Audenophiles, this passage will be most compelling for its reference to conversion, which might be taken to anticipate the poet's own return to Anglicanism in late 1939. More significant for our purposes,

however, is that it essentially reverses the theory of development propounded Rivers and promoted by Auden senior. Where George Auden
associated regression with a breakdown of the system that suppresses
selfish impulses, W. H. associates regression with an excess of suppression
that prevents desires from maturing properly. In his formulation, the difficulty arises not when a later, epicritic brain ceases to master an earlier
protopathic one but when desire is stifled and pushed "underground." It
looks very much as though W. H. is here revising some of his father's
principles in light of ideas from D. H. Lawrence and, more especially,
Homer Lane, whose "Doctrine of Original Virtue" held that goodness is
achieved where behavior is free and desire unimpeded (Carpenter 86–87;
see also Davenport-Hines 90–99).[11]

   Yet if W. H. diverges from George Auden on the question of inhibition,
he clearly exceeds his father when it comes to validating progress: by his
lights, it is not only that desires should be allowed to mature but also that
"the old life must die in giving birth to the new." Nor is this the only
instance from his early writing in which W. H. stresses the virtues of forward movement and the necessity of breaking with the past. In a journal
entry of 1929, he takes issue with Freud's construal of eros as an impulse
toward union, concluding, "The real 'life-wish' is the desire for separation, from family, from one's literary predecessors" (*English* 299). And in
the poem beginning "It was Easter as I walked in the public gardens"
(later titled "1929," for its year of composition), he presents the maturation of the "frightened soul" as a matter of painful but necessary severing:

> Moving along the track which is himself,
> He loves what he hopes will last, which gone,
> Begins the difficult work of mourning,
> And as foreign settlers to strange country come,
> By mispronunciation of native words
> And by intermarriage create a new race
> And a new language, so may the soul
> Be weaned at last to independent delight. (*English* 39 / *Selected* 11)

In the vision articulated here, growth may always involve mourning for
what has been lost, but it is not just a weaning-from; it is also a weaning
*to* independent delight—a meeting with some pleasure or desire. That this
delight also counts as a destiny, Auden indicates twice: first, in the image
of the self as a track along which some narrower kind of subjectivity (say,
consciousness as experienced from moment to moment) inexorably
moves; second, in the comparison of the soul's weaning to colonization
of a country already inhabited. Representing the assumption of a mature
identity as a practice of radical exogamy and linguistic creation ("a new
race / And a new language"), this passage thus further confirms Edward
Mendelson's observation that in these years Auden often figured entan-

gling origins in terms of the grip of the maternal or of a familial curse associated with literary forebears (*Early* 42–53).

These figurations of origin also come together in the journal entry on separation from family and literary predecessors, of course, and they seem spectrally to inhabit the first section of "It was Easter," where the poem's meditative speaker refers to "all of those whose death / Is necessary condition of the season's setting forth." The struggle with both maternal and ancestral inhibitions materializes most vividly, however, in two theatrical pieces of this period. One, a charade called *Paid on Both Sides* (written in 1928), reaches it climax when an ancient cycle of violence between two feuding families is perpetuated by the murder of the bridegroom prior to an interclan marriage; the murderer, Seth Shaw, is goaded to the deed by his mother. In *The Ascent of F6*, which Auden wrote with Christopher Isherwood and which premiered with the Birmingham Repertory Theatre in 1938, the mountaineering hero, Michael Ransom, is impelled to a climb of F6 by a yearning to be first, or at least not last, in his mother's love. To his complaint that his twin brother, James, has always received the lion's share of maternal regard, his mother responds by assuring him that he had always been her favorite, James receiving more show of affection only because he resembled the boys' late father, a man unable to "live an hour without applause" (*Plays* 312–13). In the mad finale of the play, James (or a dream-vision of James) is killed at the mountain's crest by a Demon, and when the Demon is revealed to be the boys' mother, Michael too falls dead. In both of these strange dramas, to fail to grow is to remain in thrall to the desires of one's parents; as in the review of Dibblee, the preferable path would be to embrace desires that can (in perfect repudiation of the naturalist assumption that desire signals enslavement to circumstances) authentically be called one's own.

Elsewhere in his writings, the younger Auden would parallel this onto-genetic story of necessary severing with a phylogenetic one.[12] In another journal entry of 1929, for example, he reflects:

> The progress of man seems to be in a direction away from nature. The development of consciousness may be compared with the breaking away of the child from the Oedipus relation. Just as one must be weaned from one's mother, one must be weaned from the Earth Mother (Unconscious?). Along with the growing self-consciousness of man during the last 150 years, as illustrated for example by Dostoevksy, has developed Wordsworthian nature-worship, the nostalgia for the womb of Nature which cannot be re-entered by a consciousness increasingly independent but afraid. Rousseau is a nice example of the two tendencies. (*English* 298)

Those professing regret about the growth of self-consciousness, W. H. is quite certain, are merely afraid of losing hold of mommy; the history of humankind (or rather of "man," in his telling diction) is one in which separation is self-consciousness and self-consciousness is destiny.

These sentiments certainly invite dismissal as a mere projection of post-college anxieties onto a cosmic stage: fresh out of Oxford, looking forward to earning his own wages for the first time, and just beginning to publish, Auden in 1929 was clearly transforming personal imperatives into authoritative generalizations. Yet his statements respond illuminatingly, for all that, to his father's efforts to comprehend the teleology of human development, social and individual. If the elder Auden had to negotiate between a conviction that the group instinct was more advanced than individualism and evidence that "primitive" cultures were governed by a more communal psychology, his son disposed of the problem by placing individualism unequivocally at the summit of evolution. For W. H., there was no need to imagine a bifurcation of epicritic control into suggestion and reason, as Rivers had done. The more individualistic person, or the more individualistic social formation, was simply and plainly the more evolved.

But was cross-cultural comparison on the younger Auden's mind at this point? That it was is confirmed by an article of 1932 in which he sketches the differences between primitive and advanced societies as he understands them. Speculating on the origins of language in an article for Naomi Mitchison's *Outline for Boys and Girls and Their Parents* (an innovative children's encyclopedia designed to teach children to think critically), W. H. asks his reader to imagine a part of a whole beginning to act "as if there were no larger whole." At that point, he explains, "there is a breakdown (e.g. a cancer growth in the body). And this is what has happened to us. At some time or other in human history, when and how we don't know, man became self-conscious; he began to feel, I am I, and you are not I; we are shut inside ourselves and apart from each other. There is no whole but the self" (*English* 303; see also *Prose 1* 13). Auden then goes on to speculate that language arose from the individual's urge to rejoin the group in some way—from a longing "to recover the sense of being as much part of life as the cells in his body are part of him." His principal evidence for this theory is that language is less important for "savage tribes" than for more advanced societies: among primitives, he assures his young readers, news travels "by a sympathy which we, ignorant of its nature and incapable of practising it, call telepathy. Dr. Rivers tells a story of some natives in Melanesia getting into a rowing-boat. There was no discussion as to who should stroke or steer. All found their places, as we should say, by instinct" (*English* 303).[13]

Thus does Auden adapt the passage from *Instinct and the Unconscious* that we encountered earlier. But where for Rivers and George Auden this testimony to primitive unanimity necessitated some refining of the idea that individual sacrifice implies advancement, for WH it merely confirms that higher individuation indicates higher evolution. The younger Auden does allow here, as in "It was Easter," that the breakdown of unity entails pain: it may be compared to a cancer; it makes "man" more "aware of the shortness and uncertainty of the life of the individual"; it leads him to look "round desperately for some means of prolonging" existence, as for example by writing (*English* 306; also *Prose 1* 16). Auden never suggests, however, that a less differentiated social organization or a less acute degree of individual consciousness would be the most desirable condition for human beings, even were it possible for modern societies to recover it.

In fact, this passage's acknowledgment of the suffering entailed by individualized self-consciousness would modulate into a key theme of Auden's writing from the mid-1930s on: that doubt, anxiety, sorrow, and imperfection are privileges of the most advanced species (or the most advanced cultures), and thus best apprehended not as burdens but as gifts or opportunities. In "Our hunting fathers" of 1934, for example, Auden first imagines "our" ancestors pitying the "limits and the lack / Set in" the features of animals, seeing

in the lion's intolerant look,
Behind the quarry's dying glare,
Love raging for the personal glory
That reason's gift would add,
The liberal appetite and the power,
The rightness of a god. . . .

In the second half of the poem, however, evolution's actual course defies this dim prediction of the beasts. The remaining stanza concerns the discovery that love is "by nature suited to / the intricate ways of guilt," not simple mastery, and that love's ambition, now bodied in humans, is not to acquire godly rightness but to "think no thought but ours, / To hunger, work illegally, / And be anonymous" (*English* 151 / *Collected* 122). With extraordinary economy, Auden has managed a three-stage progression, moving first from the protohumanity of animals to the imaginative pity of "our" primitive forebears, then from those ancestors to the still more intriguingly fallible and unsatisfied beings "we" are today. Human love may be guilty and hungry, but this is hardly to the discredit of either human beings or the evolutionary processes that produced them.

Auden makes roughly the same point in the first sonnet of the 1938 sequence "In Time of War." Beginning that poem with two quatrains on prehuman evolution,[14] he then goes on to tell how

finally there came a childish creature
On whom the years could model any feature,
And fake with ease a leopard or a dove;

Who by the lightest wind was changed and shaken,
And looked for truth and was continually mistaken,
And envied his few friends and chose his love.
                    (*English* 251 / see also *Collected* 184)

As in Sartrean existentialism, the human being is the first organism in
whom existence precedes essence ("On whom the years could model any
feature")—and as in Sartre, admiration for this marvel, however admixed
with pity, is unabashed. The human creature can never be satisfied, successful, or even consistent, but the elusiveness of serenity is a small price to
pay for the capacity to choose love and seek truth. Auden is scarcely hum-
bler about humankind in this passage than Alexander Pope was when he
named man the glory, jest, and riddle of the world—or than the authors
of *Biological Foundations of Education* (1931) were when they presented
readers with an evolutionary pyramid (reproduced here) atop which man
stands haloed by "Unprecedented capacities and opportunities" as well as
"Unprecedented obligations and responsibilities."[15]

"Who by the lightest wind was changed and shaken": as in Auden's *I
Believe* entry, the distinguishing mark of the human organism is its unmatched sensitivity to environmental changes, and it is this sensitivity that
permits an identification between the field of our moral choice and the
challenges posed by ever mutable milieux. But for Auden it is not only
that the opportunity to be moral coincides with the acme of evolution. It
is also that struggle with environment is the very motor of development
for individuals as well as species. In a 1935 piece on the relationship between modern psychology and modern art, he lists as an implication of
Freudian theory his own view that "[a]ll change, either progressive or
regressive, is caused by frustration or tension. Had sexual satisfaction been
completely adequate human development could never have occurred"
(*English* 340 / *Prose 1* 102). Sublimation is crucial to progress, in other
words, but it may be that sexual unfulfillment is only one of sundry dissat-
isfactions that make humanity intensely productive and intensely itself.
And indeed in a brief article printed the following year, Auden remarks
that "all intelligent people" are probably "the product of psychological
conflict in childhood, and generally share some neurotic traits. I rather
suspect that if the world consisted solely of the psychologically perfect, we
should still be eating roots in the jungle" (*English* 359).

So saying, Auden clearly echoes experts of previous decades who had
linked neurasthenia to civilization; and like some of those experts, he proposes that the intellectual and the artist be admitted the most advanced
of human types. Elsewhere in the same 1936 essay, he submits that the

artist like every other kind of "highbrow" is self-conscious, i.e., he is all of
the time what everyone is some of the time, a man who is active rather than

Figure 6.1. "Achievement and obligation." From Caldwell, Skinner, and Tietz, *Biological Foundations of Education*, 1931.

passive to his experience. A man struggling for his life in the water, a school-boy evading an imposition, or a cook getting her mistress out of the house is in the widest sense a highbrow. We only think when we are prevented from feeling or acting as we should like. Perfect satisfaction would be complete unconsciousness. (*English* 334 / *Prose 1* 95)

Auden makes this same comparison between the highbrow and the person struggling for life in an earlier piece, from 1933, adding there that the "decisive factor is a conflict between the person and his environment; most of the people who are usually called highbrows had either an unhappy childhood and adolescence or suffer from physical defects" (*English* 317 / *Prose 1* 37–38).[16] If, as the *I Believe* statement has it, the "history of life on this planet is the history of the ways in which life has gained control over and freedom within its environment," then the figure who appears to stand at the ironic, uneasy, self-conscious pinnacle of evolution is the artist or intellectual.

As it happens, Auden could have found something like this view in some of Wilde's writings. Bruce Haley has pointed out that in "The Soul of Man under Socialism," Wilde identifies evolution toward individualism as the law of life and describes art as the most intense mode of individualism the world has known; the logic, as Haley rightly observes, "is clear: if all evolution tends toward individualism, and art is the purest individualism, all evolution tends toward the development of the artist or the aesthetic critic" (222). That Auden's thinking evokes Wilde, who here builds closely upon Spencer, attests yet again to the heaviness with which Spencer's hand lay over discussions of individual, society, and evolution far into the twentieth century. We might notice also that in a Commonplace Book entry a younger Wilde had ventured, well in advance of Rivers and Auden on Melanesian unanimity, that morality arose not from an urge to preserve the individual self but from "what [W. K.] Clifford calls the 'Tribal self': individualism, private property, and a private conscience, as well as the nom. case of the personal pronoun, do not appear till late in all civilizations: it is the Tribal self wh. is the first mainspring of action, and canon of right and wrong: a savage is not only hurt when a man treads on his own foot, but when the foot of the tribe is trodden on" (*Oxford Notebooks* 129–30).[17]

One thing Wilde does not expressly say in "Soul" is that the evolutionarily climactic artist or intellectual may be seen, in immature form, in the unhappy or damaged child. But this was Auden's view, and as we might expect, it led him (at least in the thirties) to a distinct distaste for educational schemes whose principal goal was to produce cheerful, healthy, well-adjusted young people. In his "Letter to Lord Byron" of 1936, he writes:

> I hate the modern trick, to tell the truth,
> > Of straightening out the kinks in the young mind,
> Our passion for the tender plant of youth,
> > Our hatred for all weeds of any kind.
> > Slogans are bad: the best that I can find
> Is this: "Let each child have that's in our care
> As much neurosis as the child can bear."

. . . . . . . . . . .

> Goddess of bossy underlings, Normality!
> What murders are committed in thy name!
> Totalitarian is thy state Reality,
> Reeking of antiseptics and the shame
> Of faces that all look and feel the same.
> (*English* 193 / *Collected* 108)

Auden's own version of georgic suggests that, since neurosis is a kind of health, a child will develop properly only by developing perversely.

Yet this position contains an important subtlety. For in Auden's view, what unacceptably produces "straightening" of "the kinks in the young mind" is not visible strictness or the open application of authority; it is rather education that, in apparent deference to the tenderness of youth's plant, seeks to normalize children in craftier ways. In "Honour," a contribution to Graham Greene's collection of 1934, *The Old School*, Auden writes that by appealing to "loyalty and honour" in the schoolboy

> you can do almost anything you choose, you can suppress the expression of all those emotions, particularly the sexual, which are still undeveloped; like a modern dictator you can defeat almost any proposition from other parts of the psyche, but if you do, if you deny these other emotions their expression and development . . . they will not only never grow up, but they will go backward, for human nature cannot stay still; they will, like all things that are shut up, go bad on you. (*English* 325 / *Prose 1* 59)

As usual, Auden reiterates his father's warnings about regression while reversing him on regression's cause: for W. H. the danger lies in a repression of desire, not a failure of repression. The twist here is that what most efficaciously represses desire is a system that seems on the face of things to be less repressive. By Auden's lights, innovations designed to minimize visible coercion are more coercive than anything they are meant to supersede. And not the least of the bad results of such veiled manipulation is that it inhibits germination of the most advanced kind of child: the neurotic protoartist, the abnormal intellectual-to-be.

So avowing, Auden effectively puts himself at odds with a whole line of educational theory that had emphasized artful manipulation over open conflict—a line whose fountainhead was Rousseau and which included most of those we have seen advocating beautiful environments for the young. For Auden, it does not matter whether proponents of such programs want the child to have actual freedom or merely the illusion thereof; in either case, the invisibility of direction deprives the growing being of struggle with its environment, and hence threatens to eliminate the neurosis needed to form an artistic and independent-minded adult. What we encounter with Auden, then, is an important reversal of an alignment presumed by Ruskin, Downing, Dallas, Bergson, the Pater of "The Child in the House," the Wilde of the American lectures, and the West of sections of "The Strange Necessity." For all of these commentators, stealthy influences on development line up on the same side as aesthetic sensitivity, so to speak, since subtlety and mystery are of the very essence of aesthetic transactions. In Auden's scheme, by contrast, artisticness grows out of friction with milieu rather than smoothness, which suggests that faith in beautiful environments' ability to engender artistic personalities might be misplaced.

Yet it is not quite the case that in Auden an *unbeautiful* environment makes an artistic soul. It is rather that "beauty," with its connotations of gentleness and ease, appears to have fallen out of the picture, to have ceased to stand as the inevitable companion to "art." And this is hardly surprising, given that Auden was born a decade and a half after the youngest of our other focal authors (Rebecca West). Coming of age as a writer in the later 1920s, he was shaped by modernism's transvaluation of aesthetic values as none of the others could have been, not even those, such as Joyce, who had helped to activate that metamorphosis. The changes in conceptions of artistic worth that accelerated dramatically in the 1910s and early 1920s made studiously current intellectuals of later years much less likely to think of art as harnessed inevitably to something so positive, so agreeable, so adaptable to banal imperatives of spiritual uplift as beauty. And this effect was undoubtedly compounded, with respect to beautiful environments specifically, by the Great War, which had revealed a world so profoundly riven that aspiring to consonance with one's surroundings could only seem perverse in a damaging rather than a liberating sense.

Auden certainly has little to say in his writings about how physically beautiful circumstances might assist in the production of artists and intellectuals. In "Honour," which is partly a memoir, he remarks in passing that the "first condition for a successful school is a beautiful situation and in that respect we were at Holt very fortunate" (*English* 322), but loveliness of scene is not a major term in his lexicon early or late, and references to the subtle ministries of beauty in his oeuvre are notably few. Indeed he seems in most of his writings through the middle 1940s to resist conceiving of causally significant "environment" in other than social terms, even to the point of mistrusting those whose attention conspicuously veers from human circumstances to the nonhuman world. In a brief on Romanticism from his 1938 introduction to the *Oxford Book of Light Verse*, he argues that Wordsworth professed to adopt the goal of writing "in the language really used by men" but often failed to do so because he was, in truth, "a person who early in life had an intense experience or series of experiences about inanimate nature, which he spent the rest of his poetical life trying to describe. He was not really interested in farm-labourers or any one else for themselves, but only in so far as they helped to explain this vision, and his own relation to it" (*English* 366 / *Prose 1* 433–34).

Nine years earlier, Auden had associated "Wordsworthian nature-worship" with resistance to humanity's progress; now, he charges Wordsworth with mistaking worship of (his own experience of) nature for an interest in people who live close to it. We are certainly very far, here, from Pater's assertion that what was modern and important about Wordsworth was his "intimate consciousness of the expression of natural things," his "quiet, habitual observation of inanimate, or imperfectly animate, existence." Nor is Wordsworth's case unique, according to Auden: on the contrary, it is "paralleled by the history of most of the Romantic poets, both of his day and the century following. Isolated in a society with no real communal ties . . . they turned away from the life of their time to the contemplation of their own emotions and the creation of imaginary worlds" (*English* 366 / *Prose 1* 434).

The implication, of course, is that it is much better to turn toward the life of one's time, as Auden and many others were then doing in their own writing. Nor, of course, was Auden the only critic to take this line in the late twenties and the thirties: his views are of a piece with those of Edmund Wilson in *Axel's Castle* and scores of others who believed that literary art's immediate future demanded a reawakening to engagement with sociopolitical reality. If Auden's artistic sympathies began to coalesce in the immediate wake of modernism's loosening of the hold of beauty, that is to say, they started to solidify in earnest at a time when nonsocial explanations of human phenomena were especially suspect—a time when, as the defense counsel in 1939's "Public v. the Late Mr. William Butler Yeats" frames it, "liberal capitalist democracy" was expected to answer at last for its denial of "the social nature of personality" (*English* 392). Further, if the age was less than perfectly hospitable to Wordsworth's claims for the saving power of nature, it was hardly more so to aestheticism's claims for the saving power of beautiful things. From the regnant perspective of *l'entre deux guerres*, nature and works of art or craft might have significant effects, but it was surely more profitable to consider how these effects were socially mediated than to speculate, Pater-fashion, about purely formal or chemical transactions between mind and material world.

Such loyalty to the claims of the social is especially well illustrated in a remark made by Caliban in *The Sea and the Mirror*, the 1944 text that Auden called a "commentary" on *The Tempest* but which also represents his most sustained engagement with aestheticism. Auden's Caliban, who functions as a principle of immediate life or reality complementing the Ariel of the imagination (and who seems adapted from the Caliban of Wilde's preface to *Dorian Gray*), claims to know the secrets of the aspiring artist, telling that notoriously uneasy type, "Lying awake at night in your single bed you are conscious of a power by which you will survive the wallpaper of your boardinghouse or the expensive bourgeois horrors of your home" (*Collected* 431). In the bon mot from Wilde's lecture tour with which this book began, fraudulent wallpaper encourages juvenile delinquency by appearing to endorse fraud, but Auden's Caliban foregrounds how aesthetic pain is, at least partly, a matter of class coding—how furnishings can affect the spirit not by exhibiting formal goodness or badness but by playing upon anxieties of position and identity. He distantly anticipates, in other words, Pierre Bourdieu's sociology of the aesthetic, offering (to borrow the subtitle of Bourdieu's celebrated *Distinction*) a certain social critique of the judgment of taste.

Auden might, then, be said to reject Wordsworth in two ways: first, by dismissing as regressive nostalgia that poet's occupation with nature; second, by meeting with skepticism one of Wordsworth's legacies to aestheticism, his celebration of the benevolently shaping power of the physical world. It may therefore seem surprising that in his long, meditative, Augustan poem of 1940, "New Year Letter," Auden casts the relationship between self and environment in terms that evoke very closely the Wordsworthian learning of lessons from natural forms. "Whenever I begin to think / About the human creature we / Must nurse to sense and decency," he reveals, "An English area comes to mind." Observing initially that the "limestone moors that stretch from BROUGH / To HEXHAM and the ROMAN WALL" stand for him as the "symbol of us all," he soon waxes recollective and yet more personal:

> There
> In ROOKHOPE I was first aware
> Of Self and Not-self, Death and Dread:
> Adits were entrances which led
> Down to the Outlawed, to the Others,
> The Terrible, the Merciful, the Mothers;
> Alone in the hot day I knelt
> Upon the edges of shafts and felt
> The deep *Urmutterfurcht* that drives
> Us into knowledge all our lives,
> The far interior of our fate
> To civilise and to create,
> *Das Weibliche* that bids us come
> To find what we're escaping from.
> There I dropped pebbles, listened, heard
> The reservoir of darkness stirred;
> "*O deine Mutter kehrt dir nicht*
> *Wieder. Du selbst bin ich, dein' Pflicht*
> *Und Liebe. Brach sie nun mein Bild.*"
> And I was conscious of my guilt. (*Collected* 227–28)

Like the Wordsworthian child-self who in the first book of *The Prelude* is led, by a mountain that seems to chase him, to troubled dreams of "huge and mighty forms, that do not live / Like living men," Auden's child-self is led by a difficult landscape to confront several disturbing phenomena, all of which would furnish themes for the grown-up poet in the 1930s. These include *Urmutterfurcht* (fear of a primeval mother); a *Weibliche* (feminine) principle that commands reflection on the origins we must try to escape; the distant darkness that seems the self; alienation; guilt. Yet nature does not work in quite the same way here as it does in Wordsworth. In *The Prelude*, the lessons imparted to the growing soul remain less than fully articulate, leaving the boy "a dim and undetermined sense / Of unknown modes of being" (*Prelude* 51). In "New Year Letter," the young Auden seems to grasp his revelations more lucidly, to be thinking already in allegorical terms, perhaps—which possibility would align with the biographical Auden's intellectual precocity. But even if the child-Auden does not have names like "Self and Not-Self" (let alone "*Urmutterfurcht*") for the portents that reach him on the moors, the passage delineates, as *The Prelude* does not, a natural world where individual elements gesture to fairly specific existential problems and aspects of mind—and, having done so, largely retreat from the foreground of exposition.

Auden's method here is consistent with his poetic practice through the end of the thirties, which was to maintain what we might call a high allegoricity when introducing elements of landscape at all. Early poems such as "Control of the passes was, he saw, the key" (1928, later titled "The Secret Agent") and "Hearing of harvests rotting in the valleys" (1933, later titled "Paysage Moralisé") conjure notional nonurban settings but firmly resist describing them in detail or unfolding their intimate effects on the consciousness of the poet. Rather, they deploy prominent generic elements—bridges, deserts, valleys, mountains, islands, cities—as backdrops for the predicaments of exiles, explorers, spies, or migrating communities, in describing which Auden variously rehearses his favored theme of separation from origins. In the poems of the later 1930s, landscapes and cities become instrumental to human meanings in a different way, appearing less as stages for human situations than as metaphors for people or their psyches. In 1939's "Matthew Arnold," for example, Arnold becomes "a dark disordered city" (*English* 241), while another passage in "New Year Letter" imagines an interior "atlas":

> the inner space
> Of private ownership, the place
> That each of us is forced to own,
> Like his own life from which it's grown,
> The landscape of his will and need
> Where he is sovereign indeed,

> The state created by his acts
> Where he patrols the forest tracts
> Planted in childhood, farms the belt
> Of doings memorised and felt,
> And even if he find it hell
> May neither leave it nor rebel. (*Collected* 226)

The transformation of Wordsworth's narrative according to Auden's own lights is really ingenious. Where Wordsworth had shown wild nature molding the child's mind, Auden makes domesticated nature a figure for the mind of the adult who was once a child. And as metaphor replaces metonymy here, the inanimate world's capacity to shape the soul stealthily—or indeed at all—ceases to be a matter of concern: now an equivalent or symptom only, nature can no longer be a cause. Moreover, although both poets conceive of nature as at once threatening and productive, Wordsworth's idyll has the mobile child proceeding through unowned vastness to gain an intuition of a benevolent if stern universe, whereas Auden's georgic presents an adult unable to get off his own property and reaping, probably grimly, the limited fruits of his prior actions and experiences. It thus becomes clear that Auden's recourse to Augustan devices in "New Year Letter" represents more than a continuation of the antimodernist return to traditional forms that he had begun a few years earlier with poems like "Letter to Lord Byron." His employment here of the symmetry-tuned classicism, public rhetoric, and decorum of the eighteenth century suggests also an effort to resist Wordsworth by returning to forms that predate the Wordsworthian transformation of English poetry.

Of course, Auden had to have recognized that his interest in the formative power of juvenile experience put him in a genealogy that included Rousseau and Wordsworth as well as George Auden and Freud; dim portents from hallowed nature might be relegated to the background, but the fashioning of the subject by small and large events of childhood was a discovery whose Romantic provenance could not credibly be denied. Further, the period of "New Year Letter" was one in which Auden was coming to find the idea of *managing* such fashioning both less and more attractive than he had previously. In the early forties, as Nicholas Jenkins notes, he was "passing through one of the most vehement phases of his rediscovered religiousness," placing himself dramatically "in opposition to his secular, collective, politically engaged outlook of the Thirties" (2–3), and this entailed more than an extension of his critique of "liberal" education's coerciveness-disguised-as-liberty. It included, in addition, new doubts about his own (essentially if not avowedly liberal) championing of children's freedom to develop neurotically and oddly, as one can see already in the 1939 notes about the neurotic X. Moreover, as he began

to look with a colder eye on his earlier enthusiasm for the quirky operations of the unconscious, Auden started to look with a friendlier one on
forms of moral instruction that were more overt and discursive—yet also,
in their way, more cunning.

The groundwork for this change had been in place for some time,
Auden having long wondered whether the individual too drastically individuated, too ready to discard conventional principles of conduct, might
not sometimes prove a danger to society. A singular manifestation of this
anxiety can be found in *The Orators*, the 1933 work that secured his literary reputation even though few of those who acclaimed it on publication
professed to understand it. Such as it is, the plot of this gorgeously opaque
mixture of poetry and prose centers on a troubled quasi-Fascist rebel
named the Airman, who raises an army of adolescent disciples against an
"enemy" only hazily sketched but evidently inclined to the kind of paternalistic management Auden associated with liberals and liberalism. In the
end, the Airman concludes that because the "power of the enemy is a
function of our resistance," the "only efficient way to destroy it" is "self-
destruction" (*English* 93), which he then appears to undertake by crashing
his plane. This terminal insight looks very much like the revelation that
there is no escaping the formative power of one's environment (except
perhaps in suicide, that ultimate rebuke to circumstances), but a no less
vexing impasse adumbrated in *The Orators* is that of how individuals can
give unrestricted play to their individualism without impairing each other's freedom. The Airman's impulse to self-originate is precisely what the
Auden of the early 1930s theoretically endorsed, but as it plays out in
practice it seems both futile and harmful to others. Even more disturbing,
perhaps, are the impulses of his followers, who seem to find an outlet for
their own interesting eccentricities—the kinks in their young minds—in
enumerating the eccentricities that merit violent suppression when found
in others.

Auden's simmering anxieties in this area became a gripping preoccupation after he visited a German-language cinema in New York in December,
1939. There he witnessed, in his later words, "quite ordinary, supposedly
harmless Germans in the audience" of a Nazi propaganda film "shouting
'Kill the Poles.'" Remarkable to Auden was the film's "lack of hypocrisy.
Every value I had been brought up on, and assumed everybody held, was
flatly denied" (quoted in Mendelson *Later* 89). Perhaps predictably,
Auden located the enabling condition of this eschewal of basic values in
liberals' emphasis on the environmental circumstances that mitigate responsibility: in showing how "men's concepts of reason and justice were
biased by chance factors such as the character of their parents, or their
geographical and social status," he wrote in 1941, liberal "historians,

economists and psychologists" had rendered vulnerable the core tenets that alone could provide a block to Fascist expediency (*Prose 2* 106).

Accordingly, Auden began to think of education less in terms of the cultivation of neurosis and desire, more in terms of a deliberate inculcation of the kinds of principles the Fascists had cast off. In his "Note on Order," published in the *Nation* in 1940, he argues that society requires "common agreement upon a small number of carefully defined presuppositions, from which each individual can deduce the right behavior in a particular instance," though this agreement must certainly be coupled with an awareness "that these presuppositions are not knowledge," not a matter of unalterable law (*Prose 1* 102). In a Yale address of 1941, similarly, he asserts that liberalism has rightly exposed "hypocrisy and prejudice" in the attempt to instill virtue, but that in so doing it "has tended to deny that there was anything to be hypocritical about." Taking note of "the psychological damage often done to the young by faulty techniques" in the teaching of values like courage, honor, honesty, patience, industry, and so on, liberalism "has come to think that it is wrong to try and teach them at all, that the child is born good, and if allowed to express itself will develop them" (*Prose 2* 122).

But how to inculcate such values properly? How correct this disastrous error? Auden asserts in the same address that "every psychological resource, every trick of advertisement and propaganda" should be used to instill fundamental principles until "they become conditioned reflexes" (*Prose 2* 122). Where before he had reprehended efforts to straighten out the kinks in young minds, he now recommends transmitting values so unrelentingly that they will be adhered to without thought. If in the thirties his accent was on the way in which apparent freedom from coercion in fact coerced, the wartime writing argues that liberal looseness was simply too loose. It may not, after all, be possible to raise the young aright without trickery, and if there is very little to be said for Rousseau's optimism about innate goodness, there is perhaps a good deal to be said for his willingness to employ pedagogical stratagems. The startling reference to "conditioned reflexes" suggests that Auden had even come, in spite of his sense that behaviorism and totalitarianism were dangerously linked, to favor a moral training not completely unlike that recommended by behaviorists—just as West, in "The Strange Necessity," had come to credit folk songs and popular religion with an unobtrusive transmission akin to conditioning in Pavlov.

Auden was certainly not recommending that people be deprived of the ability to choose between right and wrong, of course. In these years he held quite fervently to the belief that the capacity for moral action—along with the ability to love, the chance to lament, and like opportunities for the soul—was one of the indispensable privileges of being human. In the

Smith address quoted earlier, he declares that "[a]ll freedom implies necessity, that is to say, suffering" (*Prose 2* 70), and his poetry of the early forties is studded with epigrams like "There must be sorrow if there can be love" (*Collected* 331), "The distresses of choice are our chance to be blessed" (*Collected* 388), and "It is defeat gives proof we are alive" (*Collected* 420). That the fortunate fall now becomes the most important of Christian topoi in his writing speaks to the continuity between his views in this phase and his position in the middle thirties, when he had concluded that a secular version of humankind's accession to dissatisfaction, sorrow, and loss—call it a fortunate (evolutionary) rise—marked the culmination of natural history. What is new about the writing of the early forties is that it finds him more willing to reserve the capacity for moral choice for adults. Basic moral presuppositions must be implanted in the young *as if* beyond question; and though questioning will be appropriate later on, by that point conditioning will ideally have set principles firmly enough to prevent even the most morally adventurous from entertaining an *epoche* like the Nazis'.

So maintaining, Auden comes around not only to a version of Rousseau but also to a position notably similar to one taken by Wilde. In "The Critic as Artist," as we saw in chapter 2, Gilbert recommends a Platonic education that by "slow degrees" engenders in the child "such a temperament as will lead him naturally and simply to choose the good in preference to the bad," and though eventually "this taste is to become critical and selfconscious . . . at first it is to exist purely as a cultivated instinct." In Wilde's program, beautiful environments are to teach children to "love what is beautiful and good, and hate what is evil and ugly, long before they know the reason why," whereas in Auden's, "every trick of advertisement and propaganda" is to be used to instill bedrock principles. But the lineaments of the processes are the same: in both, wise management of juvenile experience provides the foundation for freedom in maturity.

Auden's *Nation* and Yale statements are anxious and grim, as surely befits addresses to the state of Western societies in 1940 and 1941; not for such times the cheerful confidence of Wilde's American lectures. In the years after the Second World War, however, Auden seems to have found it possible to tackle the interlinked problems of education, art, morality, and environment in a more optimistic and genial register. Can there, he would wonder afresh, be a training that implants values tested by reason and custom yet does not obliterate individuality? Is there a way of acknowledging that complete transcendence of environment is impossible without sacrificing belief in moral choice, personal responsibility, and other incomparably precious dimensions of humanness? Might one meaningfully recognize the claims of social concord while at the same time holding individuation to be a cardinal good? And what in the old model of the

beautiful environment nurturing a beautiful soul can be retained or redeemed for the modern world? These questions arguably receive their
most complex, subtle, and revealing treatment in the 1948 poem that
Auden was given to calling his favorite among those he had written (Osborne 230), a meditation inspired by echoes of his own formative landscape in a place not seen before.

## SHOWING OFF, SETTING OFF

In April 1948, Auden visited his father at their family cottage in the
Wordsworth-celebrated Lake District; the following month he made his
first visit to Italy, and the poem in question evolved from his sense of an
affinity between Tuscany and the northern England of his childhood. To
his friend Elizabeth Mayer he wrote at the time, "I hadn't realized till I
came how like Italy is to my 'Mutterland,' the Pennines. Am in fact starting on a poem, 'In Praise of Limestone,' the theme of which is that that
rock creates the only human landscape, i.e. when politics, art etc. remain
on a modest ungrandiose scale. What awful ideas have been suggested to
the human mind by huge plains and gigantic mountains!" (quoted in Fuller 407). The reception of the text that resulted was curiously similar to
that of *The Orators*: critics described "In Praise of Limestone" as one of
Auden's finest poems yet tended to find its meaning elusive. To this day,
and many astute critical treatments notwithstanding, its coherence as an
enunciation of ideas seems to have gone less than fully recognized.

One thing that has been clear to readers is that its limestone landscape
is a locus whose genius is the middle way, a place proper to those who avoid
extremes, seem impure, remain moderate in goodness as in badness, and
are "human," where that word carries overtones of both imperfection and
loveableness. Indeed the heavily anthologized 1937 Auden lyric beginning
"Lay your sleeping head my love, / Human on my faithless arm" is closely
evoked both in the remark to Mayer and in the opening lines of "Praise":
"If it form the one landscape that we the inconstant ones / Are consistently
homesick for, this is chiefly / Because it dissolves in water" (*Collected* 540).
Infidelity and inconstancy being ways of failing to remain the same, it is
not surprising that a poet who had always insisted on the need for change
(and who partook of a devaluing of sexual fidelity associated in the twentieth century with a certain gay male sensibility) should put these divagations
at the head of his catalogue of laudable imperfections.

The poem's concern with moderation shows most plainly, in any case,
a few lines into the second stanza, where we learn that those who inhabit
the limestone landscape have never had to reckon with a divinity ex-
ceeding the human scale. These fortunate souls are

> unable
> To conceive a god whose temper-tantrums are moral
> And not to be pacified by a clever line
> Or a good lay: for, accustomed to a stone that responds,
> They have never had to veil their faces in awe
> Of a crater whose blazing fury could not be fixed;
> Adjusted to the local needs of valleys
> Where everything can be touched or reached by walking,
> Their eyes have never looked into infinite space . . . (*Selected* 185)

The stanza that follows concerns people of an opposite temper, the "best and worst" who "never stayed here long but sought / Immoderate soils where the beauty was not so external, / The light less public and the meaning of life / Something more than a mad camp." "Saints-to-be" thus harken to the call of granite wastes; "[i]ntendant Caesars" depart for clays and gravels bespeaking the malleability of mankind; and the "really reckless" are lured away by an ocean whispering that there is "no love," only "the various envies, all of them sad" (186). In the fourth and final stanza, Auden uses the Christian doctrine that the dead shall be raised in body to make a case for the kind of Christianity that he professed from the mid-1940s on—one consonant with the pagan pleasures of the limestone landscape in its conviction that love for heaven should not mandate contempt for the imperfect, delicious world at hand.

Some critics over the years have argued that "In Praise of Limestone" proceeds by a kind of free association, or explores a range of positions that pointedly fail to tally with each other, or eschews altogether the attempt to convey a governing idea. These impressions are certainly understandable, given the poem's slipperiness and complexity, but careful reading indicates that, like nearly every other poem Auden wrote, it has a point of view to which it adheres throughout, and that its action is to articulate a scheme of values bearing on (and thus disclosing the links between) a series of human situations one might not ordinarily consider in conjunction. Part of the reason this has been missed is surely that the third stanza, with its attention-grabbing saints and caesars, tends to invite rapid passage over stanzas one and two, even though it is in those opening units that Auden unfolds the ideas that bind the poem together. It will be worth our while to linger over that unfolding and those ideas, however, since they constitute one of Auden's most inventive approaches to the problems of individuation and environment that had long absorbed him.

To begin, then, with the first stanza, whose opening lines seem to parody the style of a lecturer on science or a writer of geographical surveys (both of which George Auden happened to be): "If it form the one landscape that we the inconstant ones / Are consistently homesick for, this is chiefly / Because it dissolves in water. Mark these rounded slopes . . . /

. . . / . . . hear the springs / . . . / . . . examine this region. . . . " An if-then statement is followed by an invitation to inspect the terrain, and both seem intended to secure the reader's assent to the rhetorical proposition that follows:

> What could be more like Mother or a fitter background
>     For her son, for the nude young male who lounges
> Against a rock displaying his dildo, never doubting
>     That for all his faults he is loved, whose works are but
> Extensions of his power to charm? (185)

But this is a strange rhetorical question indeed. "Fitter" how, and why a dildo? The answer is not obvious from the opening alone, and the next sentence seems at first to go in another direction:

>                         From weathered outcrop
>     To hill-top temple, from appearing waters to
> Conspicuous fountains, from a wild to a formal vineyard,
>     Are ingenious but short steps that a child's wish
> To receive more attention than his brothers, whether
>     By pleasing or teasing, can easily take. (185)

The capsule narrative of these lines is one in which a child looks at a natural object and imagines producing something of his own—a work of artifice miming the work of nature—that will attract parental notice. Once again, Auden gestures to the assumption that the achievements and disasters of adult life can be traced to the small dramas of childhood; once again, the artist or highbrow whose dissatisfaction may be especially fertile starts out as an anxious child. Here, however, the moral seems to be that whatever one accomplishes, one is really trying to earn love—that whatever aspirations contribute to the artifactual impulse, the most basic of all is a yearning for affectionate approval, the kind of parental recognition elicited by the exclamation, "Look, I made this!" Or as Auden put it in a sonnet from "In Time of War": those who "built / Each great coercive avenue and square" were the "really lonely with the sense of guilt / Who wanted to persist like that for ever; / The unloved had to leave material traces" (*English* 261).

A moment's further reflection then discloses that this matter of being loved is precisely what ties the lounging male in the previous sentence to the child desiring to be noticed. The latter may enjoy some quantity of parental attention but wants more; the former, secure in love and already possessed of something that will attract admiration, has no need to conceive of an artifact, though he may still devise "works" that are "[e]xtensions of his power to charm." (Auden's use of "dildo" makes the artifactual connection clearer, but at the cost of a certain disorientation. Is the dildo some limestone object, an actual dildo, or the lounging male's penis, here rhetorically replaced by an item that replaces the penis in real life? In the revised version of the poem, Auden altered the line to the less distracting, if less entertaining, "for the flirtatious male who lounges / Against a rock in the sunlight" [*Collected* 540].) In the next stanza, the speaker will explain that the yearnings of would-be saints and caesars are not suited to the limestone landscape; here, he makes clear that the yearnings of artists and protoartists naturally are. Dissatisfied highbrows are not off the human scale, but the most intensely human of all. There is nothing immoderate about the urge to make.

Nor, perhaps, is there anything immoderate about any behavior driven by the wish to receive a lot of attention. At the end of the second stanza, Auden writes, of those who have grown up in a limestone landscape,

> So, when one of them goes to the bad, the way his mind works
>   Remains comprehensible: to become a pimp
> Or deal in fake jewelry or ruin a fine tenor voice
>   For effects that bring down the house, could happen to all
> But the best and the worst of us. . . . (185)

All but the best and the worst of us would ruin a fine tenor voice for effects that bring down the house? Can such extravagance really be middle-way behavior? Auden twice tries to convince us that it is. First, he aligns this prodigal exhibitionism with pimping and dealing in fake jewelry, offenses that seem daring in neither motivation nor execution, and hence unsuited to those whose extremes of soul impel them to bold exploits. Second, he hints that saints-to-be, intendant caesars, and the "really reckless" are united by an unlovely asceticism, a turning away from the immediate richness of life and from their own ability to contribute to that richness: "The best and worst never stayed here long but sought / Immoderate soils where the beauty was not so external, / The light less public and the meaning of life / Something more than a mad camp." For Auden, the extremes are inhabited by those for whom beauty is wholly internal, light wholly private (under a bushel, perhaps), and life's insistent theatricality denied. The prodigality of the self-destroying tenor, on the other hand, is of the middle of the human range.

Indeed the moral of this section of "Praise" seems to be that the urge to fashion a work of art, the urge to exhibit one's attractive body, and the urge to sacrifice the vocal instrument for grand effects are all species of a more general behavior we ordinarily call "showing off"—and that the impulse to show off is as natural as can be imagined. To learn "the shameless / Games of man," Auden would suggest in "Memorial for the City" of the following year, is "to flatter, *to show off*, be pompous, to romp" (*Collected* 593, emphasis added), which is to say that in wanting to set oneself apart this way one in truth confirms one's deep continuity with one's fellows. And indeed "Praise" indicates that if showing off is natural, the genially competitive urge that motivates it is no less so. The lines about the child's desire to receive more attention are succeeded by the following imperative:

> Watch, then, the band of rivals as they climb up and down
> Their steep stone gennels in twos and threes, sometimes
> Arm in arm, but never, thank God, in step. . . . (185)

With this image, Auden rewrites redemptively some of the troubling scenes of his earlier imagination, even as he points out that individuals' seeking to outshine each other need not portend the end of fraternity or community. Transplanted from the very English setting of *The Orators* to an idyllic Tuscany-Yorkshire, the band of adolescent males becomes more amiable, less threatening, their energies diverted from destruction of a hazily posited enemy to affable one-upmanship among themselves. Transplanted from the shadow of F6 to the less drastic topography of limestone, similarly, sibling rivalry comes to seem the stuff not of melodrama but of comedy, the project of outshining proving not a lifetime endeavor but an activity for a sunny hour. The competitive urge does not disappear in the limestone world, then, but the behavior in which it manifests itself most purely, showing off, contributes to the communal good. Whether projecting a temple, displaying one's physique, or giving it all up in a big aria, one serves the general interest by expanding rather than inhibiting oneself. Altruistic and selfish impulses converge, while delinquency, at least as George Auden theorized it, seems almost a contradiction in terms.[18]

Considered in the dual contexts of war's immediate aftermath and Auden's long-standing occupation with the relationship between individuals and groups, "Praise" can be seen to unloose a series of hopeful and provocative questions about the arrangements of human existence. (As the poem's speaker says, the limestone landscape "calls into question / All the Great Powers assume" [*Collected* 540].) If the fundamental intersubjective desire is a desire for attention, why should society not be organized around the genially competitive display of what one is, rather than the grimly competitive counting of what one has? Instead of pathologizing the impulse to register individuality by showing off, why not prefer it to the impulse to demonstrate power through acquisition? Why subscribe to the error of capitalist and socialist political economists, who assume that competition must be competition for limited products or resources? And why, above all, fall prey to the Fascist demand that whole populations fall in step behind a single charismatic leader? Instead, watch and learn from the band of rivals as they climb up and down, at times arm in arm— but never, thank God, in step.

As we have seen, Auden's concerns about the suppression of individual desire in deference to the collective were inseparable from anxieties about the difficulty of separating oneself from one's origins and, a little later, from fears that subtly managed (or just inertly oppressive) environments might inhibit the child's freedom to develop idiosyncratically and artistically. Another of the insights of "In Praise of Limestone," however, is that such worry about the power of circumstances may in a sense be misplaced, inasmuch as people never simply replicate the environments that nurtured them. The fantasy of the child wanting more attention leads not to an outcrop but to a temple, not to a wild vineyard but to a formal one, which is to say that the imagination looks forward not to duplicating the scene but to adding something new to the world. The merely lounging young man makes the point even more elegantly, for he seems to know that he will never be mistaken for his formative scenery, no matter how well suited to each other he and it may be. Confident of his differentiation, he does not even need to bother with an artifact; all he has to do is pose, just a shade artfully, in his natural setting.

Auden clinches this point by means of a single word, placed conspicuously at the end of the enjambed line 11: "What could be more like Mother or a fitter *background* / For her son . . . ?" "Background," of course, names that from which an object of attention in the foreground is distinguished, the field that allows the contours of the object to emerge; at the same time, it names a person's family circumstances, ethnic and class origins, prior experience. To think of this double sense of background is therefore to think of how formative conditions and foil may be one and the same—as in this poem where the nurturing landscape does not absorb but rather sharpens the outlines of the individual it has helped to produce. In the journal of 1929, nostalgia for the Earth Mother was impossibly regressive, but here Mother is the environment that both shapes the subject and illuminates that subject's unique shape; here, a kind of adjustment of vision brings out how individuals are inevitably distinct from their environments. This perceptual adjustment is then nicely abetted by showing off on the part of the observed, which could be described as that object's effort to heighten the contrast between himself and his surroundings, something between a full doing and a revelation of a separation already, inevitably, there.[19]

In opening up these possibilities, Auden notably modifies his earlier picture of the artist's or intellectual's forging through resistance to environment. In "Praise," an opposition between individual and situation does remain central, but the nature of that opposition has changed: at issue now is not a contest but a contrast, not an active struggle against impediments but a difference perceived by those who care to look. The poem thus depicts something like that harmony between subject and world promised by the old dream of aesthetic formation, but in this case beauty need not be invoked as a mediating term and the quirkiness or perversity of the artistic soul is not imperiled. Moreover, this reconciliation goes hand in hand with an extension of artisticness to a much broader range of people. In subsuming the making of art under the larger behavior of showing off, which attracts all but the best and the worst, Auden here divests himself of the evolutionary scheme that had set artists and intellectuals apart as more advanced human types; in the kinder world adumbrated in this poem, anyone might have something of the artist, and the artist might be anyone.

Of course, "In Praise of Limestone" does not exactly provide a workable blueprint for the good society. One obvious problem with a scheme in which showing off is the motor of social life is that it says nothing about antisocial forms of behavior driven by more material forms of deprivation; another is that self-display has historically proven extremely difficult to separate from acquisition, domination, and varieties of competition very far from affable or benign. Yet a third conspicuous difficulty is that a comprehensive validation of showing off would seem to offer little to those inclined to leave their gifts under wraps, averse to hamming it up, or happier just blending in.

It bears noting, however, that none of these obstacles would likely have carried great weight for Auden personally. Whether owing to his basic disposition or because his early achievement of fame rendered him impervious to the comparatively vulgar credential of money, he seemed little concerned with acquisition, let alone wealth, in his own life; on the other hand, he was a natural getter of attention. In prep school, he "enjoyed music and acting" and "took a frank delight in displaying his remarkable general knowledge" (Bulley 32, H. L. Smith 35), and from his time at Oxford on, he was given to a magnetic pontificating that earned him a reputation for wisdom beyond his years and later chimed perfectly with the role of poet-sage. In the facility with which he installed himself at the center of things and the tenacity with which he held individualism to be a paramount good, in fact, Auden signally resembled another writer who was also the prolific gay son of a distinguished physician: Oscar Wilde.

The affinities between Wilde and Auden in this area have a theoretical aspect as well. For in spite of his repeated insistence on poetic honesty, Auden was at least as dedicated to the naturalizing of human theatricality as the author of "The Decay of Lying." In 1953's "'The Truest Poetry Is the Most Feigning,'" possibly the only poem in which he seems to embrace an affiliation between poetry and dissimulation, Auden describes Man as "The self-made creature who himself unmakes, / The only creature ever made who fakes" (*Collected* 621). In *The Age of Anxiety* (1944–1946), he writes that human beings "cannot become something before they have first pretended to be it; and they can be divided, not into the hypocritical and the sincere, but into the sane who know they are acting and the mad who do not" (*Collected* 518). In his 1942 poem to John Retger on his seventh birthday, he wishes the boy "first a / Sense of theatre . . . / . . . / You will any day now / Have this revelation: / 'Why, we're all like people / Acting in a play'" (*Collected* 321). In "Talking to Dogs," written near the end of his life, he begs, "Let difference remain our bond, yes, and the one trait / both have in common, a sense of theatre" (*Collected* 868). In "Cav and Pag," reprinted in 1962 in *The Dyer's Hand* but first issued with a 1953 recording of *Cavalleria Rusticana* and *I Pagliacci*, he reiterates that we "are all actors" (480). If showing off is as integral to humanness as Auden suggests, Wilde might be regarded as the epitome of humanity.

It is therefore all the more startling to come across a 1950 review of a critical study of Wilde in which Auden censures that large personality— virtually point by point—for what he himself had celebrated in "Praise" two years earlier. In "A Playboy of the Western World: St. Oscar, the Homintern Martyr," Auden asserts that Wilde "was not by nature an artist" because artists are

> primarily interested in deeds and only secondarily interested in securing the approval of others, whereas Wilde is the classic case of a man who is completely dominated by the desire to be loved for himself alone. . . . A person with this passionate need to be loved has constantly to test those around him by unconventional and provocative behavior, for what he does or says must be admired not because it is intrinsically admirable but because it is his act or remark. Further, a person with a need to be loved universally is frequently a homosexual. (391)

Thus dramatically does Auden oppose the view, articulated in "Praise," that the artifactual urge is an epiphenomenon of a more fundamental desire for attention. Showing off, attracting notice, wanting to be loved more and better here turn back into the disreputable failures of control people ordinarily think them, even as the speculative exuberance of the 1948 poem is renounced. That Auden also lapses into the less positive of his two conceptions of homosexuality, associating it with damaging rather than productive neurosis, only intensifies this essay's prim severity, a mood at the opposite swing of the pendulum from the pagan gemütlichkeit of the limestone landscape.[20]

Auden then goes on to attack the study's author, the anarchist literatus George Woodcock, for calling Wilde "an apostle of individualism." When Wilde "preaches individualism," Auden charges, "he is not advocating either . . . the concentrated discipline of one's nature in a chosen direction, like Marcus Aurelius, nor the planned exploration of all experience like Faust, but expressing the simplest and oldest of all wishes, 'let's have fun,' which may not be so impressive as a philosophy of life but is ever so much more sympathetic" (393). This indictment is particularly ill advised in that it seems elicited by Wildean pronouncements, indebted to Pater, that *do* recommend the exploring of all experience as a project of discipline; nor does Auden seem to notice that in describing the simply fun arcadia for which Wilde allegedly yearns he evokes meticulously the terrain of his own "In Praise of Limestone": "Thus when, like all the nineteenth century literary école païenne, he extols the Greeks, the Great God Pan, and the Beautiful Pagan Life, any resemblance to the historical reality is accidental and all he seems to mean is: 'I should like a world without Sunday closing, damp weather and overcooked vegetables but with plenty of sunshine and lots of yummy scantily-clad teen-agers who can't say No' " (392). Or, shall we say, a fusion of Tuscany and Yorkshire in which any god can be pacified by a good lay, flirtatious males lean against rocks in sunlight, and rent boys festively chase potential clients (lines 73–76: "these gamins, / Pursuing the scientist down the tiled colonnade / With such lively offers, rebuke his concern for Nature's / Remotest aspects" [*Selected* 186]).

Many factors, not excluding the mere contingency of a writer's bad mood, must have led Auden to repudiate so violently in 1950 what he had so disarmingly endorsed in 1948; indeed given his career-long tendency to oscillate between campily expansive provocation and guiltily dour retraction, it might be more surprising if he had never disparaged the features of Wilde's imagination that most resembled his own. But that there is a little more to the story is suggested by a subsequent passage of the review, in which Auden professes to find Wilde's sexual affairs refreshingly honest in comparison to his writings. "After all the high-falutin' talk about Beauty and the New Hedonism," he remarks, "it is such a relief to discover that Wilde was just an ordinary sinner like you and me. . . . He was a phoney prophet but a serious playboy" (393). Read in light of his earlier identification of the highbrow with the usefully neurotic, the fruitfully dissatisfied, and the productively deviant, this observation suggests that for Auden the difference between the authentic artist and the sham artist of the Wildean type is that the former at some level owns, or is unable to conceal, his departures from norms of desire and behavior, whereas the latter tries to disguise his evasion of social strictures by calling it devotion to beauty. Indeed it is as if aesthetics' long tradition of connecting the beautiful to both pleasure and social concord here stood revealed as part of the cunning ruse of the playboy aesthete, the reconciliation in this case occurring not between the universal human subject and the phenomenal world, or even (as in Eagleton) between the bourgeois subject and an alienating social order, but between the timid hedonist and the community whose disapprobation he cannot endure.

Auden is not necessarily dismissing all dedication to beauty, of course, but the tonal cues here—including the capitalization of the initial "B" and the reference to "high-falutin' talk"—do seem to partake of the midcentury weakening of beauty's claim on social optimism that we have already remarked. From this perspective, the review of Woodcock seems not only a repudiation of the enchantments of "In Praise of Limestone" but also one more putting of a period to the story that began in the eighteenth century with Schiller and Wordsworth and carried on through Ruskin, Downing, Morris, Ouida, Pater, Wilde, and all those others who saw in beautiful environments a way to a better future. But how, if at all, are these two forms of farewell connected?

An answer is suggested, perhaps, by the review's conclusion, where Auden observes that in Wilde's "daydream," as it materializes in *The Importance of Being Earnest,*

> Eden is the place where everyone is happy, poor Miss Prism, silly Dr. Chasuble and old Lady Brackwell [*sic*] just as much as the young lovers, where everyone loves everyone else and where, though the laws of nature operate—people have the same nature that they have in the real world—their operation causes neither conflict nor suffering. Given his nature, it is not surprising that this subject should have excited Wilde to write a masterpiece, for on this subject as on no other is the playboy, who is always an "alienated" soul who craves to belong, truly earnest. (394)

The last sentence further confirms that the ire Wilde excited in Auden had much to do with the playboy's claim to alienation, which seems to mock the more complex, less stridently broadcast estrangement of the real artist or highbrow. But the passage as a whole points to a still larger problem: that the situation of Eden may be essentially inhospitable to art.

As we have seen, Auden joined Rebecca West in conceiving of art as an evolutionary development arising out of the agon between human beings and their recalcitrant milieux. But in her rendering, especially in "The Strange Necessity," art's ultimate virtue is that of a tool used—pleasurably—in the struggle against a universe whose unhelpfulness cannot in any absolute sense be redeemed. West did not believe that we ought in some metaphysical way to be thankful for the uncooperativeness of the world in which we find ourselves; on the contrary, she held that a perfect creation would admit neither pain nor struggle, and that human beings' ability to master their environments in whatever small ways is excellent chiefly, if not solely, because it makes life easier and happier. Auden, on the other hand, tended to think of the struggle as good in itself, or at least as the structural or logical precondition of true moral goodness. The "distresses of choice are our chance to be blessed" not because a right choice is a little victory over a refractory world but because without distress there simply can be no blessing.

It makes sense, then, that West should have had fewer qualms than Auden about art's stealthy operations upon the soul—that she would indeed endorse, as an activity of art in the largest sense, folk songs' and traditional religion's operation on those more likely to learn through "suggestion" than from lectures emitted by Hull House. In this, and in her affirmation of the high importance of aesthetic sensitivity (*The Return of the Soldier*, "The Strange Necessity," *Black Lamb*, and other texts), she can be considered one of the heirs of the positive program of shaping by beauty that Wilde and so many others advanced. Auden, by contrast, could not conceive of either art or virtue as originating with some gentle influence by which the soul is harmonized with its world, his 1956 statement that poetry's great job is to "praise all it can for being and for happening" notwithstanding (*Dyer's* 60). For him, the emblematic figure of the highbrow was the "man struggling for his life in the water," and the crown or essence of individuality the moral choice that only struggle permits. It is thus not hard to see why the "playboy" Wilde, with his promise of a union of art and ease, would present special problems for Auden; nor is it hard to see why similar hesitations might surface around "In Praise of Limestone." The landscape of that poem does not work on its children in precisely the same way aesthetic education does—it is less a beautiful place making souls beautiful than a moderate, inconstant place making souls (mostly) moderate and inconstant[21]—but its world is certainly one in which, as in Eden and as in *Earnest*, the laws of nature cause neither conflict nor suffering.

These problems clearly did not bother Auden consistently. In other writing, much of it from after 1950, he ranges himself on the side of "Arcadians," whose dreaming on the prelapsarian is innocuous and even loveable because tied to no hope of implementation, as against "Utopians," whose fantasies of shaping the future can lead to repression and tyranny, the violence of fanatics and states. In an essay from *The Dyer's Hand*, he writes that the Arcadian "knows that his expulsion from Eden is an irrevocable fact and that his dream . . . cannot become real," then goes on to describe that dream in terms evocative of his earlier criticism of Wilde: "To be an inhabitant of Eden, it is absolutely required that one be happy and likable"; in Eden, the "self is satisfied whatever it demands" and the "only motive for an action is the pleasure it gives the actor." A few sentences later, Auden numbers Wilde among the "four great English experts on Eden," the others being Charles Dickens, Ronald Firbank, and P. G. Wodehouse (*Dyer's* 410–11). Putting all this together, we might say that Auden pulls away from Wilde when arcadian wistfulness seems in danger

of turning into utopian projection, when merely longing for perfect fulfillment gives way to planning a future (or trying to live a life) where
satisfaction would be unbroken.

This in turn helps us to see why Auden could so love "In Praise of
Limestone" and yet at times, as in the review of Woodcock's book, so
strikingly distance himself from its kind of vision. As the conjuring of a
scene, "Praise" captures the Audenian Eden perhaps more splendidly than
any of his other poems; as a meditation on human tendencies and relations,
it discloses resonant truths about experience in the world we have. But it
will not do, for Auden, to forget that the genial accord between surroundings and individual imagined in "Praise" represents a situation unlike
those in which we usually find ourselves—nor will it do to forget that such
radical harmony would, as an encompassing condition, mean the death of
art and of meaningful goodness. Given that Eden sponsors none of the
dissatisfaction Auden associated, in scientific and religious terms respec-
tively, with evolutionary ascent and expulsion from the garden, inhabiting
it would, from his standpoint, mean giving up what is most precious in
existence. It would mean evading the suffering, but also losing the significance, of life after the Fall.

To end with "In Praise of Limestone" is undoubtedly to invite some objections, among them that this landscape poem ought not to be taken as the closing exhibit in a book that has concerned itself with the interiors of human dwellings much more than with outdoor places. To this it must be rejoined, however, that one of this study's very morals has been that writers of the period in question were concerned with something that transcended any categorical division between built human spaces, on the one hand, and landscape (or pastoral, or georgic, or Wordsworth's legacies to nature writing), on the other. This something was environment, the concept of which drew its power to shape thinking—about the nature of human existence, about ways of organizing social life, about the offices of art and beauty—partly from its very abstraction, certainly, but partly too from the diversity of its concrete manifestations, from country houses to limestone landscapes, from the streets of London or Chicago to little white rooms against whose windows blossoms beat on gusty mornings. The writers we have looked at here were united by a sense that to be a person is, at least from the point of view of fundamental science, to be an organism in an environment. And they explored this way of understanding human beings, which to some ears may sound so impoverishing, in prose fictions, poems, and nonfictional commentary of extraordinary invention and complexity.

Another response to the foregoing demurral would be to point out that in moving outdoors with Auden's poem of 1948, we anticipate, if only by way of a thin figuration, something important that happened in public consciousness a few years after: the rise of "the environment" as a matter of developed ecological concern. For if the two world wars had made it difficult to imagine raising young people in conditions not subject to radical disruption, a different effect was engendered by the discovery that human manipulation had canceled all bets on the future of the physical earth and its climates. Where the wars made it harder to believe that any zone smaller than the world could be treated as a delimited environment (and hence a totality wholly manageable by watchful guardians), the newer revelations made it imperative to think how the world as a totality might indeed be managed so as to prevent catastrophe.

The intersection between solicitude about developmental environment and the new ecological awareness is nicely illustrated, as it happens, by a little book published in 1968 by the son of one of the scientists who meant so much to Theodore Dreiser. In *A Naturalistic View of Man*, George

Crile, Jr.'s main claim is one rehearsed by his father and many other writers we have examined: that "tastes and desires, prejudices and fears, are molded by environmental exposures and by experiences which occur too early to be consciously recalled" (35)—that "the decor of the child's home, the associations with people and animals, the music heard, the attitudes observed, the ideas discussed, all put their mark on the future man as firmly as physical qualities such as red hair and brown eyes, which the child inherits through the genes" (36). Crile, Jr., adds, however, that it is not only organisms in the ordinary sense of the term that go through periods in which much hangs on small things; the same may be true of the planet. "[T]here is a critical time in the life of each cell, each organ, each animal, each society, and perhaps even in the ecology of the world, at which the organism in question is particularly sensitive to its environment and best able to make an adaptive change"; and it seems to him likely that at the date of his writing, "the superorganism of the world" is "in one of these critical periods" (xiii, 152). By way of addressing this crisis, he recommends, above all, teaching the young the principles of science and the importance of international cooperation and peace.

This gesture toward the inculcation of basic values may remind us not only of Auden's midwar recommendation that courage, honesty, and so on be instilled as "conditioned reflexes" but also of that poet's long-standing occupation with the problem of how to educate children properly while not depriving them of free will. In this concern, he and Crile, Jr., were eminently representative of the middle two quarters of the twentieth century, when debates about education's methods and goals received unprecedented public attention and often turned, explicitly or implicitly, on ethical questions prompted by the (apparently secure) knowledge that environments could be engineered to induce people to develop in particular ways. For a commentator like Margaret Mead (writing in 1928 on the differences between American culture and Samoan culture, as she observed them), the need of modern education was not to impress upon children any particular ideological viewpoint but to give them—somehow—tools for choosing among the vast array of belief systems to which they would inevitably be exposed. For John Dewey (publishing a series of books on education and aesthetics that remained hugely influential through the interwar and postwar years), the best education would be one comporting with the truth that because the human organism and its environment reciprocally shape each other, the most useful experiences are those that lay the foundations for richer experience in the future. For Paul Goodman (commenting in 1960 on the causes of unrest among Beats, Hipsters, and Delinquents), American authorities needed to cease trying to manipulate the local conditions of problem juveniles and start recognizing that society as a whole was failing to offer its young people adequate environmental objects—meaningful ways of spending a life, healthy outlets for sexual desire, the freedom to invent new ways of thinking and being. For B. F. Skinner (generating research as well as utopian fiction and manifestos from the 1930s to the 1970s), high-handed refusals to apply the insights of behaviorism missed the point that children will always be conditioned by the stimuli, including the ideological ones, amid which they mature.

In other words, the idea that the way to a better world lies through thoughtful attempts to harness the environmental forces that determine human destinies—an idea pressed by Zola and Loeb and embraced in certain respects by Wilde and Dreiser—seems to have retained its ability to provoke capacious ethical reflection well into the twentieth century. If it lost some of its hold on expert and popular imaginations as the century drew to a close, a leading reason was surely that issues of troubled youth (the generation gap, adolescent rebellion, the malaise of maturation in an administered world) generally lost ground, in the news media and in public consciousness, to other concerns. Also playing its part was an increasingly aggressive challenge to progressive educators (for whom this kind of ethical problem was especially absorbing) from proponents of more traditional forms of teaching and child rearing. It may be, too, that the drift away from existentialism as a kind of broad philosophical matrix for cutting-edge anxieties made matters of free will less magnetic of intellectual regard. But perhaps the most critical element in this shift was the heightened attention to hereditary factors in development that we noted in the introduction, which implied a widening field of determinants and thus made less plausible the view that the course of a life could be set by environmental conditions alone.

In the last years of the twentieth century, moreover, neuroscience pressed an additional point bearing on anxiety about juvenile environments: that the human brain is more plastic and more resilient for a longer period than had previously been thought. Such a conclusion principally militates against premises like the one John Bruer dubbed "the myth of the first three years" (the idea that deficits of stimulation in the first thirty-six months of life are irreparable), but it also appears to warrant a drop in anxiety about the capacity of any single small event to alter a destiny. It is hardly the case that guardians of the young have ceased to worry about the damage inflicted by painful or shocking experiences: if few people today believe (with Lydia Child or Elmer Gates) that a child is scarred by the least failure of maternal serenity, many still wonder (with Ellen Key and W. H. Auden) whether casually inflicted wounds do not last forever in the child's so finely strung soul. But the new disclosures of biology—not to mention increasing attention to the influence on the young of noncustodial forces such as peers and mass media—have made it less necessary, at least theoretically, for parents and educators to imagine themselves charged with protecting children from all potentially injurious experience.

If the small, quickly forgotten blows of the quotidian may be on their way to seeming less momentous, however, the opaque operation of more seriously disruptive events seems to have become more fascinating. The 1990s in particular saw an explosion of public interest in recovered memories and posttraumatic disorders, even as scholars in several disciplines developed a body of theory around trauma—conceived (to take one influential formulation) as a structure of experience in which "the greatest confrontation with reality may also occur as an absolute numbing to it," in which "immediacy, paradoxically enough, may take the form of belatedness" (Caruth 5). Cultural critics at the beginning of the twenty-first century have also trained their sights on a trope we saw accruing force at the start of the twentieth: that of the child as bearer of society's future. In *No Future* (2004), for example, Lee Edelman writes that under the sign of "reproductive futurism," the well-being of children not yet born has taken precedence over the well-being of people alive in the present, particularly in political rhetoric: the "figural Child alone embodies the citizen as an ideal, entitled to claim full rights to its future share in the nation's good, though always at the cost of limiting the rights 'real' citizens are allowed. For the social order exists to preserve for this universalized, this fantasmatic Child, a notional freedom more highly valued than the actuality of freedom itself, which might, after all, put at risk the Child to whom such a freedom falls due" (2, 11). Together, these explorations and critiques suggest not that the links among children, experience, temporality, and injury are weaker than they had been, but that they are being reconfigured in ways that make concern about the manipulation of juvenile environments less central.

But what, in all of this, of the aesthetic? It certainly cannot be said that beauty and art were pivotal to mid- and later twentieth-century debates about the proper way to raise children or the causes of juvenile dissatisfaction. Notwithstanding Dewey's extensive meditations on "art as experience" and Herbert Read's briefs for the priority of art in all education, it does seem that one way the later twentieth century distinguished itself from the putatively more innocent age that preceded it was in the self-distancing from beauty that we have remarked at several junctures—a kind of presumptive embarrassment before the idea that so fragile, luxurious, and indeed feminized a thing could be a source of social hope. At the beginning of the twenty-first century, the single prominent residue of belief that art plays a crucial part in development seemed to lie in the widely disseminated but scientifically dubious notion that exposing children to classical music prenatally or in the first years of life gives them a cognitive advantage (the "Mozart effect"). This popular wisdom has even prompted legislation, the state of Florida requiring day-care centers to play classical music each day, Georgia and Tennessee mandating provision of classical CDs for every newborn (Gladwell 80).

Yet though beauty and art may not have dominated educational theory, policy-making, or the advice dispensed to parents in the later twentieth century, they did often assume an important role in fictions about young people and their development—and did so in ways that read like a convergence between the concerns discussed in the previous chapters of this book and the developments sketched in the preceding paragraphs of this epilogue. Consider, for example, Richard Wright's *Native Son*. Published in 1940, that novel does, certainly, precede "In Praise of Limestone" and West's treason books, but it merits consideration in this coda inasmuch as it unites paradigms familiar from earlier decades with anxieties that came into their own around the middle of the century. Famously reworking the broad outline of Dreiser's *American Tragedy*, Wright presents in Bigger Thomas a protagonist who, like Clyde Griffiths, longs for things he cannot have, murders or virtually murders at least one woman, and is convicted in a trial that occupies much of the novel. Like Dreiser, Wright dwells on the ways in which his hero is shaped by his environment, and like Dreiser he conducts a kind of naturalist experiment that raises thorny questions about individual guilt and social responsibility.

Unlike Dreiser however, Wright supplies his narrator with the terminology of behaviorism proper, which on the publication of *An American Tragedy* was only just beginning to make its way into public consciousness. Bigger, the narrator of *Native Son* tells us, "had been so conditioned in a cramped environment that hard words or kicks alone knocked him upright and made him capable of action" (240). In his essay on the origins of his novel, further, Wright refers to a "Bigger Thomas behavioristic pattern" in the lives of whites as well as blacks, to how "the pinch and pressure of the environment" gives a particular pitch to "waves of recurring crime, . . . silly fads and crazes, . . . quicksilver changes in public taste, . . . hysteria and fears." It is not exactly "that environment *makes* consciousness," Wright remarks, but it does seem "that the environment supplies the instrumentalities through which the organism expresses itself" (442).

Moreover, Bigger is affected by two kinds of forces that do not evidently affect Clyde: sensitization to the arbitrary power of another social group, and the importunings of mass media. According to the narrator, Bigger thinks of white people as "a great natural force, like a stormy sky looming overhead," one that "ruled him, even when they were far away and not thinking of him, ruled him by conditioning him in his relation to his own people" (115). One channel of this conditioning is the cinema, which exposes him to a more affluent world that, by virtue of his race as well as his social position, he has no prospect of joining. Where Clyde's intuition of a more beautiful way of living derives from cars and couples he sees on the streets, Bigger gains a glimpse into the life of the white well-to-do, at once more intimate and more mediated than Clyde's, from the movies—which whether art or not-quite-art (in the case of the particular newsreels and features he sees) certainly constitute a form in which words and images permit a feeling of immersion in experience not one's own. In the words of Boris Max, Bigger's attorney, "advertisements, radios, newspapers and movies" help to excite "the senses . . . dangle within easy reach of everyone the fulfillment of happiness"; and yet for many these are merely "daily taunts. Imagine a man walking amid such a scene, a part of it, and yet knowing that it is *not* for him!" (394). In *Native Son*, in other words, the kinds of stimulation provided by art (or forms having the structural properties of art) conduce neither to the formation of the beautiful soul imagined by Schiller and Wilde nor to the transcendence of enslaving desire imagined by Schopenhauer and Joyce. Rather, they enhance ferociously the kindling of desire treated by Dreiser; and they do so as part of an environment that, like the America Goodman would later describe, seems poor in adequate objects for those whose yearning it ignites.

Twenty-two years later, the intersection between conditioning and art would receive a grim apotheosis in Anthony Burgess's *A Clockwork Orange*. There, the brutal gang leader Alex, finally fallen into the hands of the law, is forced to watch violent films after being injected with drugs that induce feelings of intense physical illness, with the result that he becomes a law-abiding member of society because his body requires him to. As Gail Hart has observed, numerous references to Schiller in the novel (and in the film version by Stanley Kubrick) call attention to the text's engagement with the Schillerian dream in which aesthetic cultivation issues in citizens upholding a harmonious state. Burgess brings to the fore, particularly, a question that had always lurked in the Schillerian formula but would seem especially pointed for an age transfixed by the power of conditioning: how can the use of art (or anything) to fashion better behaved members of society be squared with the desideratum of nurturing free will in moral action? Schiller circumvented the problem by affiliating aesthetic education itself to the growth of freedom, but in *Clockwork*, as Hart notes, a debate among authorities about Alex's treatment "encapsulates and undermines much of Enlightenment reflection on rational and volitional freedom, including Schiller's theory" that "beauty symbolizes moral self-determination." Alex "is, in many ways, an inversion of Schiller's . . . *schöne Seele* . . . in whom duty and inclination coincide" (152).

Burgess's novel might be read in several ways, but its dominant suggestion, quite in line with Auden's "The distresses of choice are our chance to be blessed," is that the worst thing that can be done to a person is to eliminate all capacity for free exercise of the will. As Burgess wrote succinctly in a 1986 introduction, the book's "moral lesson . . . is the weary traditional one of the fundamental importance of moral choice" (lx). *Clockwork* is complicated, however, by the fact that Alex's treatment includes, in addition to conditioning by the artlike medium of violent film, an unintended sensitization to a form of high art. During his lawless days, Alex voraciously enjoys classical music, which he associates sometimes, though not always, with the pleasures of hurting people. As it happens, the films he is forced to watch while in custody are accompanied by classical music, so that after his release music too causes him to feel sick: "And I remembered especially that horrible Nazi film with the Beethoven Fifth, last movement. And now here was lovely Mozart made horrible" (162). The aesthetic faith of Schiller—and of Ruskin, Pater, and Wilde—thus seems subject to a further, double undercutting. In the so-to-speak natural circumstances that precede his treatment, Alex's love of music is bound up with antisocial and violent behavior, while in his postconditioning existence, its association with less disruptive courses depends not on harmonious feeling but on deterrent pain.

It would seem, especially given the many references to Schiller in the text, that the manipulation Burgess condemns must compass the deploying of art to the end of making good citizens. If so, *A Clockwork Orange* would ask to be read as a death knell for, or final nail in the coffin of, the utopian hope of improving society by aesthetic work upon the soul. Yet even on this front, matters are not quite so clear-cut. For the great composers themselves inspire a tenderness in preconditioning Alex, who though caring for few other people credits them with a kind of radical innocence. (While undergoing the treatment, he cries that it is a sin to use "Ludwig van" to accompany the Nazi film, for "[h]e did no harm to anyone. Beethoven just wrote music" [131].) In the final chapter of the novel, moreover, a slightly older Alex begins to dream of becoming a productive member of society when he thinks how Mozart, Mendelssohn, and Rimbaud had produced so much great art by the time they were his age (216).

The fears of an aimless and energetically destructive younger generation that propel *Clockwork* did not abate in the decades immediately following, but there does seem to have been, as just noted, a certain falling off of metaphysical solicitude about what happens to free will when juveniles are subjected to ingenious management. Indeed if Burgess and Auden record this solicitude at its lofty height, we can discern a kind of monument to its waning in Doris Lessing's 1988 novel, *The Fifth Child*. That narrative ends, emphatically, with delinquency: at the conclusion, the son of two thoughtful, generous middle-class people is leading a gang of hooligans, relishing the spectacle of violence (his mother sees him and his friends on television, "leering and jeering and shouting encouragement" to rioters in North London [126]), and almost certainly engaging in robbery and assault, perhaps rape and murder, himself. What brings Ben Lovatt to this pass, however, is neither the importuning of mass media, nor a social niche barren of opportunities for an interesting life, nor a school or home environment fundamentally out of touch with the needs of the young. It appears, rather, that Ben becomes what he becomes thanks to an exceptionally bizarre heredity.

From his birth, in fact, the violent, brooding Ben looks unlike other humans, and as the novel goes on even his parents come to compare him routinely to Neanderthals, goblins, dwarves, and trolls. His mother's speculation, which the novel seems more to endorse than to dismiss, is that aeons ago some cavern-dwelling species mixed into the population of early *Homo sapiens*, and that nowadays its residual genes occasionally meet up to produce a late representative such as Ben. (In Lessing's even stranger sequel, *Ben, in the World* [2000], scientists confirm that Ben is a "throwback" [143].) As an acknowledgment of the limits of parental control over the destinies of their offspring, *The Fifth Child* is superbly reasonable; as an effectively if unintentionally racist and xenophobic diagnosis of social problems, it is superbly mad. What makes it most striking from the point of view of our concerns, however, is its way of registering a change in thinking about human development that occurred in the last years of the twentieth century—a shift in attention, again, toward the power of genetic inheritance to set the parameters of possibility, a heightening of the conviction that environment alone cannot be destiny.

Among the authors treated at length in this study, the one whose vision seems closest to that of *The Fifth Child*, in many ways, is Rebecca West. Lessing's tale, after all, may be described as one of people who try to set up a beautiful home for beautiful souls, as Jenny and Kitty do in *The Return of the Soldier*, only to have it wrecked by an alien incursion. No more than West does Lessing appear to blame or praise the aspiration to a noble domestic environment; what seems censured, as the Lovatts' careful preparations melt away before Ben's brutality, is the expectation that things must certainly go well if sufficient care is taken to make existence lovely. (Indeed the Lovatts themselves wonder whether their strange fifth child is not some kind of punishment for the hubris of thinking they could arrange a fine life for a large family in modern times.) Yet Lessing's representation seems even bleaker than West's, and for reasons having to do partly with the power of the aesthetic. In West's framing, sensitivity to beauty helps humans in their struggle with a hostile universe—a point refracted through *The Return of the Soldier* in Margaret's appreciation for handsome things and Jenny's admiration of that woman's time-immune romance with Chris. *The Fifth Child*, on the other hand, has little to say about beauty as such, and by the novel's end even what we would call a general beauty of life seems but an achingly remembered opulence, the property of a time long ago and never to be regained.

In seeming to demonstrate how the dream of a gentle, dignified life is always fragilely suspended over an abyss of violence, Lessing's text evokes not only the Great War, around which *The Return of the Soldier* revolves, but also the Holocaust and World War II. Auden, as we have seen, was stunned in 1939 by the rapidity with which social tolerance, ethical principles, and traditions of civility could give way before a straightforward sanctioning of their casting off, and this rending of certainties has, of course, been the subject of countless works of fiction, poetry, drama, and nonfiction since then. One over which we might pause here is W. G. Sebald's novel *Austerlitz*, published both in its original German and in English translation in 2001. For this novel indicates especially acutely how some of the questions considered over the course of this book have shaped themselves in recent years.

At the heart of Sebald's story is a couple enjoying, to the end of the 1930s, hopes of a marvelous future—Agáta an aspiring opera singer, Maximilian a Czech party official who dreams "of making Czechoslovakia an island of freedom in the midst of the tide of Fascism," the two sharing an "interest in every aspect of French civilization" (154). These enlightened, cultured people are no match for the Nazis, of course: Maximilian flees to France and probably dies in a camp in the Pyrenean foothills (290), while Agáta is sent first to the Jewish ghetto of Terezín, an old town built on a star-shaped plan of fortification, and then east to her death in 1944 (204). Not the least wrenching part of their story is the breakup of their and others' physical households: Agáta having to deliver her best-loved possessions to the Compulsory Collection Center; the removal by shady officials of everything left in their apartment after they have gone; the mounds of property collected from those about to be transported out of Prague; and these forms of pillage echoed by a description of the so-called Galéries d'Austerlitz in Paris, where Nazi officers and their wives could choose from among items appropriated by the regime. "In the years from 1942 onwards," says the novel's most knowledgeable speaker, "everything our civilization has produced, whether for the embellishment of life or merely for everyday use, from Louis XVI chests of drawers, Meissen porcelain, Persian rugs and whole libraries, down to the last saltcellar and pepper mill, was stacked there in the Austerlitz-Tolbiac storage depot" (288–89).

The life Agáta and Maximilian had sought to make was not for themselves only, however; it was also for their son, who grows up to become the knowledgeable speaker of the foregoing lines. Borne away from Prague by train at the age of four and a half, Jacques Austerlitz is placed with a dour Welsh couple and then makes his way through the English school system, for many decades repressing all memory of, and avoiding all inquiry into, his past. When the narrator first meets him, in 1967, he is a slightly eccentric scholar, interested for no reason he can name in the architecture of railway stations and star-shaped fortifications; only three decades later does he appear as a man whose sleeping memories have been awakened by the buildings of Marienbad, by an old waiting room at Liverpool Street Station, by the lobby of his parents' apartment building in Prague, by "the capital of a cast-iron column" that solicits a photograph on the platform in Pilsen (221).

*Austerlitz* is thus a reworking of the bildungsroman that captures in several ways the disposition of the beginning of the twenty-first century, when literature seems singularly preoccupied with the historical past and when interest in the continuities of human development seems matched, if not exceeded, by interest in the breaks and gaps induced by individual and collective trauma. As in "The Child in the House" and *A Portrait of the Artist*, the small elements of physical environment register stealthily and irrevocably on the young mind, but what is of primary significance in *Austerlitz* is not how these may have shaped, just in themselves, the personality of the child in question. What matters more is that these impressions of early life descend into forgetfulness under the pressure of events that also deprive the soul of the chance to flower as splendidly as it might. For Sebald suggests strongly that, however extraordinary Austerlitz may be, his life has been more austere and impoverished, as well as more anguished, than it ought to have been.

Of course, no single novel can emblematize the fate, even the literary fate, of aestheticism's hope that beautiful environments might produce beautiful souls. Many people continue to believe, and many documents continue to suggest (as *Austerlitz* itself does at times), that aesthetic experience is important not just for its capacity to enrich life in the moment but also for its manner of forming the soul over spans of years. Still, Sebald's broken narrative can be said to illustrate, at a minimum, a difference in mood between the opening of the twentieth century and the start of the twenty-first—to bespeak a chastening of optimism having to do in part with changing views about the nature of art and beauty, but also with a cluster of doubts (accumulating for seven or eight decades at least) about the effectiveness, significance, ethics, and durability of efforts to arrange the circumstances of the young. In *Speaking of Beauty*, Denis Donoghue writes movingly of how "the 'tense' of beauty is the future," of how "its apprehension is propelled by a politics of hope and anticipation"; but he adds that Stendhal went too far in calling beauty the promise of happiness. "It is not even so much," Donoghue remarks, "but it is a figure of happiness, not a promise but a hint of possibility" (87). Perhaps the aesthetic turn of recent years should be seen, then, as a turn toward a figure and a hint. This would be a turn appropriate, no doubt, to a time when the embrace of anything more robust or definite may seem unwarranted—and when it may be hard to imagine anything so precious as beauty continuously surrounding and shaping, easier and truer to think of it as emerging, flickering out, and then appearing again.

# Notes

## Introduction
## Talking about Beauty

1. If slated for two dates, he would give on the second night another lecture focusing on home design, called "The House Beautiful." Much of the information on Wilde's program comes from Kevin O'Brien's superbly helpful *Oscar Wilde in Canada: An Apostle for the Arts*, 24–32.

2. All citations to works by Wilde in *Fateful Beauty* are to the Perennial Edition of the *Complete Works*, except where otherwise noted.

3. The years 1860 and 1960 delimit this book's period of focus only roughly, of course. Other markers from the same temporal neighborhoods could certainly have been used, since what is essential is only the indication that the line of thinking described in this study belonged preeminently to the second half of the nineteenth century and the first half of the twentieth. The advantage of 1860 and 1960, apart from their separation by exactly a hundred years, is that they are abstractable from the publication dates of the first and last literary texts given close attention here, Pater's "Coleridge's Writings" of 1868 and West's *New Meaning of Treason* of 1964.

4. See Steiner, *The Scandal of Pleasure*; Scarry, *On Beauty and Being Just*; and Donoghue, *Speaking of Beauty*. Other returns to the aesthetic, and analyses of the return to the aesthetic, can be found in Isobel Armstrong, *The Radical Aesthetic*; Peter de Bolla, *Art Matters*; John J. Joughin and Simon Malpas (editors), *The New Aestheticism*; George Levine (editor), *Aesthetics and Ideology*; Jonathan Loesberg, *A Return to Aesthetics*; David Wayne Thomas, *Cultivating Victorians*; and the special issue of *Diacritics* (spring 2002) edited by Simon Jarvis.

5. In *Ancient Art and Ritual*, first published in 1913, Harrison stressed ancient rites' way of involving entire communities and hoped for a reintegration of art and life in the modern age. These hopes were, of course, shared by many artists and thinkers during the age of modernism; they were also subjected to critique in polemics such as Wyndham Lewis's *Dithyrambic Spectator* (1925). Clement Greenberg is usually associated with an (approving) exploration of modern visual art's efforts to a draw a boundary between itself and the course of the world at large, but in the 1953 essay "The Plight of Culture" he concludes that because work has come to hold an absolutely central position in the modern world, "the only solution for culture" may be "to shift its center of gravity away from leisure and place it squarely in the middle of work." In " societies below a certain level of economic development," he observes, "everybody works; and where this is so, work and culture tend to be fused in a single functional complex. Art, lore and religion" are "barely distinguishable . . . from the techniques of production, healing and even war. . . . With work becoming universal once more, may it not become necessary . . . to repair the estrangement between work and culture, or rather between interested and disinterested ends . . . ?" (32–33).

6. As it happens, the line seems not to have reached the cartoon's actual first audiences. According to an online guide to censors' cuts and edits of classic cartoons, the whole sequence in which the stork leaves a bar in the clouds and delivers the baby to the wrong parents was omitted. For early viewers, then, it was not at all clear how the Sylvesters came to be the parents of a baby mouse (*Guide* 3).

### Chapter One
### Stealthy Environments

1. In *Discourse Networks 1800/1900*, Friedrich Kittler shows how this kind of change extended also to training in literacy and to the visions of poetry's role that, at least in German writing, such training inspired. "The lengthy process of reshaping the population of central Europe into modern nuclear families was directed by paternal figures only during its first phase—in Germany, up to Lessing's time"; thereafter, "[m]others stepped into the position previously held by fathers" and "a transition took place in the materiality of acculturative speech. The word of the father came . . . as articulated doctrine," but the "maternal gift is language in a nascent state, pure breath as a limit value from which the articulated speech of others begins" (27).

2. On the reception of Edgeworth's *Practical Education* by a Jewish family in the United States at the beginning of the nineteenth century, see Friedman's *Ways of Wisdom*.

3. Page numbers for three of the quotations from Child are the same for the second edition, of 1831, and the sixth edition, of 1846. The quote on the importance of the thousand little things done and said, however, only appears in the latter, which has a "Concluding Chapter" lacking in the 1831 version.

4. Among the earliest were Prussia in 1717, Austria in 1774, and Hungary in 1777.

5. On working-class schools in the nineteenth century, see especially Gardner's *Lost Elementary Schools of Victorian England*.

6. In England the first major document in the story of what Anthony Platt has named "the invention of delinquency" was the 1816 report of the Society for Investigating the Causes of the Alarming Increase of Juvenile Delinquency in the Metropolis. Efforts to implement the report's recommendation that young offenders be housed apart from adult prisoners at first went nowhere, but in subsequent decades the separate incarceration (and, eventually, separate trial) of the young became a principle of law (Colón 384). For more on antidelinquency bodies in England, see Cunningham, *Children of the Poor* 101ff., and Gillis, *Youth and History*, 156–57. The first notable public appearance of the term "juvenile delinquency" in the United States seems to have come in the 1818 report of New York's Society for the Prevention of Pauperism, formed the preceding year (Griffin and Griffin 12). An 1823 report for the same body led to the establishment of the New York House of Refuge, the first institution specifically for juvenile delinquents in the United States (Hawes 29). The first legal definition of delinquency seems to have appeared in section one of the Illinois Juvenile Court Act of 1899 (Glaser 3, Griffin and Griffin 19).

7. Hawes notes that the indeterminate sentence had already been wielded in the 1820s by judges committing juveniles to the New York House of Refuge, which though chartered and regulated by the state was operated by a private philanthropic group (40–41). Platt points out that long before the 1899 establishment of the juvenile court, Illinois had several provisions designed especially for children coming before the law.

8. For a careful account of the history of the terms "dime novel" and "penny dreadful," see Springhall, *Youth* 3–4, 39–44.

9. In 1894 a British Child Study Association was established under the leadership of Sully, a professor at University College, London (Cunningham, *Children of the Poor* 197–98).

10. The first OED-cited use of "organism" to mean "an individual animal, plant, or single-celled life form" comes from the 1834 *Philosophical Transactions of the Royal Society.* See also Shuttleworth, *George Eliot,* 3, on Kant giving in the *Critique of Judgment* (1790) "the now-classic definition of the organism as a whole in which each part is reciprocally means and end."

11. On the late Victorian obsession with the physical degeneration of the London working class, see Jones 127ff.

12. For a detailed recounting of the debate, see Hecht 227–35 and Nye 97–131.

13. Or as the proceedings themselves record Manouvrier:

> But this environment, I repeat, is indefinitely variable and one cannot suppose that two men can be subject to the same environmental conditions, if one examines this properly, that is to say in its concrete and real variations and not in its abstract totality, which is nothing more than a sort of algebraic sign.
>
> Let us imagine two brothers originally as alike as possible, and let us imagine it proposed that they be raised in the same fashion. . . . A simple change of servant that you would not note down can be, from the point of view I am taking, a great event. A single word, a gesture, a look can also be events. Later on, there will be the books read, the plays, etc., which will be different for the two brothers. . . . We are made, morally, by these small influences. . . . As for the actions of life, they depend very often on causes still smaller in appearance; that we met such a person, a certain day, was enough to modify our habits and our way of life. (*Actes* 279–80)

Leps does note that the alleged differences between French criminology and Italian could sometimes be less sharp than advertised. The Italian criminologist Enrico Ferri, for example, claimed in 1884 to have discovered a "law of criminal saturation" under which the amount of crime bears an exact relation to environmental conditions. "As a given volume of water at a definite temperature will dissolve a fixed quantity of chemical substance and not an atom more or less," he declared, "so in a given social environment with definite individual and physical conditions, a fixed number of offenses, no more and no less, can be committed" (quoted in Leps 57). On Manouvrier's response to Ferri's system, which claimed to balance biological and social causation, see particularly Nye 108.

14. Michèle Mendelssohn begins her *Henry James, Oscar Wilde, and Aesthetic Culture* by discussing a startling attestation to both the regional penetration of aestheticism and that movement's usefulness to American marketing, an 1882

advertisement featuring an image of Wilde and the suggestion that "being aesthetic" means buying sweets at the establishment of J. N. Piercy of Binghamton, New York (1).

15. Thomas Laycock, 1860: "No general fact is so well established by the experience of mankind or so universally accepted as a guide in the affairs of life, as that of unconscious life and action" (quoted in Whyte 162). Henry Maudsley, 1867: "The most important part of mental action, the essential process on which thinking depends, is unconscious mental activity" (quoted in Whyte 162). Friedrich Nietzsche: "The real continuous process takes place *below* our consciousness: the series and sequence of feelings, thoughts, and so on, are symptoms of this underlying process" (quoted in Whyte 176).

16. In his 1749 *Observations on Man, His Frame, His Duty, and His Expectations*, Hartley grounded this associationism in a material theory according to which ideas originate with vibrations of external objects impinging on the sensory receptors. These vibrations being transmitted along the nerves (porous cords filled with tiny particles of ether) to the brain, they give rise to corresponding infinitesimal vibrations called "vibratiuncles" which can remain in the brain as "dispositions" or be unleashed in motor activity (Richardson 9, Rylance 85). Hartleyan associationism was variously amended and attacked from the very first: its most vigorous eighteenth-century booster, Joseph Priestley, excised the mechanical theory as such while retaining the materiality of mental life (Richardson 10, Vallins 106, Christensen 61); Coleridge abandoned associationism because he felt it left no room for moral meaning in human existence, Hartley's identification of its necessitarian character with divine providence notwithstanding (Christensen 52, 90). Nonetheless, the doctrine of association of ideas did in one form or another enjoy a vigorous career well into the nineteenth century, helped along by adherents such as James and John Stuart Mill.

17. On habit, see further E. Darwin, *Zoonomia* 31; Lewes 56–59 and 112; Dewey, *Experience* 35; Burt 505 ("Habit formation is always the crux, alike in the making and in the unmaking of the youthful misdemeanant"); Taylor 69.

18. In *Lectures on the Philosophy of the Human Mind*, 1820, Thomas Brown had used the term "suggestion" to describe the basic process, emotional and not merely rational (as Lockean associationism would have it), by which the mind puts facts or thoughts into new combinations (Taylor 68, 77). Carpenter also discussed suggestibility at midcentury, theorizing that in a hypnotized person "unconscious cerebration" prevails over conscious action (Reed 79).

19. In *The Individual Delinquent*, Healy devotes several pages to suggestibility, writing that "within moderate limits" it is characteristic of normal people and that reliable ways of measuring it are lacking, but also that some repeat offenders have "shown themselves to be extraordinarily suggestible socially" (94). He notes as well that there is no record of a subject who "has been hypnotized into an offense which was against his nature to perform" (706).

20. This translation has been prepared for *Fateful Beauty* from the French original, as have translations from Manouvrier and Souriau. All other passages from sources originally in languages other than English have been drawn from the published English translations given in the References.

21. Schiller certainly did not go wholly unmentioned in British journals before Carlyle, nor was Carlyle the only one writing about him in the 1820s. On this, see Kooy, especially chapter 3.

22. For an extensive and fascinating treatment of Ruskin's influence in America, see Freedman 82–101. On Pater's American notoriety, see Freedman 114–16, 121, 128.

23. A believer in Darwinian sexual selection when few others were, he argued also, in his 1879 volume *The Colour-Sense* as well as in *Physiological Aesthetics*, that lower animals are attracted to bright colors because such colors (in flowers and fruits) betoken proximity to food, and that such attraction also accounts for the origin of the color sense in human beings (J. Smith 290). See Shuttleworth and Cantor 12 on the seriousness with which scientists received Allen's contributions and how, indeed, Allen's case exemplifies the blurriness of the line between journalist and scientist in the nineteenth century. On Wilde's warm appreciation of Allen's 1891 essay, "The Celt in English Art," see Smith and Helfand, "Text as Context," 80–81.

## Chapter Two
## Aestheticism's Environments

1. Donoghue comments that in this paragraph Pater "is not endorsing the scientist's account of what we call life" but only tempting himself "with the vertigo of an alien vocabulary," speculatively "suppos[ing] himself a materialist or an objectivist and let[ting] modern science have its destructive way" (*Walter Pater*, 48–49). That Pater's take on human existence is not bounded by materialist philosophy is beyond question, but this does not mean that Pater disputed materialism as a matter of scientific fact. On the contrary, he took it seriously enough (as we will see) to make it the donnée of his farthest-reaching early theories. Donoghue's assumption that materialism could not have been fully crucial to Pater's thinking—an assumption also made with respect to Wilde by several readers we will encounter here— attests how the persistent divide between the sciences and the humanities (what C. P. Snow half a century ago called the "two cultures") can skew present-day readings of nineteenth-century writers for whom the divide scarcely pertained.

The suggestion that Spencer may have been Pater's source for the language quoted here comes from Billie Andrew Inman in *Walter Pater's Reading*. Inman also shows that Pater could have taken inspiration from Johannes Müller's *Elements of Physiology*, published in English translation in the 1840s, or from an article on Darwin published by Lewes in 1868 (182–84).

2. Determinism is thus closely related to "mechanism," defined in the OED as "[t]he opinion or doctrine that all natural (esp. biological or mental) phenomena can be explained with reference to mechanical or chemical processes." Both determinism and mechanism are also associated with "materialism," in its meaning as (quoting the OED once more) the theory "that mental phenomena are nothing more than, or are wholly caused by, the operation of material or physical agencies."

3. Lytton Strachey quotes this remark for his acerbic portrait of Arnold in the 1918 *Eminent Victorians* (231). But if Strachey captures something essential to the

earlier British nineteenth century in so doing, another of his writings suggests that he grasped only partially the middle and later century's turn toward the effects of places on the soul. His 1922 memoir, "Lancaster Gate," begins as follows:

> The influences of houses on their inhabitants might well be the subject of a scientific investigation. Those curious contraptions of stones or bricks, with all their peculiar adjuncts, trimmings, and furniture, their specific immutable shapes, their intense and inspissated atmosphere, in which our lives are entangled as completely as our souls in our bodies—what powers do they not wield over us, what subtle and pervasive effects upon the whole substance of our existence may not be theirs?

The statement reads like a paraphrase of "The Child in the House," but Strachey fails to mention Pater at this point and indeed goes on to assert that his generation's "fathers," while "interested in the mental and moral implications of their surroundings," thought in terms of ancient family seats and social distinctions, and would have found absurd "the notion that the proportions of a bedroom, for instance, might be significant" (*Lytton Strachey by Himself* 16). That some Victorian fathers (as well as Oxford bachelors) would not have found this at all absurd is elegantly shown by Cohen.

Victoria Rosner calls attention to the little-read "Lancaster Gate" in her recent *Modernism and the Architecture of Private Life*, where she argues more generally for an understanding of "interiority" as a "cluster of interdependent concepts that extend from the representation of consciousness to the reorganization of home life; revised definitions of personal privacy, intimacy, and space; and new assessments of the sexualized and gendered body." Influencing and construing each other, these categories in Rosner's view hold "modernist interiority in a tension between abstraction and materiality, between metaphor and literality" (11).

4. See Plotz 54 and Richardson, *Literature*, 51–55 and 105–06. Both scholars quote Wordsworth's mockery, in the fifth book of the *Prelude* (around lines 350–63), of those ever on guard against manifestations of independent thought in children.

5. For a careful treatment of *theoria* in Ruskin, see Landow 157–59. Landow notes that Ruskin's affiliation of ideas of beauty with "moral perception" rather than "intellectual perception" must be understood with reference to a duality in the sense of "moral," which in the nineteenth century meant not only "ethical" but also "referring to all mental processes," including unconscious ones.

6. The editors of Wilde's notebooks explain that the mark following the word "follow" is the "the Greek semicolon," which "Wilde used for emphasis or internal divisions on the page" (Smith and Helfand, "Text," 2). The bracketed "[never?]" in this quotation is a speculation by the editors.

7. See Smith and Helfand, "Text as Context," 96–104. Others who read in this vein include Terri Hasseler and Heather Seagroatt. According to Hasseler, "Dorian appears to be determined by the molecular arrangement of his body" after his soul is removed to the painting: "In him, Wilde creates the essence of the Huxleyan predetermined automaton by denying him the capability of choice" (31). According to Seagroatt, Dorian early joins his friend Lord Henry Wotton in a materialist investigation with himself as subject; by means of this narrative, Wilde critiques materialist science's inability to explain psychological events.

8. According to Richard Ellmann, Wilde wrote *Dorian Gray* in the fall of 1889 and the spring of 1890; it was published on 20 June 1890 as pages 3 through 100 of the July issue of *Lippincott's* (*Oscar Wilde* 314).

9. One of the writers from whom Wilde might have drawn his sense of the dangers of ugly surroundings, of course, was Ruskin. Yet the older critic did allow at some points that aesthetically poor environments might have their own contribution to make. It was not the finish but the imperfection of Gothic that was crucial to its social importance, Ruskin insists in *The Stones of Venice*, and in the chapter of *Modern Painters* called "The Two Boyhoods" he argues that while Giorgione was inspired by the beauties of the Venice in which he lived, the great J.M.W. Turner profited, at least in some ways, from early immersion in urban squalor. Ruskin's remarks about Turner's boyhood might indeed serve as an illustration of Pater's point that the sensitive soul finds ministries to the desire of beauty in unlikely places.

10. Of the *hôtel* in which Watteau is staying, the same correspondent—whom scholars have identified as a notional ancestor of Pater's (Levey 37)—reports a few pages later, "The antiquities, beautiful curiosities of all sorts—above all, the original drawings of those old masters Antony so greatly admires—are arranged all around one there, that the influence, the genius, of those things may imperceptibly play upon, and enter into one, and form what one does" (*Imaginary* 35). "The Child in the House" and *Marius*, again, contain numerous paeans not only to natural effects but also to the powers of indoor things, and to the interweaving of aesthetic sensibility with the growth of moral seriousness.

11. Thomas Otten notes that in their *Decoration of Houses*, Wharton and Codman advise placing valuable but fragile objects within children's reach, the better to train their hands (47), a recommendation that evokes Wilde on the unconscious acquisition of refinement through exposure to delicate china. Otten's *Superficial Reading of Henry James* also points to several connections between James's work and the matters examined here, includes a reading of Dorian Gray's final act as an "attempt to destroy the artifact that has produced him" (66), and sketches how a "new materialism" in recent literary scholarship (as in studies by Elaine Scarry, Mark Seltzer, Bill Brown, Diana Fuss, and Susan Stewart) might be seen as coming "at the end of a historical movement toward the non-anxious identification of bodies and objects" (140).

12. There is not space to recount in any detail the career of art education in Britain and the United States in the late nineteenth century and beyond. It may help a little to note, however, that art training in schools was first strongly promoted in the 1830s, initially as a method for supplying the populace with skills that would enhance cognitive development and lend a competitive advantage to British or American arts and industries. As the quotes from Jarves and Tyrwhitt suggest, art education soon came to be seen as, in addition, a method for improving the masses' morals and disposition of time. In the middle and later years of the American nineteenth century, a key component of aestheticism in a broad sense was the enthusiasm of Ruskin-influenced "art crusaders," who promoted the ideal of sensitivity to beauty and the idea that in a democracy everyone should have access to training in drawing and related activities (see Efland 91–92, Stankiewicz 51–56). Throughout this period, there subsisted a powerful tension between those

who wanted art instruction geared primarily to industry and those who recommended it for the sake of individual growth; by the end of the century, movements toward vocational education had brought these tensions sharply to the fore. In subsequent years, many advocates of art education came to tout the value of children's practice in "creative self-expression," even as modernist interest in the power of "primitive" form led to new attention to art by juveniles. During the interwar period, art education suffered setbacks attendant on economic depression, but it revived again after the war, partly through the efforts of figures like Herbert Read, who insisted that art education should be central to or paradigmatic of education generally. In the last half century, of course, the role of art in the curriculum has been debated endlessly and the funding of art training subject to immense fluctuation. For general information on the trajectory of art education in Britain, see Macdonald and Efland; on art education in the United States see Efland, Korzenik, and Logan; on Read, see Read and Thistlewood.

13. When, in a lecture of April 1884 given in London's East End, Wilde offered yet another version of his critique of English education, his remarks were said by many "to be quite worthy of Ruskin" (Mason 250). In *The Vulgarization of Art*, Linda Dowling argues that "at the heart of the vision of aesthetic democracy inspiring Ruskin and Morris" as well as Wilde "lies an ideal of aristocratic sensibility unrecognized as such" (xii). For an acute analysis of how this paradox manifested itself in Wilde's American lecture tour, and in "The Soul of Man under Socialism," see Dowling 89–100.

14. Morris later presented "The Decorative Arts" as his first public lecture, under the title "The Lesser Arts."

15. For other instances in which Ouida decries ugliness or failures of aesthetic sensibility, see her *Critical Studies*, 198–206.

16. These points suggest too how wallpaper, which literally surrounds the subject as no other item of decoration does, could take on a sort of emblematic centrality when it came to concern about environmental effects. Wilde was not the only writer to acknowledge the psychological power of this furnishing in a witticism: Jan Jennings cites an 1876 comment by the editor of *Harper's Bazar* to the effect that "Indiana divorce laws may be perhaps directly traced to some frightful inharmoniousness in wall-paper" (quoted in Jennings 243). Jennings also quotes the authors of *Beautiful Homes*, 1878, on how the "beautiful picture or softly tinted wall, the peaceful drapery may perhaps be the means of opening some fount of wisdom, else closely sealed, or touching some sensitive nerve of thought, otherwise dormant" (quoted in Jennings 243). On Wilde's own domestic interiors, see Gere 97–107 (where the wallpaper, among other features, is described) and Rosner 46–58 (where his use of frames is related to *Dorian Gray*).

17. Gregory Castle offers a different analysis of *Dorian Gray* as (anti-)bildungsroman, arguing that, like Joyce's *Portrait of the Artist as a Young Man*, it critiques colonial conditions (in Ireland) for failing to "encourage and nurture Bildung" (127). Castle's larger argument is that the modernist bildungsroman plays a key role in a larger modernist project of recuperating "the Enlightenment concept of aesthetico-spiritual Bildung, which had been rationalized and bureaucratized in the course of the nineteenth century" (1). On *Dorian Gray* as a bildungsroman promoting an "organic" ideal of development, see Altieri.

18. In these same years, such questions were being considered on other fronts, of course. Published in English in 1891, for example, was Cesare Lombroso's *Man of Genius*, which argued for a connection between crime and genius, art, and education. Lombroso's very popular *Degeneration*, which reinforced the point, came out in English in 1895.

19. Zelizer is referring to the United States, but the point clearly applies to Europe in this period as well.

20. Quotations here come from Eagleton's "Ideology of the Aesthetic," which was first published in *Poetics Today* in 1988 and was reprinted in *The Politics of Pleasure: Aesthetics and Cultural Theory*, edited by Stephen Regan. This article-length version has proven handier for the purposes of quotation than Eagleton's book, *The Ideology of the Aesthetic*, though the latter offers a more extensive treatment of the subject. Locations in the book of passages similar to those quoted from the article are given here for readers' convenience; article citations are to the Regan printing.

21. In the book-length *Ideology of the Aesthetic*, Eagleton writes:

Such a belief [in virtue] naturally demands an ambitious programme of moral education and reconstruction, for there is no assurance that the human subjects who emerge from the *ancien régime* will prove refined and enlightened enough for power to found itself on their sensibilities. It is thus that Rousseau writes the *Émile* and the *Nouvelle Heloïse*. . . . Not just any subject can be "interpellated," in Althusserian phrase; the task of political hegemony is to produce the very forms of subjecthood which will form the basis of political unity. (24)

See also, in this regard, Hart 19, 29–31 on surveillance and regularity in Schiller's own education at the Hohen Karlsschule and on critical debates—Paul de Man, Theodor Adorno, and Constantin Behler as well as Eagleton—concerning coerciveness in Schiller's scheme for aesthetic education.

22. Of course, Wilde—who on this score figures once again as a link between Ruskin and modernism—also believed that the work of art itself could be understood as leveling a kind of protest against the tyranny of economic values. "You may lay up treasures by your railways," he declares at the culmination of the English Renaissance lecture, "or open your ports to the galleys of the world, but you will find the independence of art is the perfect expression of freedom" (164).

23. On the relations among contemplation, being, art, and the "critical spirit," see "The Critic as Artist" 1039–42.

Chapter Three
Aesthetics of Acuteness

1. In one of the first important long studies of Joyce, the New Directions–published *James Joyce: A Critical Introduction* (1941), Harry Levin also frames his reading of Joyce's achievement in terms of a negotiation between symbolism and naturalism—or, as Levin casts it at some points, between "richness" and "reality." Writing appreciatively of Wilson on the whole, Levin only demurs in commenting that a decade of the "*ersatz* product known as 'socialist realism'" has proven Wil-

son's forecast of a strengthening of naturalism mistaken, whereas Symbolism has turned out to be more resilient than expected (4, 209).

2. According to Smith and Helfand, the probable prompt for this entry is Spencer's *Study of Sociology*—which text Wilde also quotes in an entry coming shortly after: "Light falling on a crystal alters its molecular arrangements, but can only do so by an infinite series of millions of etherial waves, so also in the social organism any permanent change requires innumerable recurrences of thoughts• feelings• action•" (*Oxford Notebooks* 111). The succeeding entry refers to experiments by Claude Bernard. See footnote 7, below, for more on Wilde's absorption of Spencer.

3. For an extended discussion of Joyce's relation to aestheticism, see also Harkness. For an extended discussion of Wilde and Joyce as Irish writers, see Mahaffey.

4. In a now famous letter of 1906, Joyce told his publisher Grant Richards, "I have written [*Dubliners*] for the most part in a style of scrupulous meanness and with the conviction that he is a very bold man who dares to alter in the presentment, still more to deform, whatever he has seen and heard" (quoted in Gorman 150).

5. Joyce also described his project to his brother Stanislaus as that of trying "to give people some kind of intellectual pleasure or spiritual enjoyment by converting the bread of everyday life into something that has a permanent artistic life of its own . . . for their mental, moral, and spiritual uplift" (quoted in Ellmann, *James Joyce* 163).

6. Emer Nolan discusses this line from *Portrait* in showing how Stephen's scientific materialism ends up (unsettlingly) confirming his continuity with his local environment, including its religious and nationalist traditions. See especially 284–89.

7. See Smith and Helfand, "Text as Context," 28–30 for a summary of Wilde's responses to Spencer. Among the most significant of Wilde's entries, in this regard, is one in the Commonplace Book that credits Spencer and Kant with carrying on the line of dialectic. According to Wilde, Spencer did so by substituting for "individualistic empiricism" a "generalistic empiricism of the hereditary transmission of concepts: Innate Ideas have thus returned to the mind, in Kant on transcendental, in Spencer on Biological Grounds" (*Oxford Notebooks* 120).

8. Patrick convinces his audience that the Archdruid is wrong to claim that physical vision can give some people insight into noumenal reality, just as in the *Popular Lectures* Helmholtz faults Goethe for too intense fidelity "to his principle, that Nature must reveal her secrets of her own free will; that she is but the transparent representation of the ideal world" (51). Helmholtz takes this occasion to reinforce the point, discussed below, that the quality of a sensuous perception depends less on the nature of the object perceived than on that of the sensory receptor. For more on Helmholtz at this moment in the *Wake*, see Theall 173 and 180–81.

9. Or as Theall remarks, "[p]erception as a function of the machinery of the body is itself mechano-organic" in Joyce. Indeed each of the eighteen episodes of *Ulysses* grounds its action "in the nature of the body as an organo-chemico-electro-mechanical entity" (44, 45).

10. In *Adolescence*, Hall too associates a delay in the reflex with aesthetic sensitivity. An important modification occurring in adolescence, he writes, is, that

"whereas most sense stimuli before this age tend strongly to provoke reflex reactions, after it these tend to be delayed or better organized. . . . Sensations are more objectified and their pleasure and their pain effects are more keenly felt. There is a new sense esthetic or enjoyment of the sensation itself for its own sake" (2.2).

11. In *Joyce and Aquinas*, William T. Noon points out that in fact the "Aquinan contemplatio is as much kinetic as it is static" and quotes approvingly Paul Elmer More's contention that Joyce would have been truer to Aquinas had he distinguished not between a kinetic and a static art but "between art that aims to arouse physical lust or loathing, and art that seeks to move desire and joy of hyperphysical realities" (37). Noon further observes that the "epistemological accentuation" of Stephen's aesthetic theory makes it more Kantian than Scholastic: "the Scholastic aesthetic is metaphysical, whereas the Kantian aesthetic is epistemological in nature," though both associate the aesthetic with freedom from interest in physical possession of the object (38).

12. Here and elsewhere in this study, the term "beautiful soul" is used in a general and relatively casual way to indicate a person, personality, or subjectivity one might regard, by whatever criteria, as beautiful. The term is not used in the more restrictive sense of the Enlightenment concept of *schöne Seele* or *belle âme*, famously treated by (among many others) Goethe and Hegel. For more on the history of this concept, see Norton and Milne.

13. In her superb *James Joyce, Sexuality and Social Purity*, Katherine Mullin reproduces a page from F. Arthur Sibly's *Private Knowledge for Boys*, 1912, where under the heading "Rules for those who desire to lead a pure life" and the subheading "CARE OF THE MIND" the following instruction may be found: "When sexual thoughts occur to the mind, banish them *instantly*. Every moment that such thoughts remain in the mind they increase their hold on it. The least tolerance or encouragement of such thoughts is therefore fatal to real chastity" (reproduced in Mullin 102).

14. This point jibes well with Michael Levenson's discussion of a question Stephen puts in one of his diary entries in *Portrait*: "Was it an instant of enchantment only or long hours and days and years and ages?" Levenson writes,

Stephen imagines the epiphanic moment stretching endlessly outward, unfolding into eternity, but this visionary prospect coincides in disturbing ways with the image of damnation as "an evil of boundless extension, of limitless duration.". . . Indeed, one of the most forbidding implications in the plotting of Stephen's character is precisely the suggestion that the revelatory moment may prolong itself through "hours and days and years and ages," and so prevent not only a satisfying culmination but even the consolations of catastrophe. (188)

15. Late in his devotional phase, Stephen derives "an intense sense of power" from knowing "that he could by a single act of consent, in a moment of thought, undo all that he had done," and then draws another "thrill of power and satisfaction" from the knowledge "that he had not yielded nor undone all" (128). Something of this frisson certainly informs his later doctrine of aesthetic apprehension, which delineates in a different fashion how much can be staked upon a moment of consciousness.

16. Noon, once again, provides illuminating detail on Stephen's adherences to and divergences from actual Aquinan doctrine. What Aquinas means by *integritas*, Noon points out, is not the discrete unity Stephen describes but "the completeness or perfection which a being possesses when it is all that it ought to be" (47). Further, *integritas*, *consonantia*, and *claritas* "are conceived by Aquinas as qualities of things which the mind comes to know, not as 'stages' in the mind's own act of knowing" (22). And while it is true that the three elements required for beauty do apply to created beauty, the question Aquinas is addressing when he names this triad pertains to the Trinity, not to things in the world (26).

Chapter Four
Tropisms of Longing

1. In the same article, for example, Dreiser evokes the horror of a New York sweatshop, inviting the reader to picture "a small, dark, foul closet in a crowded and filthy tenement, a room in which a dozen or fifteen human beings" work from dawn until midnight every day for appalling wages (258).

2. In his first volume of autobiography, *Dawn*, Dreiser remembers the grim Catholic schoolroom he entered at age six as containing "forty or fifty hard wooden benches, much scarred . . . by knives and pencils and much bespattered with ink. . . . The floor was bare, the walls covered with blackboards" (27). He also records his delight at finally being enrolled in a public school years later: "But, ah, the charm of that seventh grade room! Its warm, bright space; clean, varnished desks; wide and bright windows, framing what lovely views!" (192).

3. In the most celebrated of modernist polemics against ornament, 1908's "Ornament and Crime," Adolf Loos argues that "the evolution of culture is synonymous with the removal of ornamentation from objects of everyday use" and that "in economic respects," ornament "is a crime, in that it leads to the waste of human labor, money, and materials" (167, 169). "[A]nyone who goes to the Ninth [Symphony of Beethoven] and then sits down to design a wallpaper pattern," according to Loos, whose rhetoric evokes Wilde taken into a higher key, "is either a fraud or a degenerate" (175).

4. Such calls for more attractive facilities were complemented, in this period, by appeals from the "schoolroom decoration movement" proper, which extolled the virtues of putting photographs and casts of great works into classrooms. Originating with the Boston Public School Art League, founded in 1892 by the Salem artist Ross Turner, the movement soon spread to arts societies in other cities. Like so much else in American arts advocacy, it seems to have drawn its principal inspiration from Ruskin, who had long argued not only for the beautification of facilities but also for the provision of images of masterpieces as aids to instruction. The school decoration movement also helped inspire the later "picture study" movement, which similarly stressed the power of art to improve the taste and elevate the spirit (Stankiewicz 54, 59–60).

5. This quotation accords with Jonathan Freedman's sketch of the American career of Pater's writings. In the 1880s and 1890s, according to Freedman, Pater increasingly found favor in the United States press, including some Christian

publications, but was still greeted with dismay by many Christian commentators. Freedman cites, for example, *Christianity and Aestheticism*, in which the Christian Socialist Washington Gladden decries the "aesthetic Paganism . . . whose degrading worship threatens the life of the church and the nation" (quoted in Freedman 115).

6. In so writing, Dreiser was entering what had been, for at least a century, an arena of vigorous debate among journalists, jurists, physicians, and members of the general public. That ordinary citizens would not utterly discount the physiological bases of behavior in assessing moral responsibility, even in 1800, is shown by the case of *Hadfield*, tried that year. The defendant having been charged with an attempt on the life of George III, his counsel maintained that he could not be held responsible for his actions because he had been suffering from delusions probably resulting from a brain injury. As Daniel N. Robinson notes, Hadfield's acquittal illustrates a "general willingness to accept neurological opinions as grounds for exoneration," so that although most educated persons in England in 1800 might not have regarded the soul as material, many might have "concede[d] that certain peculiar states of mind could be induced by pathological states of brain" (305).

7. In his *Creative and Sexual Science* of 1870, Orson Fowler describes at one point how "a POUGHKEEPSIE HUSBAND" furnished his rooms with "beautiful furniture, pictures, books, &c." during his wife's pregnancy, "in order thereby to impress taste, refinement, and love of art on their offspring." In the event, affirms Fowler, the children "were far better than" the parents, " with "[h]eads and characters" of a quality "rarely found in this wife-neglecting age." Fowler then asks, "HAD GRECIAN WORKS OF ART, lavishly erected in public, and placed in their boudoirs for their pregnant wives to impress on their unborn, nothing to do with the formation of the refined tastes of the classical people?" (796).

This legend of the Greeks' improving the unborn by exposing the mother to beauty also makes an appearance in Wilde's 1889 "Decay of Lying" ("The Greeks, with their quick artistic instinct, . . . set in the bride's chamber the statue of Hermes or Apollo, that she might bear children as lovely as the works of art that she looked at in her rapture or her pain" [983]) and in a passage from Winckelmann that Pater quotes in *The Renaissance* ("The general esteem for beauty went so far, that the Spartan women set up in their bedchambers a Nireus, a Narcissus, or a Hyacinth, that they might bear beautiful children" [quoted at *Three* 201]).

8. All citations to *Sister Carrie* are to the Oxford University Press edition.

9. In an article of 1969, Christopher Katope points out that *Sister Carrie* is permeated by the language of forces that Dreiser would have encountered in Spencer, from the first chapter's title, "The Magnet Attracting: A Waif Amid Forces" to the "repeated use of the term 'force' and related terms ('magnetism,' 'attraction,' 'lures,' 'radiating presence,' 'drawn,' 'influence,' 'fascination,' 'current of feeling,' 'power,' 'chemical reagent,' 'dissolving fire,' and more) in describing Carrie's relationship to her environment and especially to Drouet and Hurstwood" (66–67).

10. In 1936's *Phenomena of Life: A Radio-Electric Interpretation* (a copy of which he presented to Dreiser when they finally met face-to-face), Crile indexes in especially lively terms his long-standing sense of a connection between the discoveries of science and solicitude about every experiential transaction. Moving easily

from (scientifically dubious) theories about the centrality of electric potential in health to implications for the raising of the young, he refers to the "protoplasm upon which the teacher etches the action patterns of education and training," and to the "daily formation of action patterns in childhood" as shaped not only by "parents, brothers and sisters, uncles and aunts, and grandparents" but also by religion and "the radio, the movie, the theatre, the newspapers, the novels, the tale of adventure, by playmates and acquaintances" (116–17).

11. Moers and Zanine note further that while he was writing *An American Tragedy*, Dreiser was discussing with his friend Edward H. Smith ideas about criminal nature propounded by a neuropathologist named Max G. Schlapp. "[C]riminal actions are in reality reactions caused by the disturbed internal chemistry of the body," write Schlapp and Smith in their jointly authored *New Criminology* (1928), and this chemistry depends almost wholly upon constitution: "personal environment is a secondary matter, the determining factor in all cases being the mental, nervous and glandular soundness of the individual" as established partly (á la Gates) by prenatal conditions (29, 209). Though Dreiser did not accept these claims (see Zanine 105), the novel more than permits the inference that Clyde differs from Roberta in basic constitution as well as early experience. The defense attorney Jephson, for example, ventures at one point that Clyde committed his crimes because he was "a moral and mental coward—not that I am condemning you for anything that you cannot help. (After all, you didn't make yourself, did you?)" (710).

12. Preparing the house where his trysts with Aileen are to take place, Cowperwood consults with Fletcher Gray, a partner in an art-importing firm who astounds him with his aesthete's knowledge—as of the fact that there "are fifty periods of one shade of blue porcelain alone." The financier then quickly catches the enthusiasm of this namesake of Wilde's Dorian: "Wealth, in the beginning, had seemed the only goal, to which had been added the beauty of women. And now art, for art's sake—the first faint radiance of a rosy dawn—had begun to shine in upon him, and to the beauty of womanhood he was beginning to see how necessary it was to add the beauty of life—the beauty of material background—how, in fact, the only background for great beauty was great art" (*Financier*, 144–45).

13. A fascinating product of Dreiser's ambivalence appears in a piece called "Phantasmagoria" included in *Hey Rub-a-Dub-Dub!* In this bizarre allegorical drama Dreiser presents the whole course of the cosmos, beginning to end, as a struggle between powers of good led by Beauty (and including pity, love, reason, and hope) and powers of evil led by Ambition (hate, despair, fear, greed) for the attention of the precociously weary Lord of the Universe. In the first of the play's three scenes ("The House of Birth"), Beauty and Ambition present their cases; in the second ("The House of Life"), Beauty has the upper hand and life flourishes; in the third ("The House of Death"), Ambition and gloom prevail, until at the close of the drama the universe collapses. That Dreiser would choose Beauty and Ambition as the universe's archetypally contending principles says a great deal about the force of both in his imagination; it also invites a reevaluation of Cowperwood's and Witla's stories. On their own, these narratives can be understood as showing how the craving for beauty and the desire for wealth and status become competing priorities under a particular kind of social organization; read in the

strong light of "Phantasmagoria," however, they appear to describe two manifestations of a conflict absolutely fundamental to existence.

14. The editors of the Pennsylvania edition of *Sister Carrie* omit this ending as part of their effort to produce a text free from additions Dreiser seems to have made at the urging of others. Whether the reconstructed version is superior to the one originally published is an intriguing question, but it does not affect the intrinsic interest, for our purposes, of the closing pages of the *Carrie* issued in 1901.

15. See many of the entries in *Notes on Life*, including those at 72–73, 279–80, 283, 332–33.

16. Following his reading in "Darwin, Huxley, Tyndall, Lubbock," Witla in *The "Genius"* concludes that "[l]ife was nothing save dark forces moving aimlessly. . . . To think that beauty should blossom for a little while and disappear for ever seemed sad" (157).

17. It should be acknowledged that the tone of the brief entry containing this comment is difficult to read; the remark does not necessarily indicate frustration or despair. In another of his notes, Dreiser writes, "The secret of the Universe is that it has no place to go. Being all in all . . . it can only change itself, transmute its totality into endless forms with endlessly varied objectives or desires, moods, aspects, pleasures, sorrows, successes and failure, dramas and tragedies. To achieve this, it must veil itself by making each of its creatures sensorially incomplete" (208).

18. Zanine gives the book as *Beauty*, but there is no book by Santayana with that shorter title.

## Chapter Five
## Great House and Super-Cortex

1. "The country-houses of late George Eliot, of Henry James and of their etiolated successors," Williams writes, were "the country-houses of capital rather than of land. More significantly and more ritually than ever before, a rural mode was developed, as a cultural superstructure, on the profits of industrial and imperial development. It was a mode of play: an easy realisation of the old imagery of Penshurst: field sports, fishing, and above all horses; often a marginal interest in conservation and 'old country ways' " (282).

2. Marvell: "But all things are composed here / Like Nature, orderly and near. / . . . / In which we the Dimensions find / Of that more sober Age and Mind / When larger sized Men did stoop / To enter at a narrow loop; / As practising, in doors so strait, / To strain themselves through *Heavens Gate*" (quoted in Williams 55). Langhorne: "Nor lightly deem, ye Apes of modern Race, / Ye Cits that sore bedizen Nature's Face, / Of the more manly Structures here ye view; / They rose from Greatness that ye never knew" (quoted in Williams 80).

3. In *The Anglo-Irish Novel and the Big House*, Vera Kreilkamp notes that "[d]uring the struggle for independence from 1919 to 1921 and the subsequent civil war, nearly two hundred Irish country houses were destroyed as the symbols of a colonizing force, sometimes without consideration for the politics of their owners" (5–6).

4. As Williams notes, for many writers "an idea of the country is an idea of childhood: not only the local memories, or the ideally shared communal memory, but the feel of childhood: of delighted absorption in our own world, from which, eventually . . . we are distanced and separated, so that it and the world become things we observe" (297).

5. Margaret's feeling for beauty also includes frank recognition of ugliness. Her verdict on her own residence is, "It is a horrid little house isn't it?," after recording which Jenny comments, "She evidently desired sanction for a long suppressed discontent" (49).

6. In this, West certainly taps into the tradition of English country-house poetry. As Kreilkamp neatly puts matters, poems such as Jonson's "To Penshurst" and Marvell's "Upon Appleton House" attack "grand edifices that are constructed for show. . . . Houses are praised if they are places in which to live and to form organic social relations; they are not praised if they exist merely to feed the vanity of their owners" (18).

7. The curly brackets, by convention of the *Selected Letters*, indicate words West inserted above the line.

8. And so is science. West wonders, "May it not be possible that the process of collecting information about the universe which we call science when it can be most profitably extracted through real material and art when it can be most profitably extracted through imaginary material, represents the activity of a collective and external super-cortex which works on the material created by the activities of the individual cortices?" (125). According to Zola, the new novelist would deploy physiology's discoveries "to solve scientifically the question of how men behave when they are in society," conducting in fiction a scientific experiment. West's formula is closely related: the artist and the scientist both seek information about the universe, but where the one extracts it from imaginary material, the other extracts it from real material.

9. West's theories about the value of art overlap in several ways with those that John Dewey would advance in 1934's *Art as Experience*. Like West, Dewey stresses the resistance of the universe to the demands of the organism: it "is the fate of a living creature . . . that it cannot secure what belongs to it without an adventure in a world that as a whole it does not own and to which it has no native title"; an "environment that was always and everywhere congenial to the straightaway execution of our impulses would set a term to growth as surely as one always hostile would irritate and destroy" (59). Like West, Dewey asserts that increasing refinement of responses to stimuli comes with higher evolution: "As an organism increases in complexity, the rhythms of struggle and consummation in its relation to its environment are varied and prolonged, and they come to include within themselves an endless variety of sub-rhythms. . . . Fulfillment is more massive and more subtly shaded" (23). And like West again, Dewey sees in the existence of art "proof that man uses the materials and energies of nature with intent to expand his own life, and that he does so in accord with the structure of his organism— brain, sense-organs, and muscular system" (25).

10. On the power of art as a stimulus, West writes in "The Strange Necessity," "If anyone asks me how it is possible for imagined stimuli to have the same effect as real ones, I . . . point to the phenomena of hypnotism, which have proved under

controlled conditions on innumerable occasions that imagined stimuli can have precisely the same effect as real ones, and furthermore I will point out that no psychologist has ever furnished an explanation of hypnotism for which one would reward him with a drink" (103). It is not clear whether West means to include Pavlov among the psychologists, here.

11. "[T]here is no need," he writes near the beginning of *Conditioned Reflexes*, "for the physiologist to have recourse to psychology. It would be more natural that experimental investigation of the physiological activities should lay a solid foundation for a future true science of psychology. . . . The physiologist must take his own path, where a trail has already been blazed for him. Three hundred years ago Descartes evolved the idea of the reflex" (4).

12. West also presents as a third piece of evidence the cultural impoverishment of British imperial outposts. But she offers little elaboration on this point, perhaps because her take on the British empire—which she calls, earlier in the essay, "a political necessity, and a glorious one" (140)—is generally favorable.

13. In *Raising America*, Hulbert quotes the celebrated child expert Arnold Gesell's 1939 denunciation of behaviorism as "authoritarian" and "foreign to the idea of democracy and the genius of liberty" (quoted at 172). One would never know, Hulbert comments, "that back in 1930 the *New York Times* had called behaviorism 'fundamentally hopeful and democratic,' more American than any view that emphasized the 'blind forces of heredity.'" By the end of the decade, "Watson had been demoted to cold conditioner of mindless automatons, of whom America—and the world—certainly needed no more" (172).

14. In an angry 1953 letter to Arthur Schlesinger, Jr. (who, she felt, had misrepresented her), West describes herself as living by a certain creed of liberalism (*Letters* 274–75); in a letter of two years after to Bernard Kalb, she affirms, "The liberal faith still seems to me to hold its truth" (*Letters* 290). Later in 1955, she told her correspondent J. B. Priestley, "I am afraid that I am the last liberal left, and I must confess that my obstinate liberalism cannot approve of Communist civil servants packing the civil service with Communist Party members" (*Letters* 297).

Chapter Six
Growing Up Awry

1. Auden's statement first appeared in edited form in a 1938 issue of the *Nation*, as part of that weekly's "Living Philosophies" series; the collection came out shortly after.

2. Auden's phrasing also alludes to Stella Gibbons's 1932 novel *Cold Comfort Farm*, in which the elderly matriarch Ada Doom rules her family by keeping ever before them how at an early age she was scarred by "something nasty" she saw "in the woodshed" (141, 144, 221).

3. The 1962 remark comes from the expanded version of a piece Auden had first published in 1946, an introduction to an edition of Henry James's *American Scene*. Elsewhere in that introduction (both versions), Auden contrasts Old World and New World views on freedom and socially acceptable behavior, remarking that Europe has tried to preserve in some form or another the "fundamental presuppo-

sition of *romanitas* . . . that virtue is prior to liberty, i.e, what matters most is that people should think and act rightly" whether of their own free will or not, whereas America (to which he had recently immigrated) has "come, symbolically, to stand" for the assumption "that liberty is prior to virtue" in the sense that "freedom of choice is . . . the human prerequisite without which virtue and vice have no meaning" (*Dyer's* 318 / *Prose 2* 277). In spite of the evenhandedness with which Auden treats the two social formulae, it is clear from his other writings, with their frequent returns to the importance of freely exercised moral decision, that his sympathies lie mainly with the latter.

4. In a 1933 piece for the *Criterion* Auden was already writing

> The last hundred years have seen an immense advance not only in knowledge, but also in the technique of spreading and instilling it: this means that Liberalism is gone for ever. Whoever possesses the instruments of knowledge . . . is the dictator of the country. . . . If we want a decent sex life, happy human relations, if we want to be people at all, *and not behaviorist automatons,* we must see to it that our dictator can have no personal or class axe to grind and we must hurry or it will be too late. (*Prose 2* 31, emphasis added)

5. Auden begins his contribution to a 1935 collection called *Christianity and the Social Revolution* this way: "Man is an organism with certain desires existing in an environment which fails to satisfy them fully. His theories about the universe are attempts, whether religious, scientific, philosophical, or political, to explain or overcome this tension. If we regard the environment as static, then the problem is one of modifying our desires; if we take the organism as static, one of modifying the environment" (*English* 342 / *Prose 1* 109). Religion and psychology, Auden continues, dwell primarily with the first assumption (static environment, modification of desires), science and politics with the second (static organism, modification of environment). In the pages that follow, he evolves from this scheme an elaborate representation of the relations among Communism, Christianity, and psychology.

6. The major exception to the rule of scholarly neglect is Richard Davenport-Hines's fine short biography, *Auden*, which notes a number of intriguing connections—around topics as diverse as autism, juvenile delinquency, sexual perversity, and the psychology of Greek drama (20–21, 22–23, 89–90, 312–13)—between the two Audens' publications.

7. In the Smith College address, W. H. Auden notes that if he had to "list the twenty books which . . . are of the greatest potential value to the political future of mankind," he would include Mead's "great trilogy about the South Seas," *Patterns of Culture*, and *Middletown* (*Prose 2* 65). In the *I Believe* essay of the year before he comments that studies like Benedict's and the Lynds' "have shown the enormous power of a given cultural form to determine the nature of the individuals who live under it. A given cultural pattern develops those traits of character and modes of behaviour which it values, and suppresses those which it does not." But this does not "warrant ascribing to a culture a superpersonality, conscious of its parts as I can be conscious of my hand or liver" (*English* 373–74 / *Prose 1* 479).

8. Davenport-Hines reports that George Auden had "himself contracted encephalitis in the epidemic after the First World War" and wrote his "account of

its behavioural sequel in children as part of an attempt to modify perceptions of delinquency" (23). In *The Young Delinquent*, Burt devotes several pages to "Illnesses Specifically Disposing to Nervous Instability," mentioning epilepsy, brain inflammations (including encephalitis) and chorea. Burt estimates that in London at the time of writing there were "over two hundred school children who show[ed] serious disturbances of intellect or conduct as a result of" encephalitis; as mentioned above, he also cites one of George Auden's articles on the subject (258).

9. The currency of theories about the evolutionary superiority of self-control was, certainly, quite wide. In *Adolescence*, Hall writes that Henry Maudsley's "conception of adolescent insanity rests on the general conception that reason is an apparatus of restraint, superposed upon intense and brutal impulses, and that in characteristic outbreaks this curb is broken, . . . so that all that later ages of civilization and even higher barbarism have superposed is gone and dehumanization ensues" (293). In his book on crime and medicine in modern France, Nye notes that many French psychiatrists focused on pathologies of the will: "According to . . . Théodule Ribot, the French exponent of this concept, consciously directed willpower was the last of the mental qualities appropriated phylogenetically in mankind's slow evolution from savagery" (128). In Claude McKay's 1933 novel *Banana Bottom*, the missionary Priscilla Craig concludes that Jamaicans are morally lax not because "they were oversexed, but simply because they seemed to lack that check and control that was supposed to be distinguishing of humanity of a higher and more complex social order" (16). And as Matthew Gold has noted, *The Treatment of Neurasthenia by Means of Brain Control*, by Roger Vittoz (under whose care at Lausanne T. S. Eliot wrote a good deal of *The Waste Land* ), begins with the claim that neurasthenia arises from a disruption of the balance between a more primitive "subconscious brain" supplying ideas and sensations and a "conscious brain" wielding reason and will (525).

10. The specialist who helps Margaret see a way past Chris's amnesia has often been identified as a Freudian, but as G. E. Hutchinson has pointed out, "the doctor in the novel . . . is in no detailed way a psychoanalyst" and through the early 1920s English intellectuals interested in the new psychology were more likely to refer to Rivers as a leading authority (66). Rivers's positing of a selfish protopathic system controlled by a socially cooperative epicritic system does, obviously, bear a close resemblance to Freud's picture of the id checked by the superego, developed in the early 1920s; both, we might say, are the fruit of psychologists' efforts to give the conflict between individual urges and social standards a framework within the constitution of the organism. But where Freud focused on sexual desire restrained by bourgeois morality, Rivers focused on feelings of danger unacceptable in soldiers on the front lines (Rivers 120). Where Freud conceived of the superego as a psychological phenomenon without necessary cerebral localization, Rivers imagined the epicritic system as a physiological structure. And where Freud retained a certain detachment about the pluses and minuses of the superego (or about civilization and its discontents), Rivers and George Auden stressed the value of epicritic dominance.

Hutchinson's remarks come in the introduction to a 1982 reprinting of a letter West published in *The Observer* of 24 June 1928. There, she insists that *Return* is not about psychoanalysis, and that she "introduced a psycho-analyst as an unimportant device," a means of "shaking" Margaret's meditations "out of her" (68). Paul Peppis has argued that the therapist in *Return* draws upon many psychologists of the day, including Janet, Prince, and Sidis, but may be most closely associated with Bernard Hart, whom Pound famously named in defining his concept of the poetic Image and who wrote the popular *Psychology of Insanity* of 1912 (2–6).

11. Lane had died in 1925, but his ideas were transmitted to W. H. Auden by his former patient John Layard—who had accompanied Rivers on his 1914 anthropological excursion and who admired W. H. as fervently as he admired W. H. R. "[N]ext to Lane and Rivers," Layard told the younger Auden, "I think you are the most intelligent man I have ever met" (quoted in Davenport-Hines 91).

12. In his 1973 study *Man's Place*, Richard Johnson observes rightly that "Auden never lost his teleological cast of mind, his fundamental curiosity about how things developed or are developing, and he has not ceased attempting to correlate ontogenic growth with phylogenic, psychic with societal, biological with historical" (130).

13. In her introduction to an earlier draft of the *Outline* contribution, Katherine Bucknell suggests that in so theorizing, Auden was drawing upon Freud's work on group psychology as well as Gerald Heard's *Social Substance of Religion* (1931). She points out too that while Rivers offered the Melanesian boat story as "proof of the existence of group communication among primitive people," Bronislaw Malinowski (who "believed there was a high level of individualism among Melanesians which was not initially apparent to Western observers") would have regarded such convergence as a product of custom (27). On Heard, see also Mendelson, *Early* 25–26.

14. "Fish swam as fish, peach settled into peach. / And were successful at the first endeavour; / The hour of birth their only time at college, / They were content with their precocious knowledge" (*English* 251; see also *Collected* 183–84). The sequence was later retitled "Sonnets from China."

15. Other examples of Auden poems in this vein are legion; they include "Our Hunting Fathers," 1934; "Fish in the unruffled lakes," 1936; "Our Bias," 1939; and "Their Lonely Betters," 1950.

16. This claim might be compared to John Dewey's discussion of learning in *How We Think*, published in 1910 and revised in 1933.

17. Wilde also put into in his Commonplace Book the following theory, adapted (Smith and Helfand speculate) from Spencer's *Study of Sociology*: "So in the history of society we first have a chaotic aggregate of human beings corresponding to formless protoplasm• In the primitive life there is no mutual dependance [*sic*], no exchange of services, as in the rudimentary animal there is no vascular system• The developement [*sic*] of the nervous system and the differentiation of function in the individual organism corresponds to increased interdependence and the division of Labour in the social organism•" (*Oxford Notebooks* 109–10). The vision is certainly Spencerian in form, since in it human society evolves from a mere mass of uncooperative beings much like each other to a complex network of highly individuated beings working together.

18. Several critics have noted how the poem itself engages in showing off. Reviewing Auden's *Collected Poems* in 1977, Irvin Ehrenpreis wrote that in poems

like "Praise," "Auden exposes his tastes and prejudices. He celebrates his land-scapes, rises to sublimity, then stoops to the humble talk one uses with close friends or relations—or with oneself. But he stops consciously short of exhibitionism, per-haps just short: he veers away from scandal and indecency" (498). The importance of showing off in Auden's thinking—especially his thinking about poetry—has been registered most cogently by Lucy McDiarmid, who begins *Auden's Apologies for Poetry* with "The Ballad of Barnaby," a 1969 Auden libretto about a tumbler-turned-monk who delightedly performs before a statue of the Virgin in the monas-tery's crypt. (Our Lady is delighted as well.) McDiarmid shrewdly links this perfor-mer to the "pleasing and teasing" child in "Praise," and notes that as a form of pleasing and teasing, art is "a sign of individuation and separation from loving Mother limestone" (5, 135). Less convincingly, McDiarmid casts such showing off as a form of humility synecdochal of a larger apology for poetry, an advertising of poetry's "triviality" and "deviation from value" (137, 134).

19. It seems fitting, too, that the final lesson drawn from the limestone land-scape, at line 89, is that "[t]he blessed will not care what angle they are regarded from, / Having nothing to hide." In a poem that so turns on the getting of atten-tion, it seems quite natural that the blessed would want to be regarded from *some* angle. But which one it happens to be should not matter, because from any direc-tion one's distinction from the environing backdrop will be manifest.

20. Noting that "Wilde, like Auden, was the son of a doctor father and formida-ble mother," Mendelson comments that when "Auden wrote about Wilde in later years he scorned his empty frivolity as if denouncing a temptation he himself had confronted and refused" (*Early* 28). We might add that Auden seems to have pro-jected onto Wilde an exhibitionism that he feared, but at other times admired, in himself.

21. This is to say that in "Praise" we have again the allegorical correspondence mode typical of Auden's landscape poetry—a mode that would also inform still later works such as the "Bucolics" of the early 1950s. In that sequence, mountains give rise to "perfect monsters" who "have the balance, nerve, / And habit of the Spiritual" yet seem to serve a cruel and frightening God, while lakes in their calm modesty "leave aggression to ill-bred romantics / Who duel with their shadows over blasted heaths," and so on (*Collected* 560, 562).

# References

*Actes du Deuxième Congrès International d'Anthropologie Criminelle, Biologie et Sociologie (Paris, août 1889)*. Lyon: A Storck, 1890.

Adams, James Eli. "Pater's Muscular Aestheticism." *Muscular Christianity: Embodying the Victorian Age*. Edited by Donald E. Hall. Cambridge, U.K.: Cambridge University Press, 1994. 215–38.

Addams, Jane. *The Spirit of Youth and the City Streets*. 1909. Urbana: University of Illinois Press, 1972.

Allen, Grant. *Physiological Aesthetics*. New York: D. Appleton, 1877.

Altieri, Charles. "Organic and Humanist Models in Some English Bildungsroman." *Journal of General Education* 23 (1971): 220–339.

Ariès, Philippe. 1960. *Centuries of Childhood: A Social History of Family Life*. Translated by Robert Baldick. New York: Vintage, 1962.

Armstrong, Isobel. *The Radical Aesthetic*. Oxford: Blackwell, 2000.

Armstrong, Tim. *Modernism, Technology, and the Body*. Cambridge, U.K.: Cambridge University Press, 1998.

Auden, George. "The Borderlands of Feeblemindedness." *The Lancet* 29 (September 1928): 641–44.

———. "Encephalitis Lethargica—its Psychological Implications." *Journal of Mental Science* 71 (October 1925): 647–58.

———. "The Maladjusted Child." *British Journal of Educational Psychology* 1.3 (November 1931): 266–78.

———. "On Endogenous and Exogenous Factors in Character Formation." *Journal of Mental Science* 72 (January 1926): 1–25.

———. Review of the *Report of Commissioners of Prisons and Directors of Convict Prisons 1923–4*. *Journal of Mental Science* 71 (April 1925): 313–15.

———. Review of the *Report of the Commissioners of Prisons for the Year Ended March 31, 1923*. *Journal of Mental Science* 70 (January 1924): 117–20.

Auden, W. H. *Collected Poems*. New York: Vintage, 1991.

———. *The Dyer's Hand*. 1962. New York: Vintage, 1989.

———. *The English Auden: Poems, Essays, and Dramatic Writings 1927–1939*. London: Faber, 1977.

———. "A Playboy of the Western World: St. Oscar, the Homintern Martyr." *Partisan Review* 17 (April 1950): 390–94.

———. *Prose and Travel Books in Prose and Verse, 1926–1938*. Prose 1. Princeton: Princeton University Press, 1996.

———. *Prose, 1939–1948*. Prose 2. Princeton: Princeton University Press, 2002.

———. *Selected Poems*. New York: Vintage, 1989.

———. "W. H. Auden." *I Believe: The Personal Philosophies of Certain Eminent Men and Women of Our Time*. Edited by Clifton Fadiman. New York: Simon and Schuster, 1939. 3–16.

Baden-Powell, Robert. 1908. *Scouting for Boys.* Oxford: Oxford University Press, 2004.

Bain, Alexander. *The Senses and the Intellect.* London: John W. Parker, 1855.

Barnett, Maud. *The School Beautiful.* Madison: State of Wisconsin, 1907.

Beecher, Catherine, and Harriet Beecher Stowe. *The American Woman's Home.* New York: J. B. Ford, 1869.

Benedict, Ruth. *Patterns of Culture.* Boston: Houghton Mifflin, 1934.

Bergson, Henri. *Time and Free Will: An Essay on the Immediate Data of Consciousness.* Translated by F. L. Pogson. 3rd ed. London: George Allen, 1913.

Bernard, Claude. *Introduction à l'Étude de la Médecine Expérimentale.* Paris: Ballière, 1865.

Bernheim, Hyppolite. *Bernheim's New Studies in Hypnotism.* 1891. Translated by Richard S. Sandor. New York: International Universities Press, 1980.

Birney, Mrs. Theodore W. Address of Welcome. *National Congress of Mothers: The First Conventions.* Edited by David J. Rothman and Sheila M. Rothman. New York: Garland, 1987. 1.6–10.

Blanchard, Mary Warner. *Oscar Wilde's America: Counterculture in the Gilded Age.* New Haven: Yale University Press, 1998.

Boehmer, Elleke. Introduction. *Scouting for Boys.* By Robert Baden-Powell. Oxford: Oxford University Press, 2004. xi–xlix.

Bourdieu, Pierre. *Distinction: A Social Critique of the Judgement of Taste.* Translated by Richard Nice. Cambridge: Harvard University Press, 1984.

Bowen, Zack. "Wilde about Joyce." *Joyce and Popular Culture.* Edited by R. B. Kershner. Gainesville: University Press of Florida, 1996. 105–14.

Breeuwsma, Gerrit. "The Nephew of an Experimentalist: Ambivalences in Developmental Thinking." *Beyond the Century of the Child: Cultural History and Developmental Psychology.* Edited by Willem Koops and Michael Zuckerman. Philadelphia: University of Pennsylvania Press, 2003. 183–203.

Bringmann, Wolfgang G., Norma J. Bringmann, and William D. G. Balance. "Experimental Approaches to Developmental Psychology before William Preyer." *Contributions to a History of Developmental Psychology: International William T. Preyer Symposium.* Edited by George Eckardt, Wolfgang G. Bringmann, and Lothar Sprung. Berlin: Mouton, 1985. 157–73.

Bristow, Edward J. *Vice and Vigilance: Purity Movements in Britain since 1700.* Dublin: Gill and Macmillan, 1977.

Bromwich, David. Contribution to " 'In Praise of Limestone': A Symposium." *"In Solitude, for Company": W. H. Auden after 1940.* Auden Studies 3. Edited by Katherine Bucknell and Nicholas Jenkins. Oxford: Clarendon, 1995. 260–62.

Bronfenbrenner, Urie. "The Context of Development and the Development of Context." *Developmental Psychology: Historical and Philosophical Perspectives.* Edited by Richard M. Lerner. Hillsdale, New Jersey: Lawrence Erlbaum, 1983. 147–84.

Bruer, John T. *The Myth of the First Three Years.* New York: Free Press, 1999.

Buckley, Jerome Hamilton. *Season of Youth: The Bildungsroman from Dickens to Golding.* Cambridge: Harvard University Press, 1974.

Bucknell, Katherine. Introduction to "Auden's 'Writing' Essay." *"The Map of All of My Youth": Early Works, Friends, and Influences*. Auden Studies 1. Edited by Katherine Bucknell and Nicholas Jenkins. Oxford: Clarendon, 1990. 17–34.

Bulley, Rosamira. "A Prep School Reminiscence." *W. H. Auden: A Tribute*. Edited by Stephen Spender. New York: Macmillan, 1975. 31–34.

Bürger, Peter. *The Decline of Modernism*. Translated by Nicholas Walker. University Park: Pennsylvania State University Press, 1992.

Burgess, Anthony. *A Clockwork Orange*. 1962. Rev. ed. New York: Ballantine, 1988.

Burrage, Severance, and Henry Turner Bailey. *School Sanitation and Decoration: A Practical Study of Health and Beauty in Their Relation to the Public Schools*. Boston: D. C. Heath, 1899.

Burt, Cyril. *The Young Delinquent*. New York: D. Appleton, 1925.

Caldwell, Otis W., Charles Edward Skinner, and J. Winfield Tietz. *Biological Foundations of Education*. Boston: Ginn, 1931.

Calvert, Karin. "Patterns of Childrearing in America." *Beyond the Century of the Child: Cultural History and Developmental Psychology*. Edited by Willem Koops and Michael Zuckerman. Philadelphia: University of Pennsylvania Press, 2003. 62–81.

Caplan, Ruth B. *Psychiatry and the Community in Nineteenth-Century America*. New York: Basic Books, 1969.

Carpenter, William. "Of Memory." *Embodied Selves: An Anthology of Psychological Texts 1830–1890*. Edited by Jenny Bourne Taylor and Sally Shuttleworth. Oxford: Clarendon Press, 1998. 154–57. [Selections from *Principles of Mental Physiology*, 1874.]

———. "The Power of the Will over Mental Action." *Embodied Selves: An Anthology of Psychological Texts 1830–1890*. Edited by Jenny Bourne Taylor and Sally Shuttleworth. Oxford: Clarendon Press, 1998. 95–101. [Selections from *Principles of Mental Physiology*, 1874.]

Caruth, Cathy. Introduction to special issue on psychoanalysis, culture, and trauma. *American Imago* 48.1 (1991): 1–12.

Castle, Gregory. *Reading the Modernist Bildungsroman*. Gainesville: University Press of Florida, 2006.

Cavallo, Dominick. *Muscles and Morals: Organized Playgrounds and Urban Reform, 1880–1920*. Philadelphia: University of Pennsylvania Press, 1981.

Chase, Karen. *Eros and Psyche: The Representation of Personality in Charlotte Brontë, Charles Dickens, and George Eliot*. New York: Methuen, 1984.

Chesterfield, Philip Dormer Stanhope, Earl of. *Dear Boy: Lord Chesterfield's Letters to His Son*. London: Bantam, 1989.

Child, Lydia Maria. *The Mother's Book*. 2nd ed. Boston: Carter and Hendee, 1831.

———. *The Mother's Book*. 6th ed. New York: C. S. Francis, 1846.

Christensen, Jerome. *Coleridge's Blessed Machine of Language*. Ithaca: Cornell University Press, 1981.

Clark, Clifford Edward, Jr. *The American Family Home, 1800–1960*. Chapel Hill: University of North Carolina Press, 1986.

Cleverley, John, and Dennis Phillips. *Visions of Childhood: Influential Models from Locke to Spock*. Sydney: Allen and Unwin, 1987.

Cohen, Deborah. *Household Gods: The British and Their Possessions*. New Haven: Yale University Press, 2006.

Colón, A. R., and P. A. Colón. *A History of Children*. Westport: Greenwood, 2001.

Comstock, Anthony. "How to Guard Our Youth against Bad Literature." *National Congress of Mothers: The First Conventions*. Edited by David J. Rothman and Sheila M. Rothman. New York: Garland, 1987. 1.177–80.

Cook, Clarence. *The House Beautiful: Essays on Beds and Tables, Stools and Candlesticks*. New York: Scribner, Armstrong, 1878.

Crary, Jonathan. *Techniques of the Observer: On Vision and Modernity in the Nineteenth Century*. 1990. Cambridge: MIT Press, 1992.

Crile, George W. *Man—An Adaptive Mechanism*. New York: Macmillan, 1916.

———. *The Origin and Nature of the Emotions*. Philadelphia: W. B. Saunders, 1915.

———. *The Phenomena of Life: A Radio-Electric Interpretation*. New York: W. W. Norton, 1936.

Crile, George, Jr. *A Naturalistic View of Man*. New York: World Publishing, 1969.

Cunningham, Hugh. *Children and Childhood in Western Society since 1500*. London: Longman, 1995.

———. *The Children of the Poor: Representations of Childhood since the Seventeenth Century*. Oxford: Blackwell, 1991.

Daley, Kenneth. *The Rescue of Romanticism: Walter Pater and John Ruskin*. Athens: Ohio University Press, 2001.

Dallas, Eneas Sweetland. *The Gay Science*. London: Chapman and Hall, 1866.

Darwin, Erasmus. *A Plan for the Conduct of Female Education in Boarding Schools*. Derby: J. Drewry, 1797.

———. *Zoonomia: or, The Laws of Organic Life*. London: J. Johnson, 1794.

Davenport-Hines, Richard. *Auden*. New York: Vintage, 1999.

de Bolla, Peter. *Art Matters*. Cambridge: Harvard University Press, 2001.

De Man, Paul. *Aesthetic Ideology*. Minneapolis: University of Minnesota Press, 1996.

De Quincey, Thomas. *Confessions of an English Opium-Eater and Other Writings*. Oxford: Oxford University Press, 1985.

Dewey, John. *Art as Experience*. 1934. New York: Perigee, 1980.

———. *Experience and Education*. 1938. New York: Touchstone, 1997.

———. *How We Think*. 1910. Boston: D. C. Heath, 1933.

*Diacritics* 32.1 (Spring 2002).

Dickinson, Mary Lowe. Response to Address of Welcome. *National Congress of Mothers: The First Conventions*. Edited by David J. Rothman and Sheila M. Rothman. New York: Garland, 1987. 1.11–21.

Donoghue, Denis. "The Oxford of Pater, Hopkins and Wilde." *Rediscovering Oscar Wilde*. Edited by C. George Sandulescu. Gerrards Cross, England: Colin Smythe, 1994. 94–117

———. *Speaking of Beauty*. New Haven: Yale University Press, 2003.

———. *Walter Pater: Lover of Strange Souls*. New York: Knopf, 1995.

Donzelot, Jacques. *The Policing of Families*. Translated by Robert Hurley. New York: Pantheon, 1979.

Dowling, Linda. *The Vulgarization of Art: The Victorians and Aesthetic Democracy*. Charlottesville: University Press of Virginia, 1996.

Downing, Andrew Jackson. *The Architecture of Country Houses.* 1850. New York: Da Capo, 1968.

——. *Victorian Cottage Residences.* 1842. New York: Dover, 1981.

Dreiser, Theodore. *An American Tragedy.* 1925. New York: Signet, 2000.

——. *Dawn.* 1931. Santa Rosa: Black Sparrow, 2000.

——. *The Financier.* 1912. New York: Meridian, 1995.

——. *The "Genius."* 1915. Cleveland: World Publishing, 1943.

——. *The Hand of the Potter.* New York: Boni and Liveright, 1918.

——. *Hey Rub-a-Dub-Dub: A Book of the Mystery and Wonder and Terror of Life.* New York: Boni and Liveright, 1920. N.p.: Kessinger, n.d.

——. *Jennie Gerhardt.* 1911. New York: Schocken, 1982.

——. *Journalism.* Edited by T. D. Nostwich. Vol. 1. Philadelphia: University of Pennsylvania Press, 1988.

——. *Newspaper Days.* 1931. Santa Rosa: Black Sparrow, 2000.

——. *Notes on Life.* Tuscaloosa: University of Alabama Press, 1974.

——. *Sister Carrie.* 1900. Oxford: Oxford University Press, 1991.

——. *Sister Carrie.* Pennsylvania ed. Philadephia: University of Pennysylvania Press, 1981.

——. *The Stoic.* 1947. New York: Signet, 1981.

——. *Theodore Dreiser's Ev'ry Month.* Athens: University of Georgia Press, 1996.

——. *The Titan.* 1914. New York: Signet, 1965.

——. "The Training of the Senses," ts. Theodore Dreiser Papers. Annenberg Rare Book and Manuscript Library, University of Pennsylvania.

Eagleton, Terry. *The Ideology of the Aesthetic.* Oxford: Blackwell, 1990.

——. "The Ideology of the Aesthetic." *The Politics of Pleasure: Aesthetics and Cultural Theory.* Edited by Stephen Regan. Buckingham: Open University Press, 1992. 17–31.

Eastlake, Charles L. *Hints on Household Taste.* 4th ed. 1878. New York: Dover, 1986.

Edelman, Lee. *No Future: Queer Theory and the Death Drive.* Durham, N.C.: Duke University Press, 2004.

Edgeworth, Maria, and Richard Lovell Edgeworth. *Practical Education.* 2 vols. London: J. Johnson, 1798.

Edis, Robert W. *Decoration and Furniture of Town Houses.* 2nd edition. London: C. Kegan Paul, 1881.

Efland, Arthur. *A History of Art Education: Intellectual and Social Currents in Teaching the Visual Arts.* New York: Teacher's College Press, 1990.

Ehrenpreis, Irvin. "Inside Auden's Landsape." *W. H. Auden: The Critical Heritage.* Edited by John Haffenden. London: Routledge, 1983. 496–504.

Elias, Robert H. *Theodore Dreiser: Apostle of Nature.* Emended ed. Ithaca: Cornell University Press, 1970.

Ellenberger, Henri F. *The Discovery of the Unconscious: The History and Evolution of Dynamic Psychiatry.* New York: Basic Books, 1970.

Elliotson, John. "From *Surgical Operations without Pain in the Mesmeric State* (1843)." *Literature and Science in the Nineteenth Century: An Anthology.* Edited by Laura Otis. Oxford: Oxford University Press, 2002. 396–401.

Ellmann, Richard. *James Joyce.* Rev. ed. Oxford: Oxford University Press, 1982.

Ellmann, Richard. *Oscar Wilde*. New York: Vintage, 1988.

Fadiman, Clifton, ed., *I Believe: The Personal Philosophies of Certain Eminent Men and Women of Our Time*. New York: Simon and Schuster, 1939.

Fisher, Philip. *Hard Facts: Setting and Form in the American Novel*. New York: Oxford University Press, 1987.

Fletcher, Horace. Response to Address of Welcome. *National Congress of Mothers: The First Conventions*. Edited by David J. Rothman and Sheila M. Rothman. New York: Garland, 1987. 202–203.

Foucault, Michel. *Discipline and Punish: The Birth of the Prison*. 1975. Translated by Alan Sheridan. New York: Vintage, 1979.

Fowler, O. S. *Creative and Sexual Science*. New York: Baird and Dillon, 1875.

Freedman, Jonathan. *Professions of Taste: Henry James, British Aestheticism, and Commodity Culture*. Stanford: Stanford University Press, 1990.

Freud, Sigmund. *Standard Edition of the Complete Psychological Works of Sigmund Freud*. Translated and edited by James Strachey. 24 vols. London: Hogarth Press, 1953–1974.

Friedman, Jean E. *Ways of Wisdom. Moral Education in the Early National Period*. Athens: University of Georgia Press, 2001.

Frye, Northrop. *Anatomy of Criticism*. 1957. Princeton: Princeton University Press, 1971.

Fuchs, Rachel. "Charity and Welfare." *Family Life in the Long Nineteenth Century, 1789–1913*. Edited by David I. Kertzer and Marzio Barbagli. The History of the European Family 2. New Haven: Yale University Press, 2002. 155–94.

Fuller, John. *W. H. Auden: A Commentary*. Princeton: Princeton University Press, 1998.

Gardner, Phil. *The Lost Elementary Schools of Victorian England*. London: Croom Helm, 1984.

Gates, Elmer. *The Relations and Development of the Mind and Brain*. New York: Philosophic Company, 1903.

Geller, Evelyn. *Forbidden Books in American Public Libraries, 1876–1939*. Westport, Conn.: Greenwood, 1984.

Gere, Charlotte. *The House Beautiful: Oscar Wilde and the Aesthetic Interior*. London: Lund Humphries, 2000.

Gigante, Denise. *Taste: A Literary History*. New Haven: Yale University Press, 2005.

Gillis, John. "The Birth of the Virtual Child: A Victorian Progeny." *Beyond the Century of the Child: Cultural History and Developmental Psychology*. Edited by Willem Koops and Michael Zuckerman. Philadelphia: University of Pennsylvania Press, 2003. 82–95.

———. *Youth and History: Tradition and Change in European Age Relations, 1770–Present*. Expanded student ed. New York: Academic Press, 1981.

Gladwell, Malcolm. "Baby Steps." *New Yorker* 10 January 2000: 80–87.

Glaser, Daniel. "Dimensions of the Problem." *Juvenile Delinquency*. Edited by Joseph S. Roucek. New York: Philosophical Library, 1958. 3–28.

Gold, Matthew K. "The Expert Hand and the Obedient Heart: Dr. Vittoz, T. S. Eliot, and the Therapeutic Possibilities of *The Waste Land*." *Journal of Modern Literature* 23.3–4 (2000): 519–33.

Goodman, Paul. *Growing up Absurd: Problems of Youth in the Organized System.* New York: Random House, 1960.

Gordon, John. *Joyce and Reality: The Empirical Strikes Back.* Syracuse: Syracuse University Press, 2004.

———. *Physiology and the Literary Imagination: Romantic to Modern.* Gainesville: University Press of Florida, 2003.

Gordon, Rae Beth. "From Charcot to Charlot: Unconscious Imitation and Spectatorship in French Cabaret and Early Cinema." *The Mind of Modernism: Medicine, Psychology, and the Cultural Arts in Europe and America, 1880–1940.* Edited by Mark S. Micale. Stanford: Stanford University Press, 2004. 93–124.

Gorman, Herbert. *James Joyce.* New York: Farrar and Rinehart, 1939.

Greenberg, Clement. *Art and Culture.* Boston: Beacon Press, 1961.

Griffin, Brenda S., and Charles T. Griffin. *Juvenile Delinquency in Perspective.* New York: Harper and Row, 1978.

Grinder, Robert E. *A History of Genetic Psychology: The First Science of Human Development.* New York: John Wiley, 1967.

*A Guide to Censored Looney Tunes and Merrie Melodies.* 9 July 2007 http://looney .goldenagecartoons.com/ltcuts/ltcutsm.html.

Haley, Bruce. "Wilde's 'Decadence' and the Positivist Tradition." *Victorian Studies* 28.2 (1985): 215–29.

Hall, G. Stanley. *Adolescence: Its Psychology and Its Relations to Physiology, Anthropology, Sociology, Sex, Crime, Religion, and Education.* 2 vols. 1904. New York: D. Appleton, 1921.

———. "The Contents of Children's Minds." *Historical Readings in Developmental Psychology.* Edited by Wayne Dennis. New York: Appleton-Century-Crofts, 1972. 119–37.

Hamilton, Elizabeth. *Letters on the Elementary Principles of Education.* 6th ed. Vol. 1. London: Baldwin, Craddock, and Joy, 1818.

Hamilton, William. "Three Degrees of Mental Latency." *Embodied Selves: An Anthology of Psychological Texts 1830–1890.* Edited by Jenny Bourne Taylor and Sally Shuttleworth. Oxford: Clarendon Press, 1998. 80–83. [Selections from *Lectures on Metaphysics and Logic*, 1859.]

Harkness, Marguerite. *The Aesthetics of Dedalus and Bloom.* Lewisburg, Penn.: Bucknell University Press, 1984.

Harrington, Anne. *Medicine, Mind, and the Double Brain: A Study in Nineteenth-Century Thought.* Princeton: Princeton University Press, 1987.

Harrison, Jane. *Ancient Art and Ritual.* New York: Henry Holt, 1913.

Hart, Gail K. *Friedrich Schiller: Crime, Aesthetics, and the Poetics of Punishment.* Newark: University of Delaware Press, 2005.

Hartley, David. *Observations on Man, His Frame, His Duty, and His Expectations.* London: S. Richardson, 1749.

Hasseler, Terri A. "The Physiological Determinism Debate in Oscar Wilde's *The Picture of Dorian Gray.*" *Victorian Newsletter* 84 (1993): 31–35.

Hawes, Joseph M. *Children in Urban Society: Juvenile Delinquency in Nineteenth-Century America.* New York: Oxford University Press, 1971.

Healy, William. *The Individual Delinquent.* 1915. Montclair, New Jersey: Patterson Smith, 1969.

Hecht, Jennifer Michael. *The End of the Soul: Scientific Modernity, Atheism, and Anthropology in France.* New York: Columbia University Press, 2003.

Helmholtz, Hermann von. *Helmholtz's Treatise on Physiological Optics.* Translated by James P. C. Southall. 3 vols. Rochester, New York: Optical Society of America, 1924–25.

———. *Popular Lectures on Scientific Subjects.* Translated by E. Atkinson. 1873. New York: D. Appleton, 1885.

Heywood, Colin. *A History of Childhood.* Cambridge, U.K.: Polity, 2001.

Higgins, Lesley. *The Modernist Cult of Ugliness: Aesthetics and Gender Politics.* New York: Palgrave, 2002.

Hill, Rosemary. "Ruskin and Pugin." *Ruskin and Architecture.* Edited by Rebecca Daniels and Geoff Brandwood. Reading, U.K.: Spire, 2003. 223–45.

Hollinghurst, Alan. *The Line of Beauty.* London: Picador, 2004.

Howells, John G. *World History of Psychiatry.* New York: Brunner/Mazel, 1975.

Hulbert, Ann. *Raising America: Experts, Parents, and a Century of Advice about Children.* New York: Knopf, 2003.

Hutchinson, G. E. Prefatory note to "On *The Return of the Soldier,*" by Rebecca West. *Yale University Library Gazette* 57.1–2 (1982): 66–67.

Illick, Joseph E. *American Childhoods.* Philadelphia: University of Pennsylvania Press, 2002.

Inman, Billie Andrew. *Walter Pater's Reading: A Bibliography of His Library Borrowings and Literary References, 1858–1873.* New York: Garland, 1981.

James, William. *The Principles of Psychology.* Vol. 1. 1890. New York: Dover, 1950.

Jenkins, Nicholas. Introduction to "Vocation and Society (1943)." *"In Solitude, for Company": W. H. Auden after 1940.* Auden Studies 3. Edited by Katherine Bucknell and Nicholas Jenkins. Oxford: Clarendon, 1995. 1–14.

Jennings, Jan. "Controlling Passion: The Turn-of-the-Century Wallpaper Dilemma." *Winterthur Portfolio* 31.4 (1996): 243–64.

Jeune, Mary. "The Children of a Great City—I." *The Woman's World* 1 (1888): 27–31.

Johnson, Richard. *Man's Place: An Essay on Auden.* Ithaca: Cornell University Press, 1973.

Jones, Gareth Stedman. *Outcast London.* Oxford: Clarendon Press, 1971.

Jordan, Thomas E. *Victorian Childhood: Themes and Variations.* Albany: State University of New York Press, 1987.

Joughin, John J., and Simon Malpas, eds. *The New Aestheticism.* Manchester, U.K.: Manchester University Press, 2003.

Joyce, James. *Finnegans Wake.* 1939. New York: Penguin, 1976.

———. *Occasional, Critical, and Political Writing.* Oxford: Oxford University Press, 2000.

———. *A Portrait of the Artist as a Young Man.* 1916. Oxford: Oxford University Press, 2000.

———. *Stephen Hero.* New York: New Directions, 1963.

———. *Ulysses.* 1922. Corrected text. New York: Vintage, 1986.

Kagan, Jerome. "Developmental Categories and the Premise of Connectivity." *Developmental Psychology: Historical and Philosophical Perspectives.* Edited by Richard M. Lerner. Hillsdale, New Jersey: Lawrence Erlbaum, 1983. 29–54.

Kant, Immanuel. *Critique of Judgement*. Translated by J. H. Bernard. New York: Hafner, 1951.

Kaplan, Amy. *The Social Construction of American Realism*. Chicago: University of Chicago Press, 1988.

Katope, Christopher G. "*Sister Carrie* and Spencer's *First Principles*." *American Literature* 41.1 (1969): 64–75.

Kett, Joseph F. *Rites of Passage: Adolescence in America 1790 to the Present*. New York: Basic Books, 1977.

Key, Ellen. *The Century of the Child*. New York: G. P. Putnam's Sons, 1909.

Kincaid, James R. *Child-Loving: The Erotic Child and Victorian Culture*. New York: Routledge, 1992.

King, Julia. "Physical Culture." *National Congress of Mothers: The First Conventions*. Edited by David J. Rothman and Sheila M. Rothman. New York: Garland, 1987. 1.193–99.

Kittler, Friedrich A. *Discourse Networks, 1800/1900*. Translated by Michael Metteer. Stanford University Press, 1900.

Kooy, Michael John. *Coleridge, Schiller and Aesthetic Education*. Houndmills: Palgrave, 2002.

Korzenik, Diana. *Drawn to Art: A Nineteenth-Century American Dream*. Hanover, N.H.: University Press of New England, 1985.

Kreilkamp, Vera. *The Anglo-Irish Novel and the Big House*. Syracuse: Syracuse University Press, 1998.

Landow, George P. *The Aesthetic and Critical Theories of John Ruskin*. Princeton: Princeton University Press, 1971.

Lee, Vernon, and C. Anstruther-Thomson. *Beauty and Ugliness*. London: John Lane, 1912.

Leps, Marie-Christine. *Apprehending the Criminal: The Production of Deviance in Nineteenth-Century Discourse*. Durham, N.C.: Duke University Press, 1992.

Lessing, Doris. *Ben, in the World*. New York: HarperCollins, 2000.

———. *The Fifth Child*. 1988. New York: Vintage, 1989.

Levenson, Michael. "Stephen's Diary in Joyce's *Portrait*—The Shape of Life." *James Joyce's A Portrait of the Artist as a Young Man: A Casebook*. Edited by Mark A. Wollaeger. New York: Oxford University Press, 2003. 183–205.

Levey, Michael. *The Case of Walter Pater*. N.p.: Thames and Hudson, 1978.

Levin, Harry. *James Joyce: A Critical Introduction*. Norfolk, Conn.: New Directions, 1941.

Levine, George, ed. *Aesthetics and Ideology*. New Brunswick: Rutgers University Press, 1994.

Lewes, George Henry. *Problems of Life and Mind*. 3rd Series. Boston: Houghton, Osgood, 1880.

Lewis, Wyndham. *The Dithyrambic Spectator*. 1925. London: Chatto and Windus, 1931.

Locke, John. *Some Thoughts concerning Education*. 1693. Oxford: Clarendon, 1989.

Loeb, Jacques. *Forced Movements, Tropisms, and Animal Conduct*. J. B. Lippincott, 1918.

———. *The Mechanistic Conception of Life*. Cambridge: Harvard University Press, 1964.

Loeb, Jacques. *The Organism as a Whole*. New York: G. P. Putnam's Sons, 1916.

Loesberg, Jonathan. *A Return to Aesthetics: Autonomy, Indifference, and Postmodernism*. Stanford: Stanford University Press, 2005.

Loftie, Rev. W. J. *A Plea for Art in the House*. Philadelphia: Porter and Coates, 1876.

Logan, Frederick. *Growth of Art in American Schools*. New York: Harper, 1955.

Loos, Adolf. *Ornament and Crime: Selected Essays*. Trans. Michael Mitchell. Riverside, Calif.: Ariadne, 1998.

Lukács, Georg [Gyorgy]. *The Meaning of Contemporary Realism*. London: Merlin, 1963.

Lynd, Robert and Helen. *Middletown*. New York: Harcourt, Brace, 1937.

Macdonald, Stuart. *The History and Philosophy of Art Education*. London: University of London Press, 1970.

Mack, Edward C. *Public Schools and British Opinion since 1860*. 1941. Westport, Conn.: Greenwood, 1971.

Magnin, Émile. *L'Art et l'Hypnose: Interpretation Plastique d'Oeuvres Littéraires et Musicales*. Paris, Félix Alcan, 1907.

———. *"Magdeleine": Étude sur le Geste au moyen de l'Hypnose*. With photographs by Frédéric Boissonnas. Geneva: n.p., n.d.

Mahaffey, Vicki. *States of Desire: Wilde, Yeats, Joyce, and the Irish Experiment*. New York: Oxford University Press, 1998.

Maltz, Diana. "Engaging 'Delicate Brains': From Working-Class Enculturation to Upper-Class Lesbian Liberation in Vernon Lee and Kit Anstruther-Thomson's Psychological Aesthetics." *Women and British Aestheticism*. Edited by Talia Schaffer and Kathy Alexis Psomiades. Charlottesville: University Press of Virginia, 1999. 211–29.

Manganiello, Dominic. "Through a Cracked Looking Glass: *The Picture of Dorian Gray* and *A Portrait of the Artist as a Young Man*." *James Joyce and His Contemporaries*. Edited by Diana A. Ben-Merre and Maureen Murphy. New York: Greenwood, 1989. 89–96.

Martin, Ronald E. *American Literature and the Universe of Force*. Durham, N.C.: Duke University Press, 1981.

Martineau, Harriet. "From *Letters on Mesmerism* (1845)." *Literature and Science in the Nineteenth Century: An Anthology*. Edited by Laura Otis. Oxford: Oxford University Press, 2002. 406–10.

Mason, Stuart. Introduction to "Impressions of America." *Works of Oscar Wilde*. Vol. 11. New York: Lamb, 1909. 250.

Maynes, Mary Jo. "Class Cultures and Images of Proper Family Life." *Family Life in the Long Nineteenth Century, 1789–1913*. Edited by David I. Kertzer and Marzio Barbagli. The History of the European Family 2. New Haven: Yale University Press, 2002. 195–226.

McDiarmid, Lucy. *Auden's Apologies for Poetry*. Princeton: Princeton University Press, 1990.

McGrath, F. C. *The Sensible Spirit: Walter Pater and the Modernist Paradigm*. Tampa: University of South Florida Press, 1986.

McKay, Claude. *Banana Bottom*. San Diego: Harvest, 1933.

McKeever, William A. *Outlines of Child Study: A Text Book for Parent-Teacher Associations, Mothers' Clubs, and All Kindred Organizations*. New York: Macmillan, 1915.

Mead, Margaret. *Coming of Age in Samoa*. 1928. New York: Morrow Quill, 1973.

Meisel, Perry. *The Myth of the Modern: A Study in British Literature and Criticism after 1850*. New Haven: Yale University Press, 1987.

Mendelson, Edward. *Early Auden*. New York: Farrar, 1981.

———. *Later Auden*. New York: Farrar, 1999.

Mendelssohn, Michèle. *Henry James, Oscar Wilde and Aesthetic Culture*. Edinburgh: Edinburgh University Press, 2007.

Merish, Lori. *Sentimental Materialism: Gender, Commodity Culture, and Nineteenth-Century American Literature*. Durham, N.C.: Duke University Press, 2000.

Michaels, Walter Benn. *The Gold Standard and the Logic of Naturalism*. Berkeley: University of California Press, 1987.

Miller, A. Jennesse. "Mother's Relation to the Sound Physical Development of Her Child." *National Congress of Mothers: The First Conventions*. Edited by David J. Rothman and Sheila M. Rothman. New York: Garland, 1987. 117–23.

Milne, Drew. "The Beautiful Soul: From Hegel to Beckett." *Diacritics* 32.1 (2002): 63–82.

Mitchell, Lee Clark. *Determined Fictions: American Literary Naturalism*. New York: Columbia University Press, 1989.

Moers, Ellen. *Two Dreisers*. New York: Viking, 1969.

Moliterno, Frank. *The Dialectics of Sense and Spirit in Pater and Joyce*. Greensboro, N.C.: ELT Press, 1998.

Moretti, Franco. *The Way of the World: The* Bildungsroman *in European Culture*. 1987. New ed. Translated by Albert Sbragia. London: Verso, 2000.

Morgan, C. Lloyd, and James Mark Baldwin. "Environment." *Dictionary of Philosophy and Psychology*. Edited by James Mark Baldwin. Vol 1. New York: Macmillan, 1901. 328–29.

Morris, William. *Selected Writings and Designs*. 1962. Baltimore: Penguin, 1968.

*A Mouse Divided*. Dir. Friz Freleng. Warner Brothers, 1953.

Mullin, Katherine. *James Joyce, Sexuality, and Social Purity*. Cambridge, U.K.: Cambridge University Press, 2003.

Mulvey, Laura. *Visual and Other Pleasures*. Bloomington: Indiana University Press, 1989.

Myers, Frederic W. H. *Human Personality and Its Survival of Bodily Death*. Vol. 1. London: Longmans, Green, 1903.

Nasaw, David. "Children and Commercial Culture: Moving Pictures in the Early Twentieth Century." *Small Worlds: Children and Adolescents in America, 1850–1950*. Edited by Elliott West and Paula Petrik. Lawrence: University Press of Kansas, 1992. 14–25.

Newsome, David. *Godliness and Good Learning: Four Studies on a Victorian Ideal*. London: John Murray, 1961.

Newton, Frances. "The Mother's Greatest Needs." *National Congress of Mothers: The First Conventions*. Edited by David J. Rothman and Sheila M. Rothman. New York: Garland, 1987. 1.148–54.

Nolan, Emer. "Portrait of an Aesthete." *James Joyce's* A Portrait of the Artist as a Young Man: *A Casebook.* Edited by Mark A. Wollaeger. New York: Oxford University Press, 2003. 281–96.

Noon, William T. *Joyce and Aquinas.* 1957. N.p.: Archon, 1970.

Nord, Deborah Epstein. *The Apprenticeship of Beatrice Webb.* Amherst: University of Massachusetts Press, 1985.

Norton, Robert E. *The Beautiful Soul: Aesthetic Morality in the Eighteenth Century.* Ithaca: Cornell University Press, 1995.

Nye, Robert A. *Crime, Madness, and Politics in Modern France: The Medical Concept of National Decline.* Princeton: Princeton University Press, 1984.

O'Brien, Kevin. *Oscar Wilde in Canada: An Apostle for the Arts.* Toronto: Personal Library, 1982.

Ortega y Gasset, José. *The Dehumanization of Art and Other Essays on Art, Culture, and Literature.* 1925, 1948. Princeton: Princeton University Press, 1968.

Osborne, Charles. *W. H. Auden: The Life of a Poet.* New York: Harcourt Brace, 1979.

Otten, Thomas J. *A Superficial Reading of Henry James.* Columbus: Ohio State University Press, 2006.

Ouida.*Critical Studies.* Leipzig: Bernhard Tauchnitz, 1901.

———. "The Streets of London." *The Woman's World* 1 (1888): 481–84.

Pater, Walter. "Coleridge's Writings." *Westminster Review* 85 (1866): 106–32.

———. *Imaginary Portraits.* New York: Allworth, 1997.

———. *Marius the Epicurean.* 1885. Harmondsworth: Penguin, 1985.

———. *Plato and Platonism.* 1893. New York: Macmillan, 1894.

———. *Three Major Texts (The Renaissance, Appreciations, and Imaginary Portraits).* New York: New York University Press, 1986.

Pavlov, Ivan Petrovich. *Conditioned Reflexes.* Translated by G. V. Anrep. Humphrey Milford: Oxford University Press, 1927.

Peppis, Paul. "Treating War Shock, Modernizing Narrative: Rebecca West and British Psychoanalysis." Unpublished paper.

Perlis, Alan D. "Beyond Epiphany: Pater's Aesthetic Hero in the Works of Joyce." *James Joyce Quarterly* 17.2 (1980): 272–79.

Platt, Anthony M. *The Child Savers: The Invention of Delinquency.* 2nd ed. Chicago: University of Chicago Press, 1977.

Plotz, Judith. *Romanticism and the Vocation of Childhood.* New York: Palgrave, 2001.

Poirier, Richard. "The Pater of Joyce and Eliot." *Addressing Frank Kermode: Essays in Criticism and Interpretation.* Urbana: University of Illinois Press, 1991.

Pollock, Linda A. *A Lasting Relationship: Parents and Children over Three Centuries.* Hanover, N.H.: University Press of New England, 1987.

Pound, Ezra. *Gaudier-Brzeska.* 1916. New York: New Directions, 1970.

Power, Arthur. *Conversations with James Joyce.* Dublin: Lilliput, 1999.

Prince, Morton. *The Unconscious: The Fundamentals of Human Personality Normal and Abnormal.* New York: Macmillan, 1914.

Ragland-Sullivan, Ellie. "The Phenomenon of Aging in Oscar Wilde's *Picture of Dorian Gray:* A Lacanian View." *Memory and Desire: Aging—Literature—Psy-*

*choanalysis.* Edited by Kathleen Woodward and Murray M. Schwartz. Bloomington: Indiana University Press, 1986. 114–33.

Read, Herbert. *Education through Art.* 1943. New York: Pantheon, 1958.

Redfield, Marc. *Phantom Formations: Aesthetic Ideology and the Bildungsroman.* Ithaca: Cornell University Press, 1996.

Reed, Edward S. *From Soul to Mind: The Emergence of Psychology from Erasmus Darwin to William James.* New Haven: Yale University Press, 1997.

Richardson, Alan. *British Romanticism and the Science of Mind.* Cambridge, U.K.: Cambridge University Press, 2001.

———. *Literature, Education, and Romanticism.* Cambridge, U.K.: Cambridge University Press, 1994.

Rivers, W.H.R. *Instinct and the Unconscious.* 1920. 2nd ed. Cambridge, U.K.: Cambridge University Press, 1924.

Robinson, Daniel N. *An Intellectual History of Psychology.* 3rd ed. Madison: University of Wisconsin Press, 1995.

Rollyson, Carl. *Rebecca West: A Life.* New York: Scribner, 1996.

Rosner, Victoria. *Modernism and the Architecture of Private Life.* New York: Columbia University Press, 2005.

Rousseau, Jean-Jacques. *Emile, or, On Education.* Translated by Allan Bloom. N. p.: Basic Books, 1979.

Ruggiero, Guido de. *The History of European Liberalism.* 1927. Translated by R. G. Collingwood. Boston: Beacon Press, 1959.

Ruskin, John. *The Seven Lamps of Architecture.* New York: John Wiley, 1854.

———. *The Works of John Ruskin.* 39 vols. Edited by E. T. Cook and Alexander Wedderburn. London: George Allen, 1903–12.

Rylance, Rick. *Victorian Psychology and British Culture 1850–1880.* Oxford: Oxford University Press, 2000.

Scarry, Elaine. *On Beauty and Being Just.* Princeton: Princeton University Press, 1999.

Schiller, Friedrich. *On the Aesthetic Education of Man.* 1795. Translated by Reginald Snell. New York: Continuum, 1965.

Schlapp, Max G., and Edward H. Smith. *The New Criminology: A Consideration of the Chemical Causation of Abnormal Behavior.* New York: Boni and Liveright, 1928.

Schleifer, Ronald. *Modernism and Time: The Logic of Abundance in Literature, Science, and Culture 1880–1930.* Cambridge, U.K.: Cambridge University Press, 2000.

Scholes, Robert, and Richard M. Kain. *The Workshop of Daedalus: James Joyce and the Raw Materials for* A Portrait of the Artist as a Young Man. Evanston, Ill.: Northwestern University Press, 1965.

Schopenhauer, Arthur. *The World as Will and Representation.* Translated by E.F.J. Payne. Vol. 2. New York: Dover, 1958.

Scotto, Robert M. " 'Visions' and 'Epiphanies': Fictional Technique in Pater's *Marius* and Joyce's *Portrait.*" *James Joyce Quarterly* 11.1 (1973): 41–50.

Seagroatt, Heather. "Hard Science, Soft Psychology, and Amorphous Art in *The Picture of Dorian Gray.*" *Studies in English Literature 1500–1900* 38.4 (1998): 741–59.

Sebald, W. G. *Austerlitz*. Translated by Anthea Bell. New York: Modern Library, 2001.

Shaffer, Talia. *The Forgotten Female Aesthetes: Literary Culture in Late-Victorian England*. Charlottesville: University Press of Virginia, 2000.

Sharpe, Lesley. *Schiller's Aesthetic Essays: Two Centuries of Criticism*. Columbia, S.C.: Camden House, 1995.

Shuttleworth, Sally. *George Eliot and Nineteenth-Century Science*. Cambridge, U.K.: Cambridge University Press, 1984.

Shuttleworth, Sally, and Geoffrey Cantor. Introduction. *Science Serialized: Representations of the Sciences in Nineteenth-Century Periodicals*. Edited by Geoffrey Cantor and Sally Shuttleworth. Cambridge: MIT Press, 2004. 1–15.

Sidis, Boris. *The Psychology of Suggestion*. New York: D. Appleton, 1899.

Smith, Harold Llewellyn. "At St Edmund's 1915–1920." *W. H. Auden: A Tribute*. Edited by Stephen Spender. New York: Macmillan, 1975. 34–36.

Smith, Jonathan. "Grant Allen, Physiological Aesthetics, and the Dissemination of Darwin's Botany." *Science Serialized: Representations of the Sciences in Nineteenth-Century Periodicals*. Edited by Geoffrey Cantor and Sally Shuttleworth. Cambridge: MIT Press, 2004. 285–305.

Smith, Philip E., II, and Michael S. Helfand. "The Context of the Text." *Oscar Wilde's Oxford Notebooks: A Portrait of Mind in the Making*. By Oscar Wilde. Edited by Philip E. Smith, II, and Michael S. Helfand. New York: Oxford University Press, 1989. 5–34.

———. "The Text." *Oscar Wilde's Notebooks: A Portrait of Mind in the Making*. By Oscar Wilde. Edited by Philip E. Smith, II, and Michael S. Helfand, New York: Oxford University Press, 1989. 1–4.

———. "The Text as Context." *Oscar Wilde's Oxford Notebooks: A Portrait of Mind in the Making*. By Oscar Wilde. Edited by Philip E. Smith, II, and Michael S. Helfand. New York: Oxford University Press, 1989. 35–106.

Smith, Walter. *Arts Education, Scholastic and Industrial*. Boston: James R. Osgood, 1873.

Smith, Zadie. *On Beauty*. New York: Penguin, 2005.

Souriau, Paul. *La Suggestion dans l'art*. Paris: Félix Alcan, 1893.

Spacks, Patricia Meyer. *The Adolescent Idea: Myths of Youth and the Adult Imagination*. New York: Basic Books, 1981.

Spencer, Herbert. *Education: Intellectual, Moral, and Physical*. London: G. Manwaring, 1861.

———. *First Principles*. 1862. 4th ed. New York: D. Appleton, 1898.

———. *The Principles of Psychology*. London: Longman, Brown, Green, and Longmans, 1855.

Springhall, John. *Youth, Popular Culture, and Moral Panics: Penny Gaffs to Gangsta-Rap, 1830–1996*. New York: St. Martin's, 1998.

Stankiewicz, Mary Ann. " 'The Eye Is a Nobler Organ': Ruskin and American Art Education." *Journal of Aesthetic Education* 18.2 (1984): 51–64.

Stanley, Arthur Penrhyn. *The Life and Correspondence of Thomas Arnold, D. D.* 12th ed. Vol. 1. London: John Murray, 1881.

Staub, Susan C. Introductory Note. *Mother's Advice Books*. Edited by Susan C. Staub. *The Early Modern Englishwoman: A Facsimile Library of Essential Works* 1.3. Aldershot, U.K.: Ashgate, 2002.

Steedman, Carolyn. *Strange Dislocations: Childhood and the Idea of Human Interiority, 1780–1930*. Cambridge: Harvard University Press, 1995.

Stein, Roger B. *John Ruskin and Aesthetic Thought in America, 1840–1900*. Cambridge: Harvard University Press, 1967.

Steiner, Wendy. *The Scandal of Pleasure*. Chicago: University of Chicago Press, 1995.

Strachey, Lytton. *Eminent Victorians*. San Diego: Harvest, 1918.

———. *Lytton Strachey by Himself*. New York: Holt, Rinehart and Winston, 1971.

Strang, Ruth. *An Introduction to Child Study*. New York: Macmillan, 1930.

Sully, James. "Babies and Science." *Embodied Selves: An Anthology of Psychological Texts 1830–1890*. Edited by Jenny Bourne Taylor and Sally Shuttleworth. Oxford: Clarendon Press, 1998. 341–44. ["Babies and Science," *The Cornhill*, 1881.]

Symons, Arthur. *The Symbolist Movement in Literature*. London: William Heinemann, 1899.

Taine, Hippolyte. *On Intelligence*. Vol. 1. Translated by T. D. Haye. London: L. Reeve, 1871.

Taylor, Jenny Bourne, and Sally Shuttleworth. *Embodied Selves: An Anthology of Psychological Texts 1830–1890*. Oxford: Clarendon Press, 1998.

Theall, Donald F. *James Joyce's Techno-Poetics*. Toronto: University of Toronto Press, 1997.

Thistlewood, David. "From Imperialism to Internationalism: Policy Making in British Art Education, 1853–1944, with Special Reference to the Work of Herbert Read." *Curriculum, Culture, and Art Education: Comparative Perspectives*. Edited by Kerry Freedman and Fernando Hernandez. New York: State University of New York Press, 1998. 133–48.

Thomas, David Wayne. *Cultivating Victorians: Liberal Culture and the Aesthetic*. Philadelphia: University of Pennsylvania Press, 2004.

Tyndall, John. *Fragments of Science*. 8th ed. Vol. 2. London: Longmans, Green, 1892. Westmead, U.K.: Gregg, 1970.

Tyrwhitt, Richard St. John. *A Handbook of Pictorial Art*. London: Macmillan, 1868.

Vallins, David. *Coleridge and the Psychology of Romanticism: Feeling and Thought*. Houndmills: Macmillan, 2000.

Watson, John B. *Behavior: An Introduction to Comparative Psychology*. New York: Henry Holt, 1914.

———. *Behaviorism*. New York: W. W. Norton, 1924.

Wells, Helen R. "Children's Rights." *National Congress of Mothers: The First Conventions*. Edited by David J. Rothman and Sheila M. Rothman. New York: Garland, 1987. 2.13–15.

West, Rebecca. *Black Lamb and Grey Falcon: A Journey through Yugoslavia*. 1941. New York: Penguin, 1994.

———. *The Meaning of Treason*. New York: Viking, 1947.

West, Rebecca. *The New Meaning of Treason*. New York: Viking, 1964.

———. "On *The Return of the Soldier*." *Yale University Library Gazette* 57.1–2 (1982): 66–67.

———. "Rebecca West." *I Believe: The Personal Philosophies of Certain Eminent Men and Women of Our Time*. Edited by Clifton Fadiman. New York: Simon and Schuster, 1939. 321–39.

———. *The Return of the Soldier*. 1918. New York: Penguin, 1998.

———. *Selected Letters of Rebecca West*. New Haven: Yale University Press, 2000.

———. *The Strange Necessity*. 1928. London: Virago, 1987.

———. *The Young Rebecca: Writings of Rebecca West 1911–1917*. New York: Viking, 1982.

Wharton, Edith, and Ogden Codman, Jr. *The Decoration of Houses*. 1897. New York: Scribner, 1907.

White, Sheldon H. "The Idea of Development in Developmental Psychology." *Developmental Psychology: Historical and Philosophical Perspectives*. Edited by Richard M. Lerner. Hillsdale, New Jersey: Lawrence Erlbaum, 1983. 55–77.

Whyte, Lancelot Law. *The Unconscious before Freud*. 1960. London: Julian Friedmann, 1978.

Wilde, Oscar. *Aristotle at Afternoon Tea: The Rare Oscar Wilde*. Edited by John Wyse Jackson. London: Fourth Estate, 1991.

———. *The Artist as Critic: Critical Writings of Oscar Wilde*. Edited by Richard Ellmann. New York: Random House, 1969.

———. *Complete Works of Oscar Wilde*. 1966. New York: Perennial, 1989.

———. "The Decorative Arts." *Oscar Wilde in Canada: An Apostle for the Arts*. By Kevin O'Brien. Toronto: Personal Library, 1982. 151–65.

———. *Oscar Wilde's Oxford Notebooks: A Portrait of Mind in the Making*. Edited by Philip E. Smith, II, and Michael S. Helfand. New York: Oxford University Press, 1989.

Williams, Carolyn. *Transfigured World: Walter Pater's Aesthetic Historicism*. Ithaca: Cornell University Press, 1989.

Williams, Raymond. *The Country and the City*. New York: Oxford University Press, 1973.

Wilson, Edmund. *Axel's Castle: A Study in the Imaginative Literature of 1870–1930*. 1931. New York: W. W. Norton, 1984.

Winter, James. *Secure from Rash Assault: Sustaining the Victorian Environment*. Berkeley: University of California Press, 1999.

Wollaeger, Mark A. Introduction. *James Joyce's* A Portrait of the Artist as a Young Man*: A Casebook*. Edited by Mark A. Wollaeger. New York: Oxford University Press, 2003. 3–26.

Wordsworth, William. *The Poetical Works of William Wordsworth*. 2nd ed. Vol. 2. Oxford: Clarendon Press, 1952.

———. *The Prelude: 1799, 1805, 1850*. New York: W. W. Norton, 1979.

Wright, Richard. *Native Son*. Restored text ed. New York: Perennial Classics, 1998.

Yeats, W. B. *The Collected Poems of W. B. Yeats*. New ed. New York: Collier, 1989.

Youmans, E. L. "Observations on the Scientific Study of Human Nature." *The Culture Demanded by Modern Life*. Edited by E. L. Youmans. New York: D. Appleton, 1867. 371–411.

Zanine, Louis J. *Mechanism and Mysticism: The Influence of Science on the Thought and Work of Theodore Dreiser*. Philadelphia: University of Pennsylvania Press, 1993.

Zelizer, Viviana A. *Pricing the Priceless Child: The Changing Social Value of Children*. New York: Basic Books, 1985.

Zola, Émile. *The Experimental Novel and Other Essays*. Translated by Belle M. Sherman. New York: Cassell, 1893.

# Index

CPSIA information can be obtained at www.ICGtesting.com
Printed in the USA
270692BV00005B/17/P